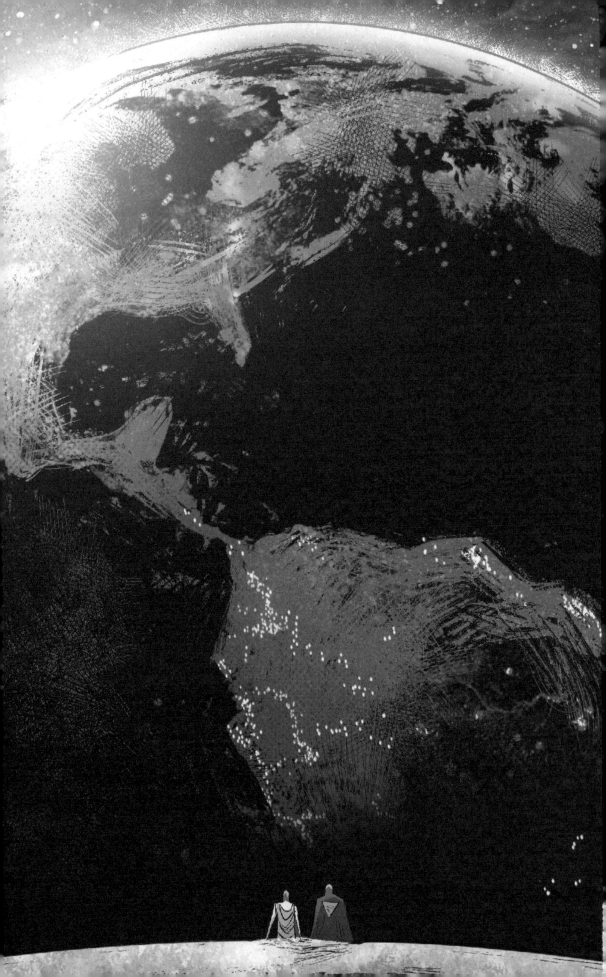

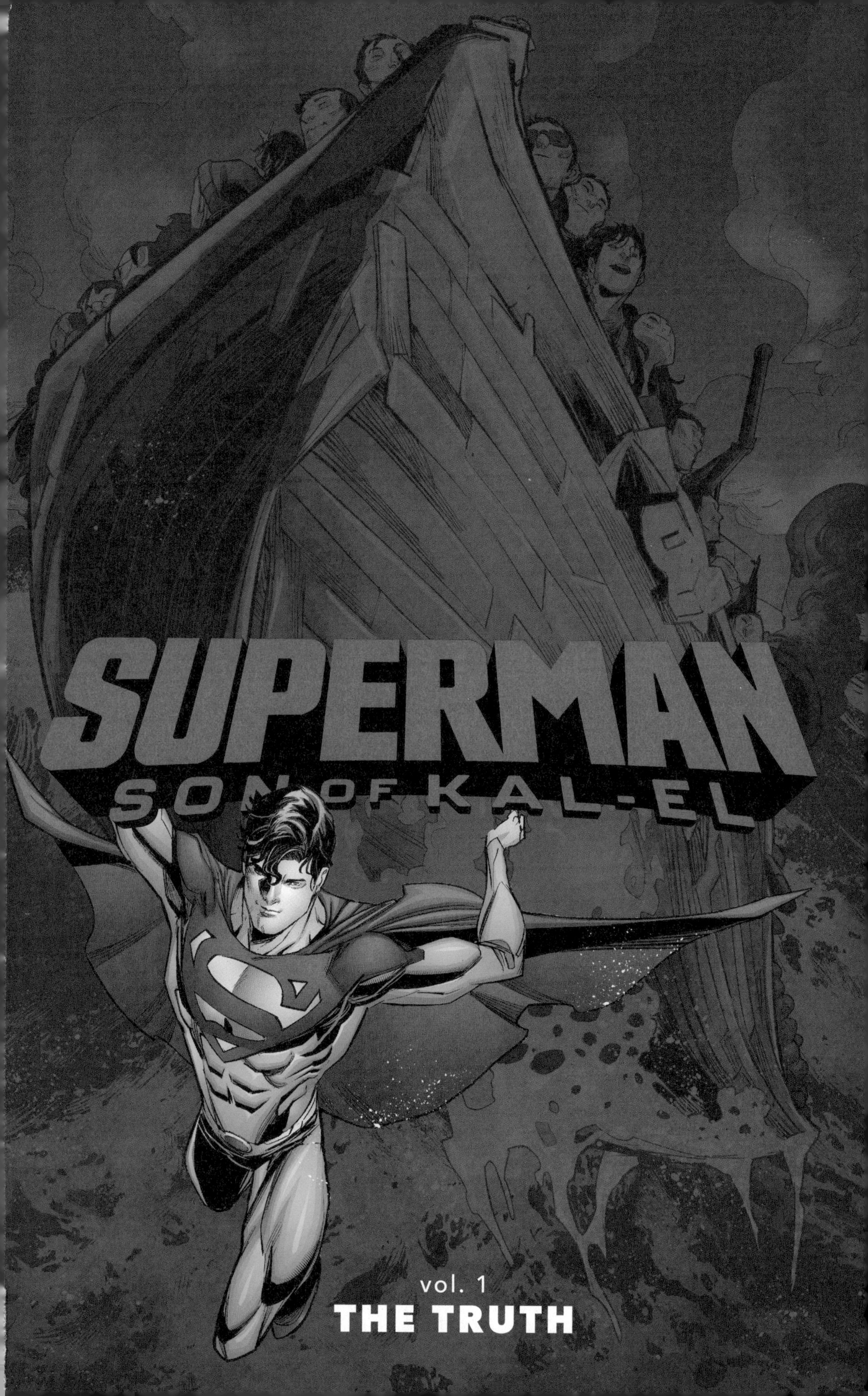
SUPERMAN
SON OF KAL-EL
vol. 1
THE TRUTH

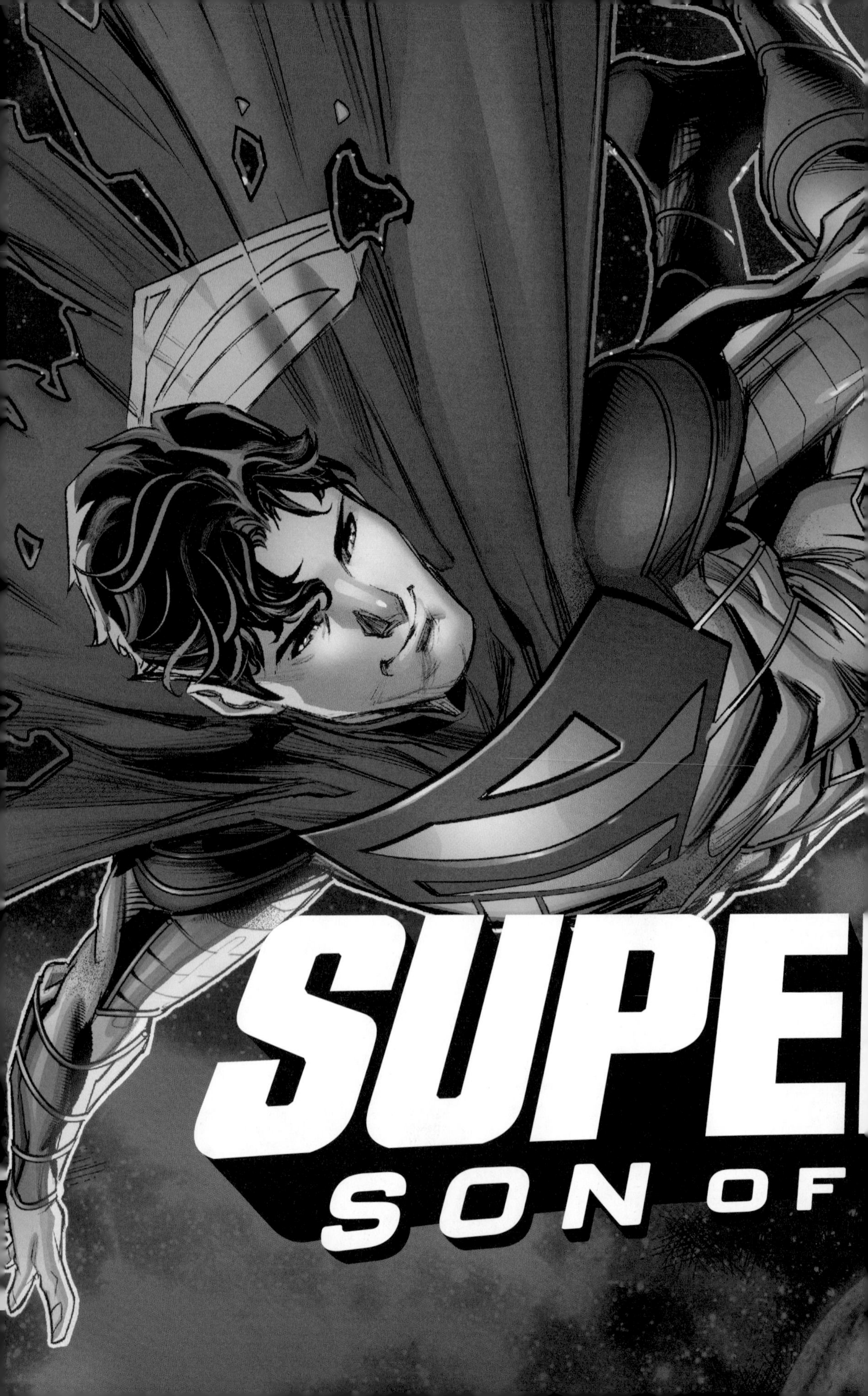
SUPE
SON OF

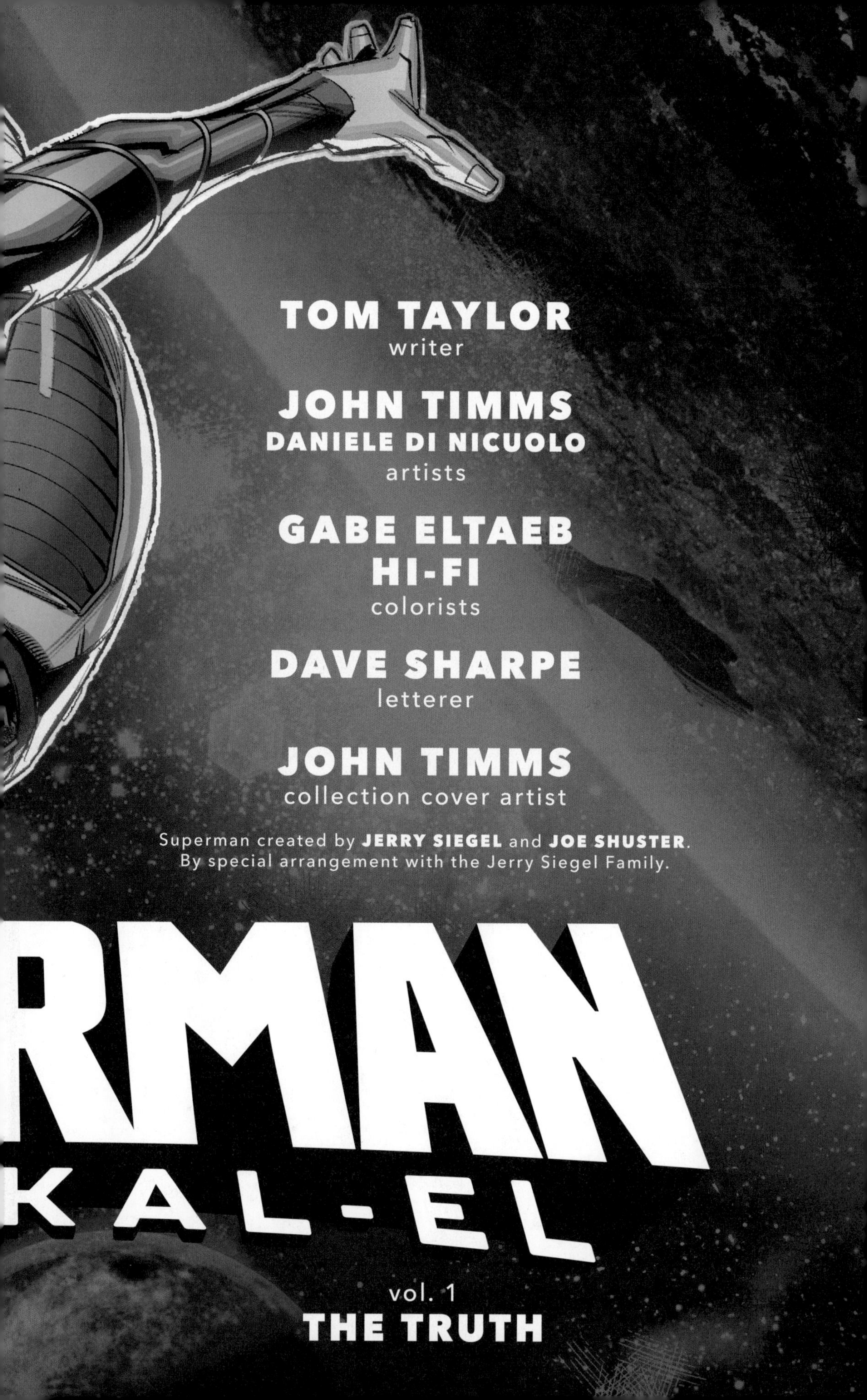
RMAN
KAL-EL

TOM TAYLOR
writer

JOHN TIMMS
DANIELE DI NICUOLO
artists

GABE ELTAEB
HI-FI
colorists

DAVE SHARPE
letterer

JOHN TIMMS
collection cover artist

Superman created by **JERRY SIEGEL** and **JOE SHUSTER**.
By special arrangement with the Jerry Siegel Family.

vol. 1
THE TRUTH

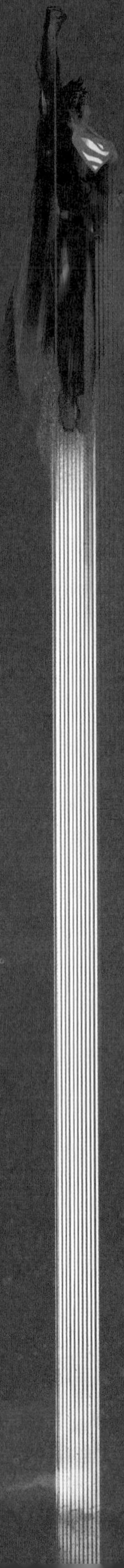

JAMIE S. RICH, **MIKE COTTON** Editors – Original Series
DIEGO LOPEZ Associate Editor – Original Series
JILLIAN GRANT Assistant Editor – Original Series
STEVE BUCCELLATO and **PAUL KAMINSKI** Editors – Collected Edition
STEVE COOK Design Director – Books
DAMIAN RYLAND Publication Design
CHRISTY SAWYER Publication Production

MARIE JAVINS Editor-in-Chief, DC Comics

ANNE DePIES Senior VP – General Manager
JIM LEE Publisher & Chief Creative Officer
DON FALLETTI VP – Manufacturing Operations & Workflow Management
LAWRENCE GANEM VP – Talent Services
ALISON GILL Senior VP – Manufacturing & Operations
JEFFREY KAUFMAN VP – Editorial Strategy & Programming
NICK J. NAPOLITANO VP – Manufacturing Administration & Design
NANCY SPEARS VP – Revenue

SUPERMAN: SON OF KAL-EL VOL. 1: THE TRUTH

DC Comics, 2900 West Alameda Ave., Burbank, CA 91505
Printed by Transcontinental Interglobe, Beauceville, QC, Canada. 4/22/22.
First Printing. ISBN: 978-1-77951-532-2

Library of Congress Cataloging-in-Publication Data is available.

PEFC Certified
This product is from sustainably managed forests and controlled sources
PEFC
PEFC/01-31-106
www.pefc.org

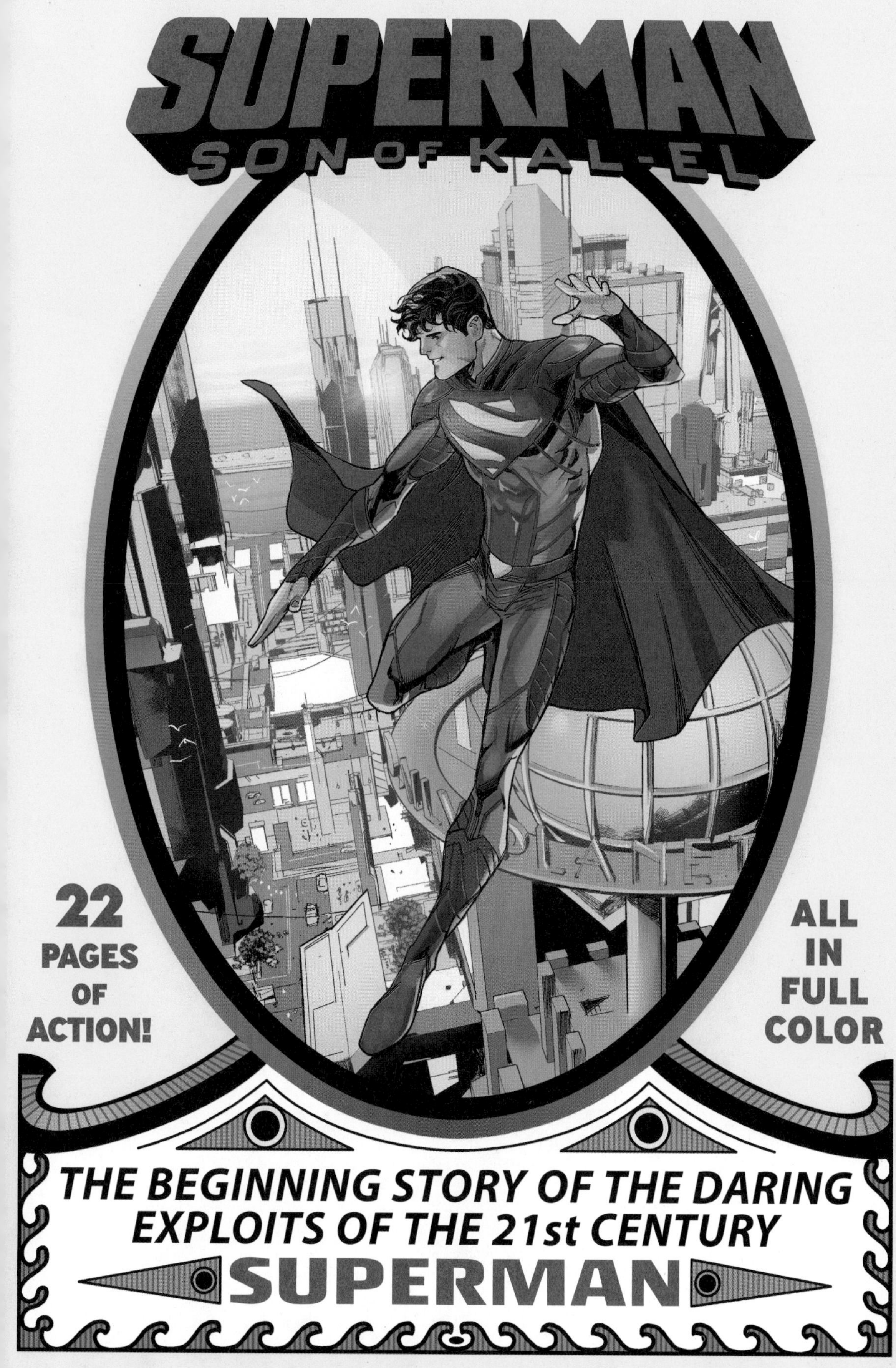
SUPERMAN
SON OF KAL-EL
22 PAGES OF ACTION!
ALL IN FULL COLOR
THE BEGINNING STORY OF THE DARING EXPLOITS OF THE 21st CENTURY
SUPERMAN

Superman: Son of Kal-El #1 variant cover art by **INHYUK LEE**

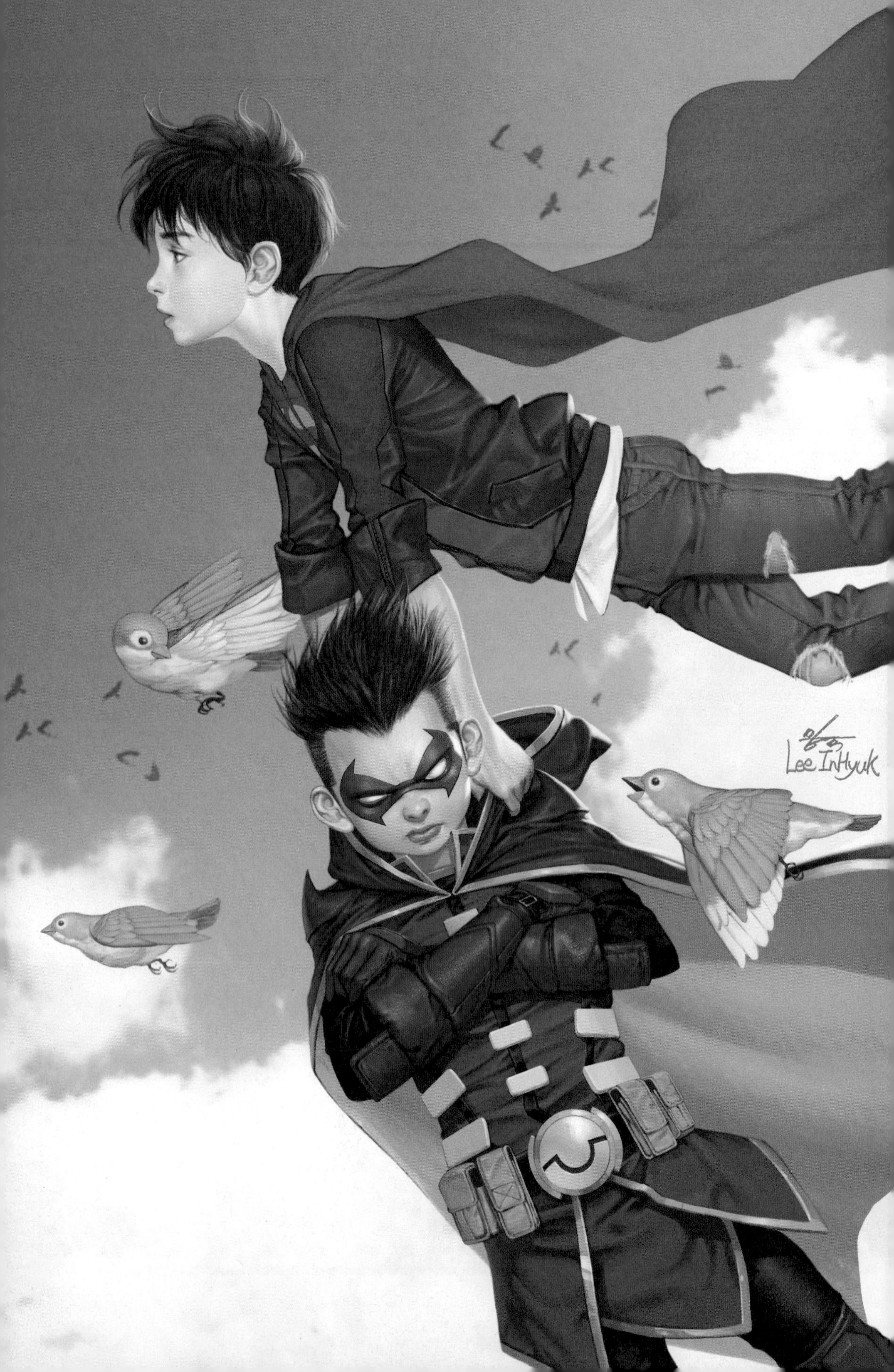
Lee InHyuk

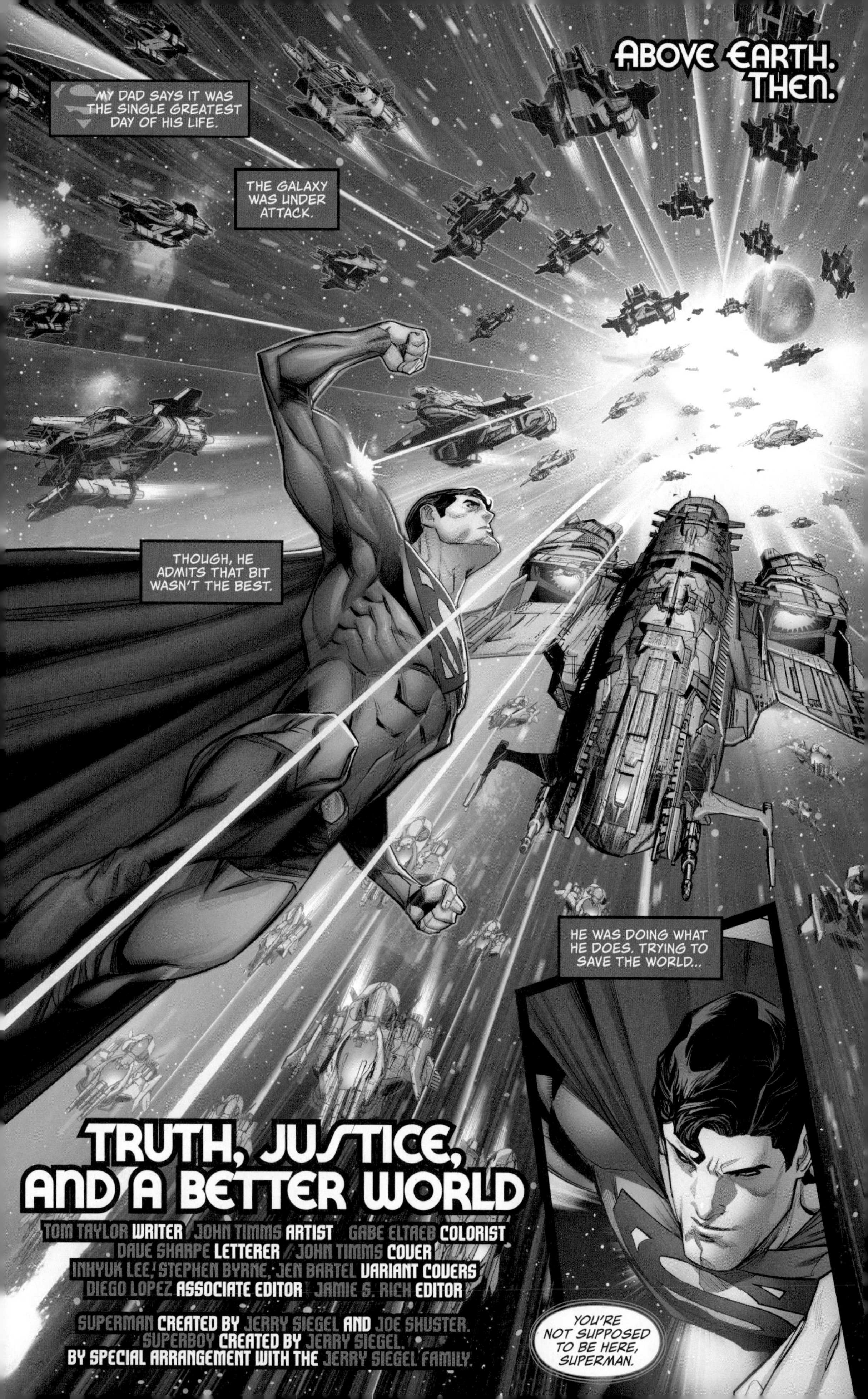
ABOVE EARTH. THEN.
MY DAD SAYS IT WAS THE SINGLE GREATEST DAY OF HIS LIFE.
THE GALAXY WAS UNDER ATTACK.
THOUGH, HE ADMITS THAT BIT WASN'T THE BEST.
HE WAS DOING WHAT HE DOES. TRYING TO SAVE THE WORLD...
TRUTH, JUSTICE, AND A BETTER WORLD
TOM TAYLOR WRITER JOHN TIMMS ARTIST GABE ELTAEB COLORIST
DAVE SHARPE LETTERER JOHN TIMMS COVER
INHYUK LEE, STEPHEN BYRNE, JEN BARTEL VARIANT COVERS
DIEGO LOPEZ ASSOCIATE EDITOR JAMIE S. RICH EDITOR
SUPERMAN CREATED BY JERRY SIEGEL AND JOE SHUSTER.
SUPERBOY CREATED BY JERRY SIEGEL.
BY SPECIAL ARRANGEMENT WITH THE JERRY SIEGEL FAMILY.
YOU'RE NOT SUPPOSED TO BE HERE, SUPERMAN.

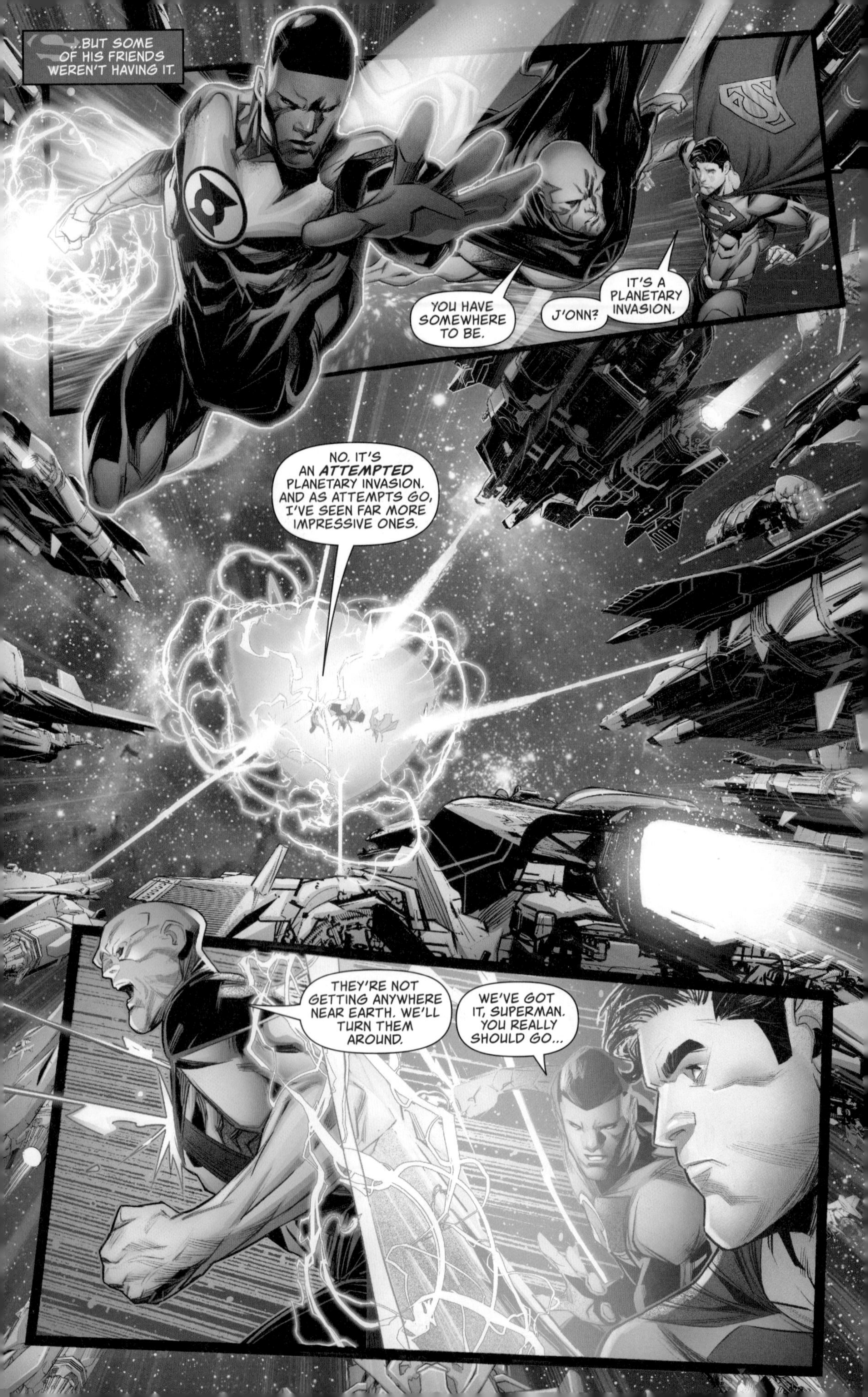
...BUT SOME OF HIS FRIENDS WEREN'T HAVING IT.
YOU HAVE SOMEWHERE TO BE.
J'ONN?
IT'S A PLANETARY INVASION.
NO. IT'S AN ATTEMPTED PLANETARY INVASION. AND AS ATTEMPTS GO, I'VE SEEN FAR MORE IMPRESSIVE ONES.
THEY'RE NOT GETTING ANYWHERE NEAR EARTH. WE'LL TURN THEM AROUND.
WE'VE GOT IT, SUPERMAN. YOU REALLY SHOULD GO...

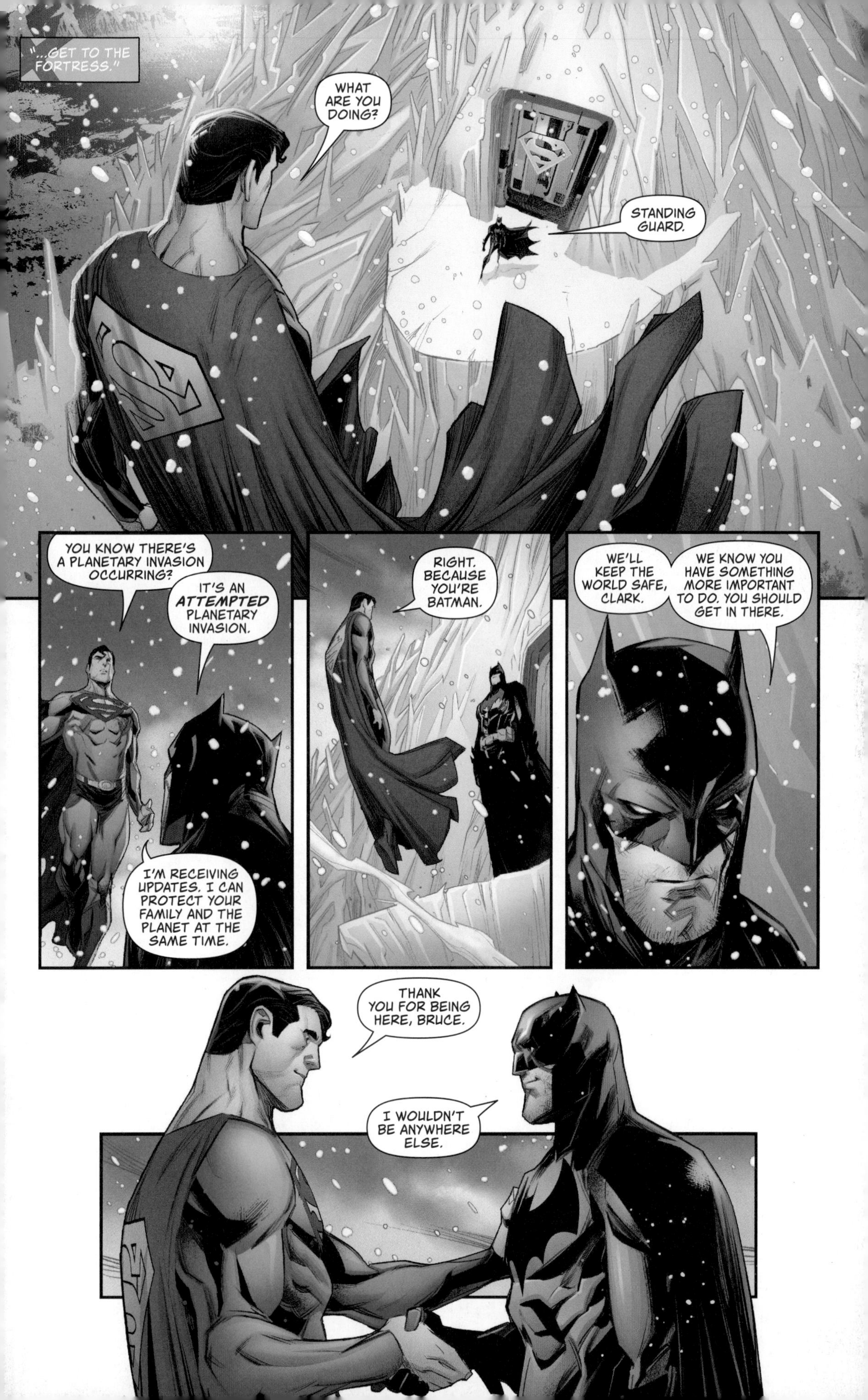
"...GET TO THE FORTRESS."
WHAT ARE YOU DOING?
STANDING GUARD.
YOU KNOW THERE'S A PLANETARY INVASION OCCURRING?
IT'S AN *ATTEMPTED* PLANETARY INVASION.
I'M RECEIVING UPDATES. I CAN PROTECT YOUR FAMILY AND THE PLANET AT THE SAME TIME.
RIGHT. BECAUSE YOU'RE BATMAN.
WE'LL KEEP THE WORLD SAFE, CLARK.
WE KNOW YOU HAVE SOMETHING MORE IMPORTANT TO DO. YOU SHOULD GET IN THERE.
THANK YOU FOR BEING HERE, BRUCE.
I WOULDN'T BE ANYWHERE ELSE.

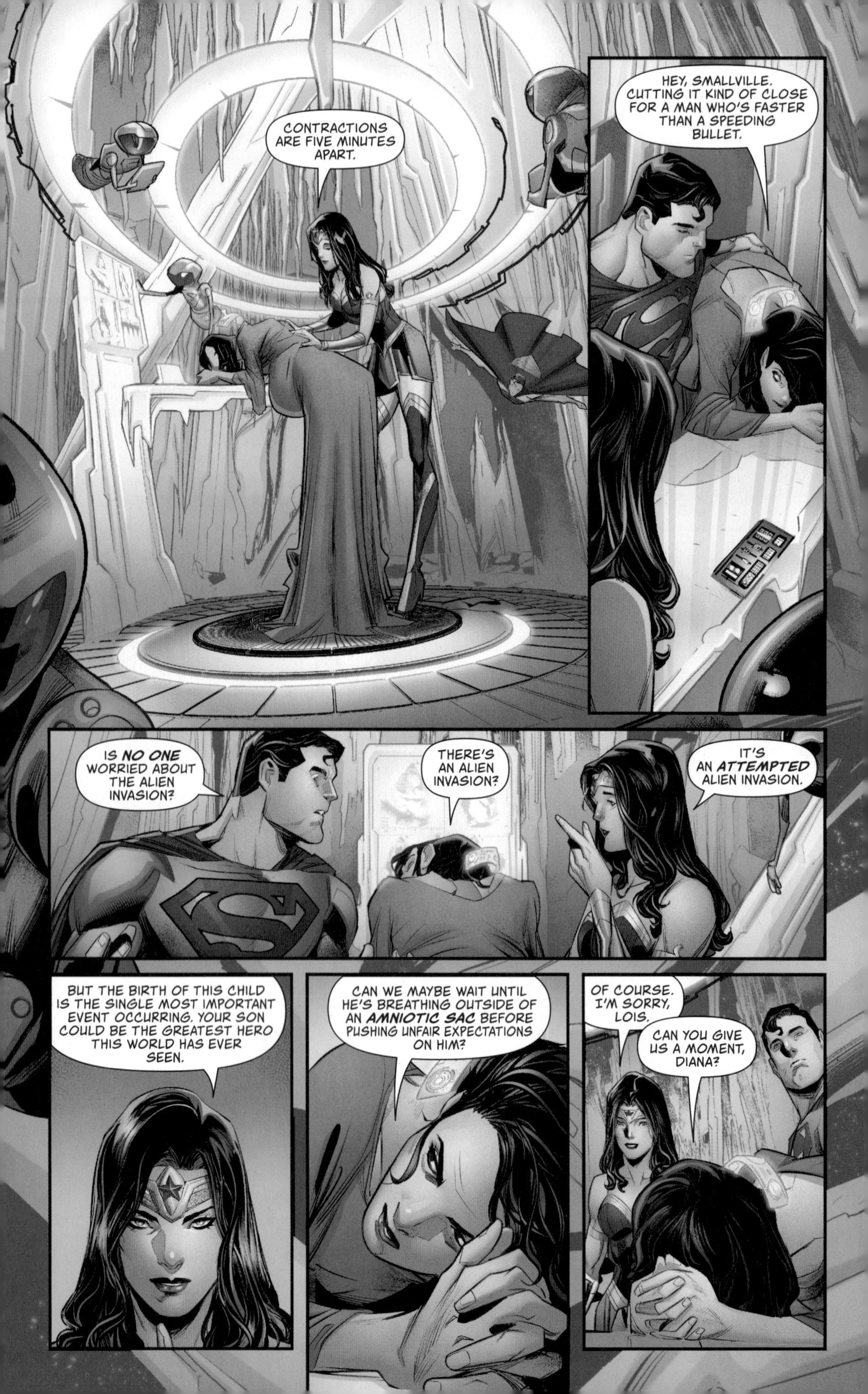
CONTRACTIONS ARE FIVE MINUTES APART.
HEY, SMALLVILLE. CUTTING IT KIND OF CLOSE FOR A MAN WHO'S FASTER THAN A SPEEDING BULLET.
IS NO ONE WORRIED ABOUT THE ALIEN INVASION?
THERE'S AN ALIEN INVASION?
IT'S AN ATTEMPTED ALIEN INVASION.
BUT THE BIRTH OF THIS CHILD IS THE SINGLE MOST IMPORTANT EVENT OCCURRING. YOUR SON COULD BE THE GREATEST HERO THIS WORLD HAS EVER SEEN.
CAN WE MAYBE WAIT UNTIL HE'S BREATHING OUTSIDE OF AN AMNIOTIC SAC BEFORE PUSHING UNFAIR EXPECTATIONS ON HIM?
OF COURSE. I'M SORRY, LOIS.
CAN YOU GIVE US A MOMENT, DIANA?

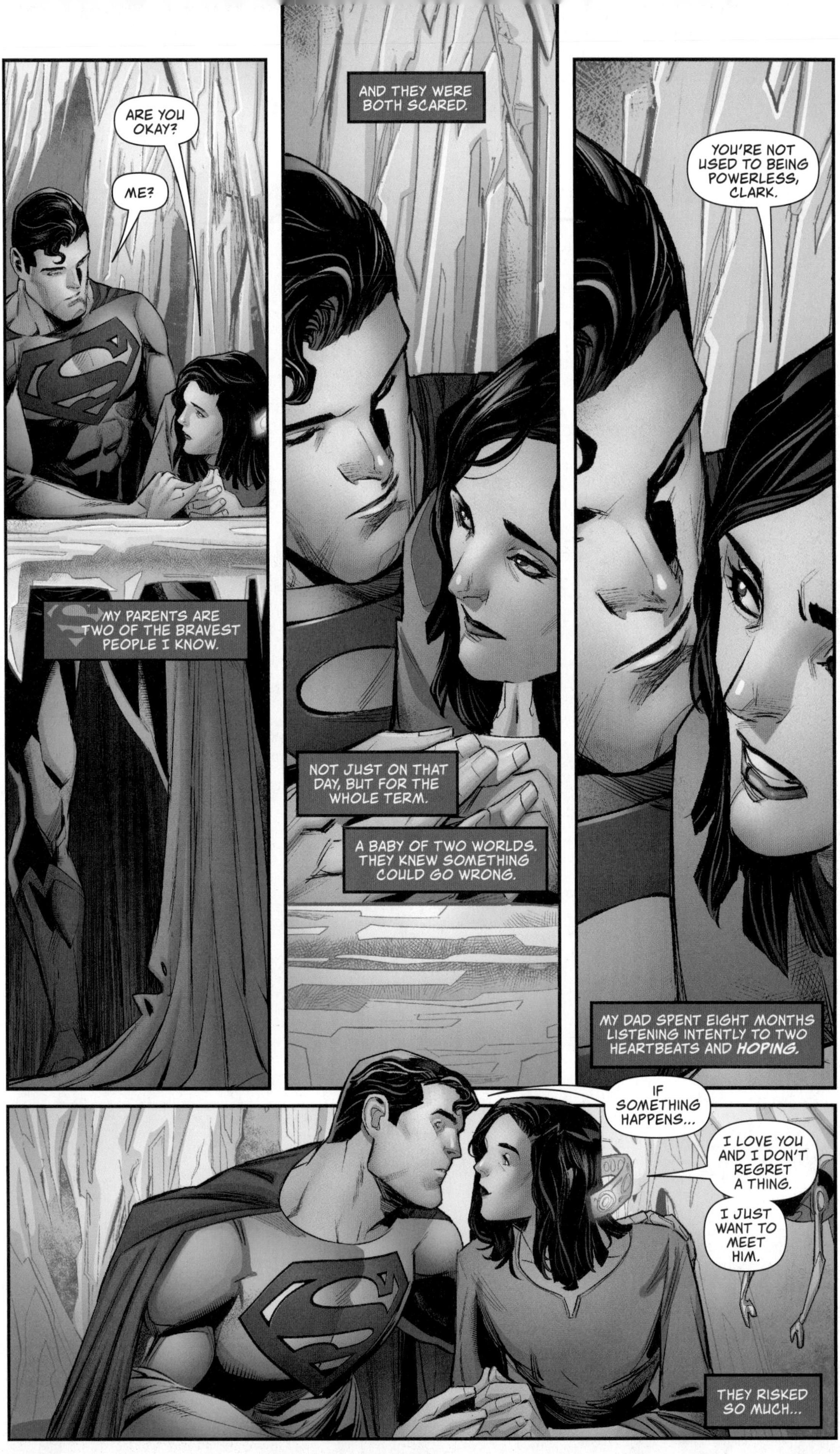
ARE YOU OKAY?
ME?
MY PARENTS ARE TWO OF THE BRAVEST PEOPLE I KNOW.
AND THEY WERE BOTH SCARED.
NOT JUST ON THAT DAY, BUT FOR THE WHOLE TERM.
A BABY OF TWO WORLDS. THEY KNEW SOMETHING COULD GO WRONG.
YOU'RE NOT USED TO BEING POWERLESS, CLARK.
MY DAD SPENT EIGHT MONTHS LISTENING INTENTLY TO TWO HEARTBEATS AND HOPING.
IF SOMETHING HAPPENS...
I LOVE YOU AND I DON'T REGRET A THING.
I JUST WANT TO MEET HIM.
THEY RISKED SO MUCH...

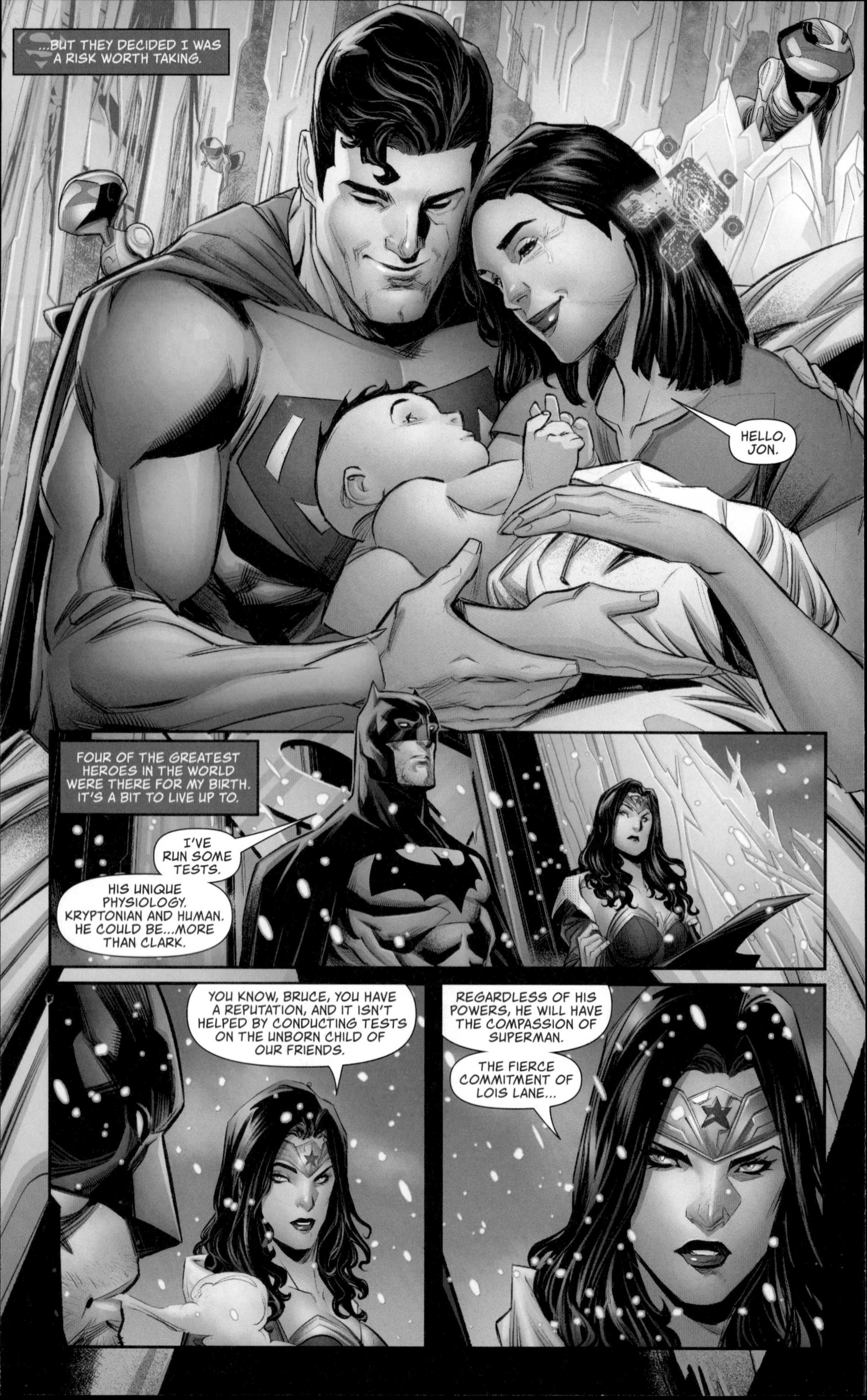
...BUT THEY DECIDED I WAS A RISK WORTH TAKING.
HELLO, JON.
FOUR OF THE GREATEST HEROES IN THE WORLD WERE THERE FOR MY BIRTH. IT'S A BIT TO LIVE UP TO.
I'VE RUN SOME TESTS.
HIS UNIQUE PHYSIOLOGY. KRYPTONIAN AND HUMAN. HE COULD BE...MORE THAN CLARK.
YOU KNOW, BRUCE, YOU HAVE A REPUTATION, AND IT ISN'T HELPED BY CONDUCTING TESTS ON THE UNBORN CHILD OF OUR FRIENDS.
REGARDLESS OF HIS POWERS, HE WILL HAVE THE COMPASSION OF SUPERMAN.
THE FIERCE COMMITMENT OF LOIS LANE...

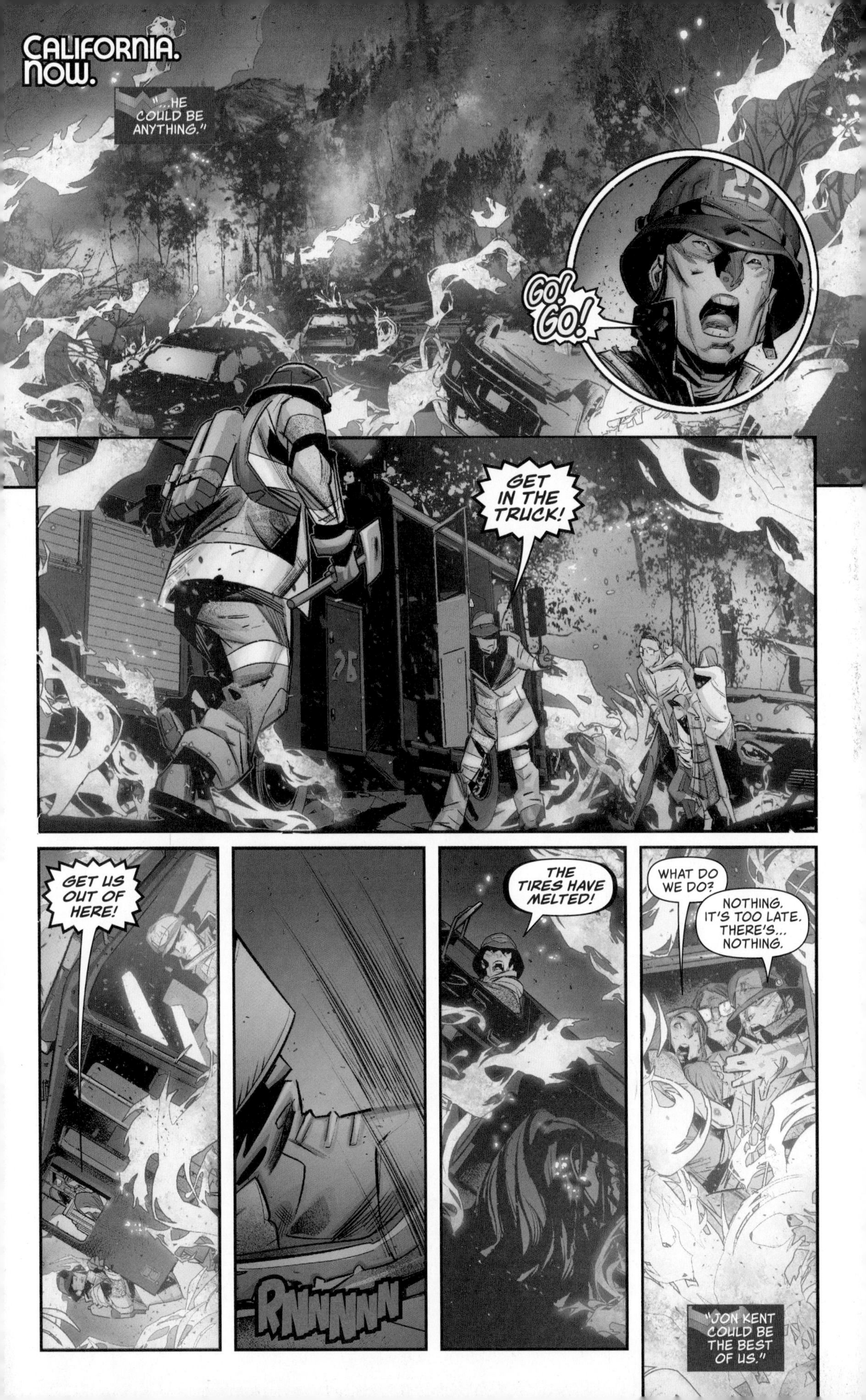
CALIFORNIA. NOW.
"...HE COULD BE ANYTHING."
GO! GO!
GET IN THE TRUCK!
GET US OUT OF HERE!
RNNNNNN
THE TIRES HAVE MELTED!
WHAT DO WE DO?
NOTHING. IT'S TOO LATE. THERE'S... NOTHING.
"JON KENT COULD BE THE BEST OF US."

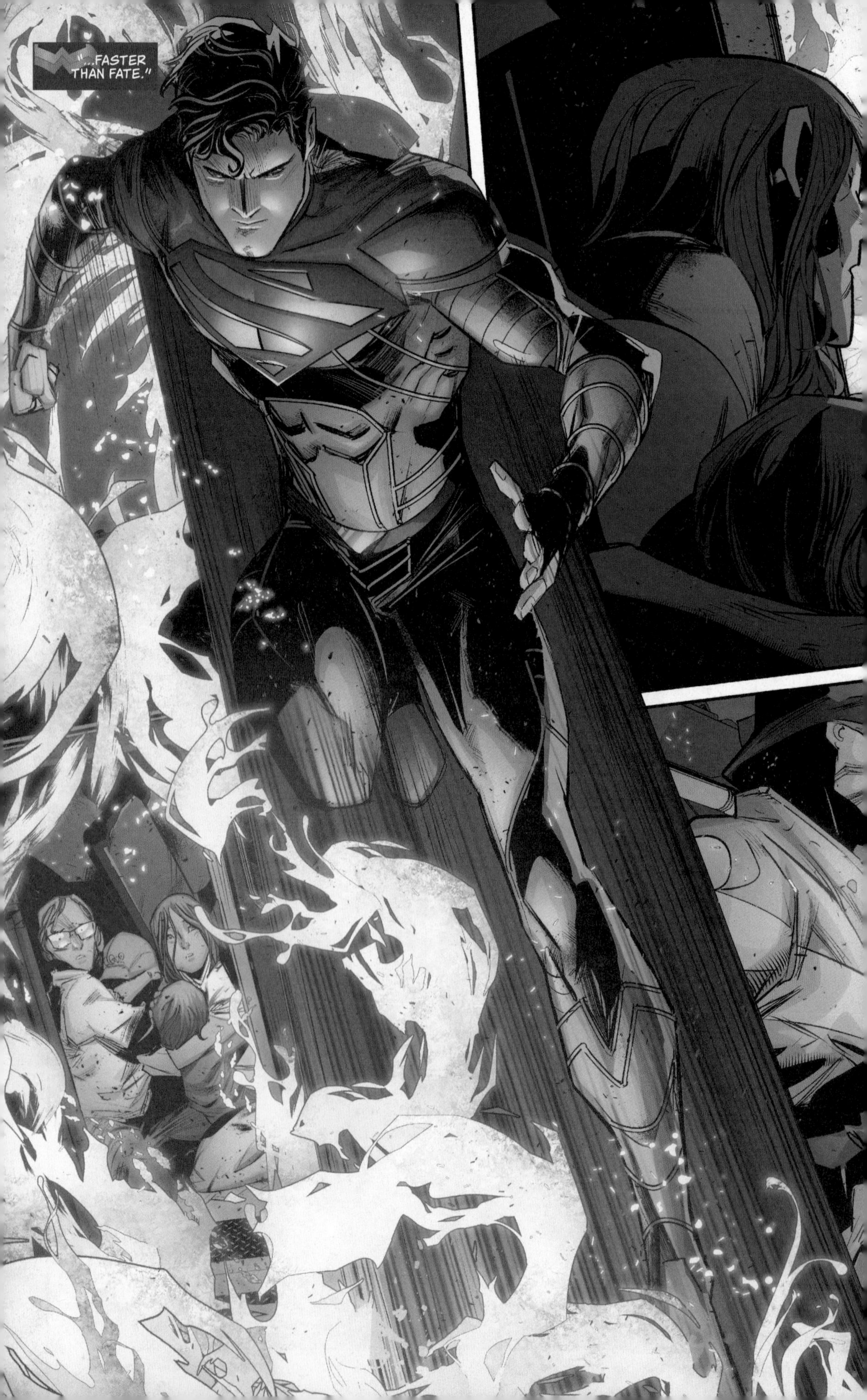
"...FASTER THAN FATE."

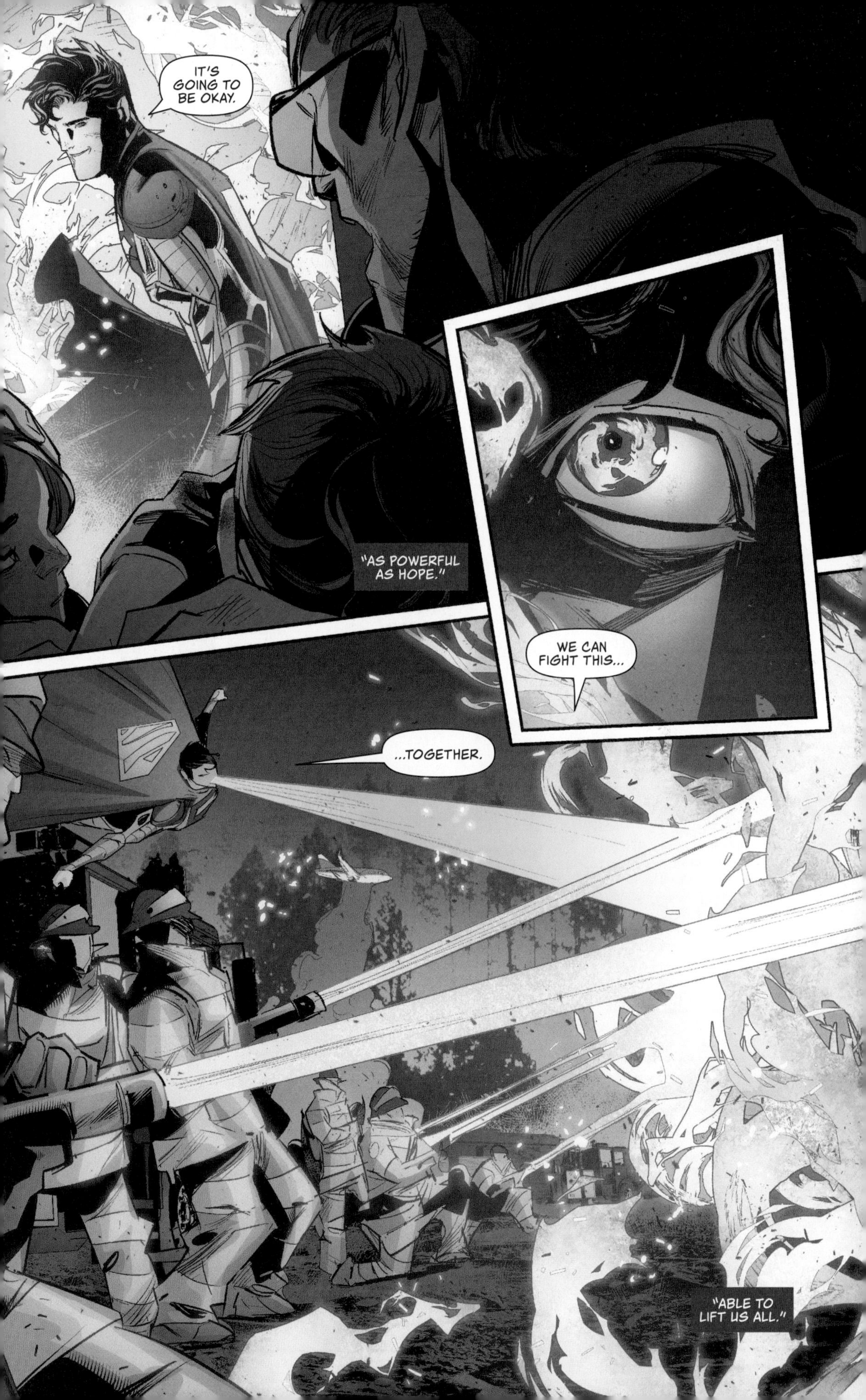
IT'S GOING TO BE OKAY.
"AS POWERFUL AS HOPE."
WE CAN FIGHT THIS...
...TOGETHER.
"ABLE TO LIFT US ALL."

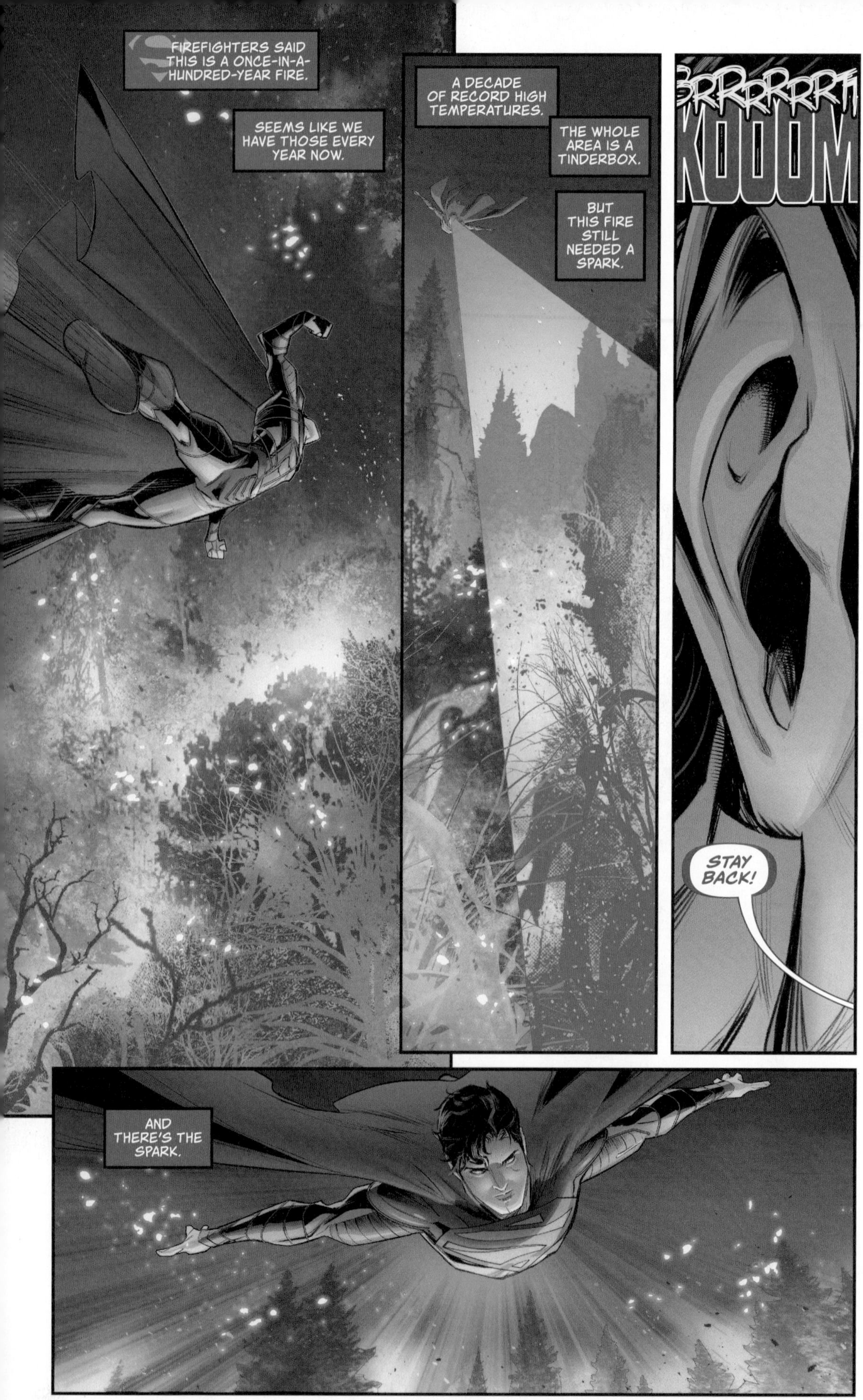

FIREFIGHTERS SAID THIS IS A ONCE-IN-A-HUNDRED-YEAR FIRE.
SEEMS LIKE WE HAVE THOSE EVERY YEAR NOW.
A DECADE OF RECORD HIGH TEMPERATURES.
THE WHOLE AREA IS A TINDERBOX.
BUT THIS FIRE STILL NEEDED A SPARK.
RRRRR
KOOOM
STAY BACK!
AND THERE'S THE SPARK.

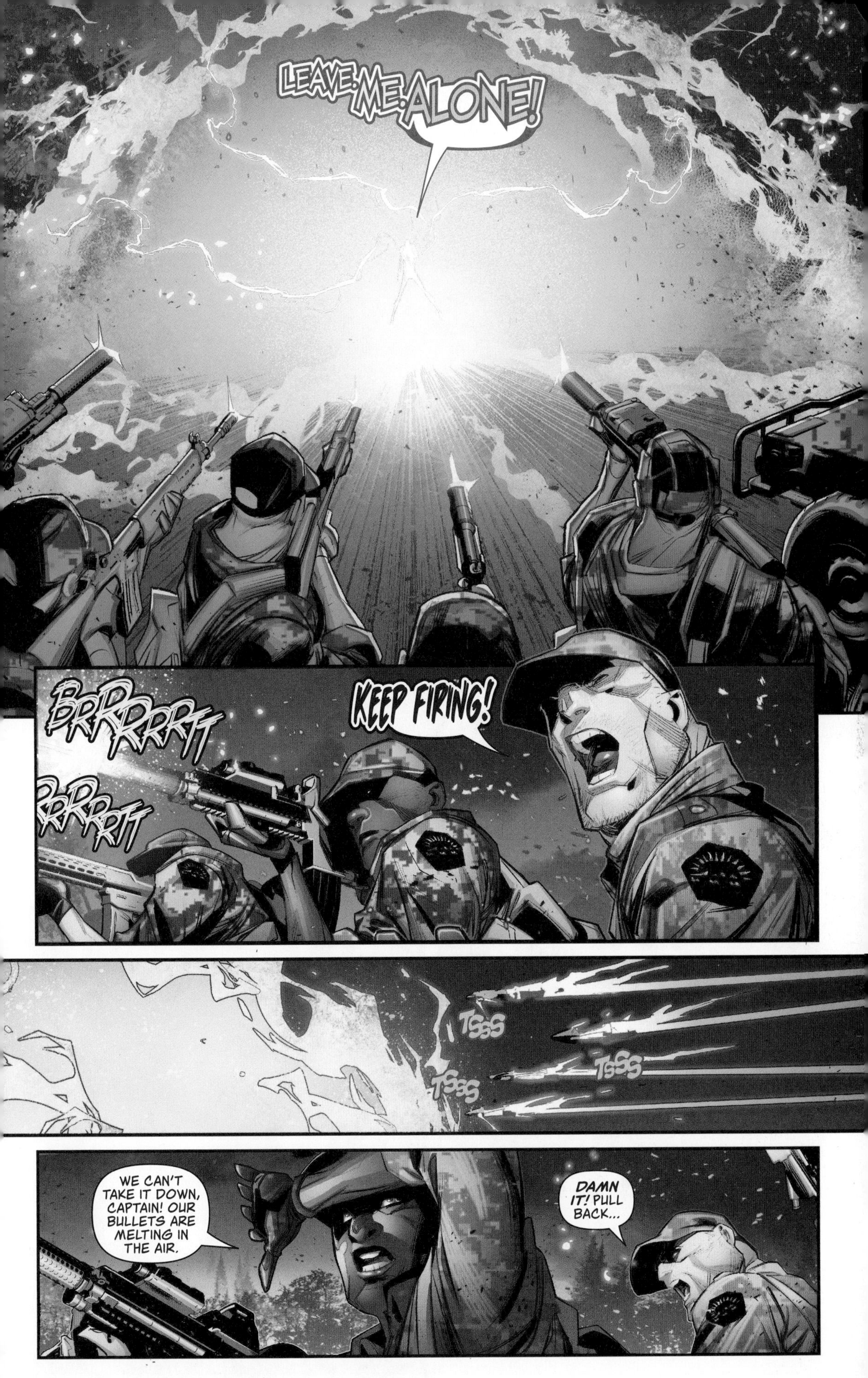
LEAVE ME ALONE!
BRRRRRRTT
BRRRRRTT
KEEP FIRING!
TSSS
TSSS
TSSS
WE CAN'T TAKE IT DOWN, CAPTAIN! OUR BULLETS ARE MELTING IN THE AIR.
DAMN IT! PULL BACK...

"...I'M CALLING IN AIR SUPPORT."

FWDOOM

NOPE.

CHZZZZRR

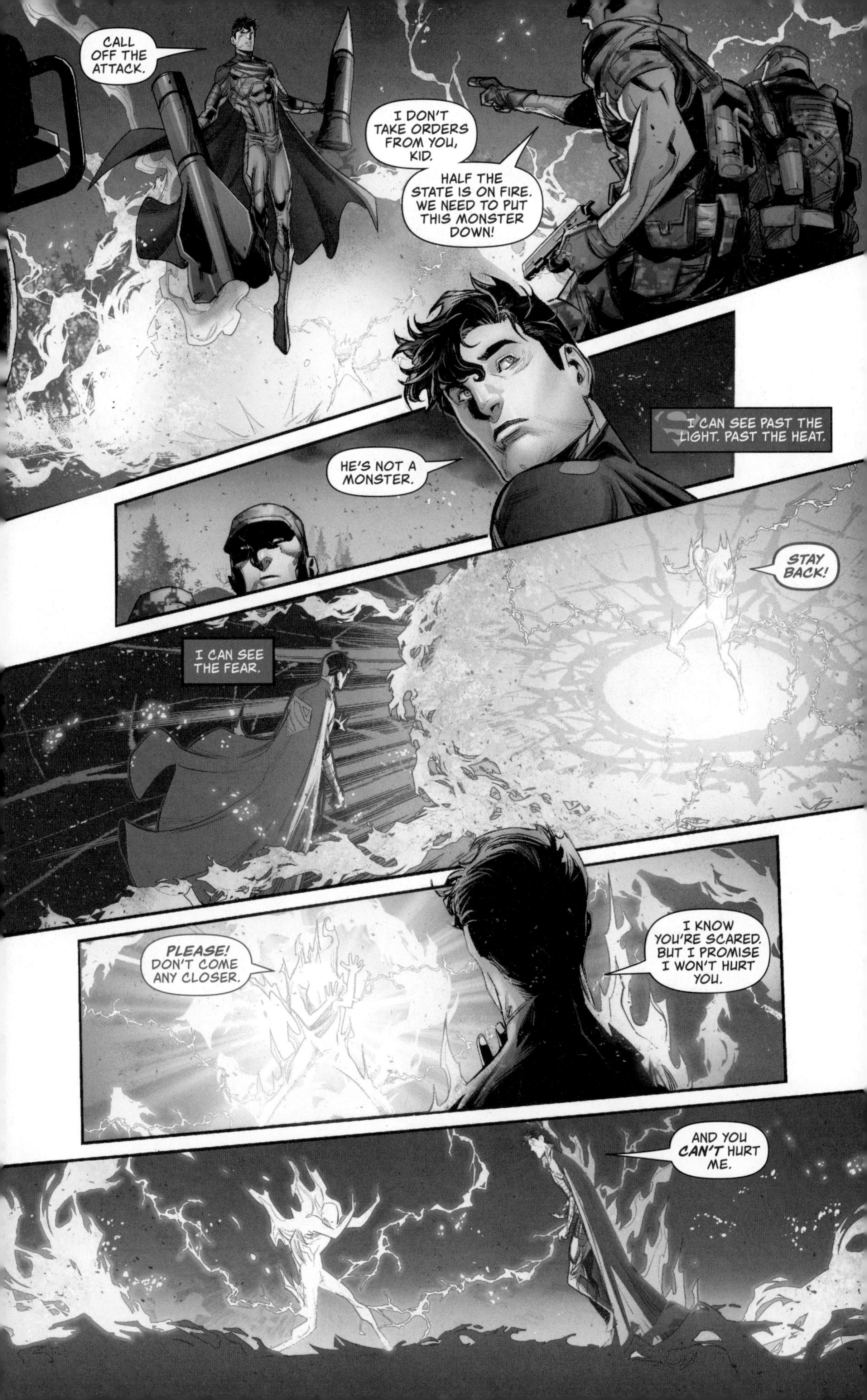
CALL OFF THE ATTACK.
I DON'T TAKE ORDERS FROM YOU, KID.
HALF THE STATE IS ON FIRE. WE NEED TO PUT THIS MONSTER DOWN!
I CAN SEE PAST THE LIGHT. PAST THE HEAT.
HE'S NOT A MONSTER.
STAY BACK!
I CAN SEE THE FEAR.
PLEASE! DON'T COME ANY CLOSER.
I KNOW YOU'RE SCARED. BUT I PROMISE I WON'T HURT YOU.
AND YOU CAN'T HURT ME.

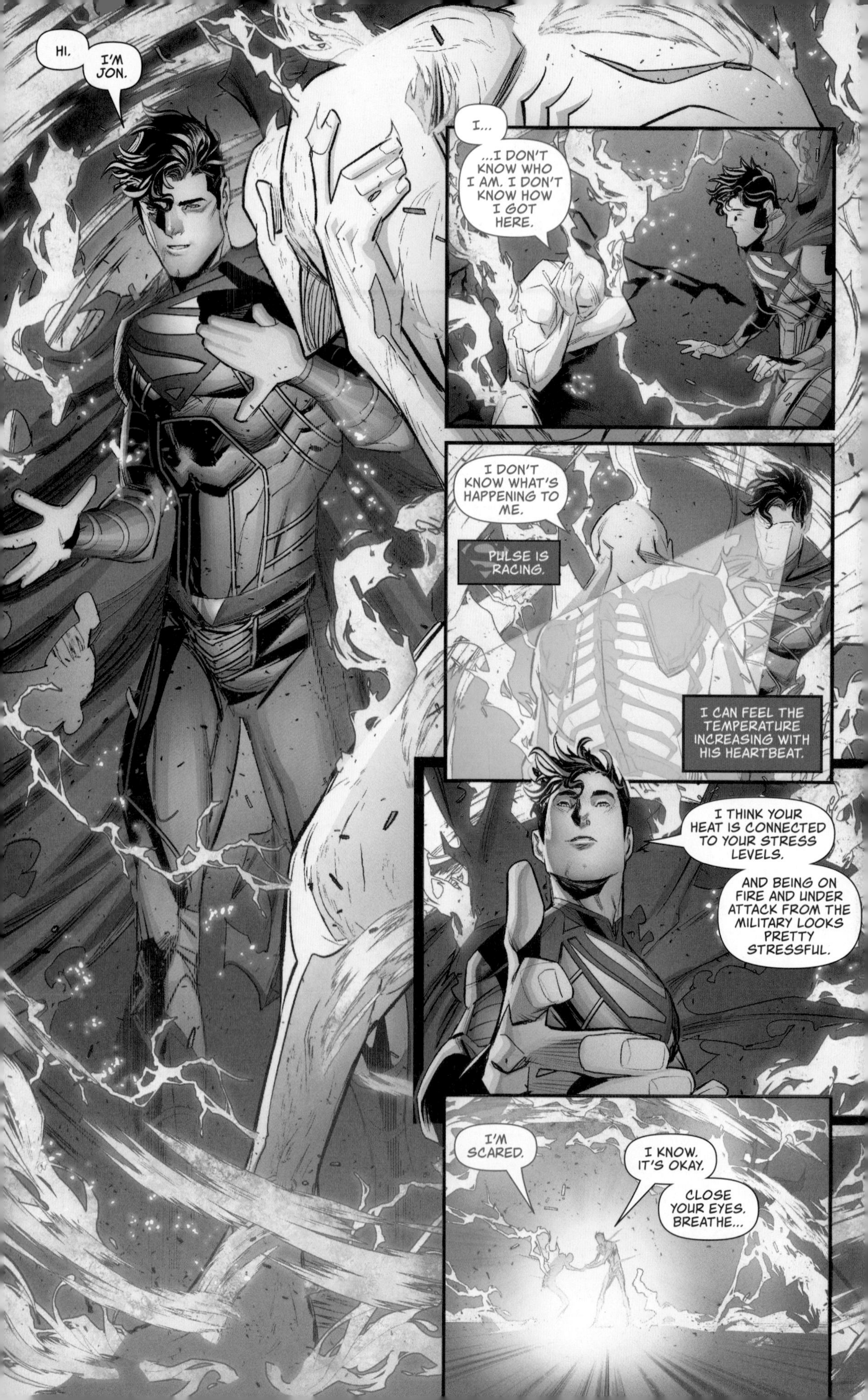
HI.
I'M JON.
I...
...I DON'T KNOW WHO I AM. I DON'T KNOW HOW I GOT HERE.
I DON'T KNOW WHAT'S HAPPENING TO ME.
PULSE IS RACING.
I CAN FEEL THE TEMPERATURE INCREASING WITH HIS HEARTBEAT.
I THINK YOUR HEAT IS CONNECTED TO YOUR STRESS LEVELS.
AND BEING ON FIRE AND UNDER ATTACK FROM THE MILITARY LOOKS PRETTY STRESSFUL.
I'M SCARED.
I KNOW. IT'S OKAY.
CLOSE YOUR EYES. BREATHE...

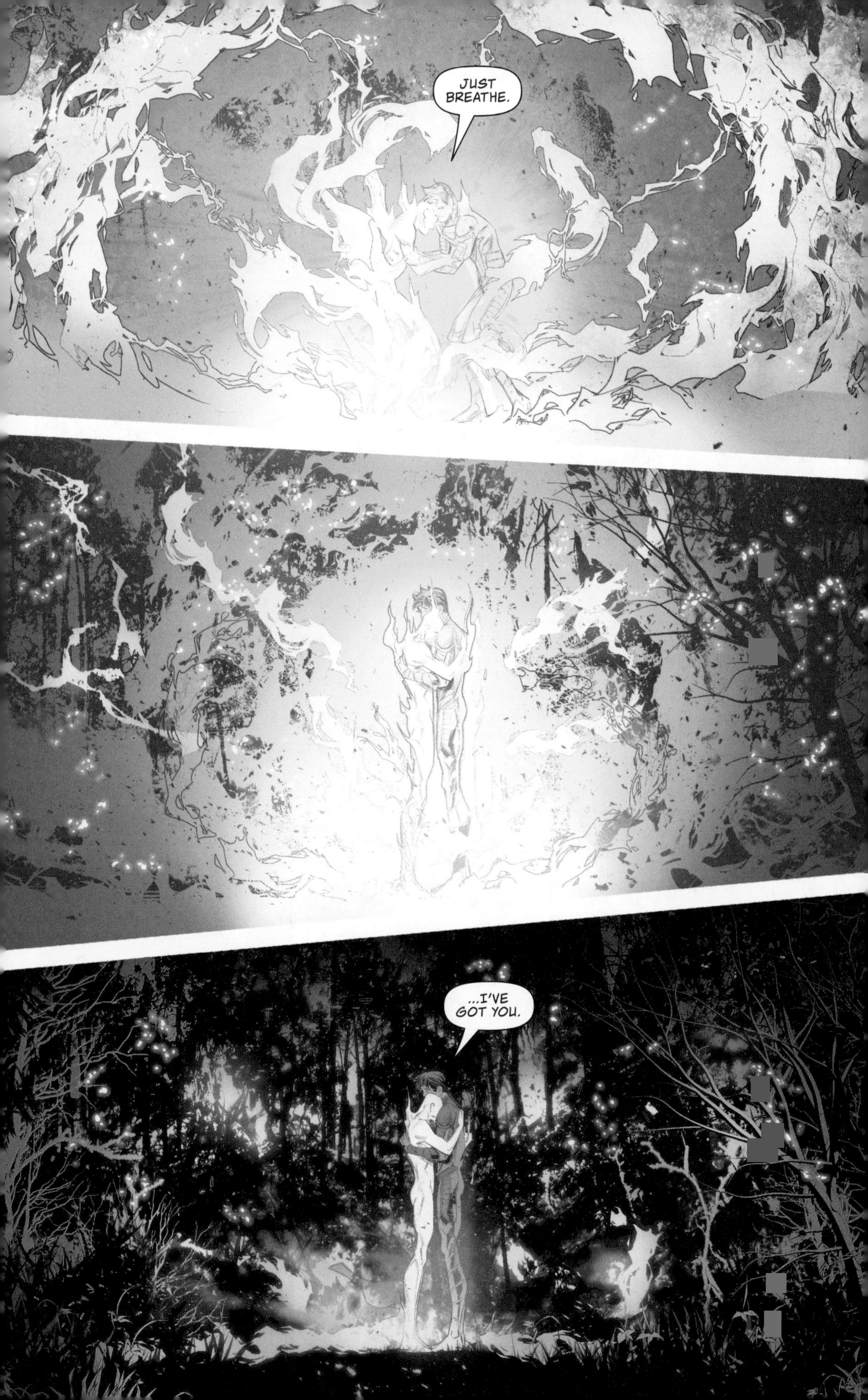
JUST BREATHE.
...I'VE GOT YOU.

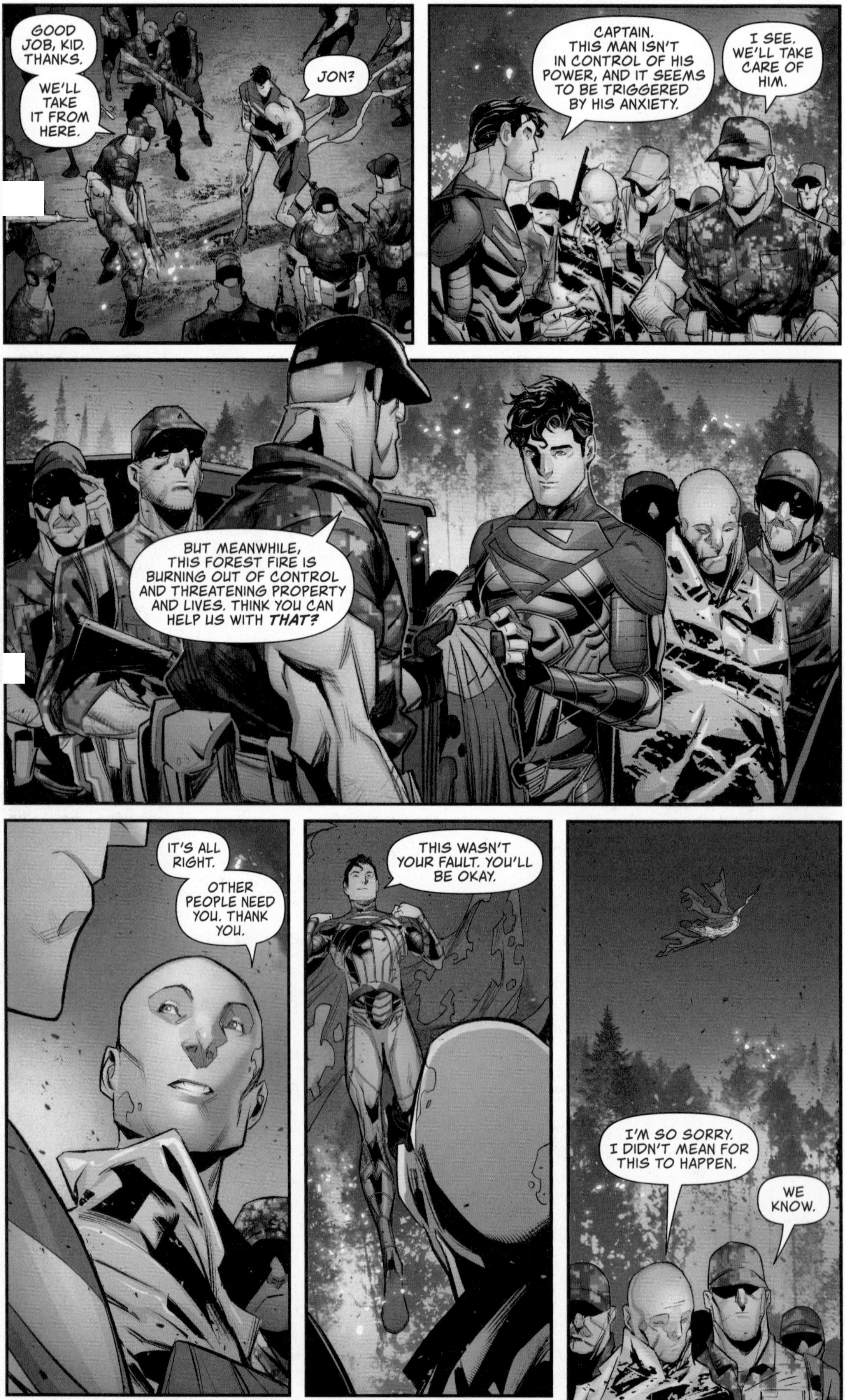
GOOD JOB, KID. THANKS.
WE'LL TAKE IT FROM HERE.
JON?
CAPTAIN. THIS MAN ISN'T IN CONTROL OF HIS POWER, AND IT SEEMS TO BE TRIGGERED BY HIS ANXIETY.
I SEE. WE'LL TAKE CARE OF HIM.
BUT MEANWHILE, THIS FOREST FIRE IS BURNING OUT OF CONTROL AND THREATENING PROPERTY AND LIVES. THINK YOU CAN HELP US WITH *THAT?*
IT'S ALL RIGHT.
OTHER PEOPLE NEED YOU. THANK YOU.
THIS WASN'T YOUR FAULT. YOU'LL BE OKAY.
I'M SO SORRY. I DIDN'T MEAN FOR THIS TO HAPPEN.
WE KNOW.

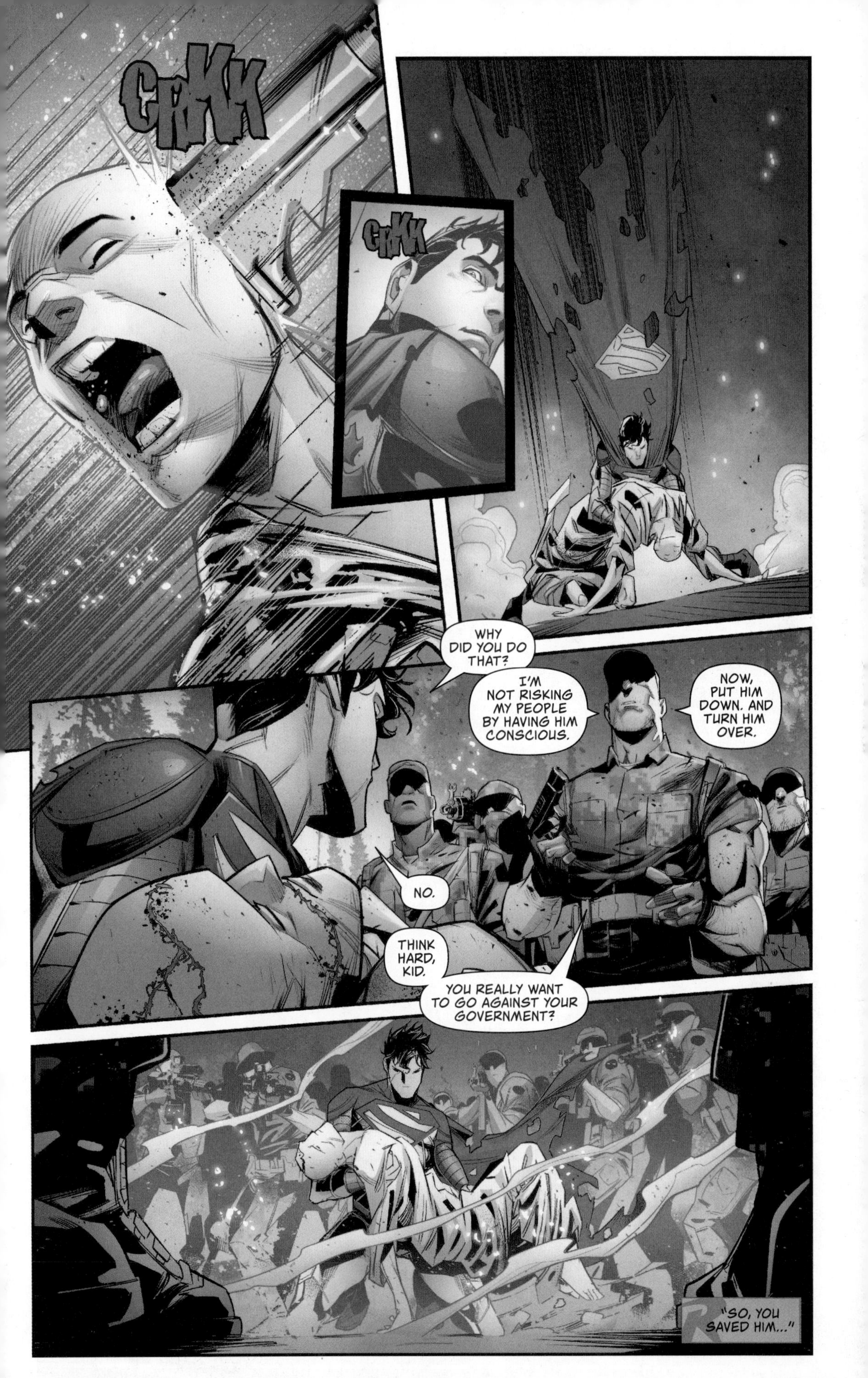
CRKK
CRKK
WHY DID YOU DO THAT?
I'M NOT RISKING MY PEOPLE BY HAVING HIM CONSCIOUS.
NOW, PUT HIM DOWN. AND TURN HIM OVER.
NO.
THINK HARD, KID.
YOU REALLY WANT TO GO AGAINST YOUR GOVERNMENT?
"SO, YOU SAVED HIM..."

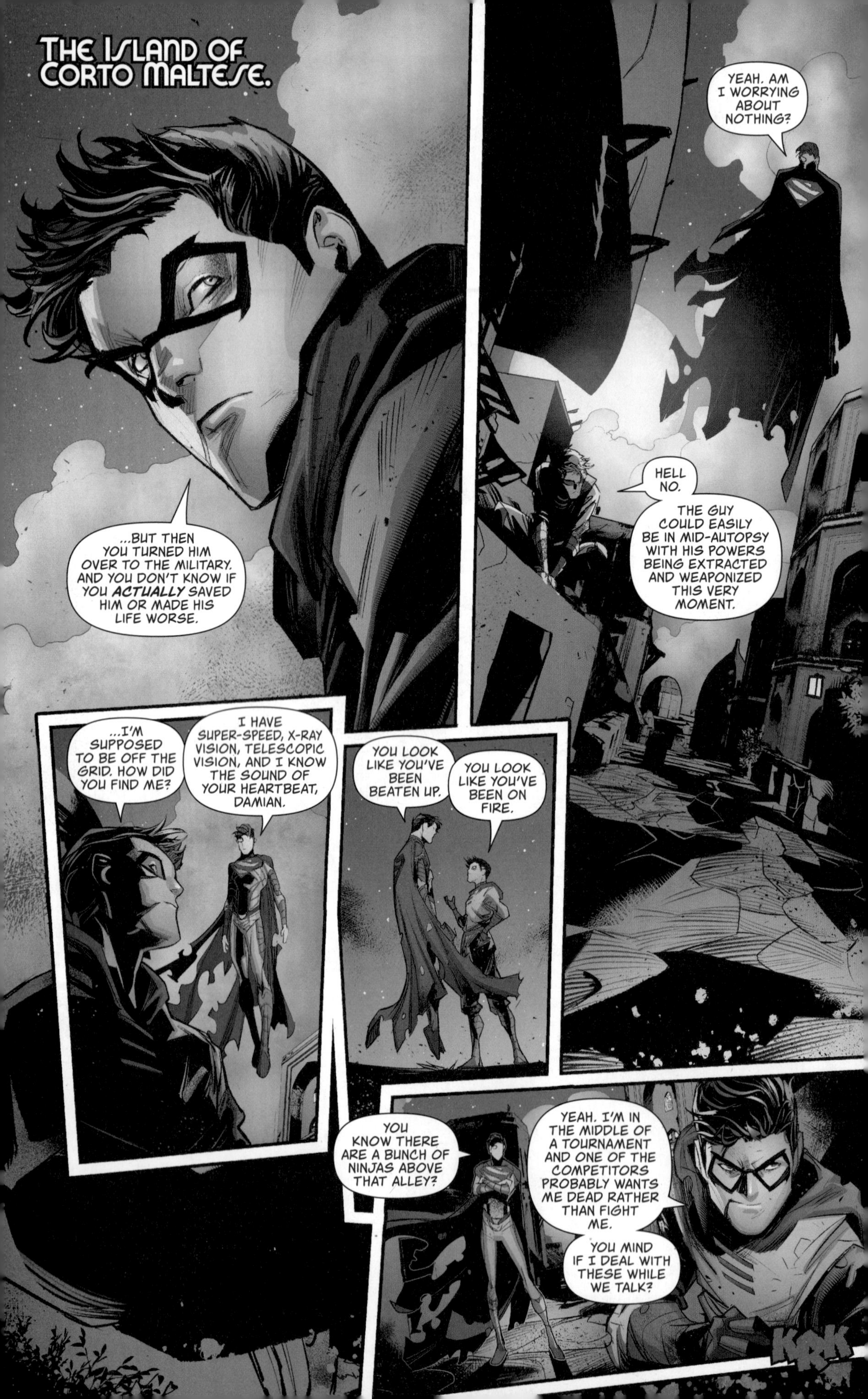
THE ISLAND OF CORTO MALTESE.
...BUT THEN YOU TURNED HIM OVER TO THE MILITARY. AND YOU DON'T KNOW IF YOU ACTUALLY SAVED HIM OR MADE HIS LIFE WORSE.
YEAH. AM I WORRYING ABOUT NOTHING?
HELL NO.
THE GUY COULD EASILY BE IN MID-AUTOPSY WITH HIS POWERS BEING EXTRACTED AND WEAPONIZED THIS VERY MOMENT.
...I'M SUPPOSED TO BE OFF THE GRID. HOW DID YOU FIND ME?
I HAVE SUPER-SPEED, X-RAY VISION, TELESCOPIC VISION, AND I KNOW THE SOUND OF YOUR HEARTBEAT, DAMIAN.
YOU LOOK LIKE YOU'VE BEEN BEATEN UP.
YOU LOOK LIKE YOU'VE BEEN ON FIRE.
YOU KNOW THERE ARE A BUNCH OF NINJAS ABOVE THAT ALLEY?
YEAH. I'M IN THE MIDDLE OF A TOURNAMENT AND ONE OF THE COMPETITORS PROBABLY WANTS ME DEAD RATHER THAN FIGHT ME.
YOU MIND IF I DEAL WITH THESE WHILE WE TALK?
KRK

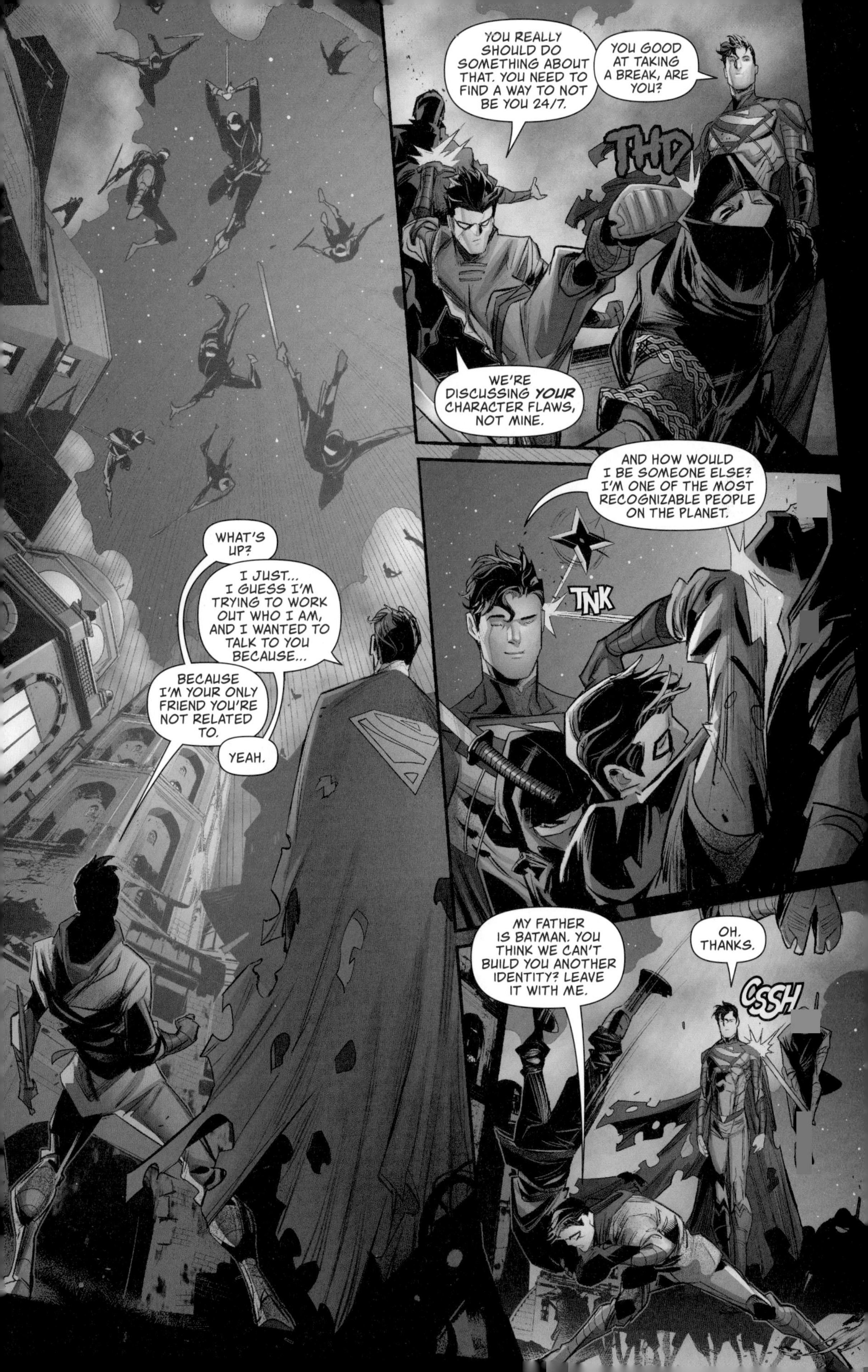
YOU REALLY SHOULD DO SOMETHING ABOUT THAT. YOU NEED TO FIND A WAY TO NOT BE YOU 24/7.
YOU GOOD AT TAKING A BREAK, ARE YOU?
THD
WE'RE DISCUSSING YOUR CHARACTER FLAWS, NOT MINE.
AND HOW WOULD I BE SOMEONE ELSE? I'M ONE OF THE MOST RECOGNIZABLE PEOPLE ON THE PLANET.
TNK
WHAT'S UP?
I JUST... I GUESS I'M TRYING TO WORK OUT WHO I AM, AND I WANTED TO TALK TO YOU BECAUSE...
BECAUSE I'M YOUR ONLY FRIEND YOU'RE NOT RELATED TO.
YEAH.
MY FATHER IS BATMAN. YOU THINK WE CAN'T BUILD YOU ANOTHER IDENTITY? LEAVE IT WITH ME.
OH. THANKS.
CSSH

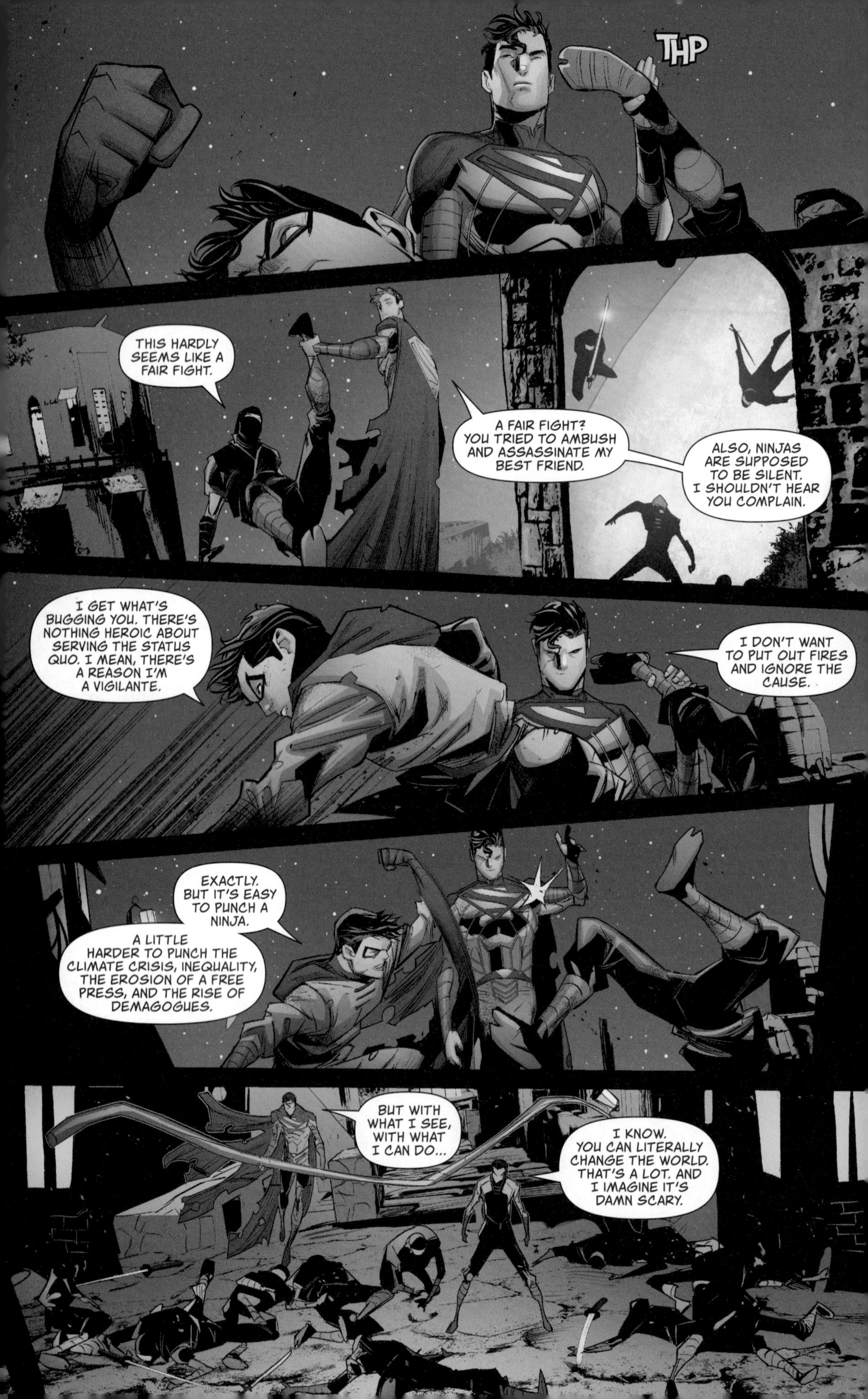
THP
THIS HARDLY SEEMS LIKE A FAIR FIGHT.
A FAIR FIGHT? YOU TRIED TO AMBUSH AND ASSASSINATE MY BEST FRIEND.
ALSO, NINJAS ARE SUPPOSED TO BE SILENT. I SHOULDN'T HEAR YOU COMPLAIN.
I GET WHAT'S BUGGING YOU. THERE'S NOTHING HEROIC ABOUT SERVING THE STATUS QUO. I MEAN, THERE'S A REASON I'M A VIGILANTE.
I DON'T WANT TO PUT OUT FIRES AND IGNORE THE CAUSE.
EXACTLY. BUT IT'S EASY TO PUNCH A NINJA.
A LITTLE HARDER TO PUNCH THE CLIMATE CRISIS, INEQUALITY, THE EROSION OF A FREE PRESS, AND THE RISE OF DEMAGOGUES.
BUT WITH WHAT I SEE, WITH WHAT I CAN DO...
I KNOW. YOU CAN LITERALLY CHANGE THE WORLD. THAT'S A LOT. AND I IMAGINE IT'S DAMN SCARY.

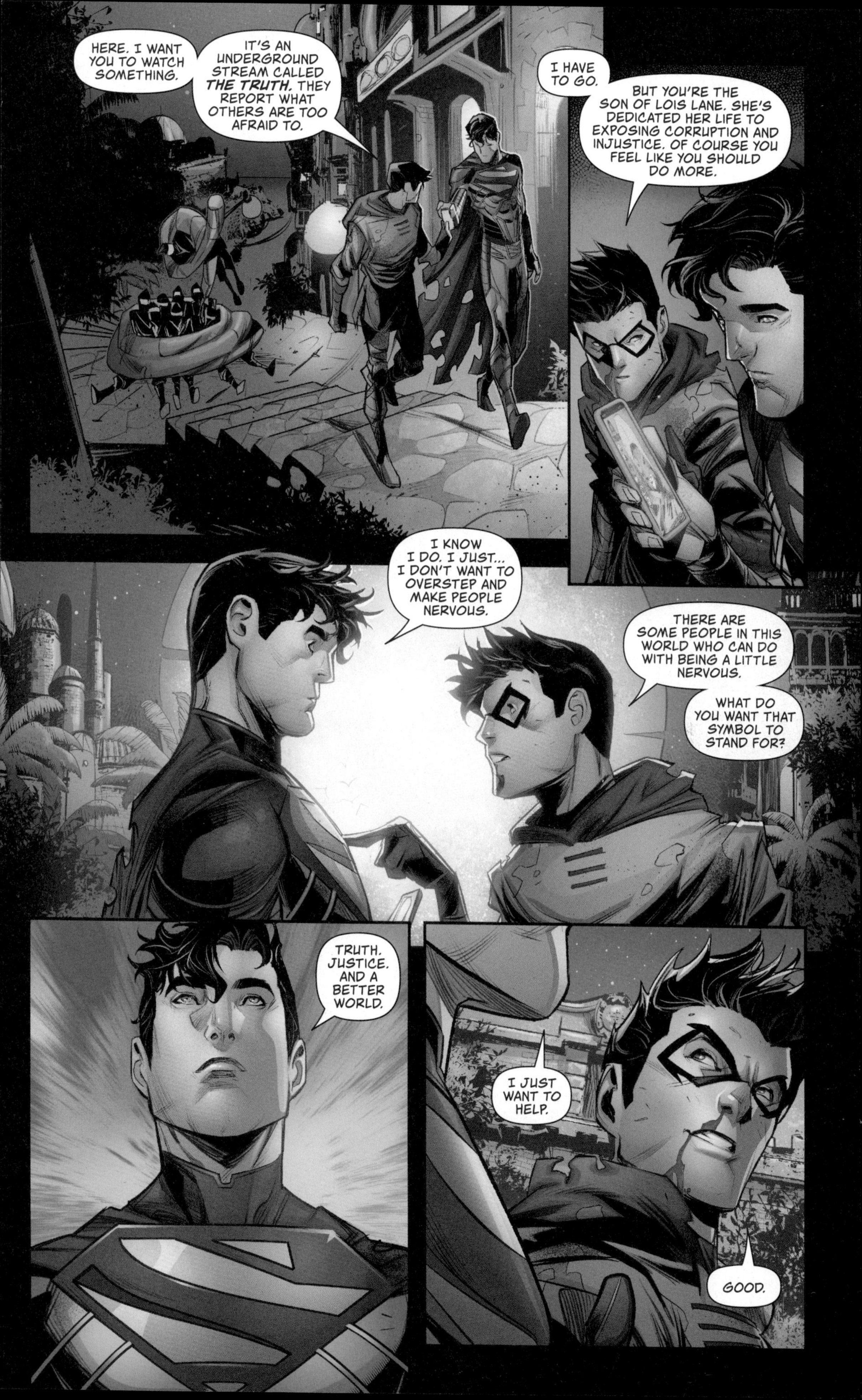
HERE. I WANT YOU TO WATCH SOMETHING.
IT'S AN UNDERGROUND STREAM CALLED THE TRUTH. THEY REPORT WHAT OTHERS ARE TOO AFRAID TO.
I HAVE TO GO.
BUT YOU'RE THE SON OF LOIS LANE. SHE'S DEDICATED HER LIFE TO EXPOSING CORRUPTION AND INJUSTICE. OF COURSE YOU FEEL LIKE YOU SHOULD DO MORE.
I KNOW I DO. I JUST... I DON'T WANT TO OVERSTEP AND MAKE PEOPLE NERVOUS.
THERE ARE SOME PEOPLE IN THIS WORLD WHO CAN DO WITH BEING A LITTLE NERVOUS.
WHAT DO YOU WANT THAT SYMBOL TO STAND FOR?
TRUTH. JUSTICE. AND A BETTER WORLD.
I JUST WANT TO HELP.
GOOD.

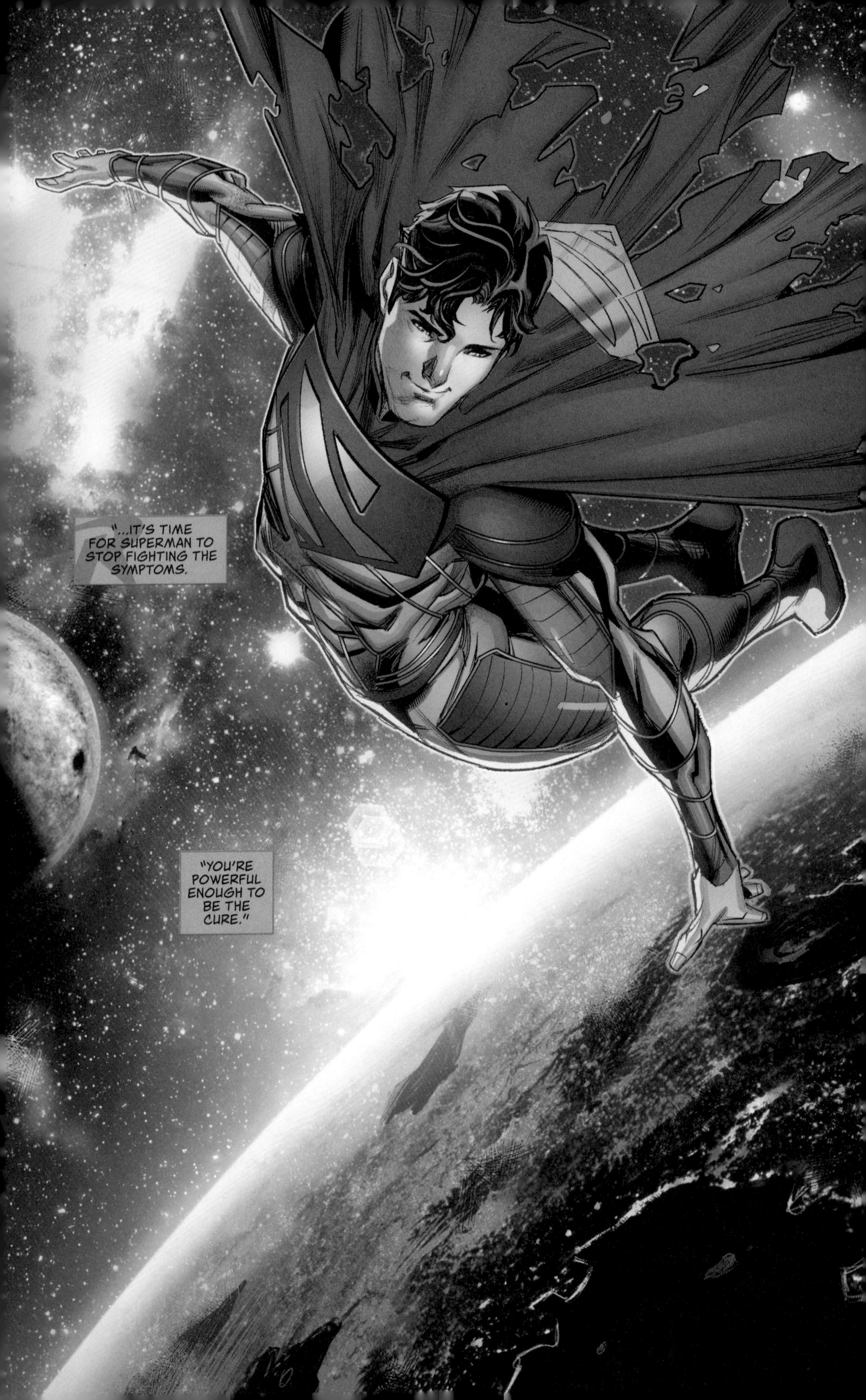
"...IT'S TIME FOR SUPERMAN TO STOP FIGHTING THE SYMPTOMS.
"YOU'RE POWERFUL ENOUGH TO BE THE CURE."

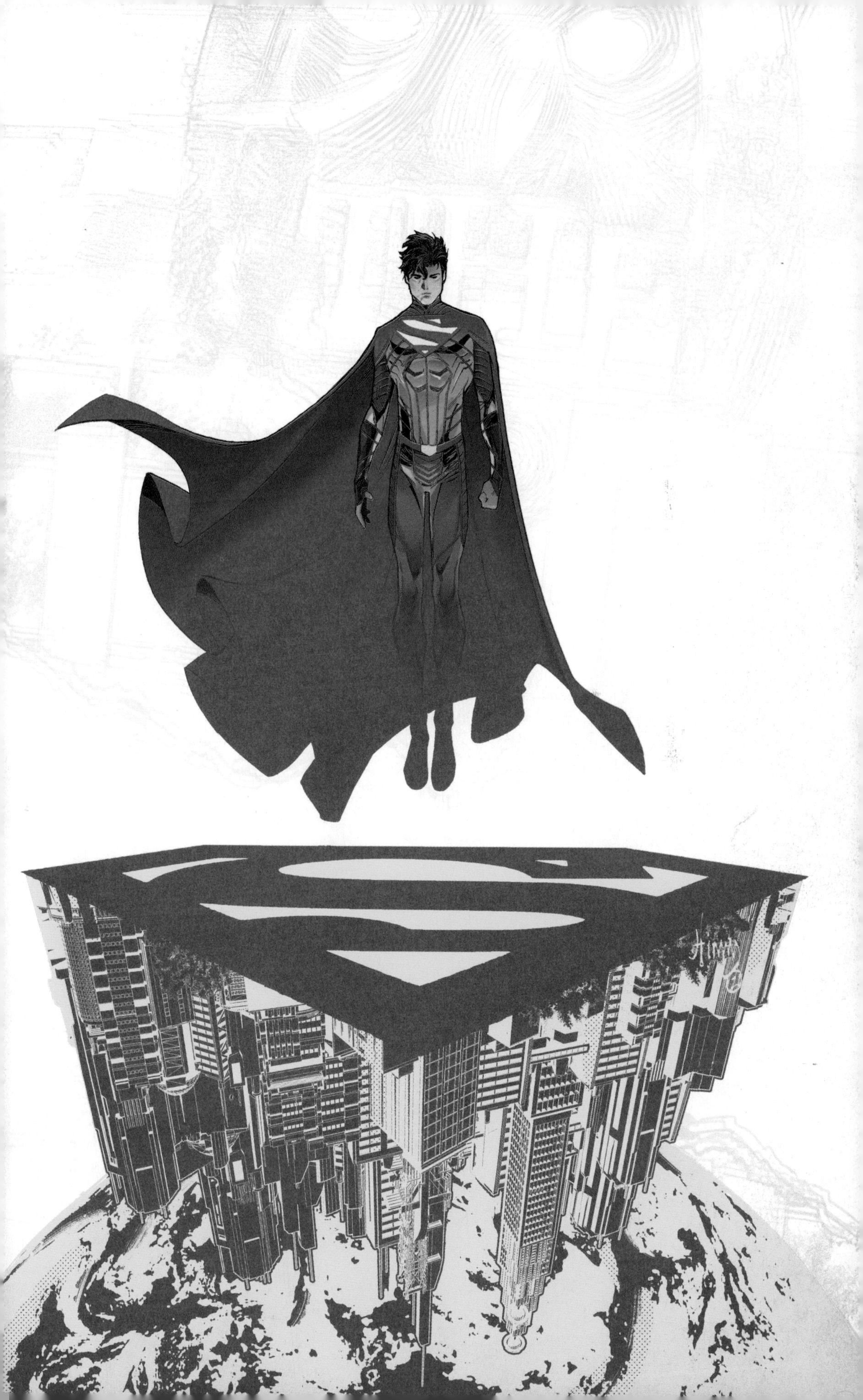

Superman: Son of Kal-El #2 variant cover art by **INHYUK LEE**

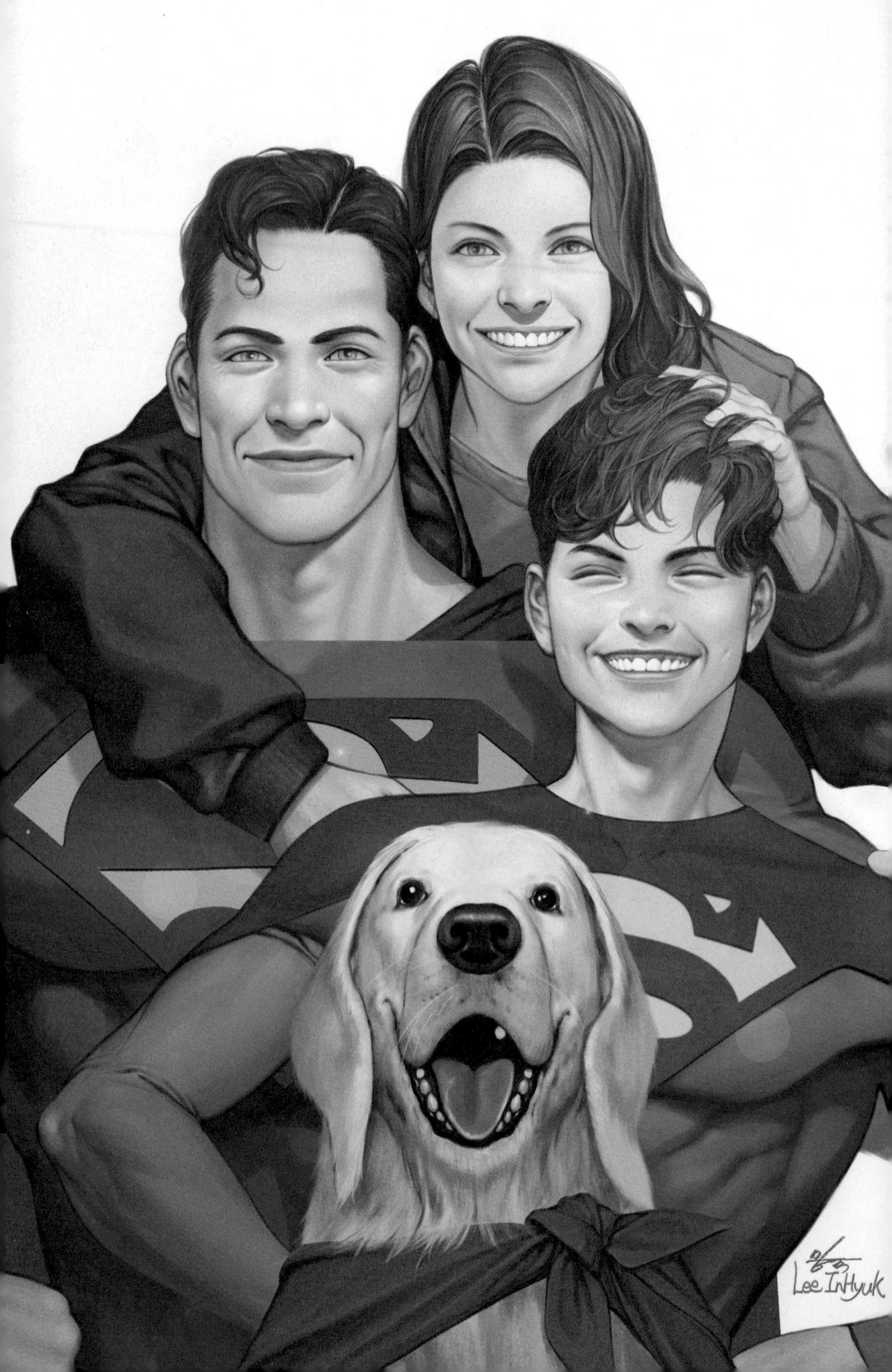
Lee InHyuk

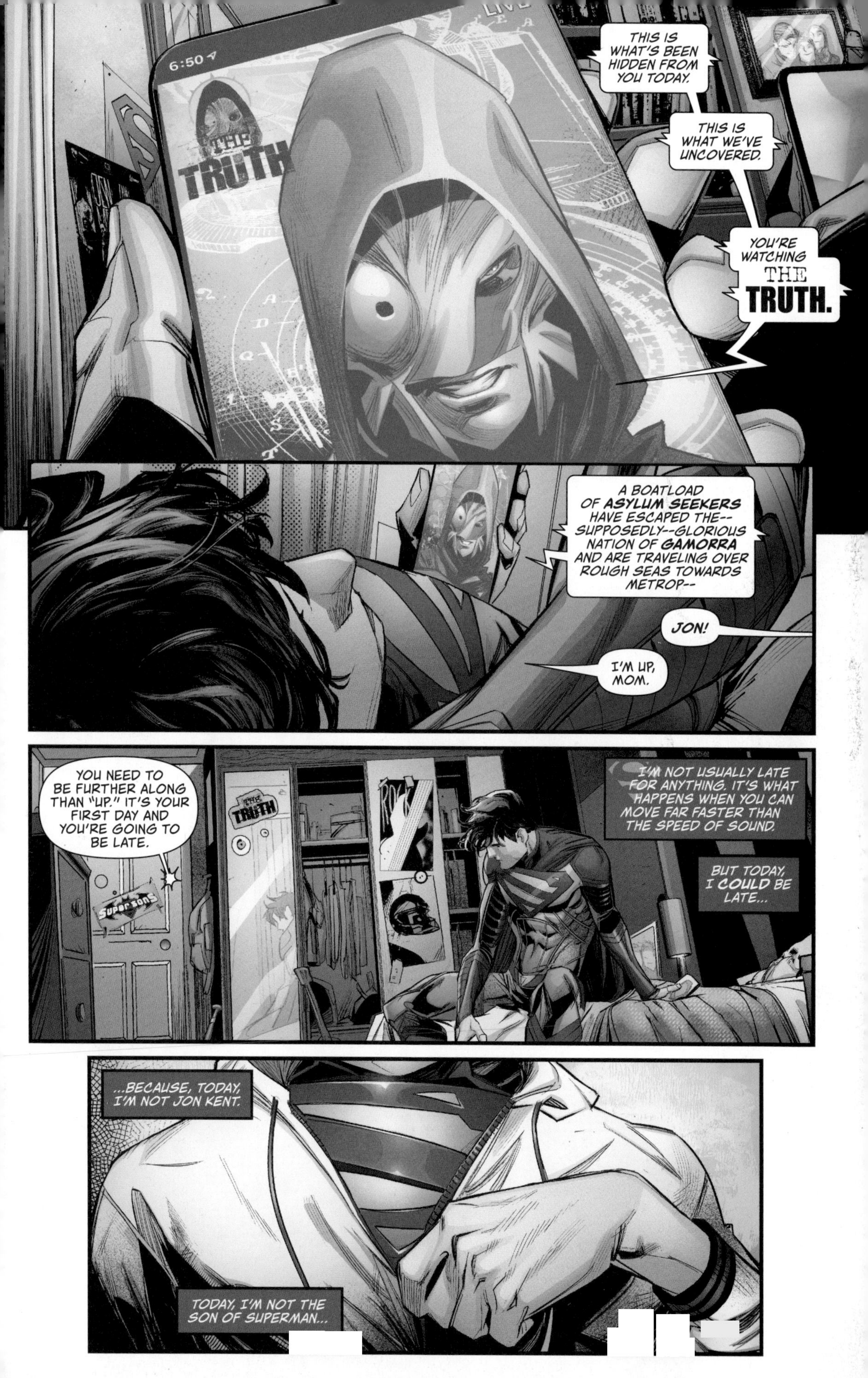
6:50
THE TRUTH
THIS IS WHAT'S BEEN HIDDEN FROM YOU TODAY.
THIS IS WHAT WE'VE UNCOVERED.
YOU'RE WATCHING THE TRUTH.
A BOATLOAD OF ASYLUM SEEKERS HAVE ESCAPED THE--SUPPOSEDLY--GLORIOUS NATION OF GAMORRA AND ARE TRAVELING OVER ROUGH SEAS TOWARDS METROP--
JON!
I'M UP, MOM.
YOU NEED TO BE FURTHER ALONG THAN "UP." IT'S YOUR FIRST DAY AND YOU'RE GOING TO BE LATE.
THE TRUTH
Super Sons
I'M NOT USUALLY LATE FOR ANYTHING. IT'S WHAT HAPPENS WHEN YOU CAN MOVE FAR FASTER THAN THE SPEED OF SOUND.
BUT TODAY, I COULD BE LATE...
...BECAUSE, TODAY, I'M NOT JON KENT.
TODAY, I'M NOT THE SON OF SUPERMAN...

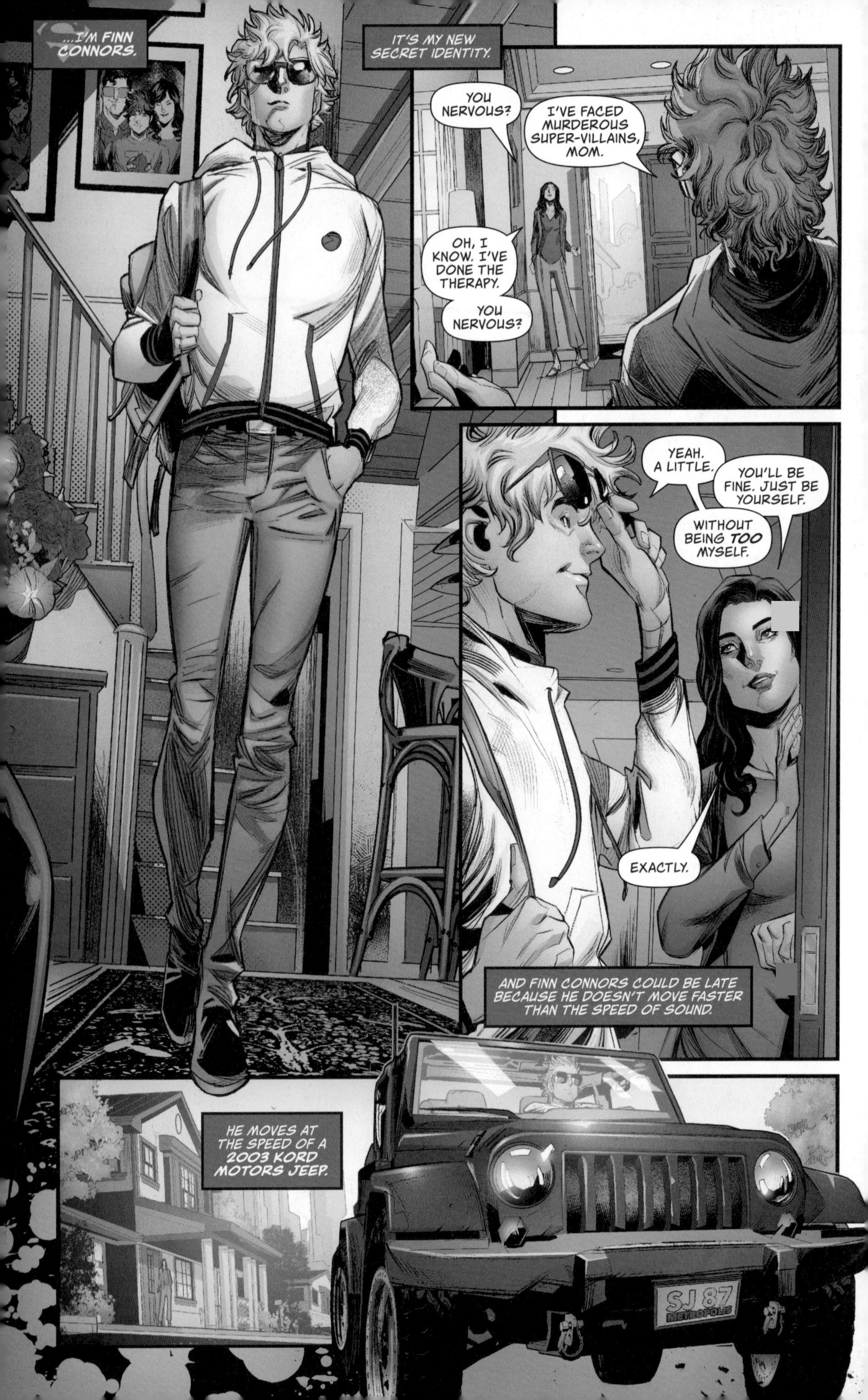
...I'M FINN CONNORS.
IT'S MY NEW SECRET IDENTITY.
YOU NERVOUS?
I'VE FACED MURDEROUS SUPER-VILLAINS, MOM.
OH, I KNOW. I'VE DONE THE THERAPY.
YOU NERVOUS?
YEAH. A LITTLE.
YOU'LL BE FINE. JUST BE YOURSELF.
WITHOUT BEING TOO MYSELF.
EXACTLY.
AND FINN CONNORS COULD BE LATE BECAUSE HE DOESN'T MOVE FASTER THAN THE SPEED OF SOUND.
HE MOVES AT THE SPEED OF A 2003 KORD MOTORS JEEP.
SJ 87
METROPOLIS

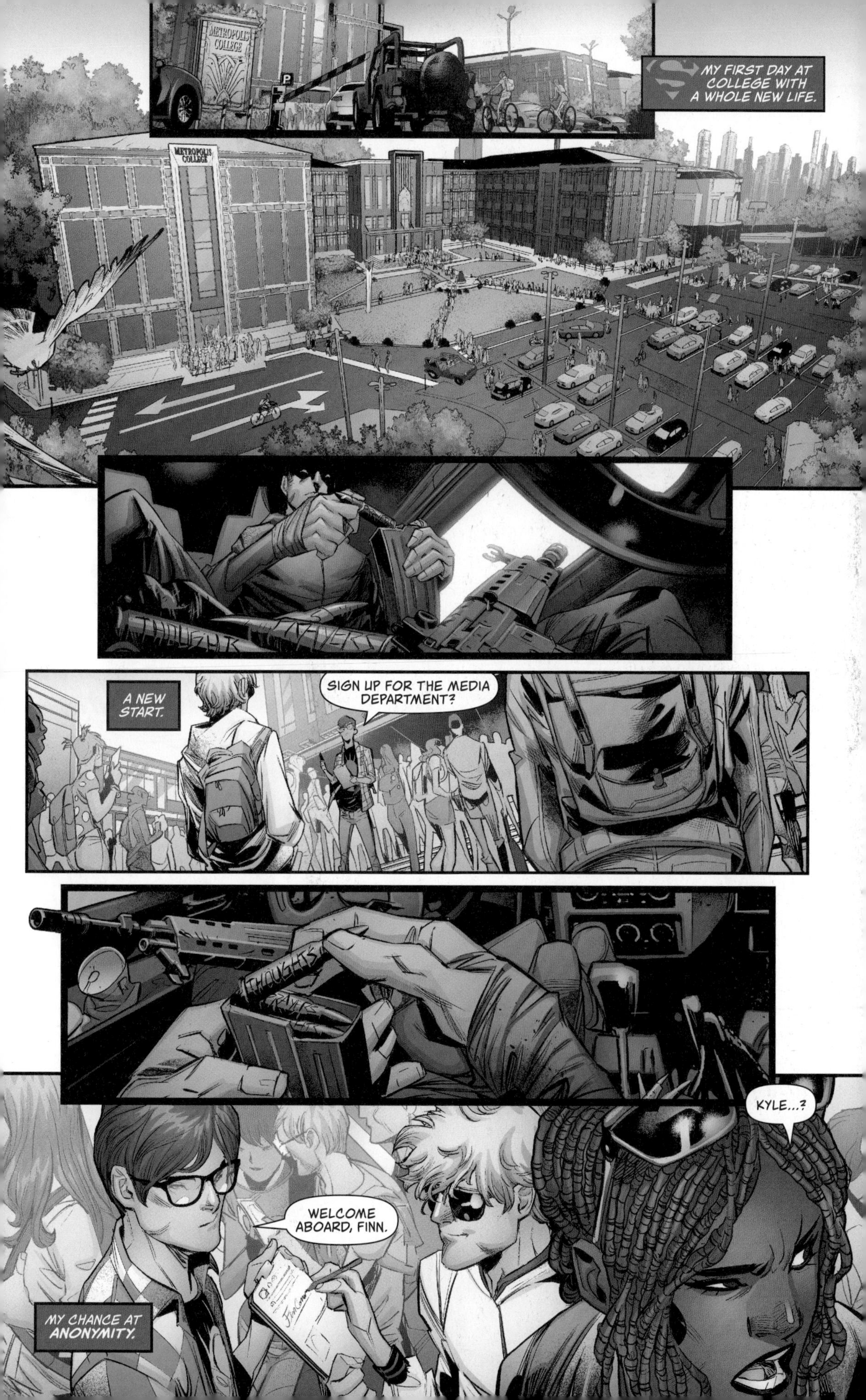
METROPOLIS COLLEGE
MY FIRST DAY AT COLLEGE WITH A WHOLE NEW LIFE.
A NEW START.
SIGN UP FOR THE MEDIA DEPARTMENT?
KYLE...?
WELCOME ABOARD, FINN.
MY CHANCE AT ANONYMITY.

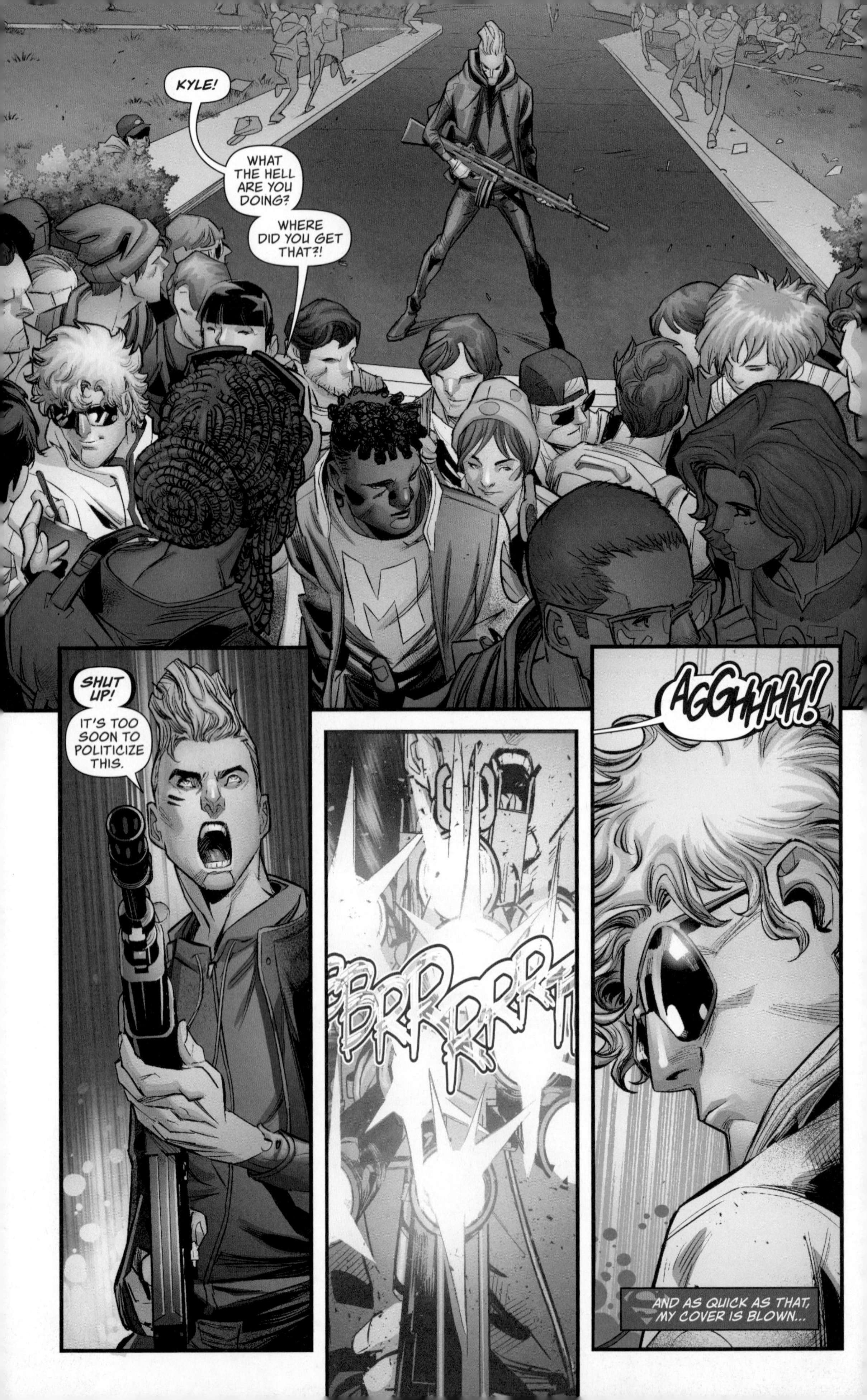
KYLE!
WHAT THE HELL ARE YOU DOING?
WHERE DID YOU GET THAT?!
SHUT UP!
IT'S TOO SOON TO POLITICIZE THIS.
BRRRRRT
AGGHHHH!
AND AS QUICK AS THAT, MY COVER IS BLOWN...

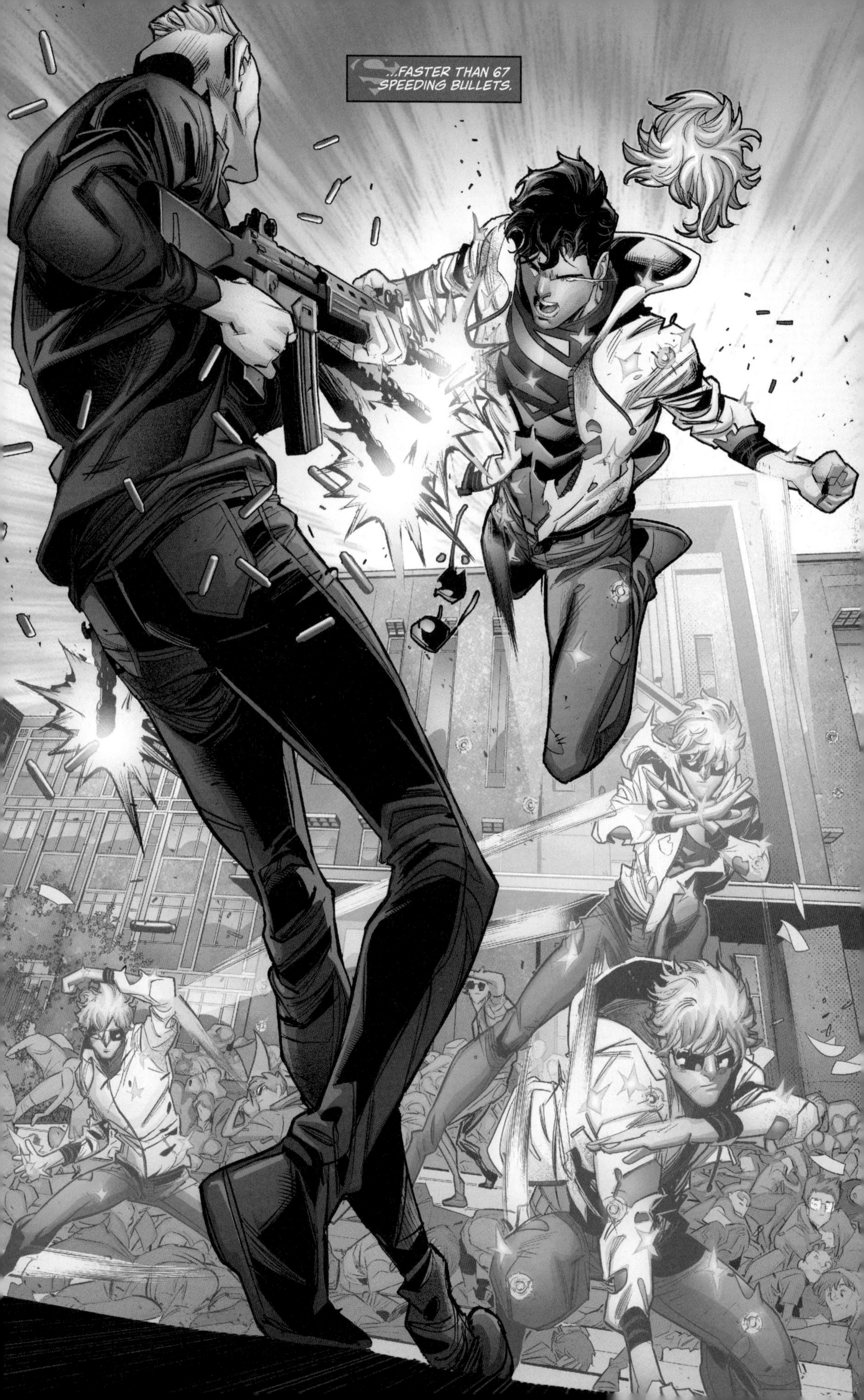
...FASTER THAN 67 SPEEDING BULLETS.

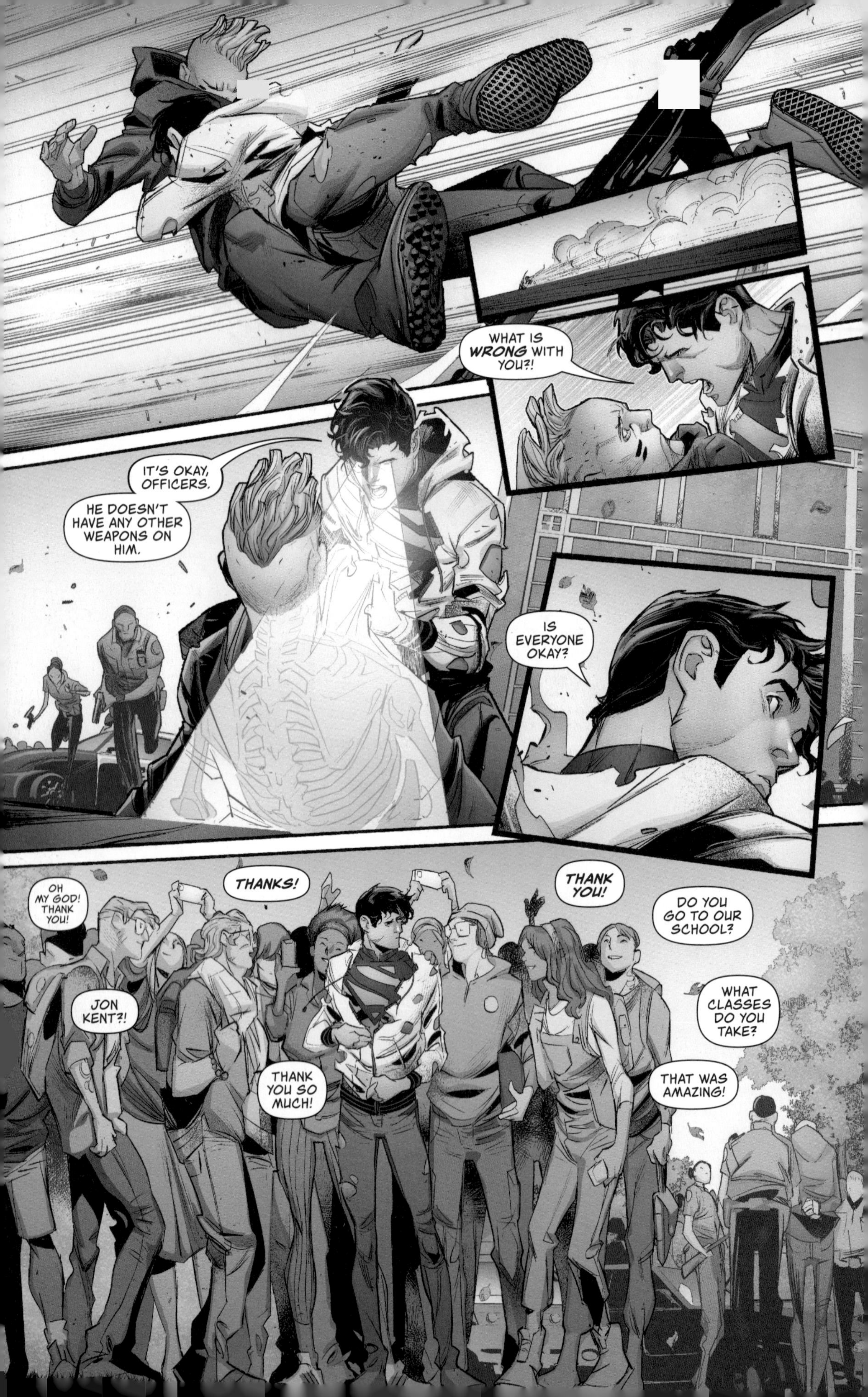
WHAT IS WRONG WITH YOU?!
IT'S OKAY, OFFICERS.
HE DOESN'T HAVE ANY OTHER WEAPONS ON HIM.
IS EVERYONE OKAY?
OH MY GOD! THANK YOU!
THANKS!
THANK YOU!
DO YOU GO TO OUR SCHOOL?
JON KENT?!
WHAT CLASSES DO YOU TAKE?
THANK YOU SO MUCH!
THAT WAS AMAZING!

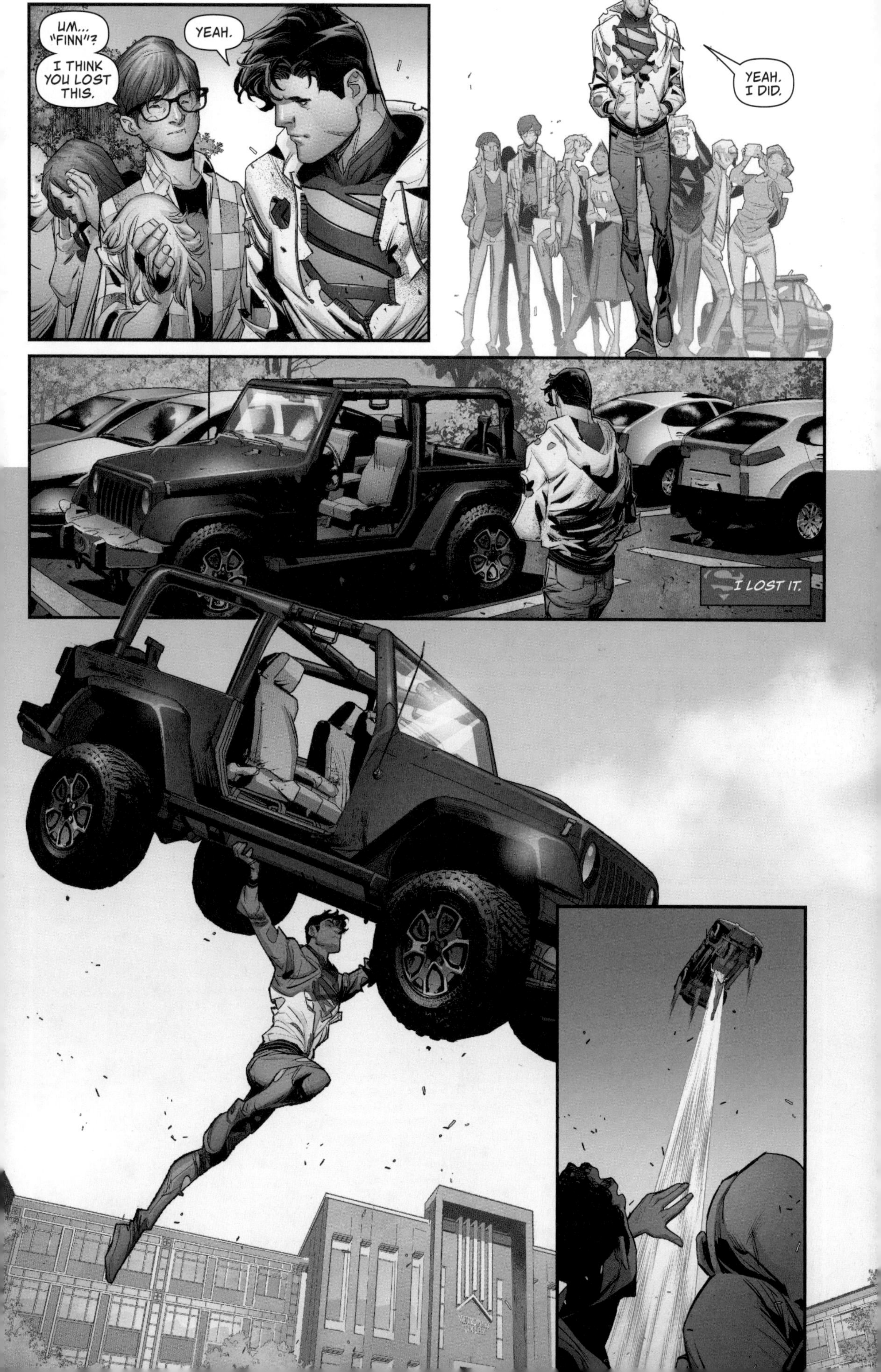
UM... "FINN"?
I THINK YOU LOST THIS.
YEAH.
YEAH. I DID.
I LOST IT.

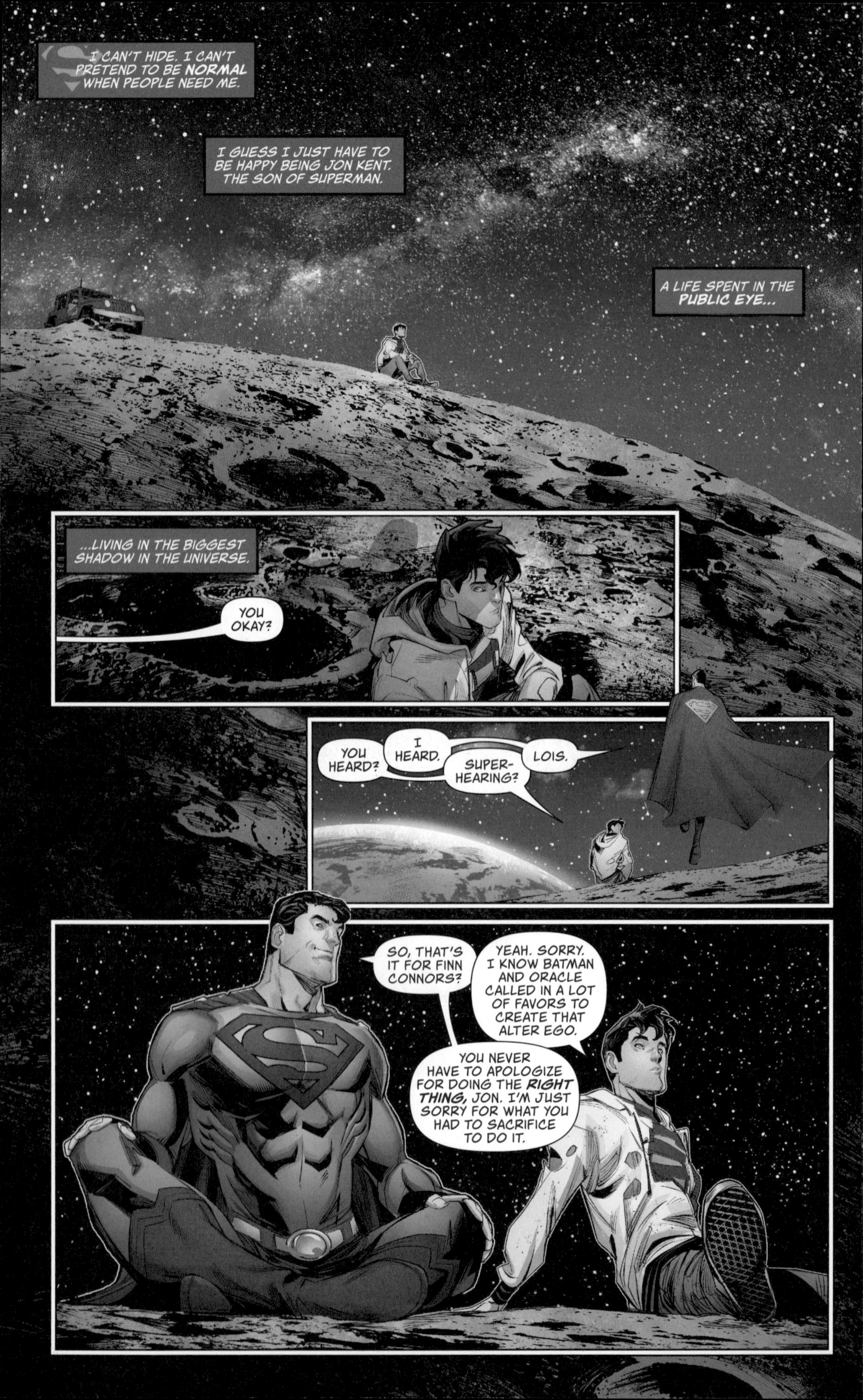
I CAN'T HIDE. I CAN'T PRETEND TO BE NORMAL WHEN PEOPLE NEED ME.
I GUESS I JUST HAVE TO BE HAPPY BEING JON KENT. THE SON OF SUPERMAN.
A LIFE SPENT IN THE PUBLIC EYE...
...LIVING IN THE BIGGEST SHADOW IN THE UNIVERSE.
YOU OKAY?
LOIS.
YOU HEARD?
I HEARD.
SUPER-HEARING?
SO, THAT'S IT FOR FINN CONNORS?
YEAH. SORRY. I KNOW BATMAN AND ORACLE CALLED IN A LOT OF FAVORS TO CREATE THAT ALTER EGO.
YOU NEVER HAVE TO APOLOGIZE FOR DOING THE RIGHT THING, JON. I'M JUST SORRY FOR WHAT YOU HAD TO SACRIFICE TO DO IT.

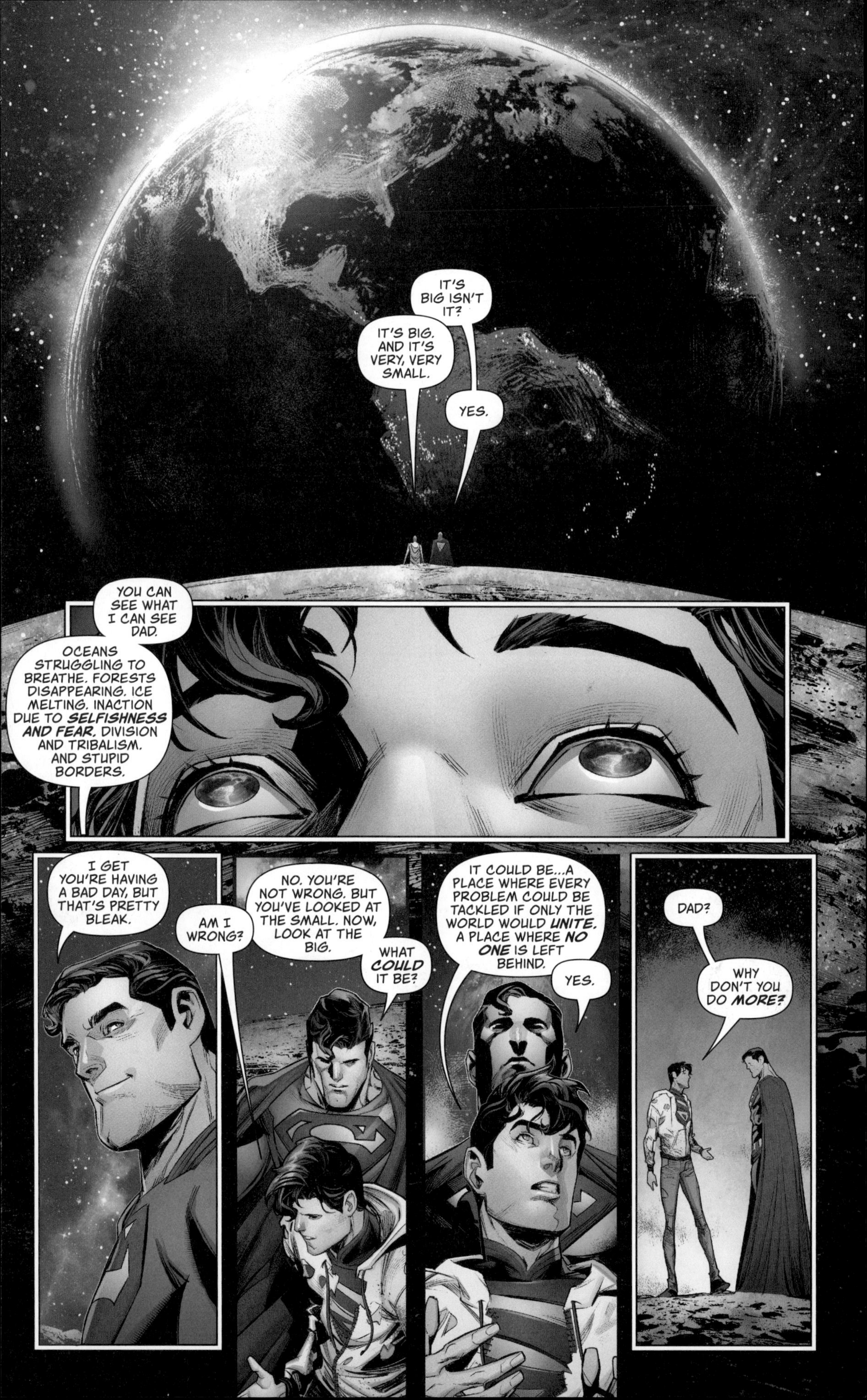
IT'S BIG ISN'T IT?
IT'S BIG. AND IT'S VERY, VERY SMALL.
YES.
YOU CAN SEE WHAT I CAN SEE DAD.
OCEANS STRUGGLING TO BREATHE. FORESTS DISAPPEARING. ICE MELTING. INACTION DUE TO ***SELFISHNESS AND FEAR.*** DIVISION AND TRIBALISM. AND STUPID BORDERS.
I GET YOU'RE HAVING A BAD DAY, BUT THAT'S PRETTY BLEAK.
AM I WRONG?
NO. YOU'RE NOT WRONG. BUT YOU'VE LOOKED AT THE SMALL. NOW, LOOK AT THE BIG.
WHAT ***COULD*** IT BE?
IT COULD BE...A PLACE WHERE EVERY PROBLEM COULD BE TACKLED IF ONLY THE WORLD WOULD ***UNITE.*** A PLACE WHERE ***NO ONE*** IS LEFT BEHIND.
YES.
DAD?
WHY DON'T YOU DO ***MORE?***

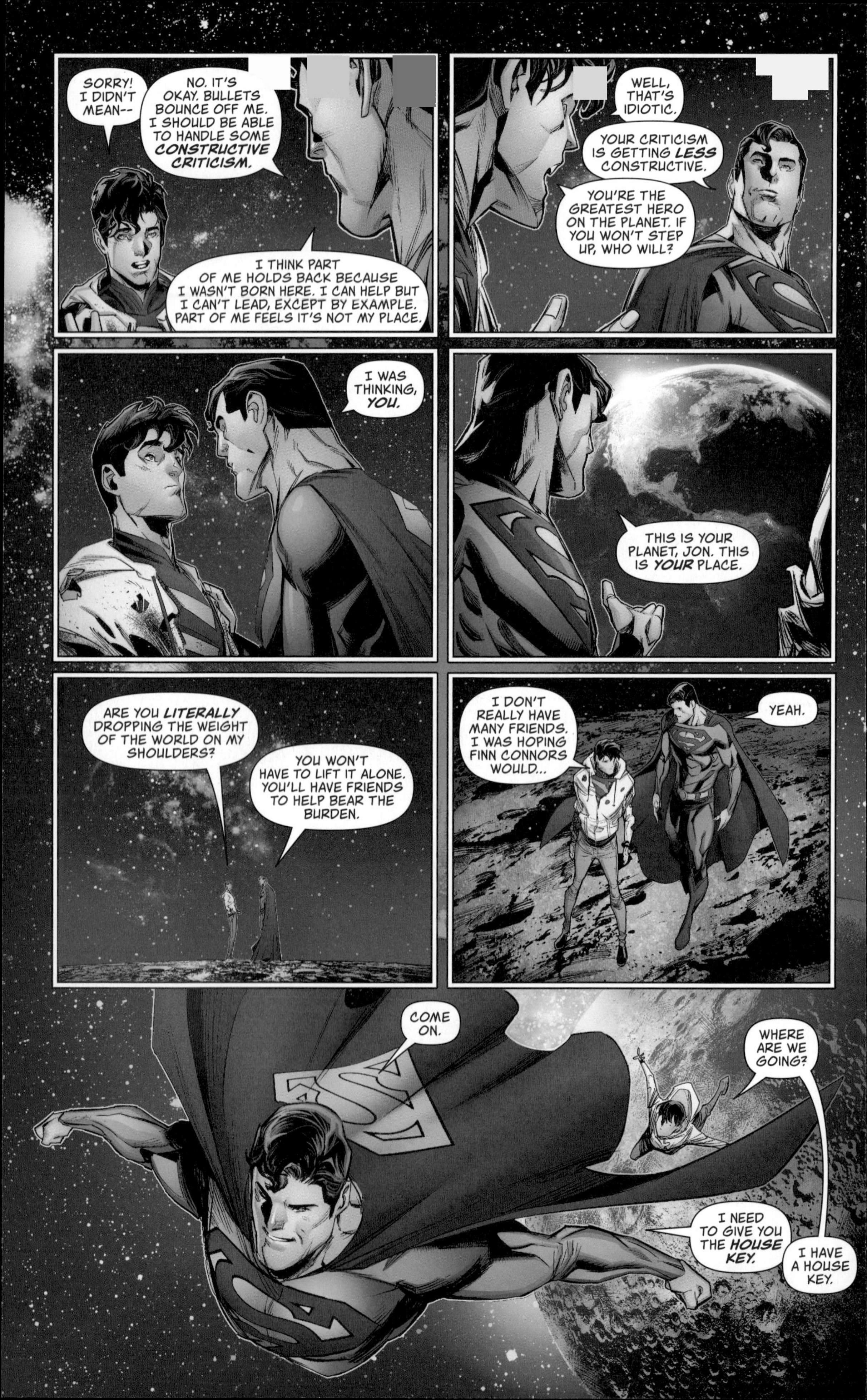
SORRY! I DIDN'T MEAN--
NO. IT'S OKAY. BULLETS BOUNCE OFF ME. I SHOULD BE ABLE TO HANDLE SOME CONSTRUCTIVE CRITICISM.
I THINK PART OF ME HOLDS BACK BECAUSE I WASN'T BORN HERE. I CAN HELP BUT I CAN'T LEAD, EXCEPT BY EXAMPLE. PART OF ME FEELS IT'S NOT MY PLACE.
WELL, THAT'S IDIOTIC.
YOUR CRITICISM IS GETTING LESS CONSTRUCTIVE.
YOU'RE THE GREATEST HERO ON THE PLANET. IF YOU WON'T STEP UP, WHO WILL?
I WAS THINKING, YOU.
THIS IS YOUR PLANET, JON. THIS IS YOUR PLACE.
ARE YOU LITERALLY DROPPING THE WEIGHT OF THE WORLD ON MY SHOULDERS?
YOU WON'T HAVE TO LIFT IT ALONE. YOU'LL HAVE FRIENDS TO HELP BEAR THE BURDEN.
I DON'T REALLY HAVE MANY FRIENDS. I WAS HOPING FINN CONNORS WOULD...
YEAH.
COME ON.
WHERE ARE WE GOING?
I NEED TO GIVE YOU THE HOUSE KEY.
I HAVE A HOUSE KEY.

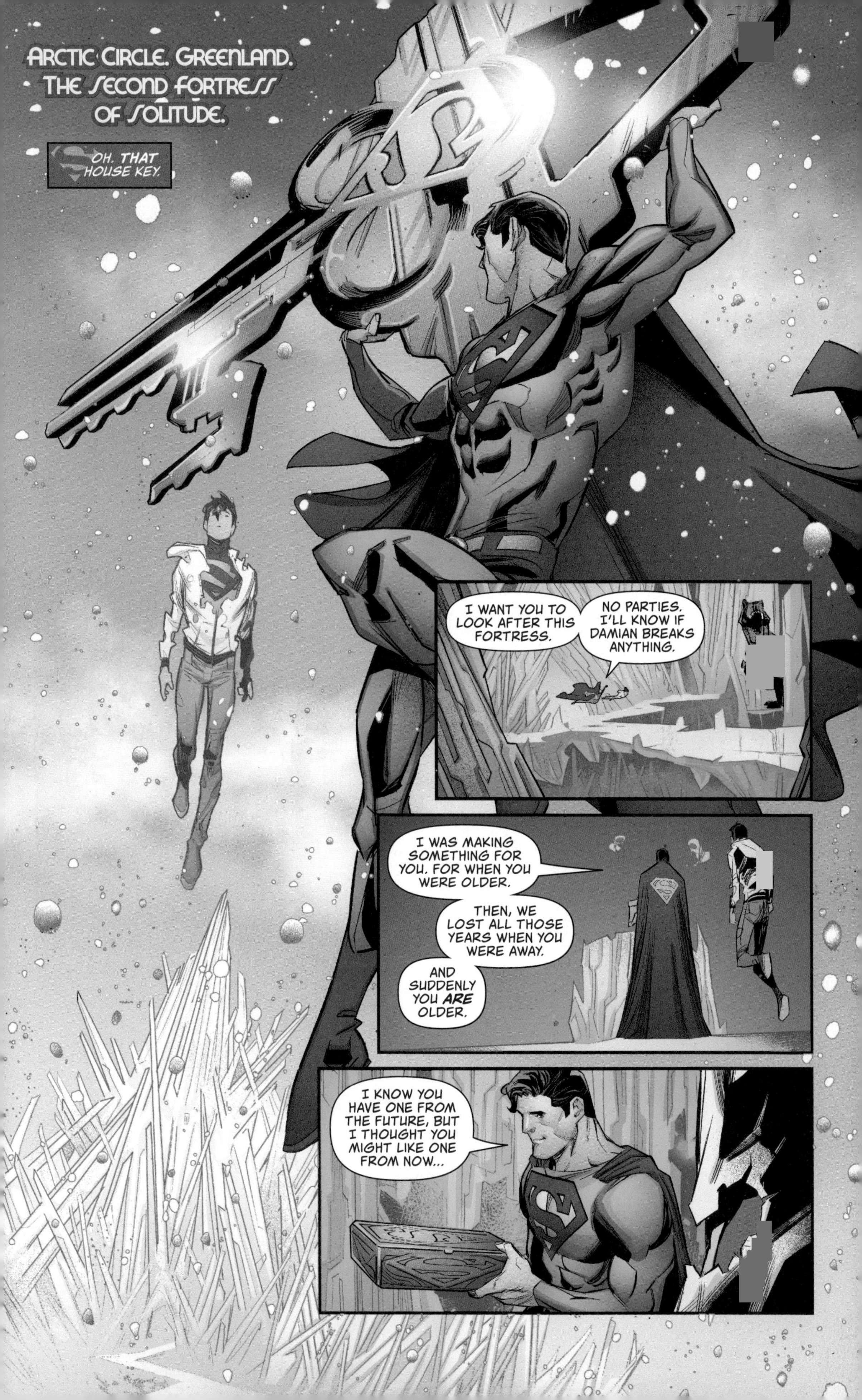
ARCTIC CIRCLE. GREENLAND. THE SECOND FORTRESS OF SOLITUDE.
OH. THAT HOUSE KEY.
I WANT YOU TO LOOK AFTER THIS FORTRESS.
NO PARTIES. I'LL KNOW IF DAMIAN BREAKS ANYTHING.
I WAS MAKING SOMETHING FOR YOU. FOR WHEN YOU WERE OLDER.
THEN, WE LOST ALL THOSE YEARS WHEN YOU WERE AWAY.
AND SUDDENLY YOU ARE OLDER.
I KNOW YOU HAVE ONE FROM THE FUTURE, BUT I THOUGHT YOU MIGHT LIKE ONE FROM NOW...

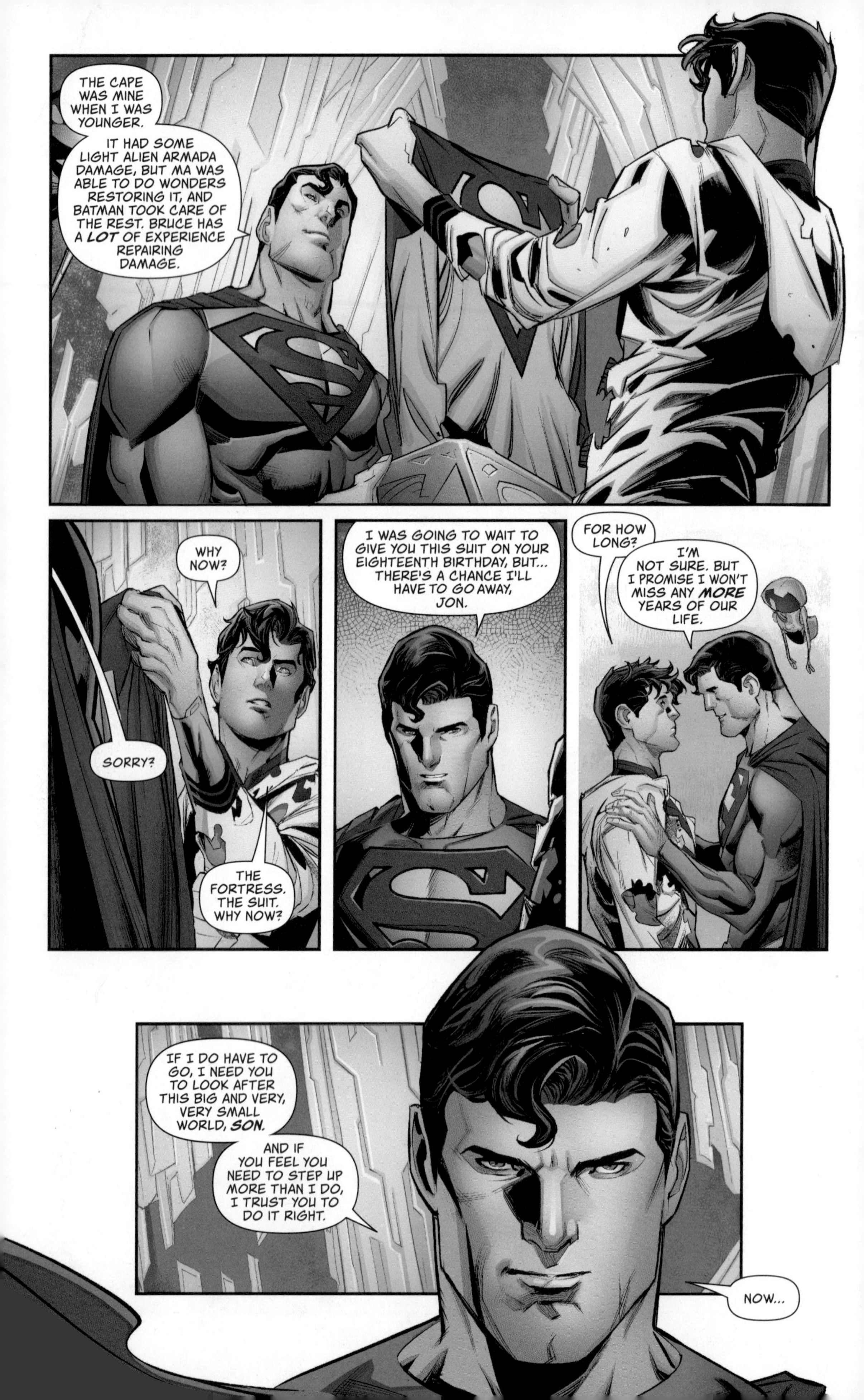
THE CAPE WAS MINE WHEN I WAS YOUNGER.
IT HAD SOME LIGHT ALIEN ARMADA DAMAGE, BUT MA WAS ABLE TO DO WONDERS RESTORING IT, AND BATMAN TOOK CARE OF THE REST. BRUCE HAS A LOT OF EXPERIENCE REPAIRING DAMAGE.
WHY NOW?
SORRY?
THE FORTRESS. THE SUIT. WHY NOW?
I WAS GOING TO WAIT TO GIVE YOU THIS SUIT ON YOUR EIGHTEENTH BIRTHDAY, BUT... THERE'S A CHANCE I'LL HAVE TO GO AWAY, JON.
FOR HOW LONG?
I'M NOT SURE. BUT I PROMISE I WON'T MISS ANY MORE YEARS OF OUR LIFE.
IF I DO HAVE TO GO, I NEED YOU TO LOOK AFTER THIS BIG AND VERY, VERY SMALL WORLD, SON.
AND IF YOU FEEL YOU NEED TO STEP UP MORE THAN I DO, I TRUST YOU TO DO IT RIGHT.
NOW...

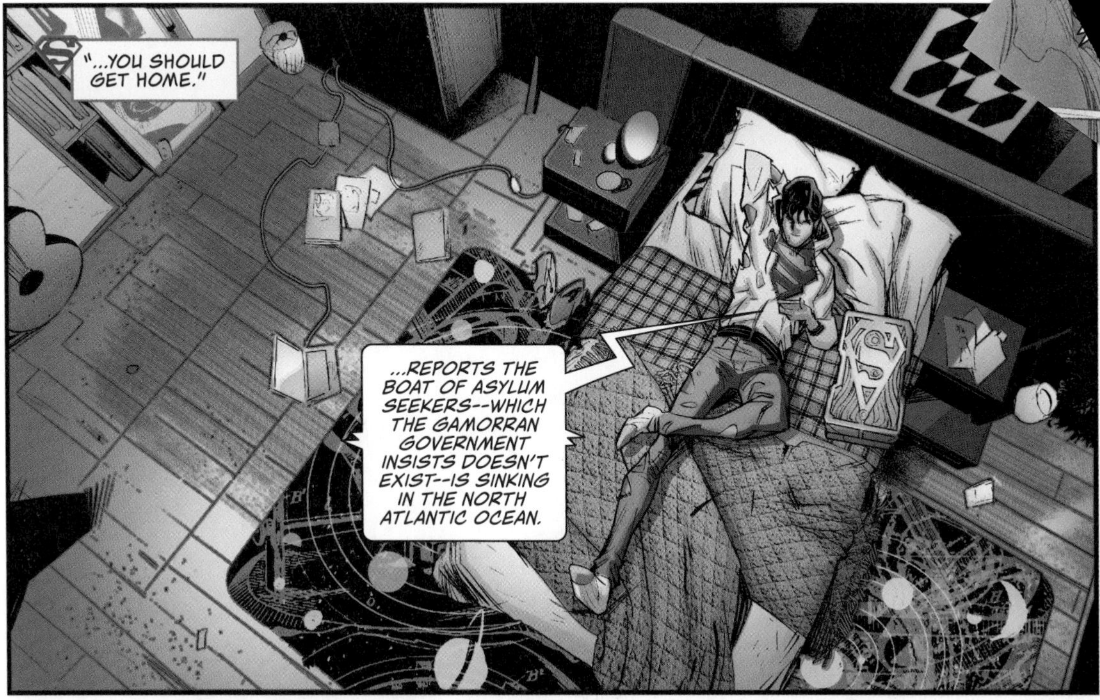
"...YOU SHOULD GET HOME."
...REPORTS THE BOAT OF ASYLUM SEEKERS--WHICH THE GAMORRAN GOVERNMENT INSISTS DOESN'T EXIST--IS SINKING IN THE NORTH ATLANTIC OCEAN.

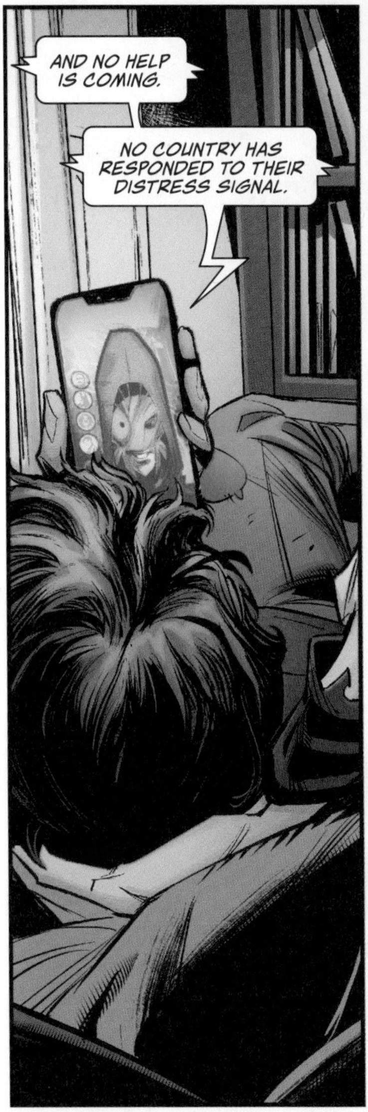
AND NO HELP IS COMING.
NO COUNTRY HAS RESPONDED TO THEIR DISTRESS SIGNAL.

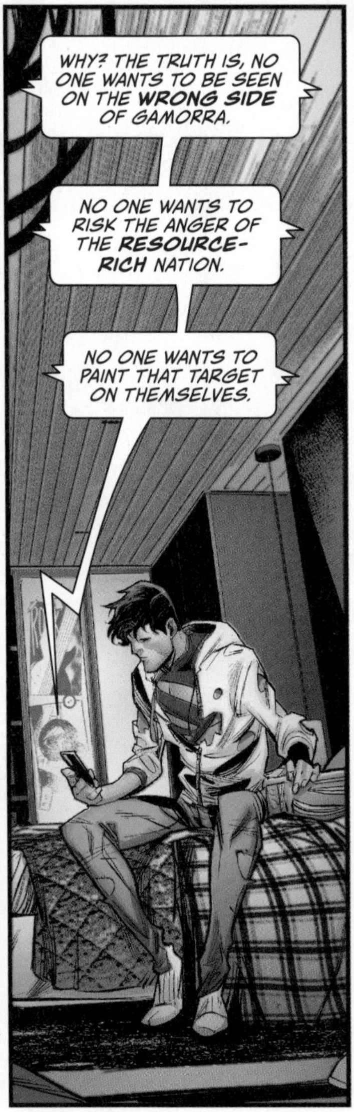
WHY? THE TRUTH IS, NO ONE WANTS TO BE SEEN ON THE WRONG SIDE OF GAMORRA.
NO ONE WANTS TO RISK THE ANGER OF THE RESOURCE-RICH NATION.
NO ONE WANTS TO PAINT THAT TARGET ON THEMSELVES.

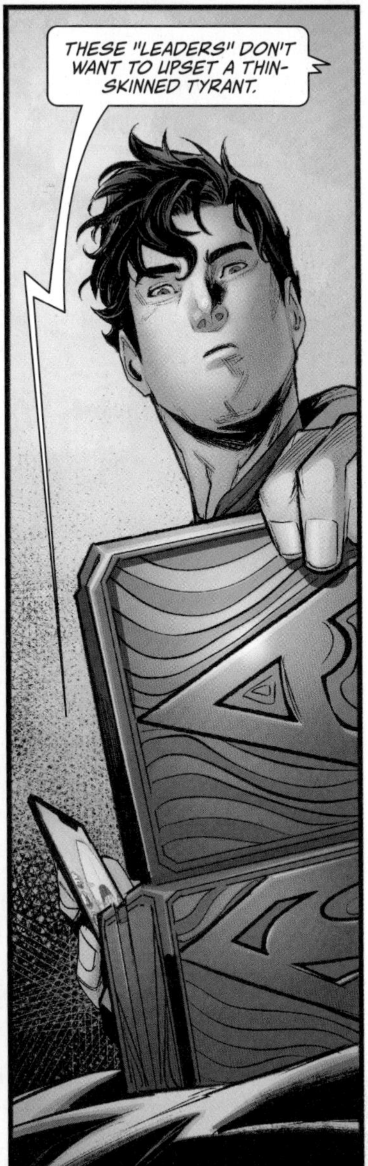
THESE "LEADERS" DON'T WANT TO UPSET A THIN-SKINNED TYRANT.

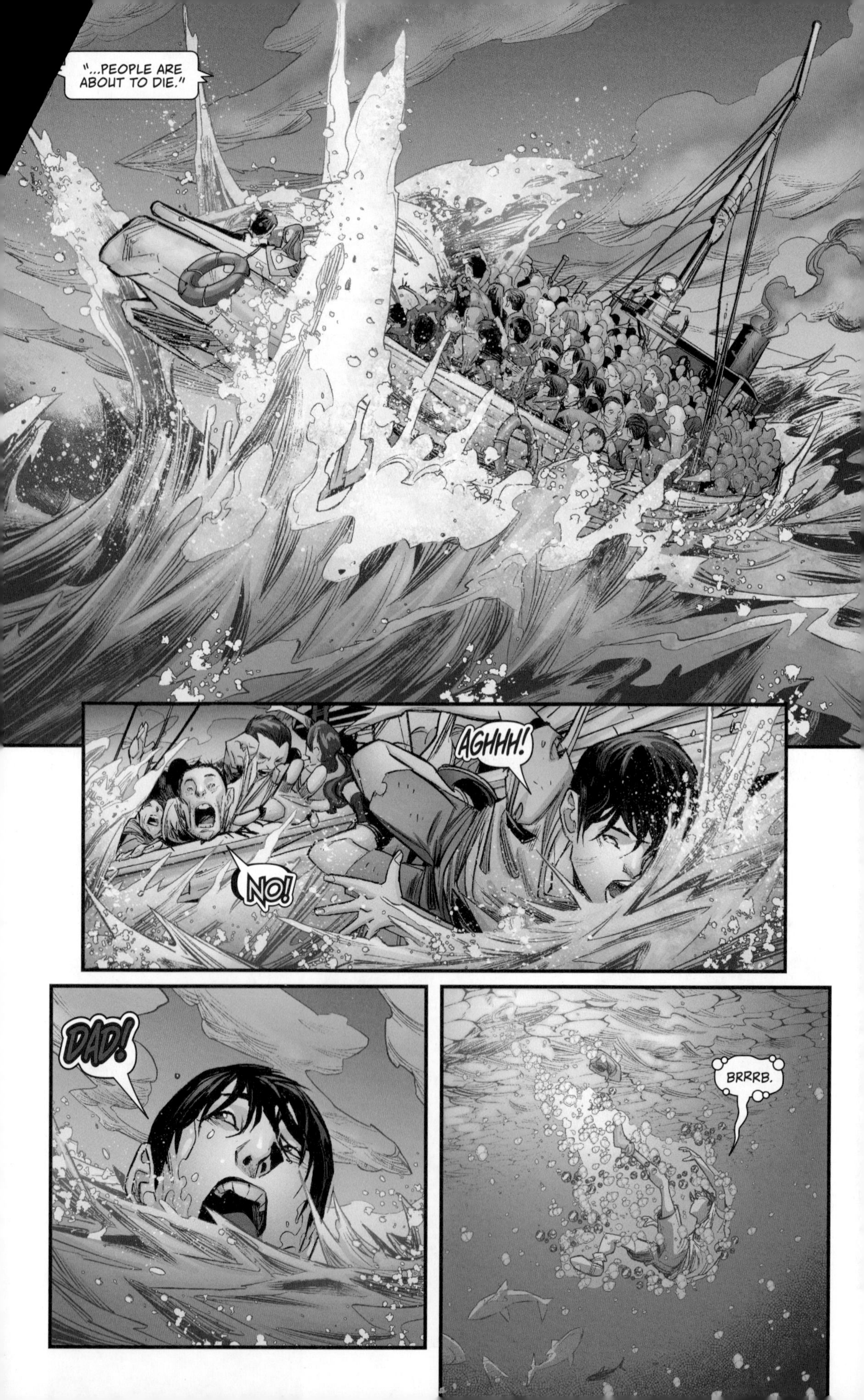
"...PEOPLE ARE ABOUT TO DIE."
AGHHH!
NO!
DAD!
BRRRB.

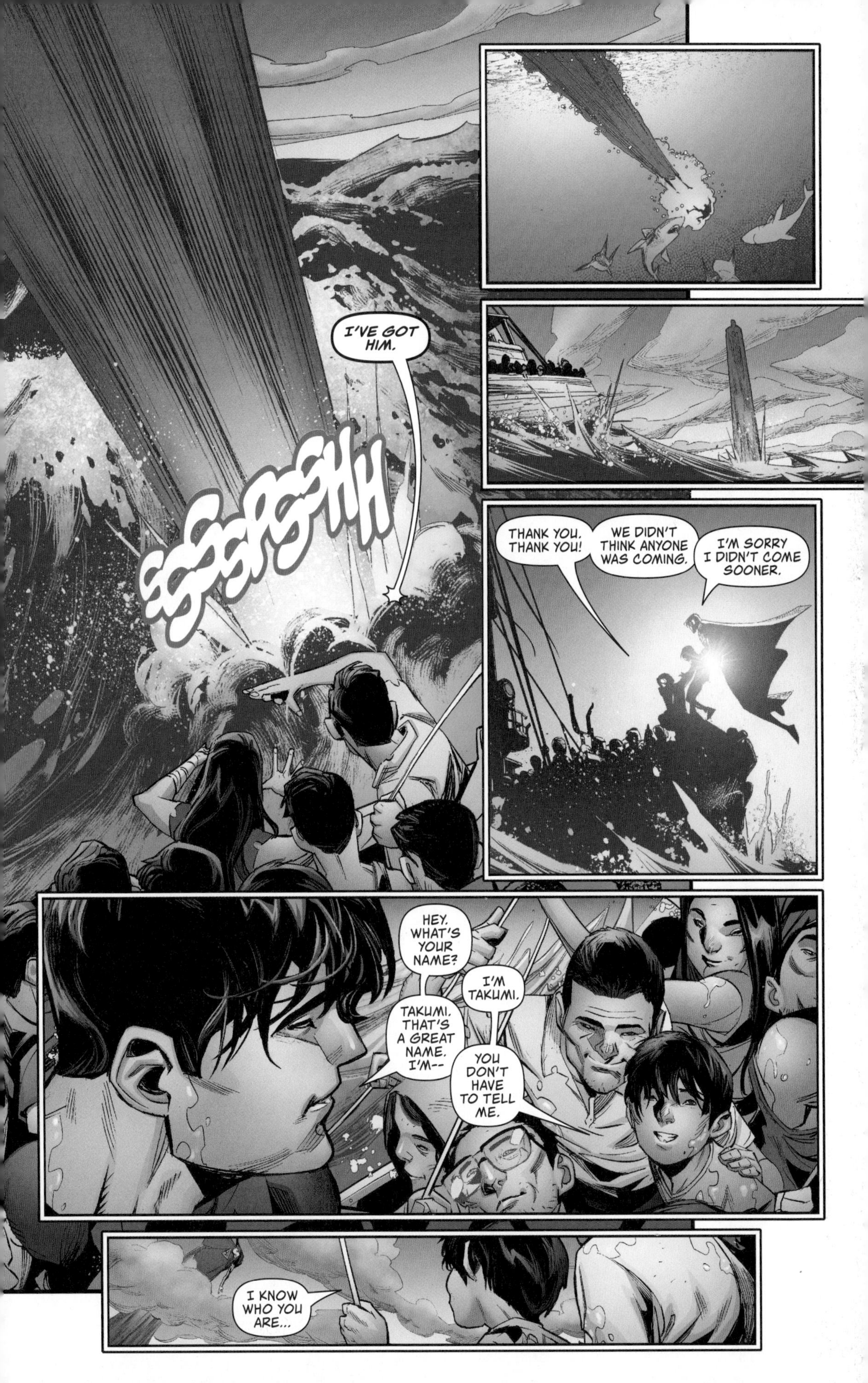
I'VE GOT HIM.
SSSPSSHH
THANK YOU. THANK YOU!
WE DIDN'T THINK ANYONE WAS COMING.
I'M SORRY I DIDN'T COME SOONER.
HEY. WHAT'S YOUR NAME?
I'M TAKUMI.
TAKUMI. THAT'S A GREAT NAME. I'M--
YOU DON'T HAVE TO TELL ME.
I KNOW WHO YOU ARE...

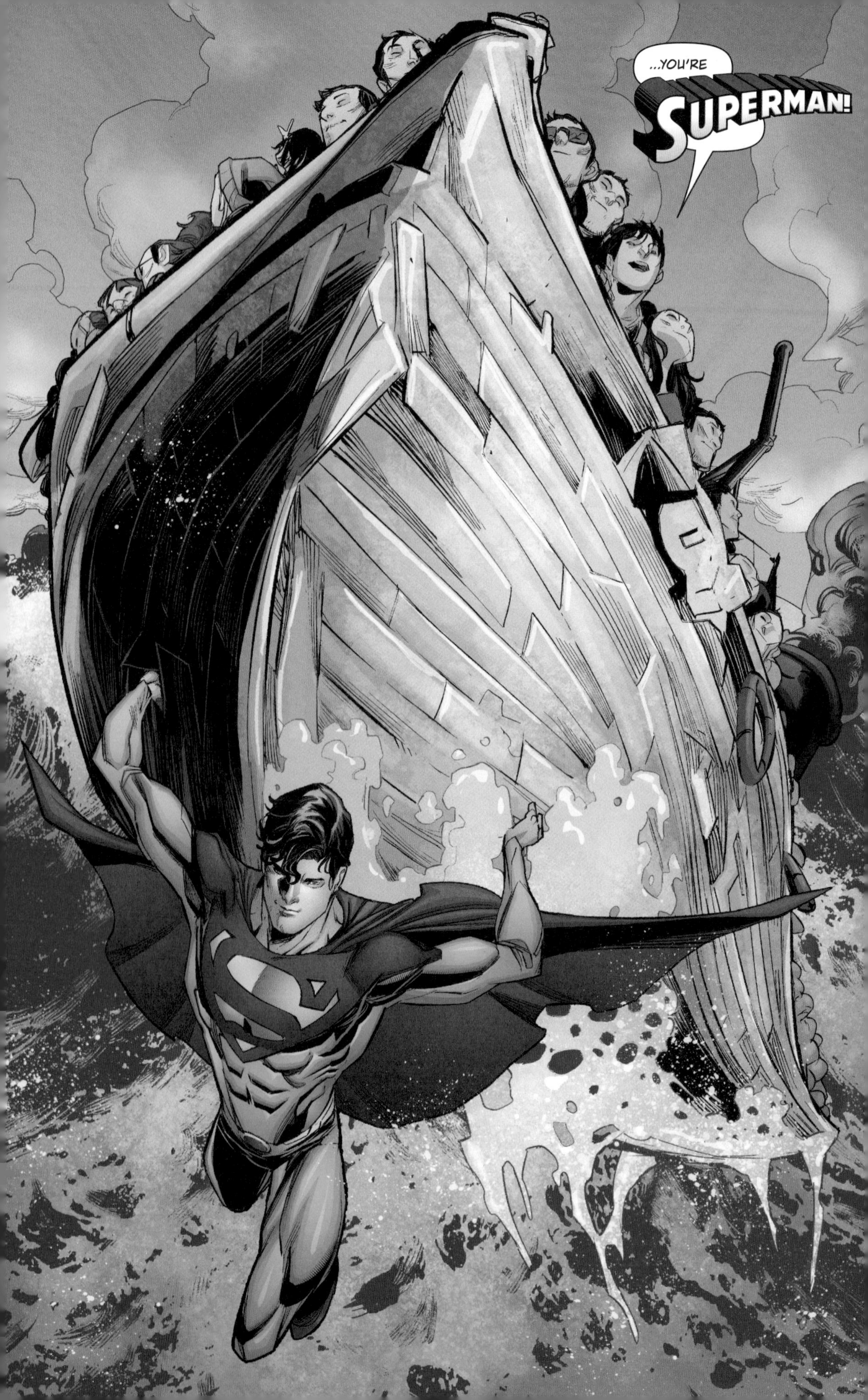
...YOU'RE
SUPERMAN!

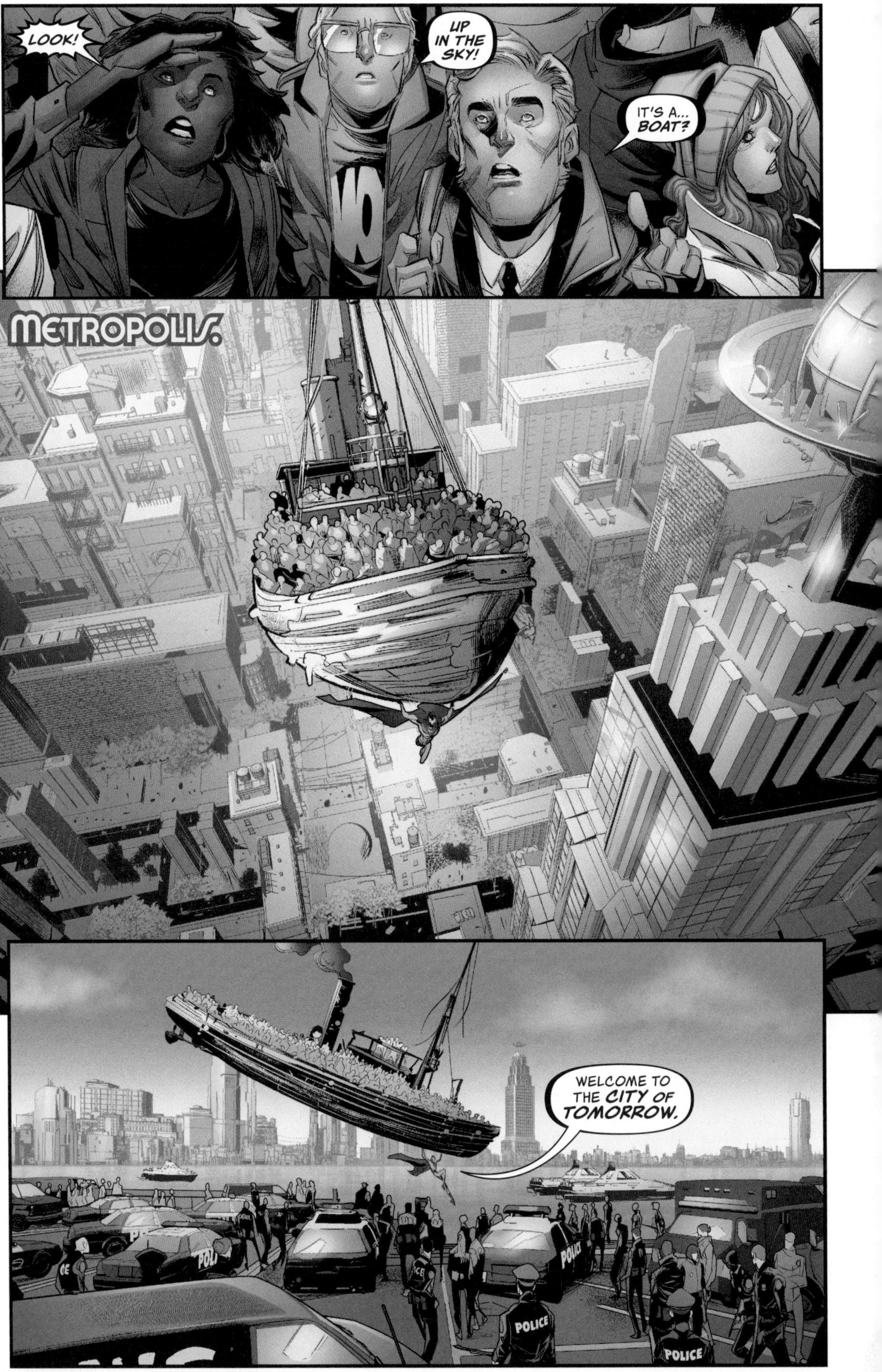
LOOK!
UP IN THE SKY!
IT'S A... BOAT?
METROPOLIS.
WELCOME TO THE CITY OF TOMORROW.

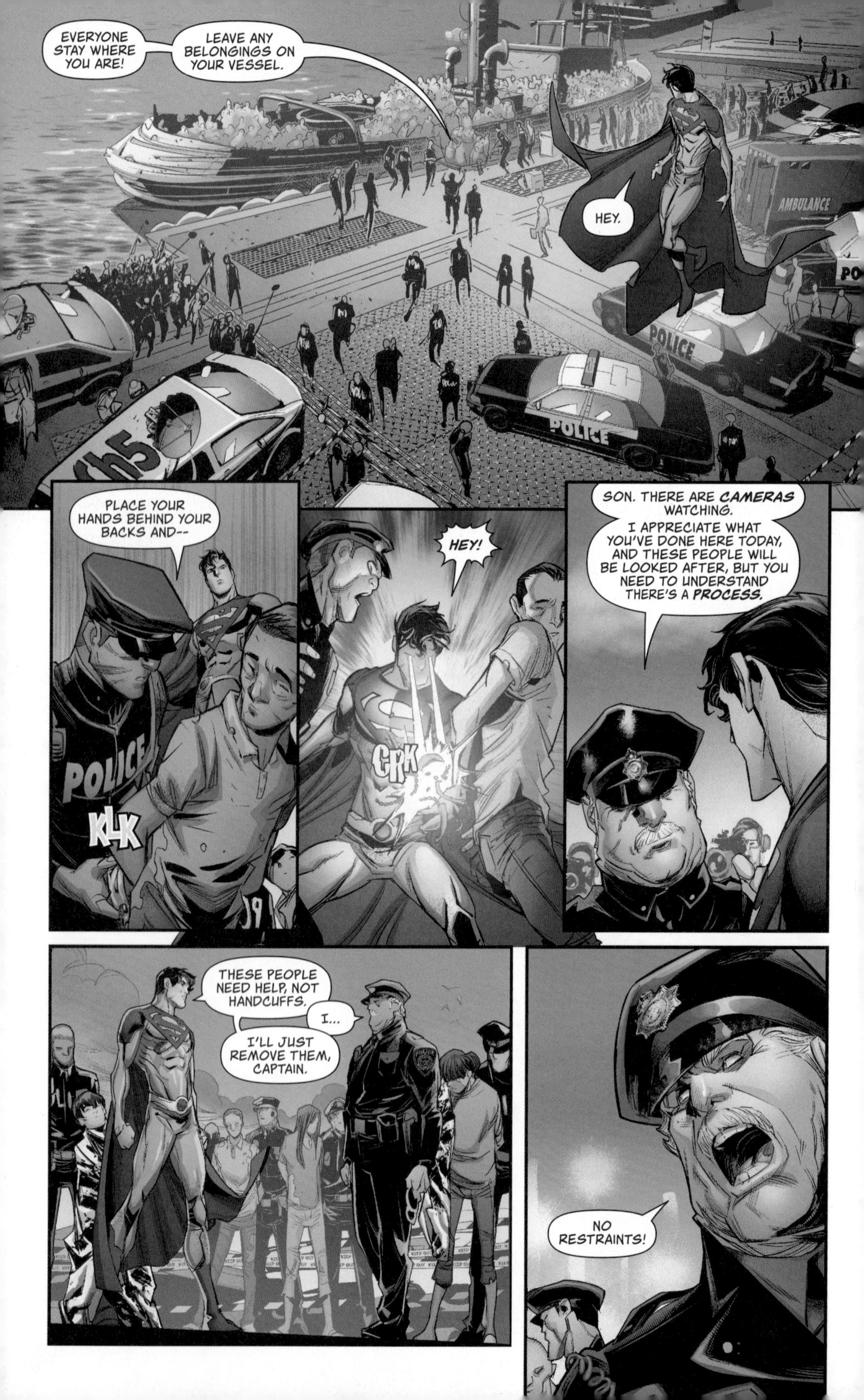
EVERYONE STAY WHERE YOU ARE!
LEAVE ANY BELONGINGS ON YOUR VESSEL.
HEY.
AMBULANCE
POLICE
POLICE
PLACE YOUR HANDS BEHIND YOUR BACKS AND--
POLICE
KLK
HEY!
CRK
SON. THERE ARE CAMERAS WATCHING.
I APPRECIATE WHAT YOU'VE DONE HERE TODAY, AND THESE PEOPLE WILL BE LOOKED AFTER, BUT YOU NEED TO UNDERSTAND THERE'S A PROCESS.
THESE PEOPLE NEED HELP, NOT HANDCUFFS.
I...
I'LL JUST REMOVE THEM, CAPTAIN.
NO RESTRAINTS!

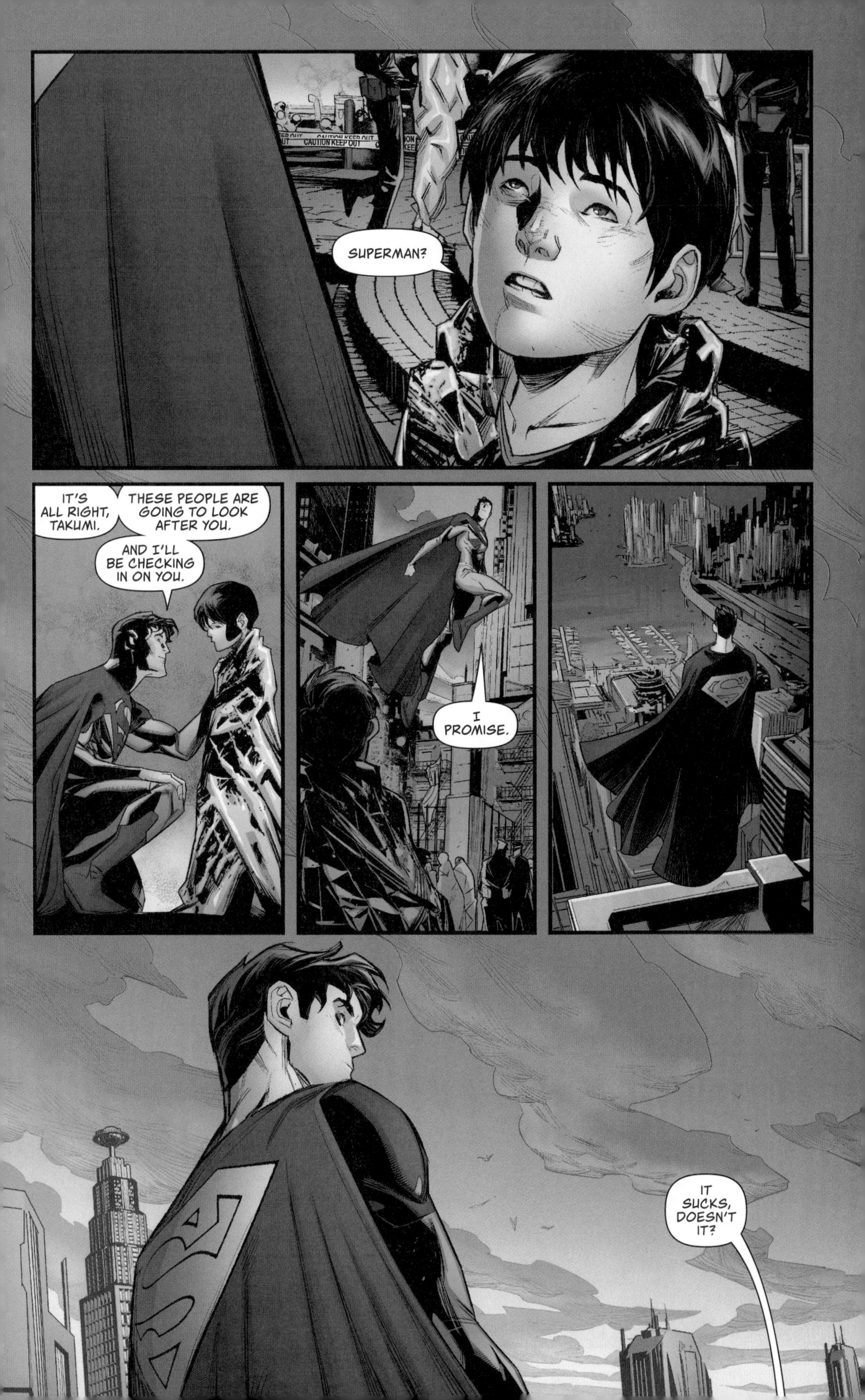
SUPERMAN?
IT'S ALL RIGHT, TAKUMI.
THESE PEOPLE ARE GOING TO LOOK AFTER YOU.
AND I'LL BE CHECKING IN ON YOU.
I PROMISE.
IT SUCKS, DOESN'T IT?

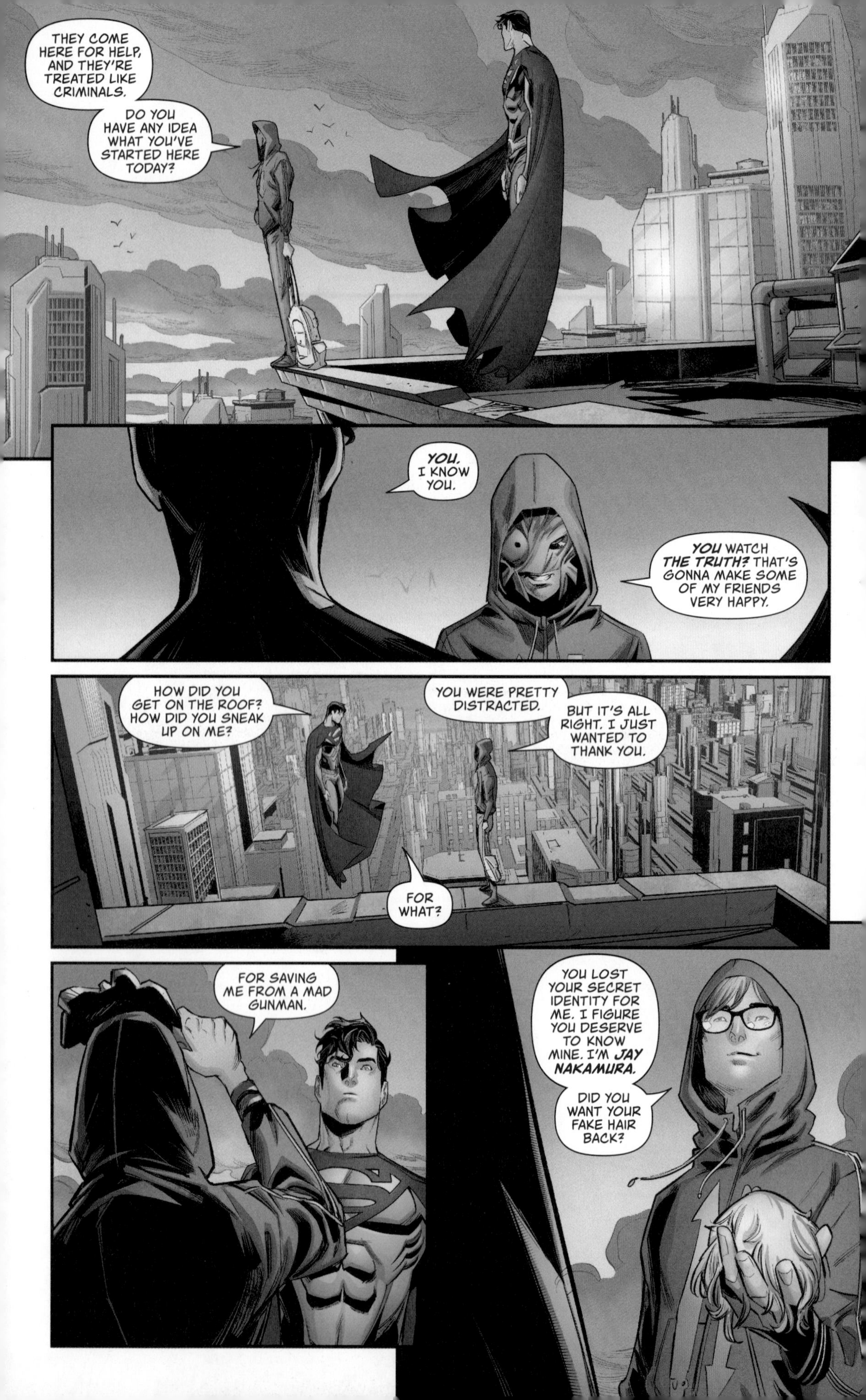
THEY COME HERE FOR HELP, AND THEY'RE TREATED LIKE CRIMINALS.
DO YOU HAVE ANY IDEA WHAT YOU'VE STARTED HERE TODAY?
YOU. I KNOW YOU.
YOU WATCH THE TRUTH? THAT'S GONNA MAKE SOME OF MY FRIENDS VERY HAPPY.
HOW DID YOU GET ON THE ROOF? HOW DID YOU SNEAK UP ON ME?
YOU WERE PRETTY DISTRACTED.
BUT IT'S ALL RIGHT. I JUST WANTED TO THANK YOU.
FOR WHAT?
FOR SAVING ME FROM A MAD GUNMAN.
YOU LOST YOUR SECRET IDENTITY FOR ME. I FIGURE YOU DESERVE TO KNOW MINE. I'M JAY NAKAMURA.
DID YOU WANT YOUR FAKE HAIR BACK?

I THINK I UNDERSTAND WHY YOU WERE WEARING A TERRIBLE WIG.

WAS IT REALLY THAT BAD?

OH, YEAH.

IT DID ABSOLUTELY NOTHING FOR YOU.

THIS IS THE PROBLEM WITH HAVING HAIR THAT'S IMPERVIOUS TO BLEACH.

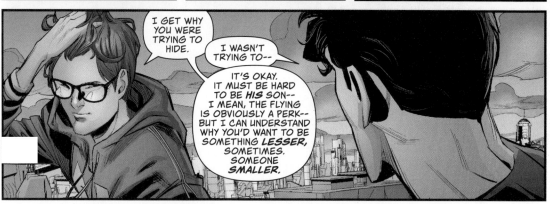

I GET WHY YOU WERE TRYING TO HIDE.

I WASN'T TRYING TO--

IT'S OKAY. IT MUST BE HARD TO BE *HIS* SON-- I MEAN, THE FLYING IS OBVIOUSLY A PERK-- BUT I CAN UNDERSTAND WHY YOU'D WANT TO BE SOMETHING *LESSER*, SOMETIMES. SOMEONE *SMALLER*.

I ACTUALLY MAY BE ABLE TO HELP WITH THAT.

BUT WE NEED TO HAVE ANOTHER CONVERSATION FIRST.

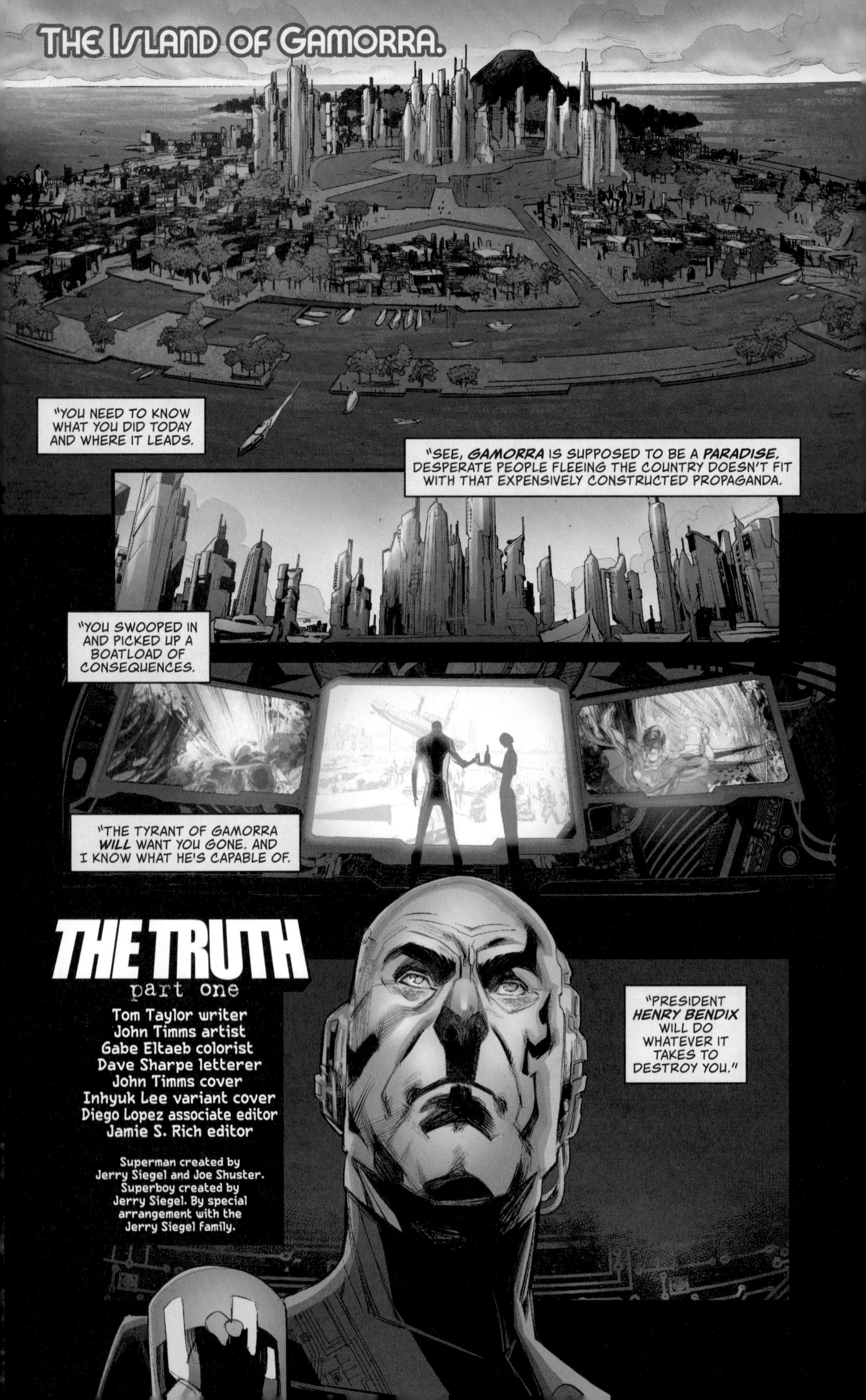
THE ISLAND OF GAMORRA.
"YOU NEED TO KNOW WHAT YOU DID TODAY AND WHERE IT LEADS.
"SEE, *GAMORRA* IS SUPPOSED TO BE A *PARADISE.* DESPERATE PEOPLE FLEEING THE COUNTRY DOESN'T FIT WITH THAT EXPENSIVELY CONSTRUCTED PROPAGANDA.
"YOU SWOOPED IN AND PICKED UP A BOATLOAD OF CONSEQUENCES.
"THE TYRANT OF GAMORRA *WILL* WANT YOU GONE. AND I KNOW WHAT HE'S CAPABLE OF.
THE TRUTH
part one
Tom Taylor writer
John Timms artist
Gabe Eltaeb colorist
Dave Sharpe letterer
John Timms cover
Inhyuk Lee variant cover
Diego Lopez associate editor
Jamie S. Rich editor
Superman created by Jerry Siegel and Joe Shuster. Superboy created by Jerry Siegel. By special arrangement with the Jerry Siegel family.
"PRESIDENT *HENRY BENDIX* WILL DO WHATEVER IT TAKES TO DESTROY YOU."

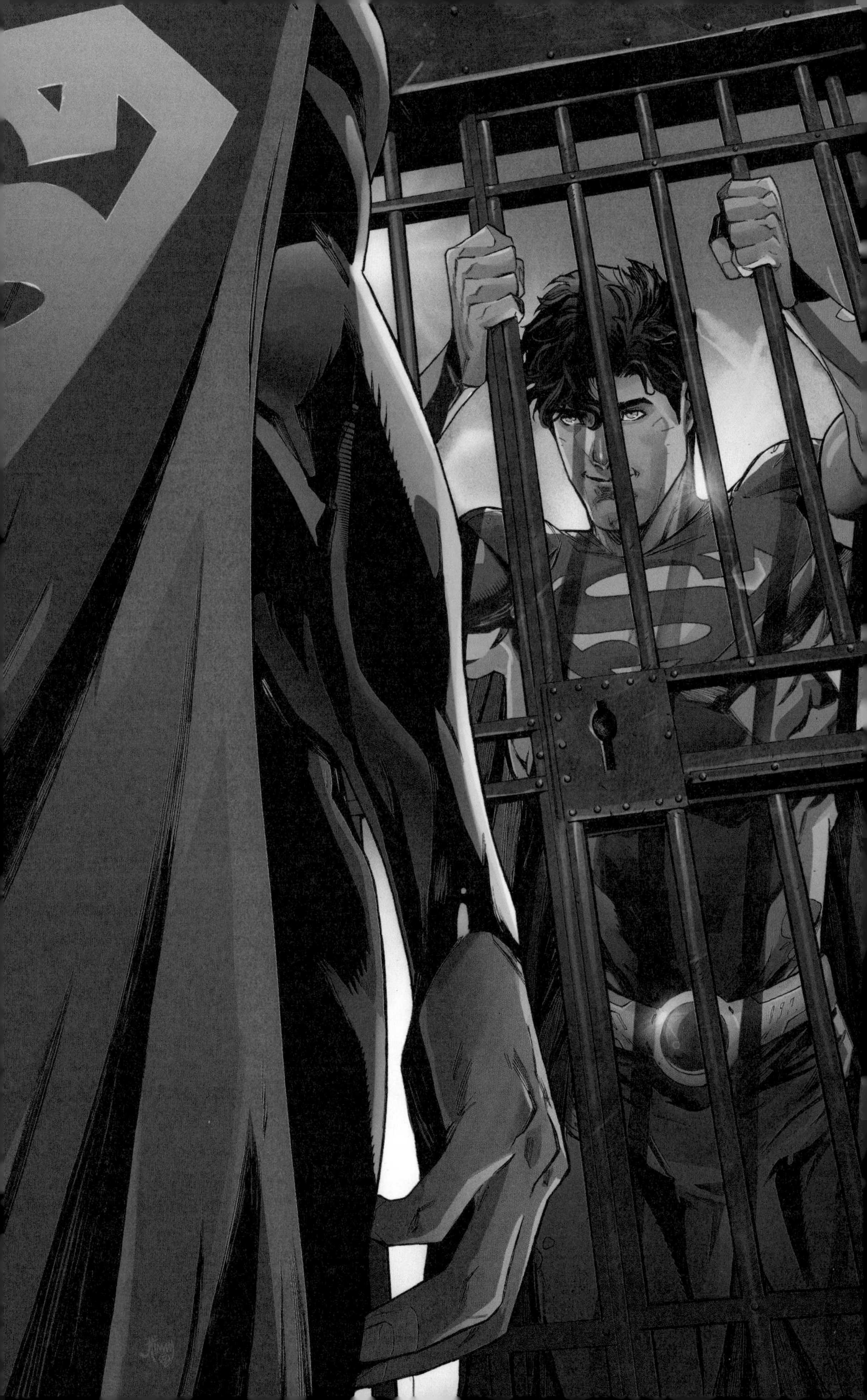

Superman: Son of Kal-El #3 variant cover art by **INHYUK LEE**

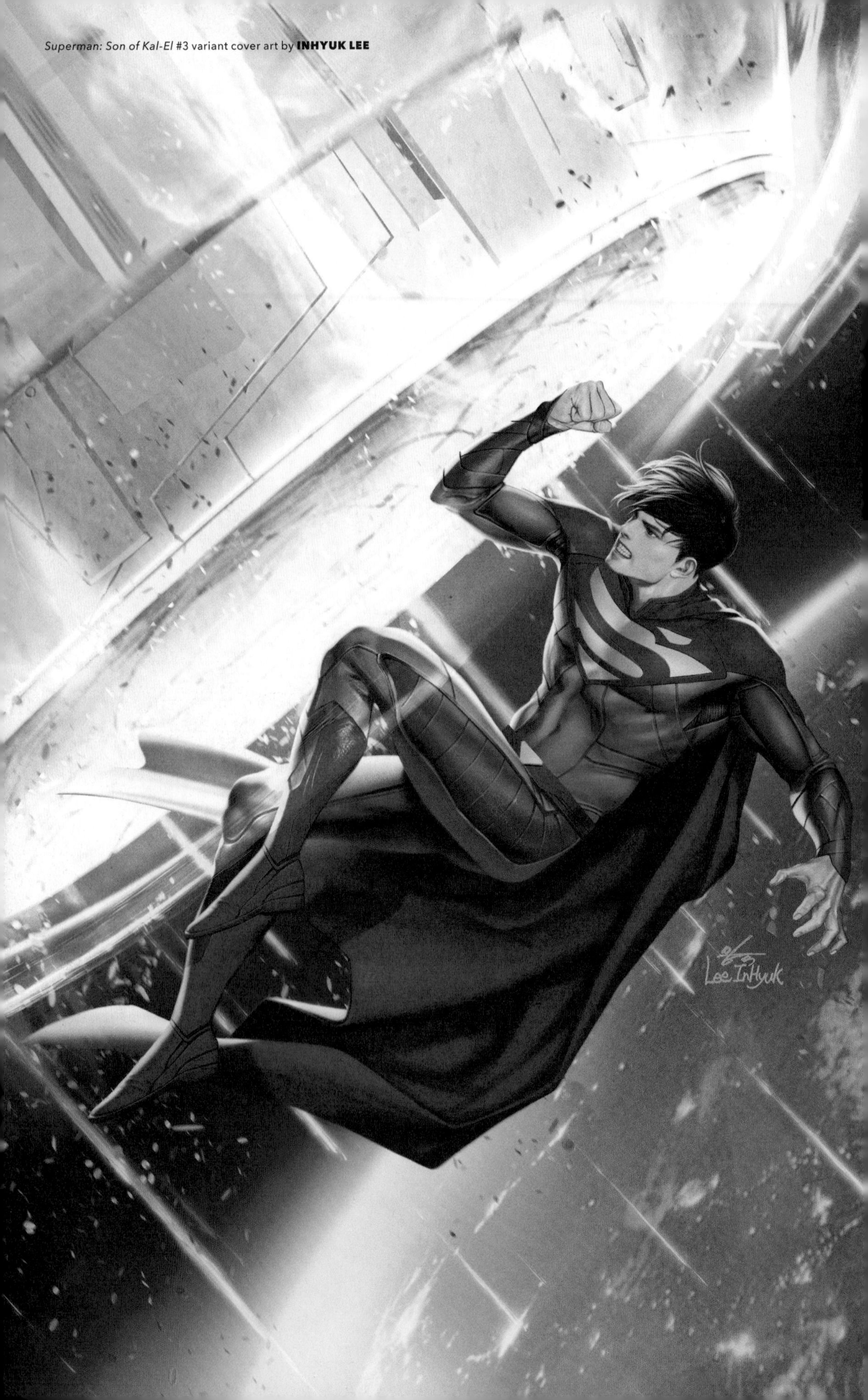
Lee InHyuk

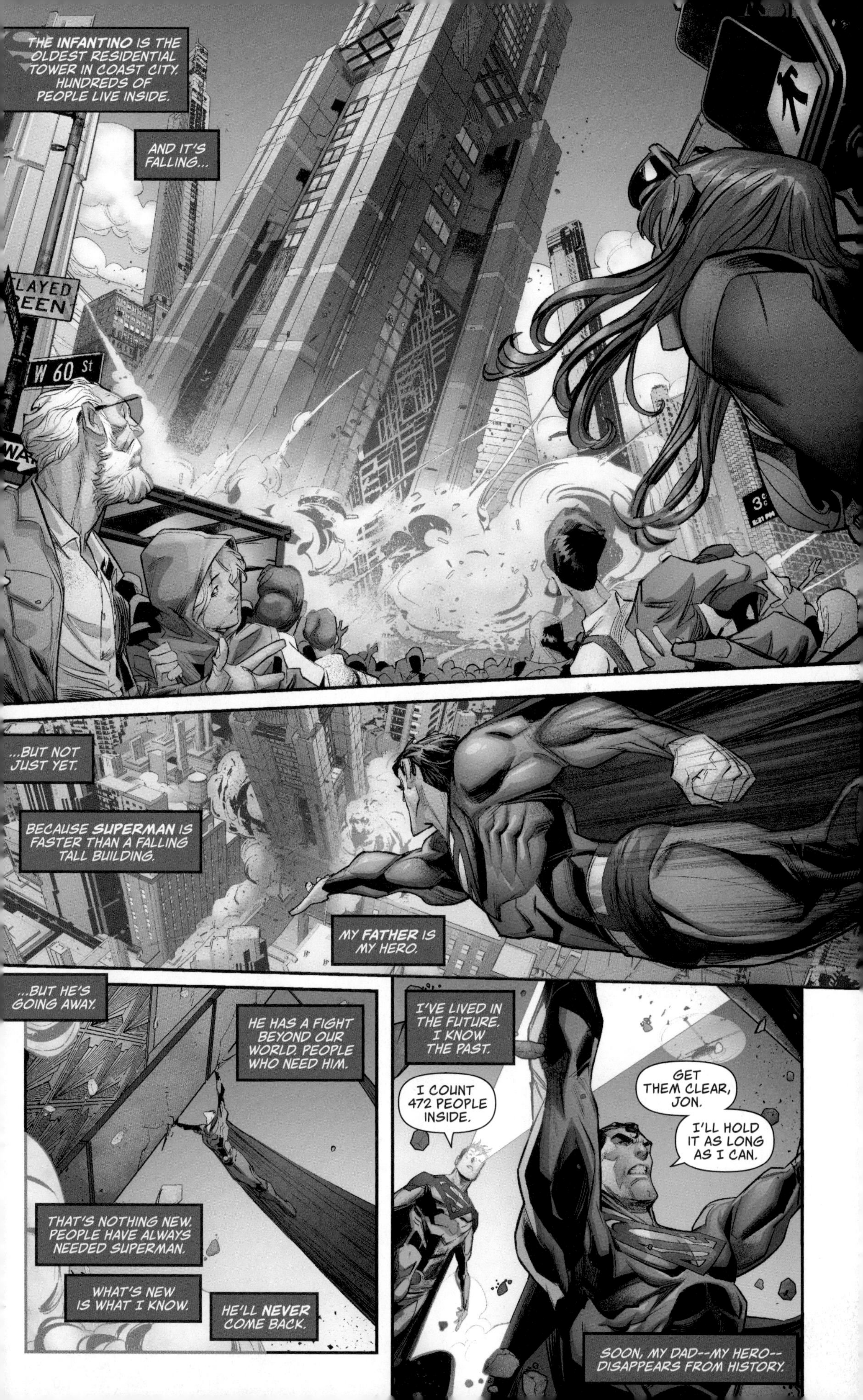
THE INFANTINO IS THE OLDEST RESIDENTIAL TOWER IN COAST CITY. HUNDREDS OF PEOPLE LIVE INSIDE.
AND IT'S FALLING...
W 60 St
...BUT NOT JUST YET.
BECAUSE SUPERMAN IS FASTER THAN A FALLING TALL BUILDING.
MY FATHER IS MY HERO.
...BUT HE'S GOING AWAY.
HE HAS A FIGHT BEYOND OUR WORLD. PEOPLE WHO NEED HIM.
THAT'S NOTHING NEW. PEOPLE HAVE ALWAYS NEEDED SUPERMAN.
WHAT'S NEW IS WHAT I KNOW.
HE'LL NEVER COME BACK.
I'VE LIVED IN THE FUTURE. I KNOW THE PAST.
I COUNT 472 PEOPLE INSIDE.
GET THEM CLEAR, JON.
I'LL HOLD IT AS LONG AS I CAN.
SOON, MY DAD--MY HERO--DISAPPEARS FROM HISTORY.

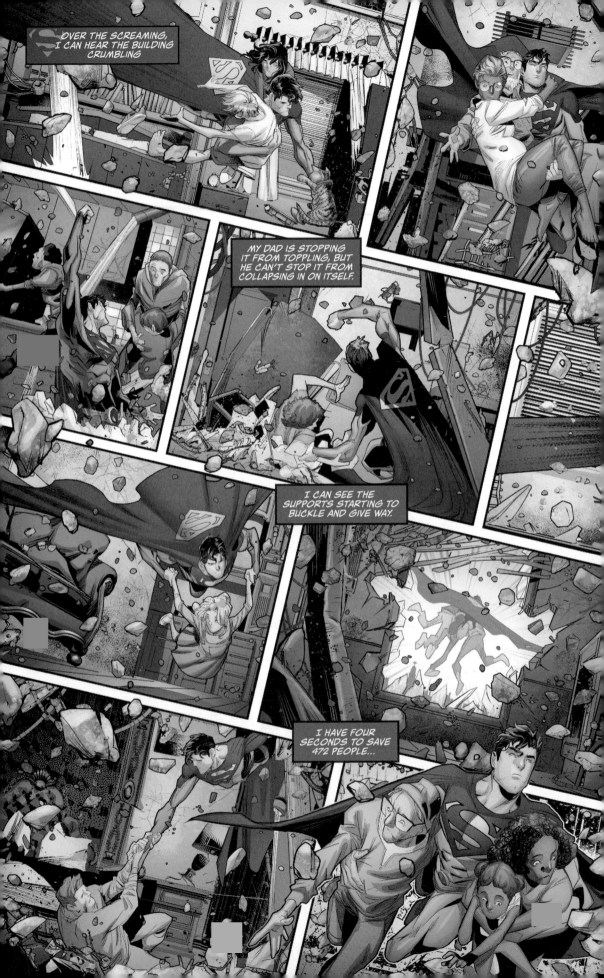

OVER THE SCREAMING, I CAN HEAR THE BUILDING CRUMBLING

MY DAD IS STOPPING IT FROM TOPPLING, BUT HE CAN'T STOP IT FROM COLLAPSING IN ON ITSELF.

I CAN SEE THE SUPPORTS STARTING TO BUCKLE AND GIVE WAY.

I HAVE FOUR SECONDS TO SAVE 472 PEOPLE...

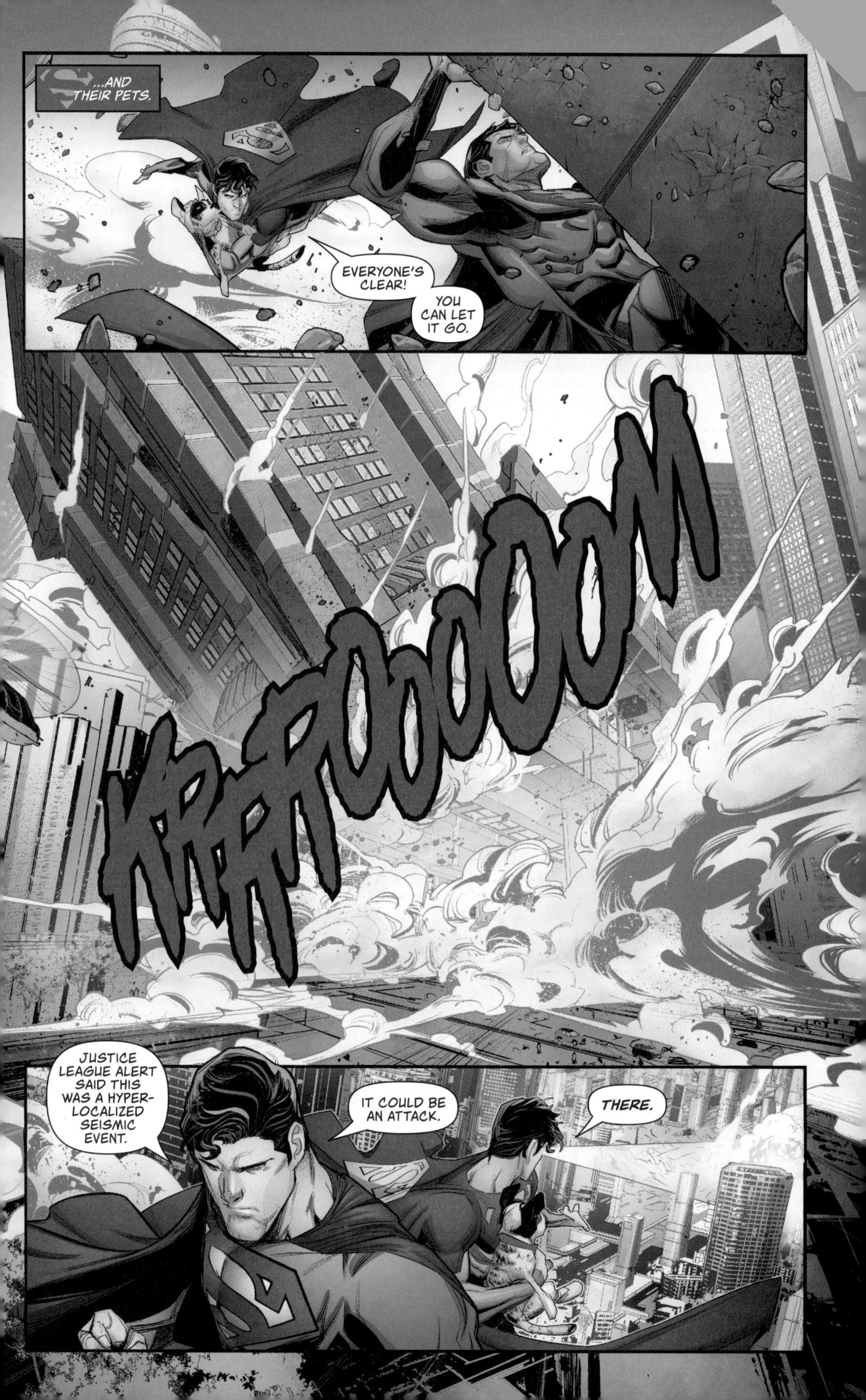
...AND THEIR PETS.
EVERYONE'S CLEAR!
YOU CAN LET IT GO.
KRRROOOOOOM
JUSTICE LEAGUE ALERT SAID THIS WAS A HYPER-LOCALIZED SEISMIC EVENT.
IT COULD BE AN ATTACK.
THERE.

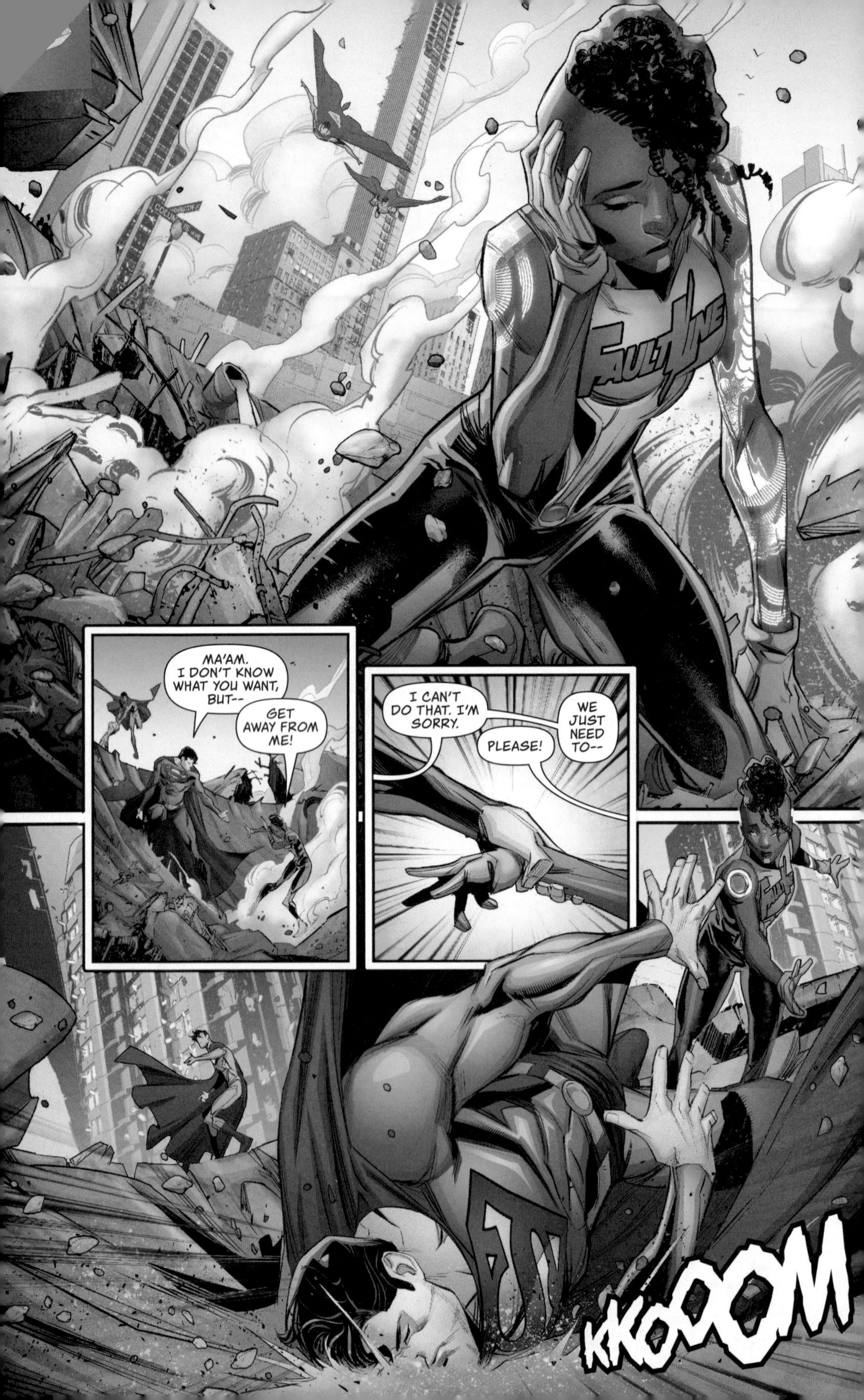
MA'AM. I DON'T KNOW WHAT YOU WANT, BUT--
GET AWAY FROM ME!
I CAN'T DO THAT. I'M SORRY.
WE JUST NEED TO--
PLEASE!
KKOOOOM

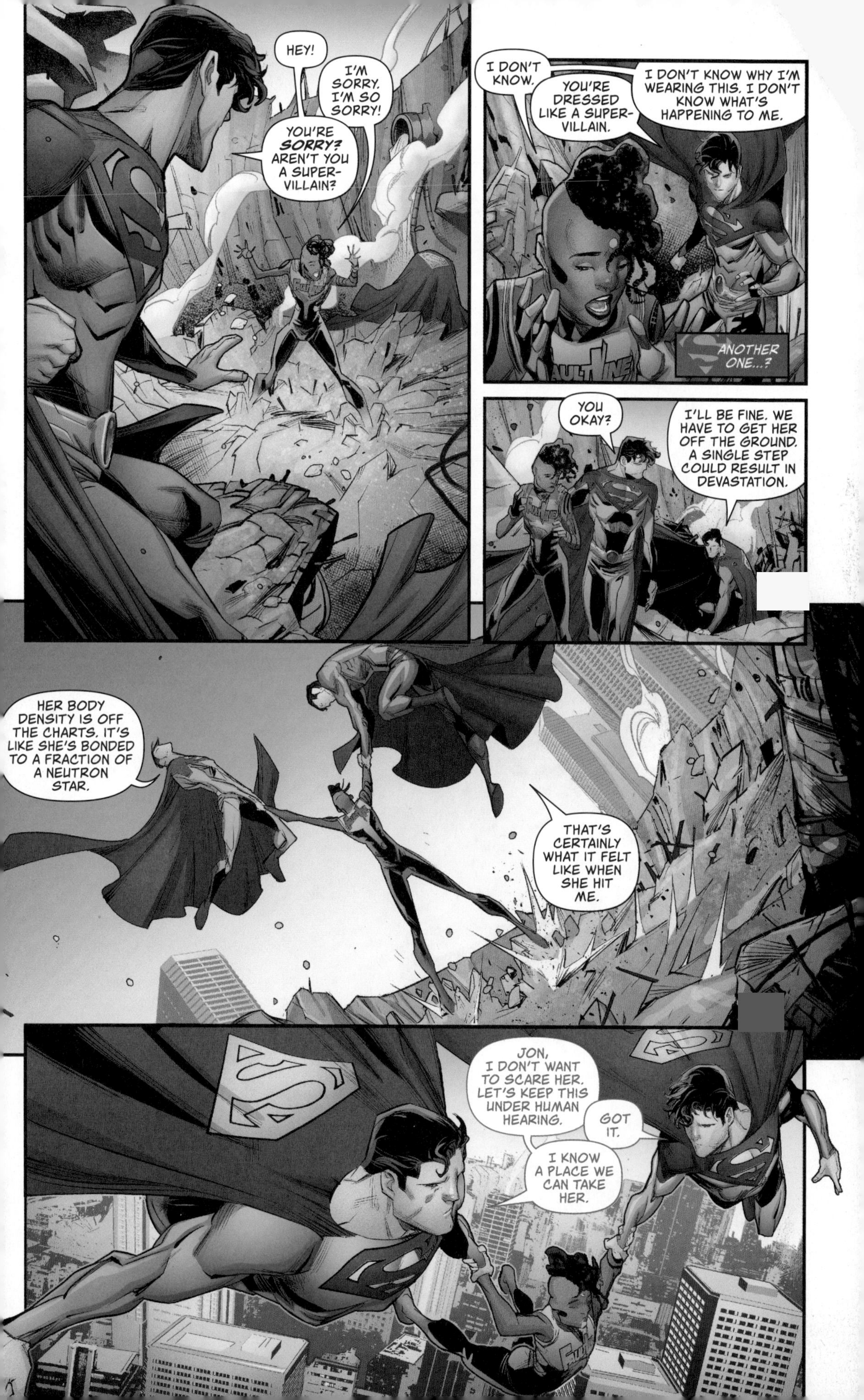
HEY!
I'M SORRY. I'M SO SORRY!
YOU'RE **SORRY?** AREN'T YOU A SUPER-VILLAIN?
I DON'T KNOW.
YOU'RE DRESSED LIKE A SUPER-VILLAIN.
I DON'T KNOW WHY I'M WEARING THIS. I DON'T KNOW WHAT'S HAPPENING TO ME.
ANOTHER ONE...?
YOU OKAY?
I'LL BE FINE. WE HAVE TO GET HER OFF THE GROUND. A SINGLE STEP COULD RESULT IN DEVASTATION.
HER BODY DENSITY IS OFF THE CHARTS. IT'S LIKE SHE'S BONDED TO A FRACTION OF A NEUTRON STAR.
THAT'S CERTAINLY WHAT IT FELT LIKE WHEN SHE HIT ME.
JON, I DON'T WANT TO SCARE HER. LET'S KEEP THIS UNDER HUMAN HEARING.
GOT IT.
I KNOW A PLACE WE CAN TAKE HER.

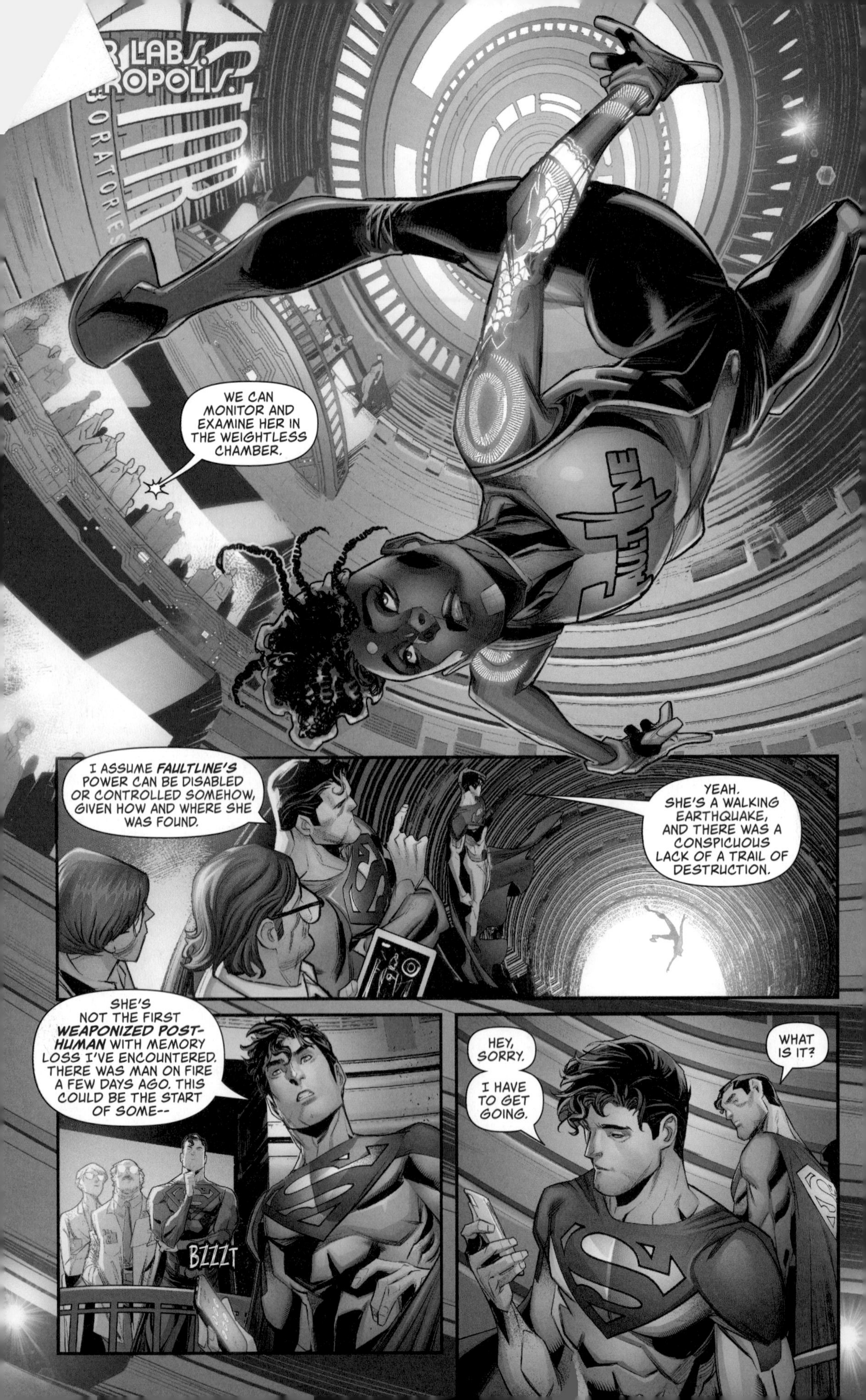
WE CAN MONITOR AND EXAMINE HER IN THE WEIGHTLESS CHAMBER.
I ASSUME FAULTLINE'S POWER CAN BE DISABLED OR CONTROLLED SOMEHOW, GIVEN HOW AND WHERE SHE WAS FOUND.
YEAH. SHE'S A WALKING EARTHQUAKE, AND THERE WAS A CONSPICUOUS LACK OF A TRAIL OF DESTRUCTION.
SHE'S NOT THE FIRST WEAPONIZED POST-HUMAN WITH MEMORY LOSS I'VE ENCOUNTERED. THERE WAS MAN ON FIRE A FEW DAYS AGO. THIS COULD BE THE START OF SOME--
BZZZT
HEY, SORRY.
I HAVE TO GET GOING.
WHAT IS IT?

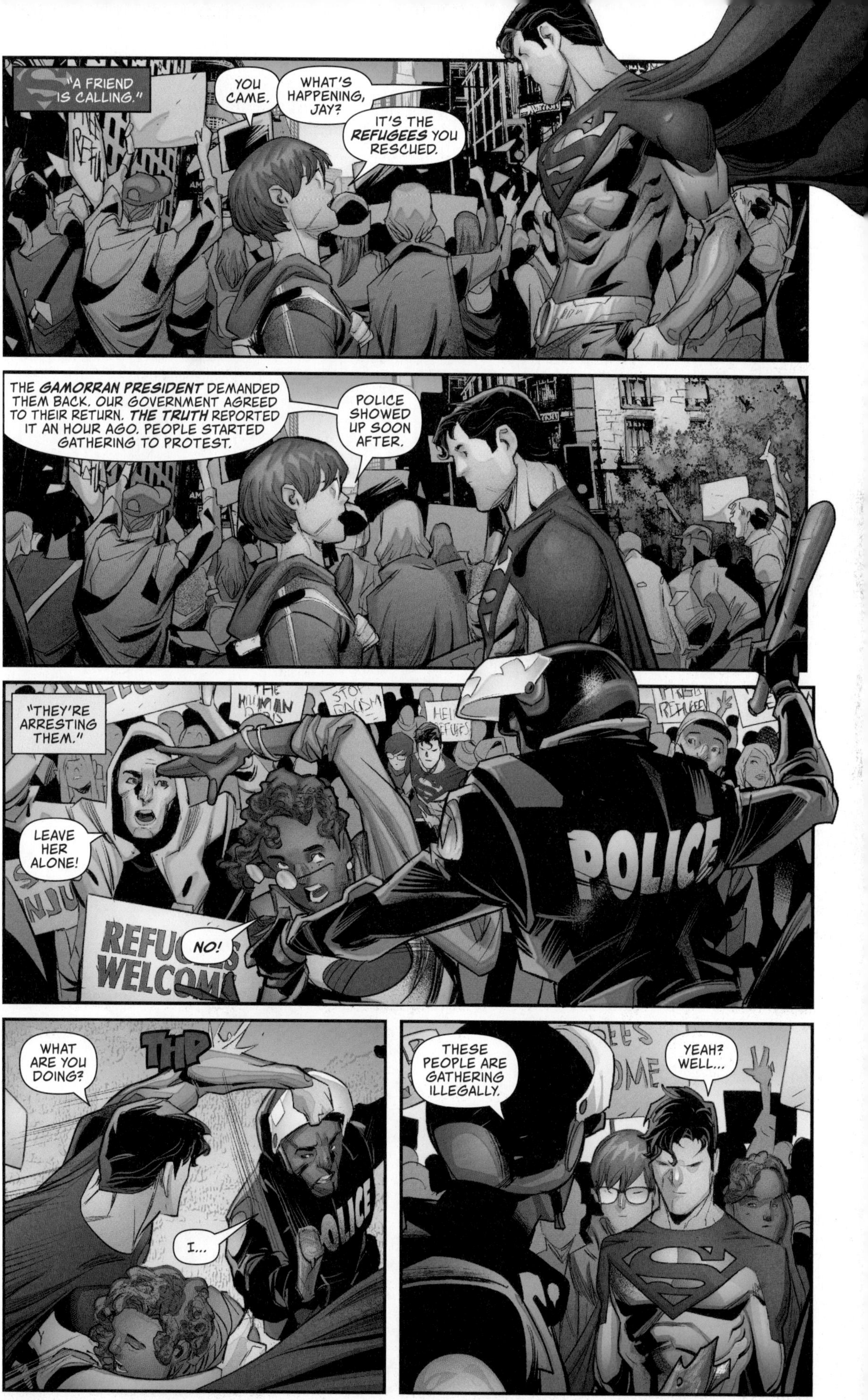
"A FRIEND IS CALLING."
YOU CAME.
WHAT'S HAPPENING, JAY?
IT'S THE ***REFUGEES*** YOU RESCUED.
THE ***GAMORRAN PRESIDENT*** DEMANDED THEM BACK. OUR GOVERNMENT AGREED TO THEIR RETURN. ***THE TRUTH*** REPORTED IT AN HOUR AGO. PEOPLE STARTED GATHERING TO PROTEST.
POLICE SHOWED UP SOON AFTER.
"THEY'RE ARRESTING THEM."
LEAVE HER ALONE!
POLICE
REFUGEES WELCOM
NO!
WHAT ARE YOU DOING?
THP
POLICE
I...
THESE PEOPLE ARE GATHERING ILLEGALLY.
YEAH? WELL...

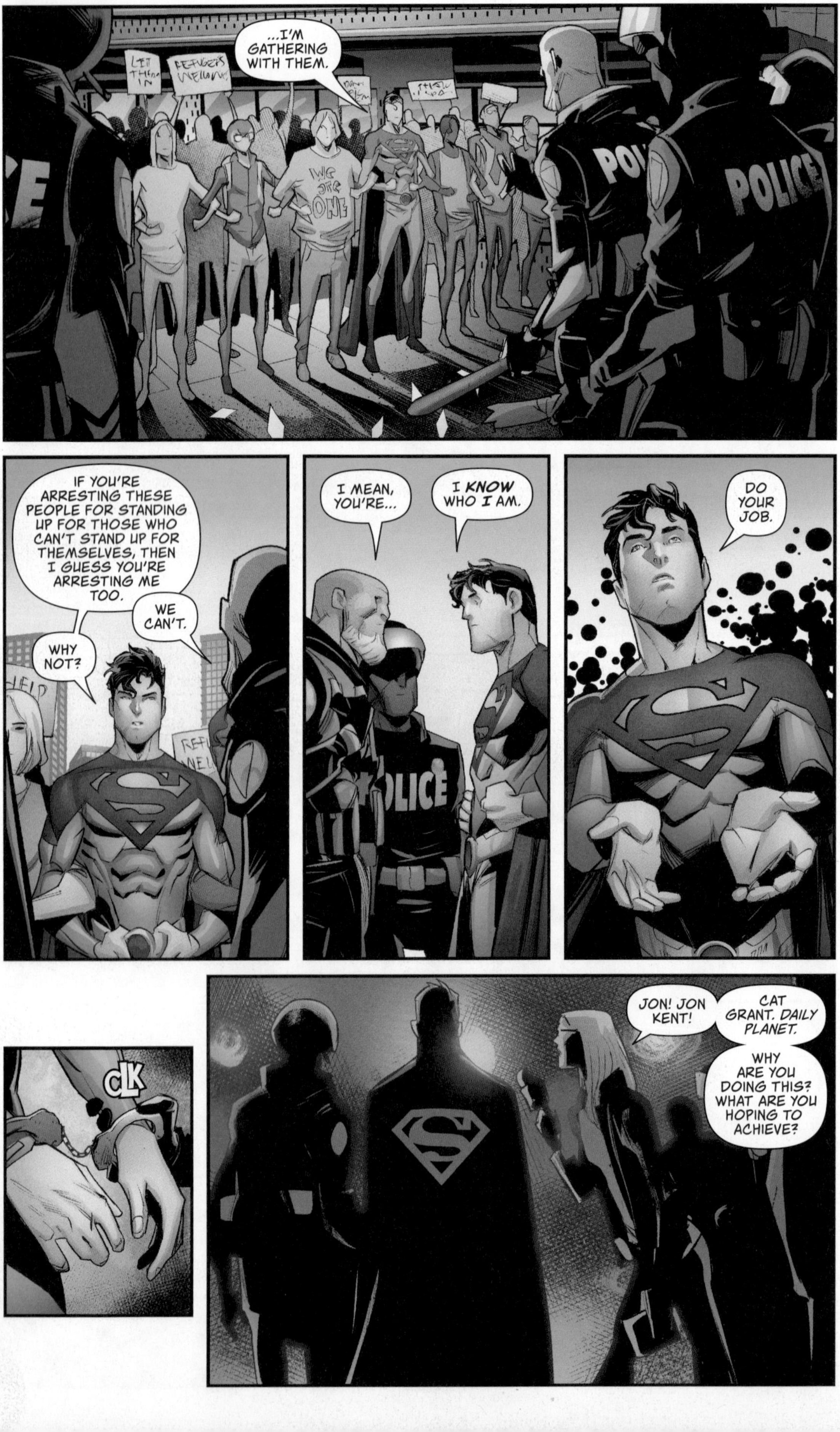

...I'M GATHERING WITH THEM.
POLICE
POLICE
IF YOU'RE ARRESTING THESE PEOPLE FOR STANDING UP FOR THOSE WHO CAN'T STAND UP FOR THEMSELVES, THEN I GUESS YOU'RE ARRESTING ME TOO.
WE CAN'T.
WHY NOT?
I MEAN, YOU'RE...
I *KNOW* WHO I AM.
POLICE
DO YOUR JOB.
CLK
JON! JON KENT!
CAT GRANT. *DAILY PLANET.*
WHY ARE YOU DOING THIS? WHAT ARE YOU HOPING TO ACHIEVE?

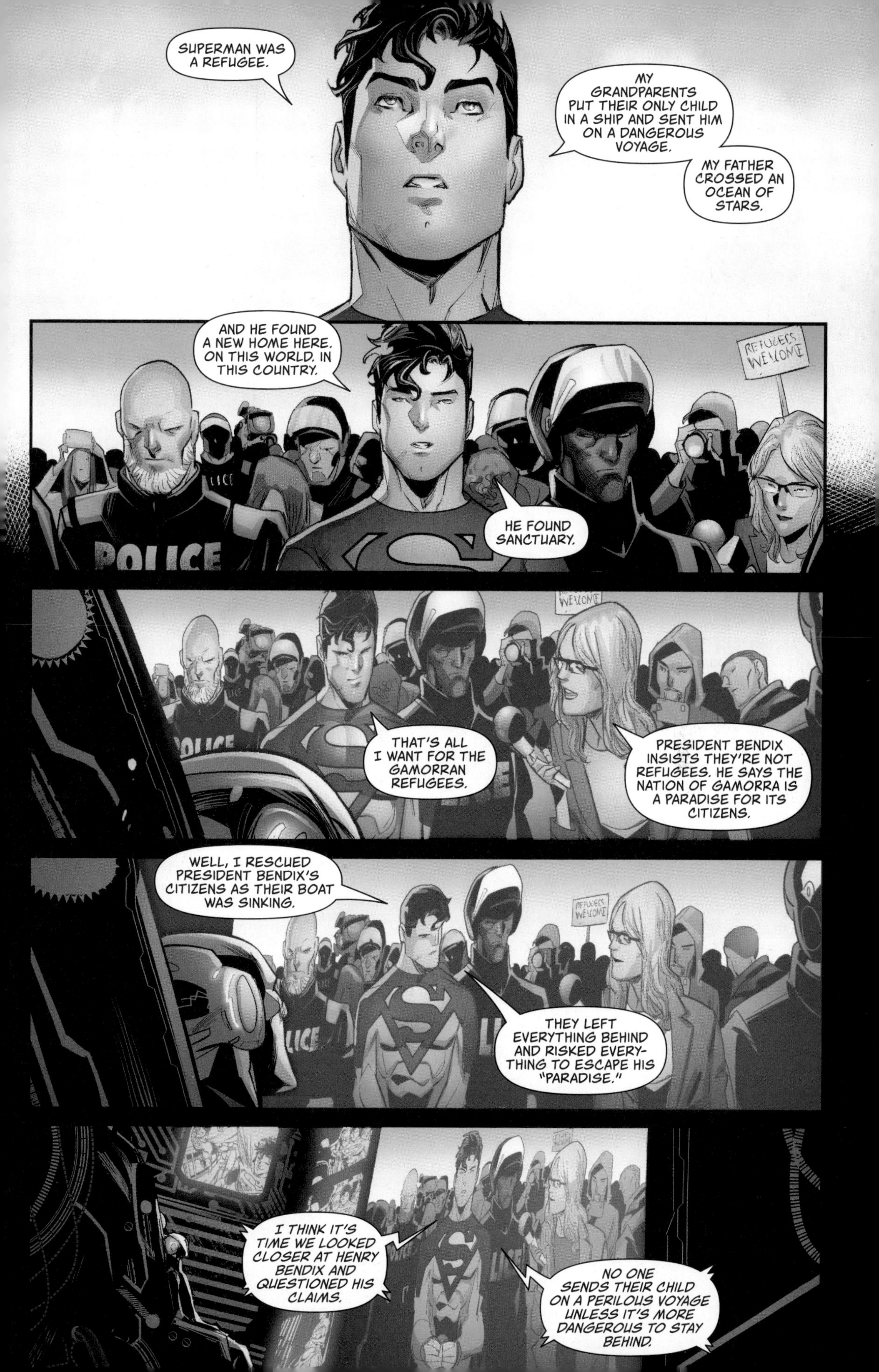
SUPERMAN WAS A REFUGEE.
MY GRANDPARENTS PUT THEIR ONLY CHILD IN A SHIP AND SENT HIM ON A DANGEROUS VOYAGE.
MY FATHER CROSSED AN OCEAN OF STARS.
AND HE FOUND A NEW HOME HERE. ON THIS WORLD. IN THIS COUNTRY.
REFUGEES WELCOME
HE FOUND SANCTUARY.
POLICE
THAT'S ALL I WANT FOR THE GAMORRAN REFUGEES.
PRESIDENT BENDIX INSISTS THEY'RE NOT REFUGEES. HE SAYS THE NATION OF GAMORRA IS A PARADISE FOR ITS CITIZENS.
WELL, I RESCUED PRESIDENT BENDIX'S CITIZENS AS THEIR BOAT WAS SINKING.
THEY LEFT EVERYTHING BEHIND AND RISKED EVERY-THING TO ESCAPE HIS "PARADISE."
I THINK IT'S TIME WE LOOKED CLOSER AT HENRY BENDIX AND QUESTIONED HIS CLAIMS.
NO ONE SENDS THEIR CHILD ON A PERILOUS VOYAGE UNLESS IT'S MORE DANGEROUS TO STAY BEHIND.

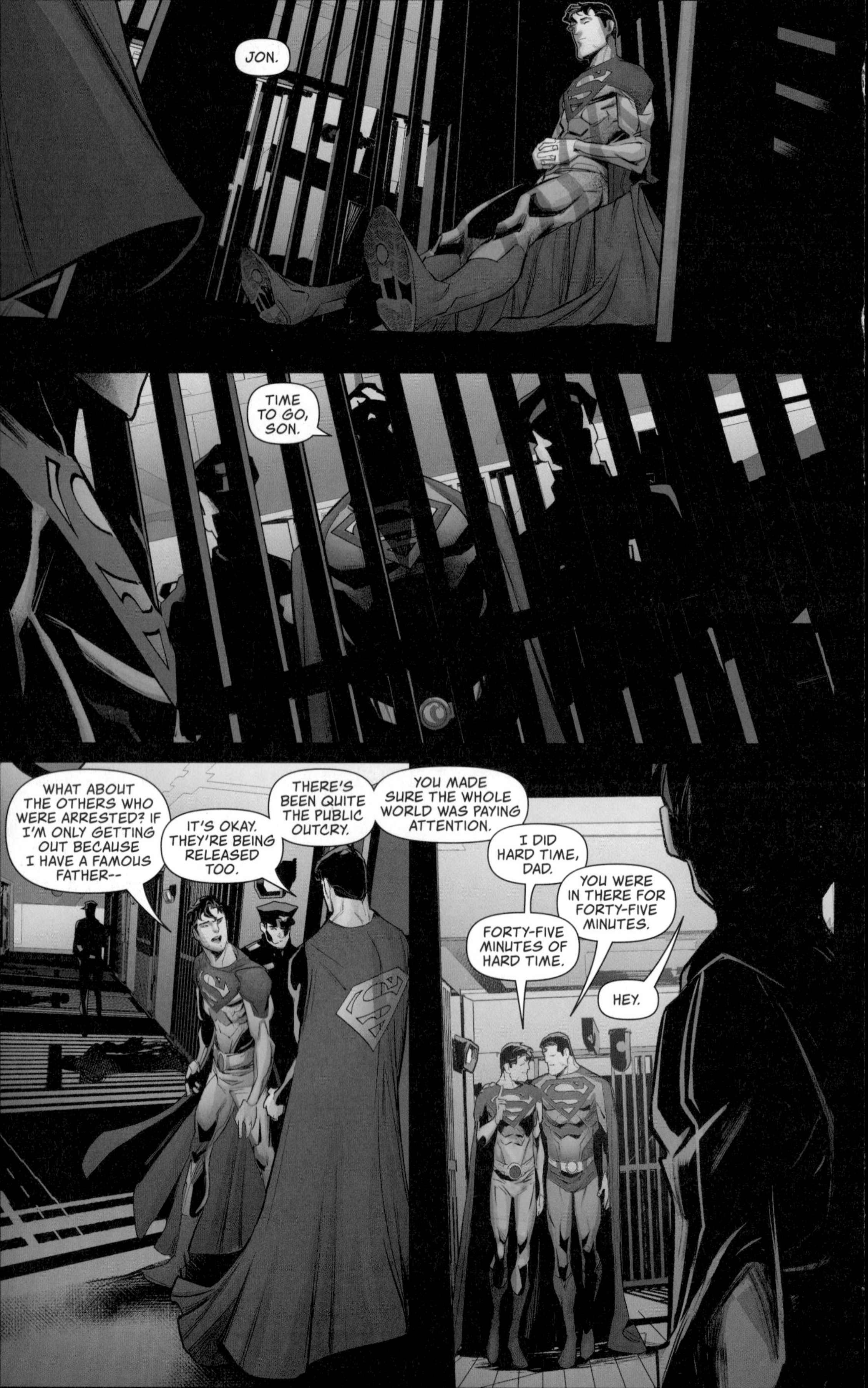
JON.
TIME TO GO, SON.
WHAT ABOUT THE OTHERS WHO WERE ARRESTED? IF I'M ONLY GETTING OUT BECAUSE I HAVE A FAMOUS FATHER--
IT'S OKAY. THEY'RE BEING RELEASED TOO.
THERE'S BEEN QUITE THE PUBLIC OUTCRY.
YOU MADE SURE THE WHOLE WORLD WAS PAYING ATTENTION.
I DID HARD TIME, DAD.
YOU WERE IN THERE FOR FORTY-FIVE MINUTES.
FORTY-FIVE MINUTES OF HARD TIME.
HEY.

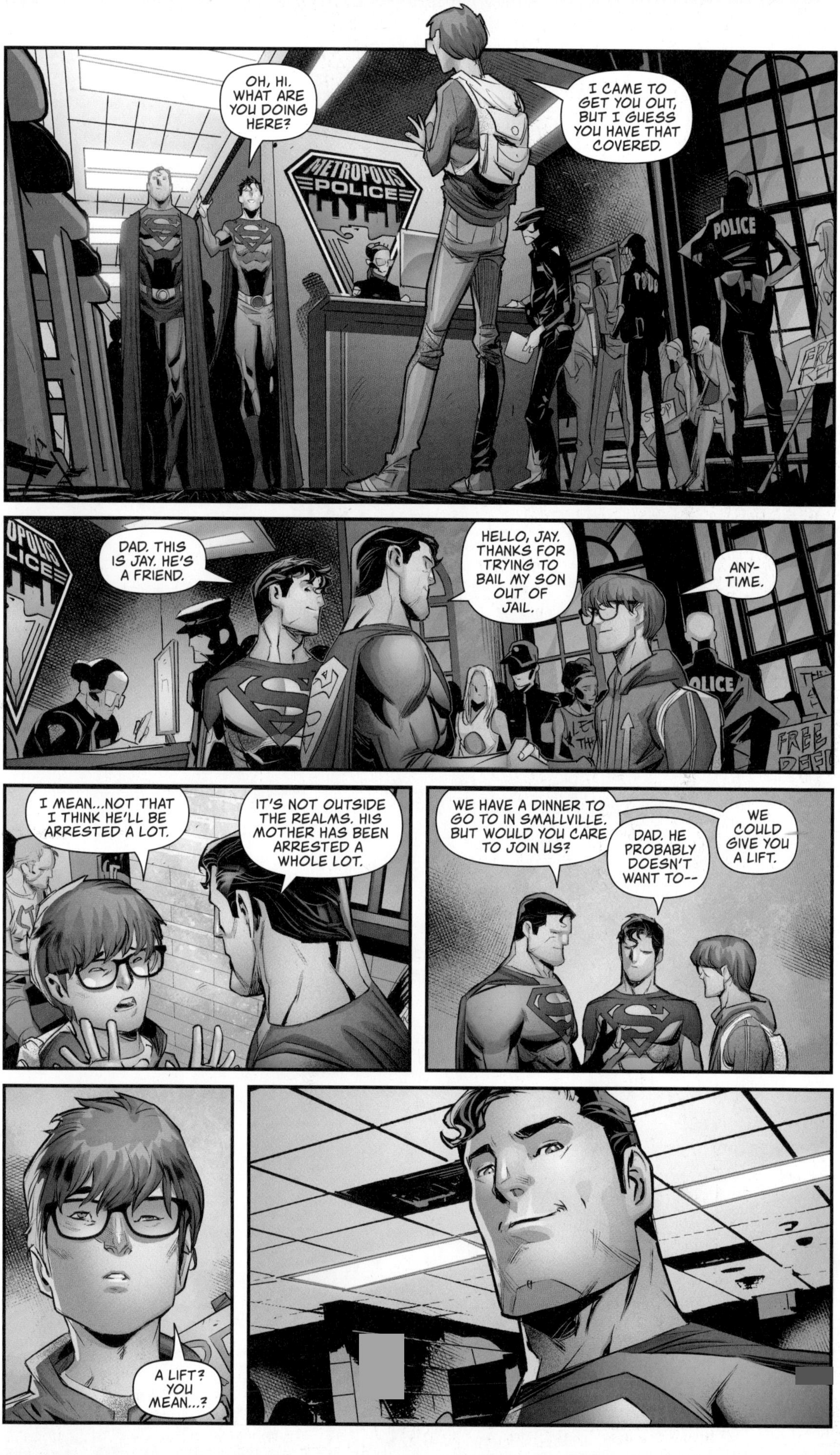
OH, HI. WHAT ARE YOU DOING HERE?
I CAME TO GET YOU OUT, BUT I GUESS YOU HAVE THAT COVERED.
METROPOLIS POLICE
POLICE
DAD. THIS IS JAY. HE'S A FRIEND.
HELLO, JAY. THANKS FOR TRYING TO BAIL MY SON OUT OF JAIL.
ANY-TIME.
I MEAN...NOT THAT I THINK HE'LL BE ARRESTED A LOT.
IT'S NOT OUTSIDE THE REALMS. HIS MOTHER HAS BEEN ARRESTED A WHOLE LOT.
WE HAVE A DINNER TO GO TO IN SMALLVILLE. BUT WOULD YOU CARE TO JOIN US?
WE COULD GIVE YOU A LIFT.
DAD. HE PROBABLY DOESN'T WANT TO--
A LIFT? YOU MEAN...?

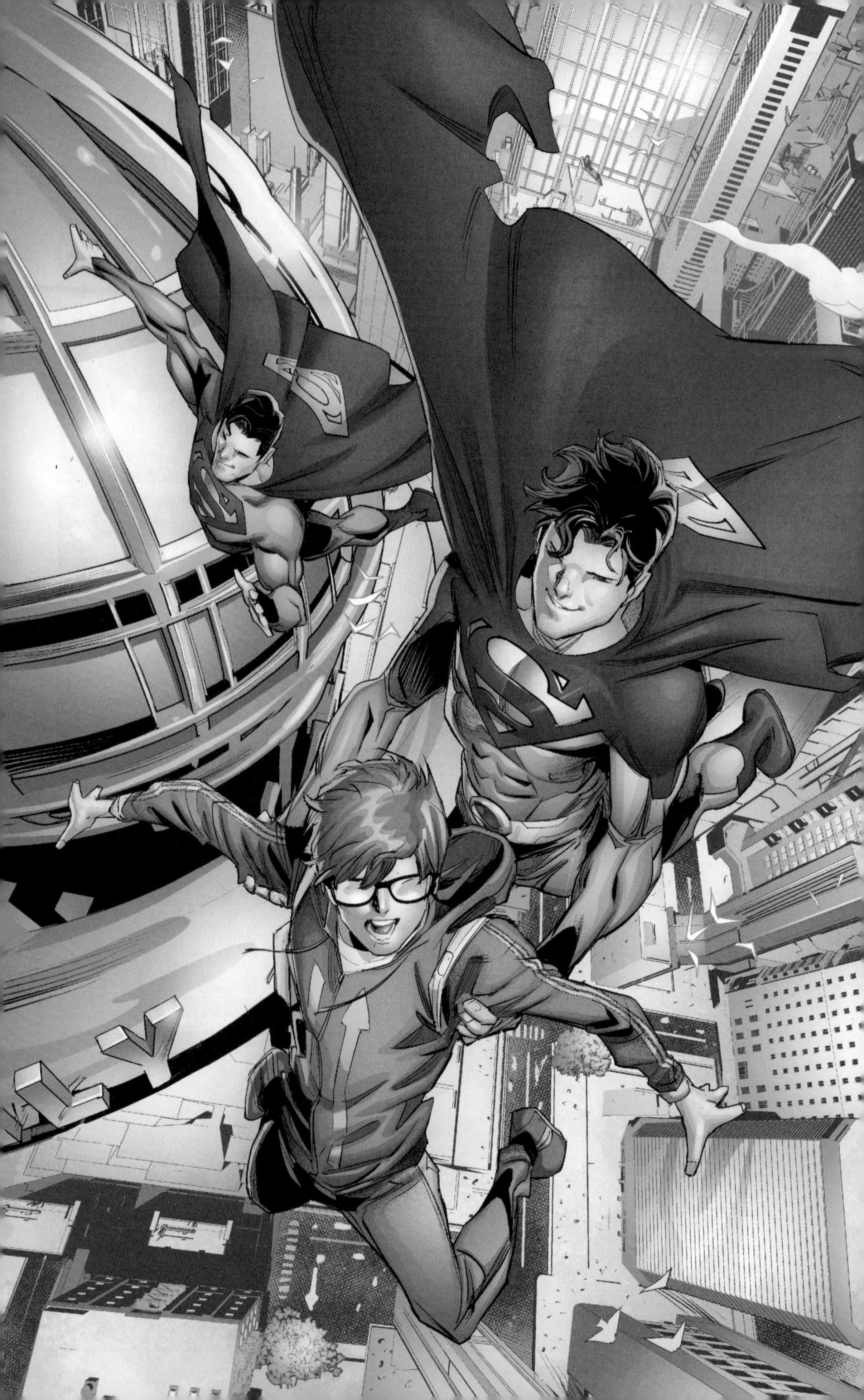

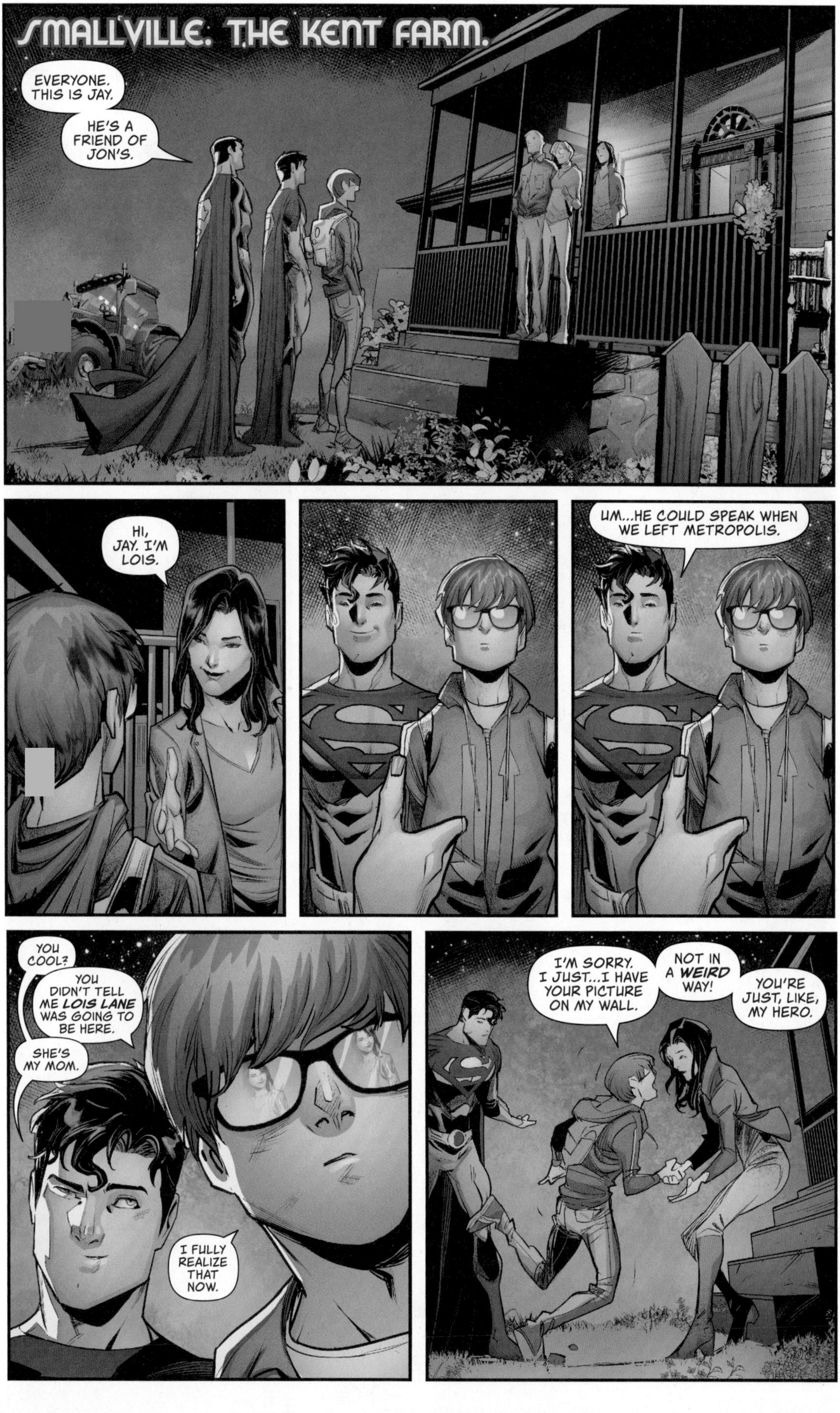
SMALLVILLE. THE KENT FARM.
EVERYONE. THIS IS JAY.
HE'S A FRIEND OF JON'S.
HI, JAY. I'M LOIS.
UM...HE COULD SPEAK WHEN WE LEFT METROPOLIS.
YOU COOL?
YOU DIDN'T TELL ME LOIS LANE WAS GOING TO BE HERE.
SHE'S MY MOM.
I FULLY REALIZE THAT NOW.
I'M SORRY. I JUST...I HAVE YOUR PICTURE ON MY WALL.
NOT IN A WEIRD WAY!
YOU'RE JUST, LIKE, MY HERO.

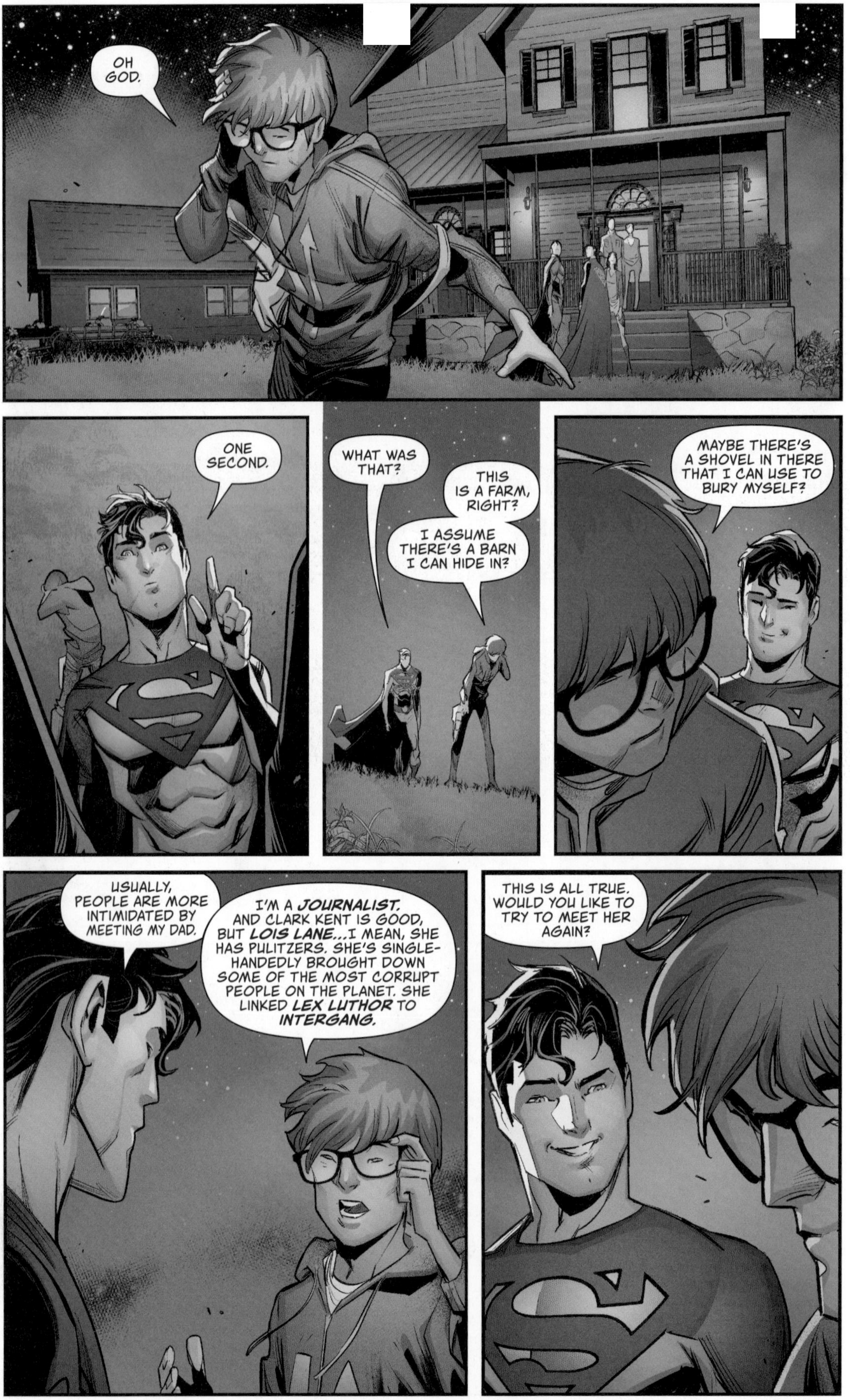
OH GOD.
ONE SECOND.
WHAT WAS THAT?
THIS IS A FARM, RIGHT?
I ASSUME THERE'S A BARN I CAN HIDE IN?
MAYBE THERE'S A SHOVEL IN THERE THAT I CAN USE TO BURY MYSELF?
USUALLY, PEOPLE ARE MORE INTIMIDATED BY MEETING MY DAD.
I'M A JOURNALIST. AND CLARK KENT IS GOOD, BUT LOIS LANE...I MEAN, SHE HAS PULITZERS. SHE'S SINGLE-HANDEDLY BROUGHT DOWN SOME OF THE MOST CORRUPT PEOPLE ON THE PLANET. SHE LINKED LEX LUTHOR TO INTERGANG.
THIS IS ALL TRUE. WOULD YOU LIKE TO TRY TO MEET HER AGAIN?

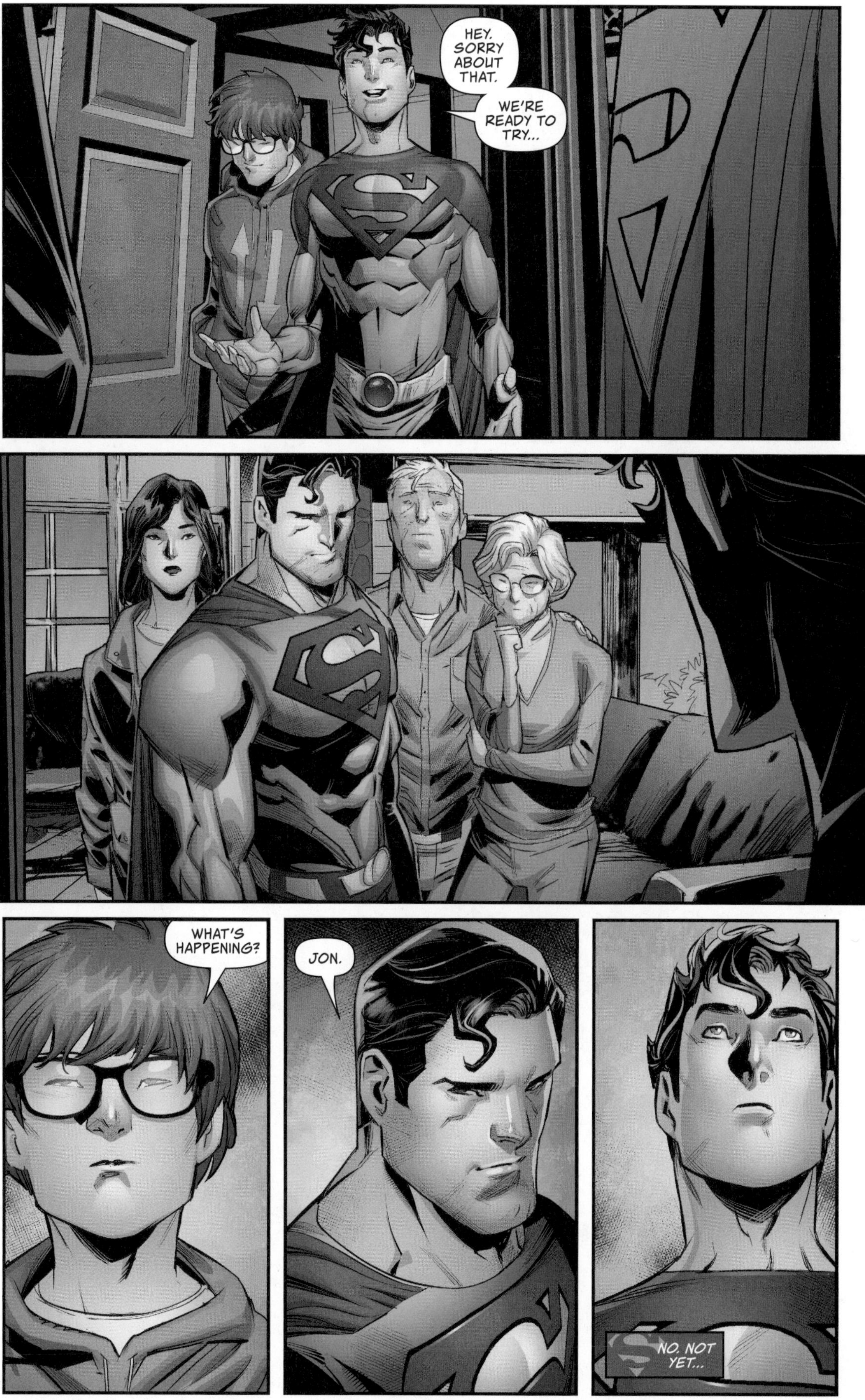
HEY. SORRY ABOUT THAT.
WE'RE READY TO TRY...
WHAT'S HAPPENING?
JON.
NO. NOT YET...

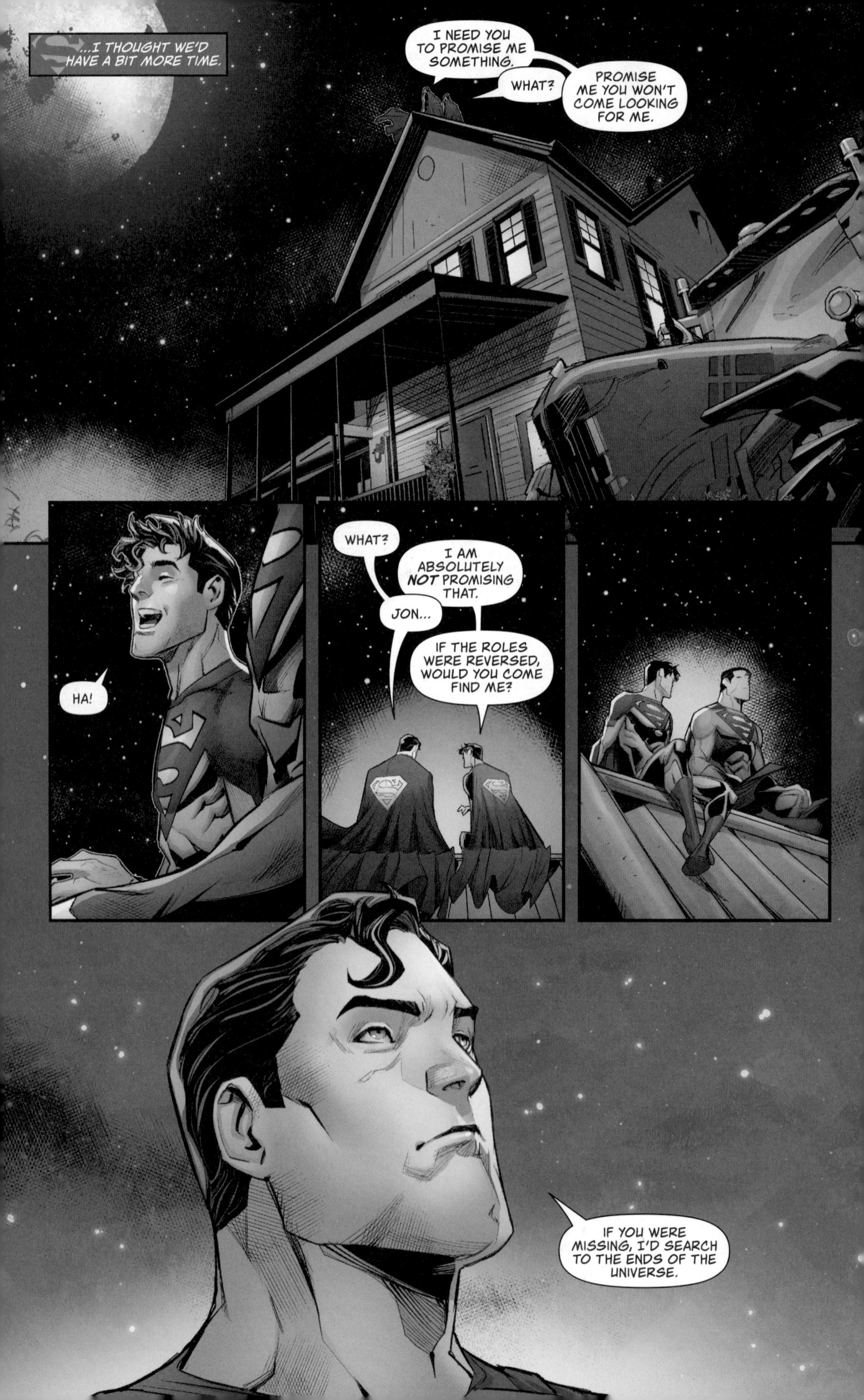
...I THOUGHT WE'D HAVE A BIT MORE TIME.
I NEED YOU TO PROMISE ME SOMETHING.
WHAT?
PROMISE ME YOU WON'T COME LOOKING FOR ME.
HA!
WHAT?
I AM ABSOLUTELY **NOT** PROMISING THAT.
JON...
IF THE ROLES WERE REVERSED, WOULD YOU COME FIND ME?
IF YOU WERE MISSING, I'D SEARCH TO THE ENDS OF THE UNIVERSE.

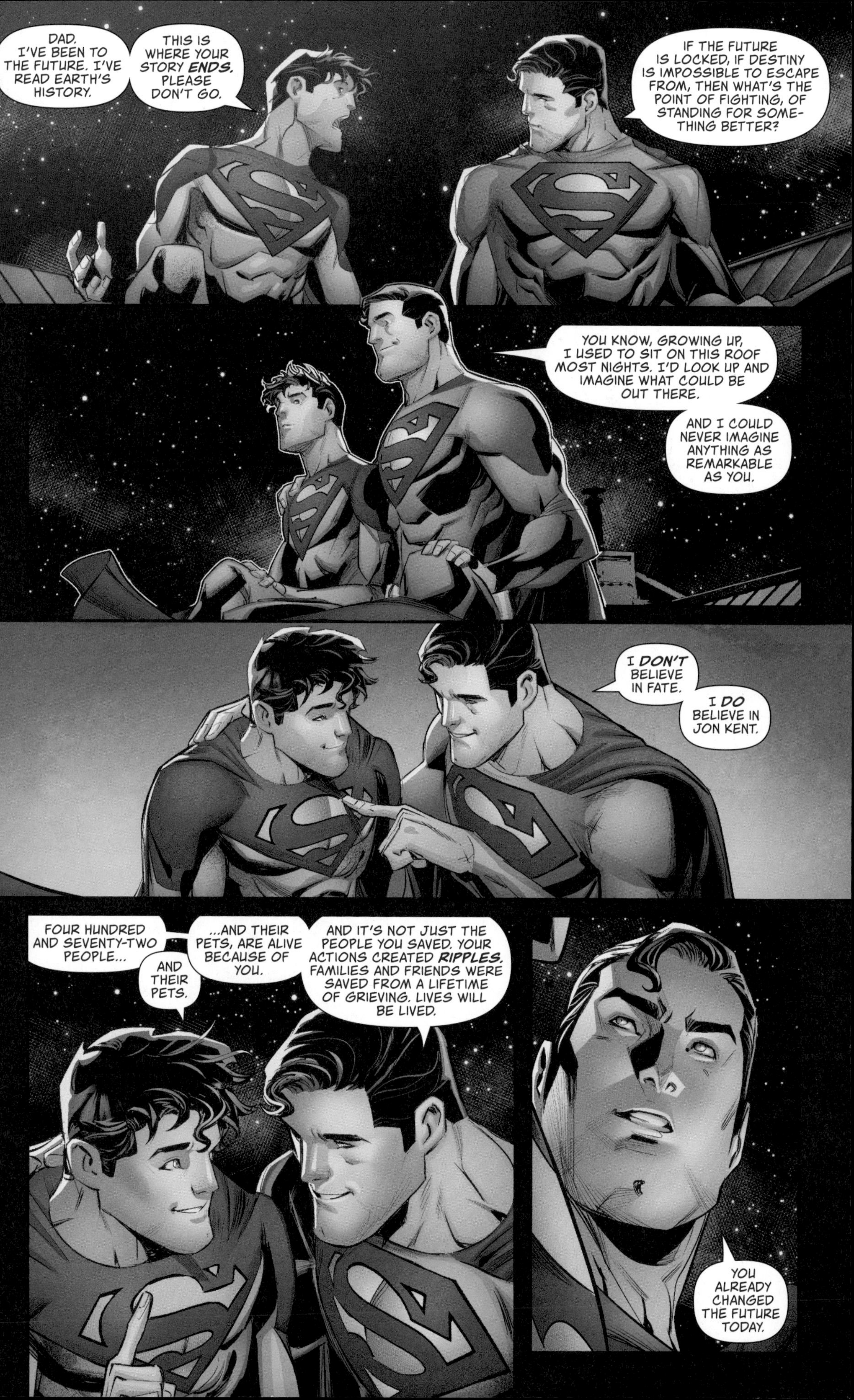
DAD. I'VE BEEN TO THE FUTURE. I'VE READ EARTH'S HISTORY.
THIS IS WHERE YOUR STORY **ENDS.** PLEASE DON'T GO.
IF THE FUTURE IS LOCKED, IF DESTINY IS IMPOSSIBLE TO ESCAPE FROM, THEN WHAT'S THE POINT OF FIGHTING, OF STANDING FOR SOMETHING BETTER?
YOU KNOW, GROWING UP, I USED TO SIT ON THIS ROOF MOST NIGHTS. I'D LOOK UP AND IMAGINE WHAT COULD BE OUT THERE.
AND I COULD NEVER IMAGINE ANYTHING AS REMARKABLE AS YOU.
I ***DON'T*** BELIEVE IN FATE.
I ***DO*** BELIEVE IN JON KENT.
FOUR HUNDRED AND SEVENTY-TWO PEOPLE...
AND THEIR PETS.
...AND THEIR PETS, ARE ALIVE BECAUSE OF YOU.
AND IT'S NOT JUST THE PEOPLE YOU SAVED. YOUR ACTIONS CREATED ***RIPPLES.*** FAMILIES AND FRIENDS WERE SAVED FROM A LIFETIME OF GRIEVING. LIVES WILL BE LIVED.
YOU ALREADY CHANGED THE FUTURE TODAY.

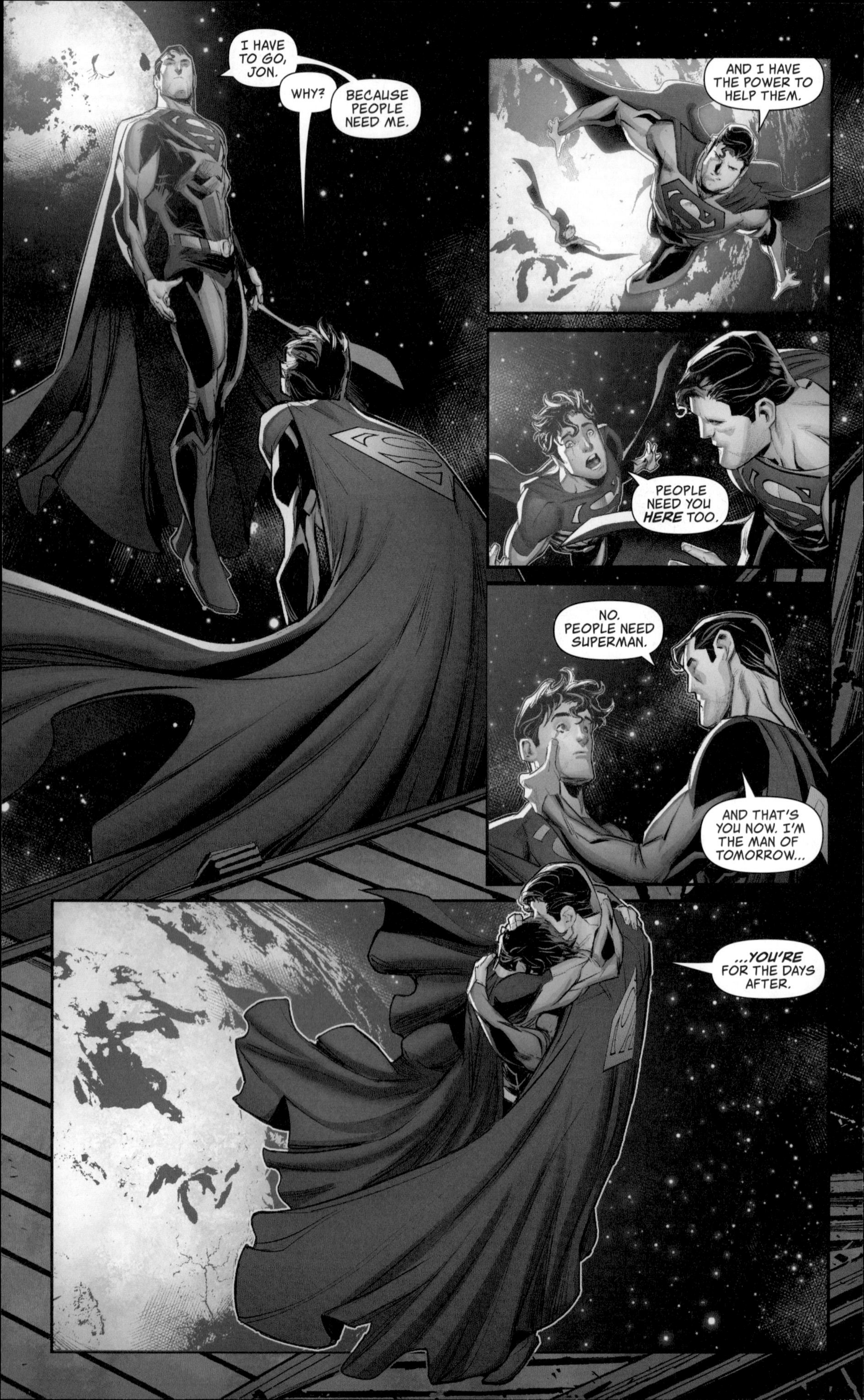

I HAVE TO GO, JON.
WHY?
BECAUSE PEOPLE NEED ME.
AND I HAVE THE POWER TO HELP THEM.
PEOPLE NEED YOU **HERE** TOO.
NO. PEOPLE NEED SUPERMAN.
AND THAT'S YOU NOW. I'M THE MAN OF TOMORROW...
...YOU'RE FOR THE DAYS AFTER.

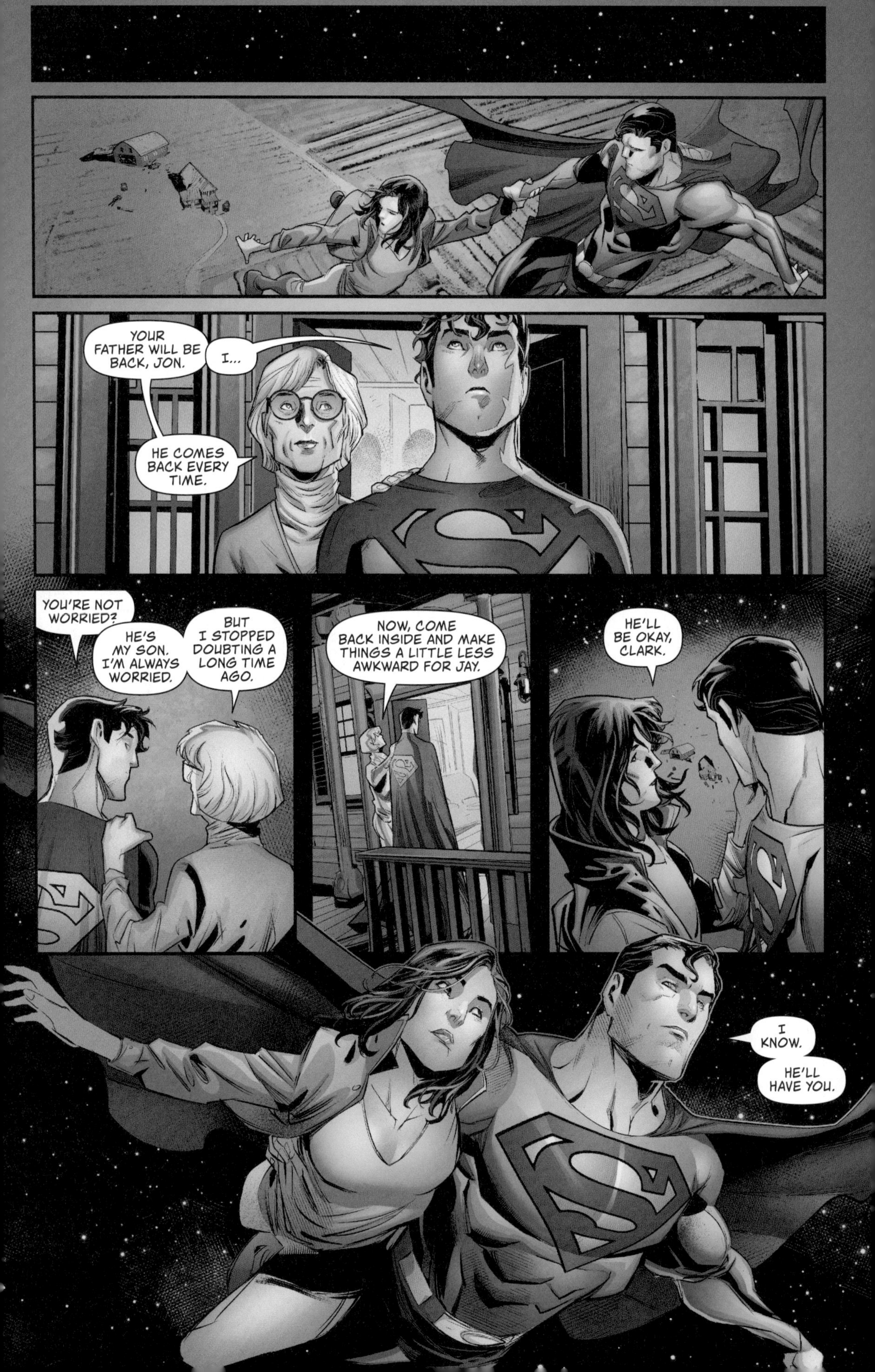

YOUR FATHER WILL BE BACK, JON.
I...
HE COMES BACK EVERY TIME.
YOU'RE NOT WORRIED?
HE'S MY SON. I'M ALWAYS WORRIED.
BUT I STOPPED DOUBTING A LONG TIME AGO.
NOW, COME BACK INSIDE AND MAKE THINGS A LITTLE LESS AWKWARD FOR JAY.
HE'LL BE OKAY, CLARK.
I KNOW.
HE'LL HAVE YOU.

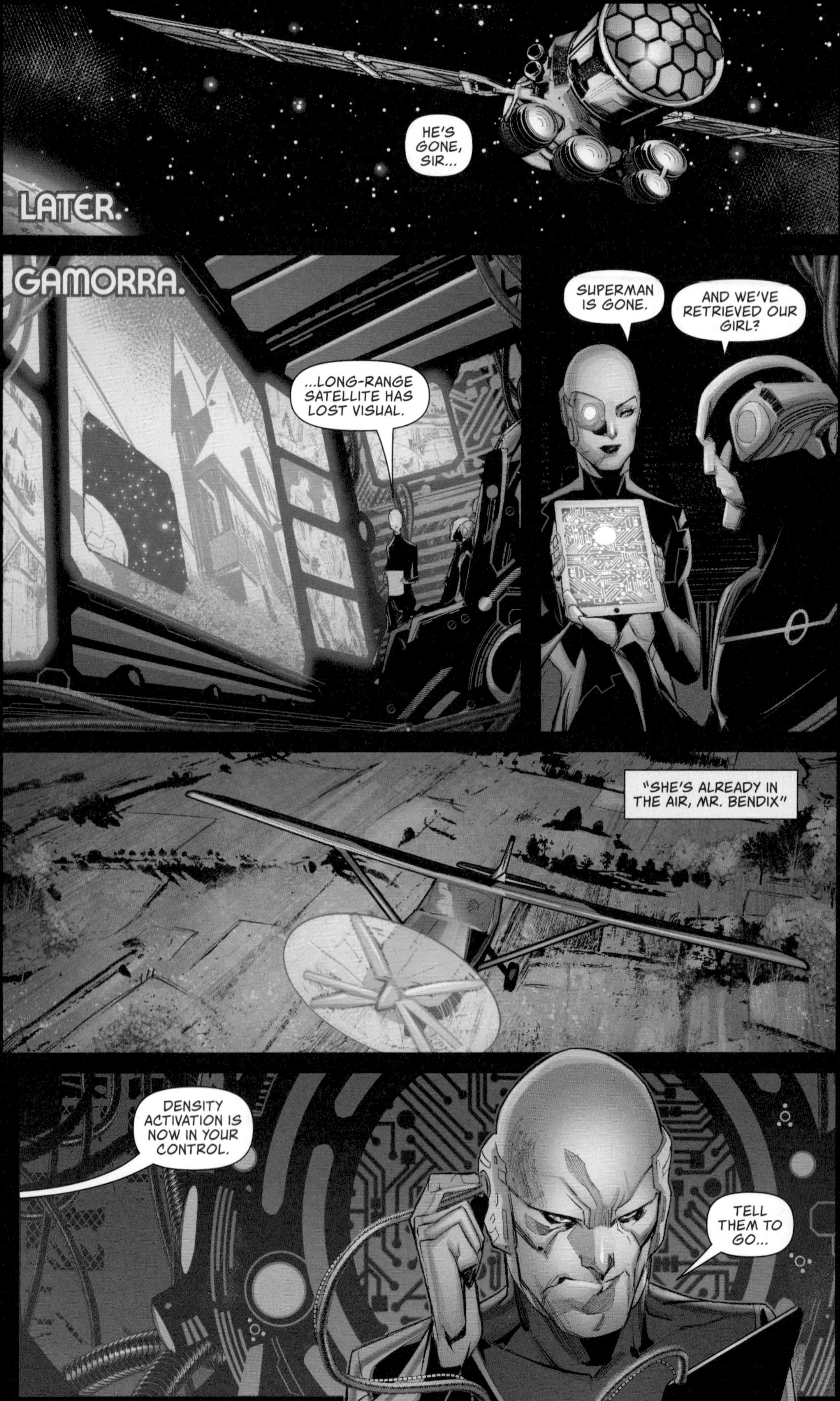
HE'S GONE, SIR...
LATER.
GAMORRA.
...LONG-RANGE SATELLITE HAS LOST VISUAL.
SUPERMAN IS GONE.
AND WE'VE RETRIEVED OUR GIRL?
"SHE'S ALREADY IN THE AIR, MR. BENDIX"
DENSITY ACTIVATION IS NOW IN YOUR CONTROL.
TELL THEM TO GO...

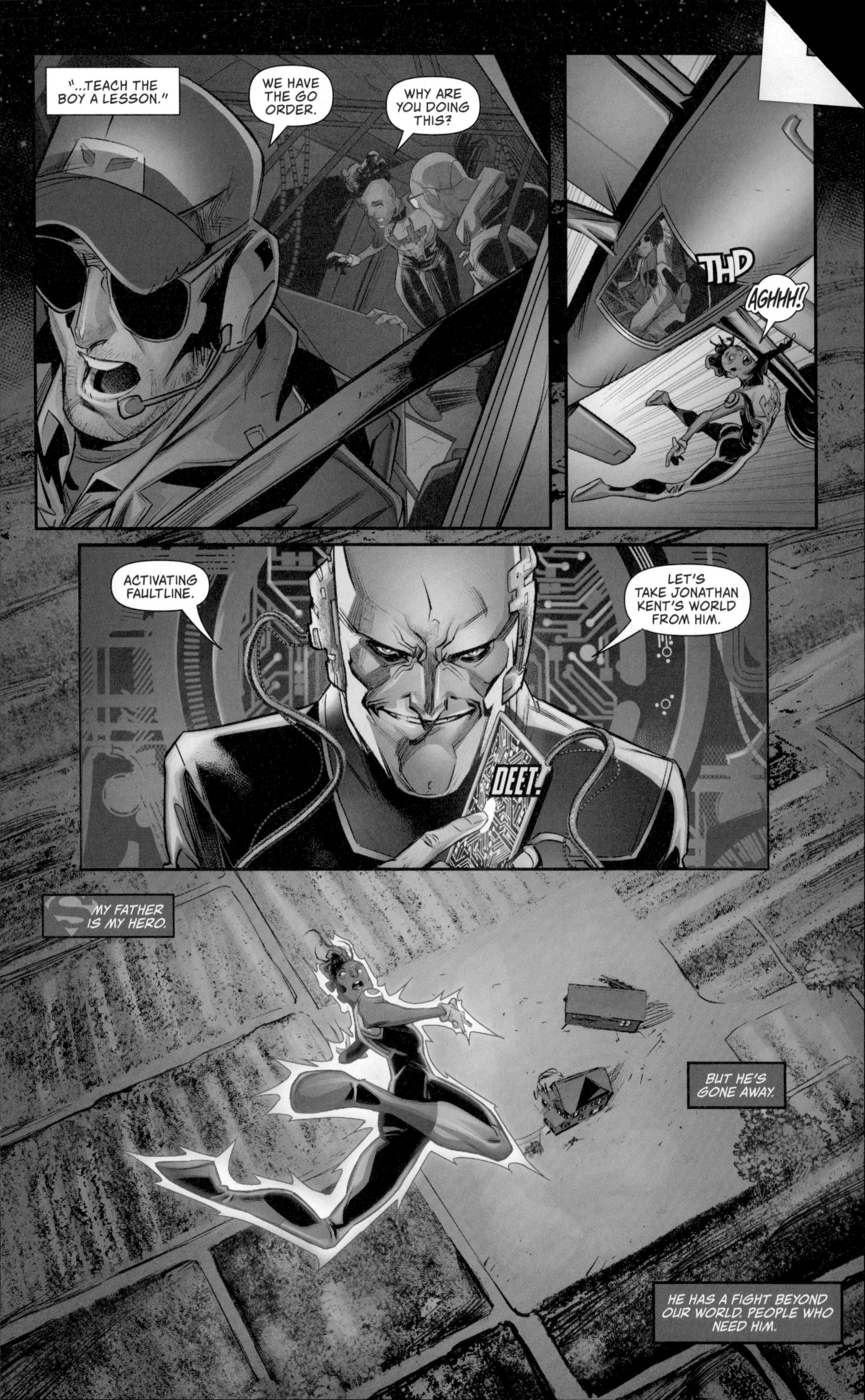
"...TEACH THE BOY A LESSON."
WE HAVE THE GO ORDER.
WHY ARE YOU DOING THIS?
THD
AGHHH!
ACTIVATING FAULTLINE.
LET'S TAKE JONATHAN KENT'S WORLD FROM HIM.
DEET!
MY FATHER IS MY HERO.
BUT HE'S GONE AWAY.
HE HAS A FIGHT BEYOND OUR WORLD. PEOPLE WHO NEED HIM.

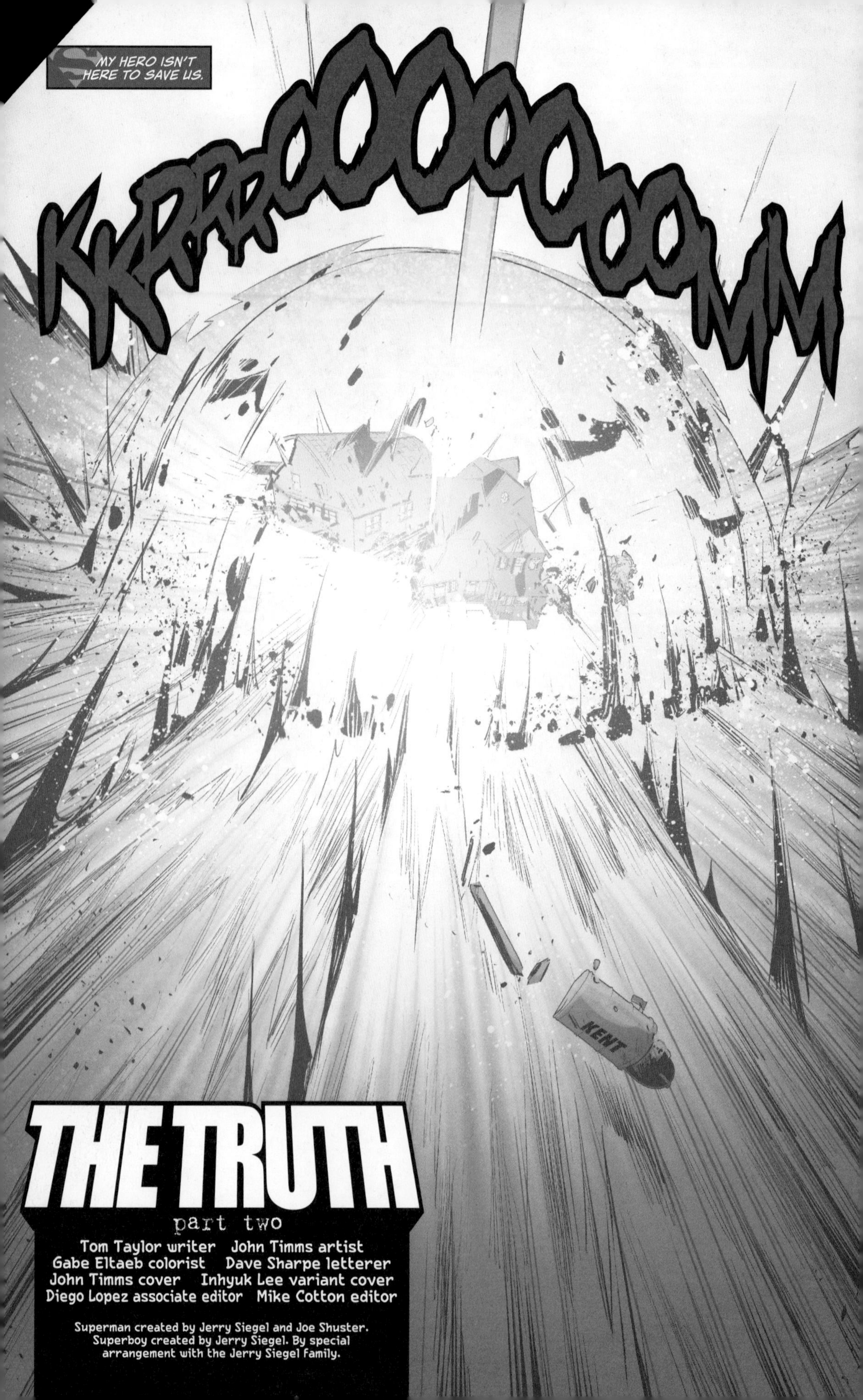
MY HERO ISN'T HERE TO SAVE US.
KKRRROOOOOOOMM
KENT

THE TRUTH

part two

Tom Taylor writer John Timms artist
Gabe Eltaeb colorist Dave Sharpe letterer
John Timms cover Inhyuk Lee variant cover
Diego Lopez associate editor Mike Cotton editor

Superman created by Jerry Siegel and Joe Shuster.
Superboy created by Jerry Siegel. By special
arrangement with the Jerry Siegel family.

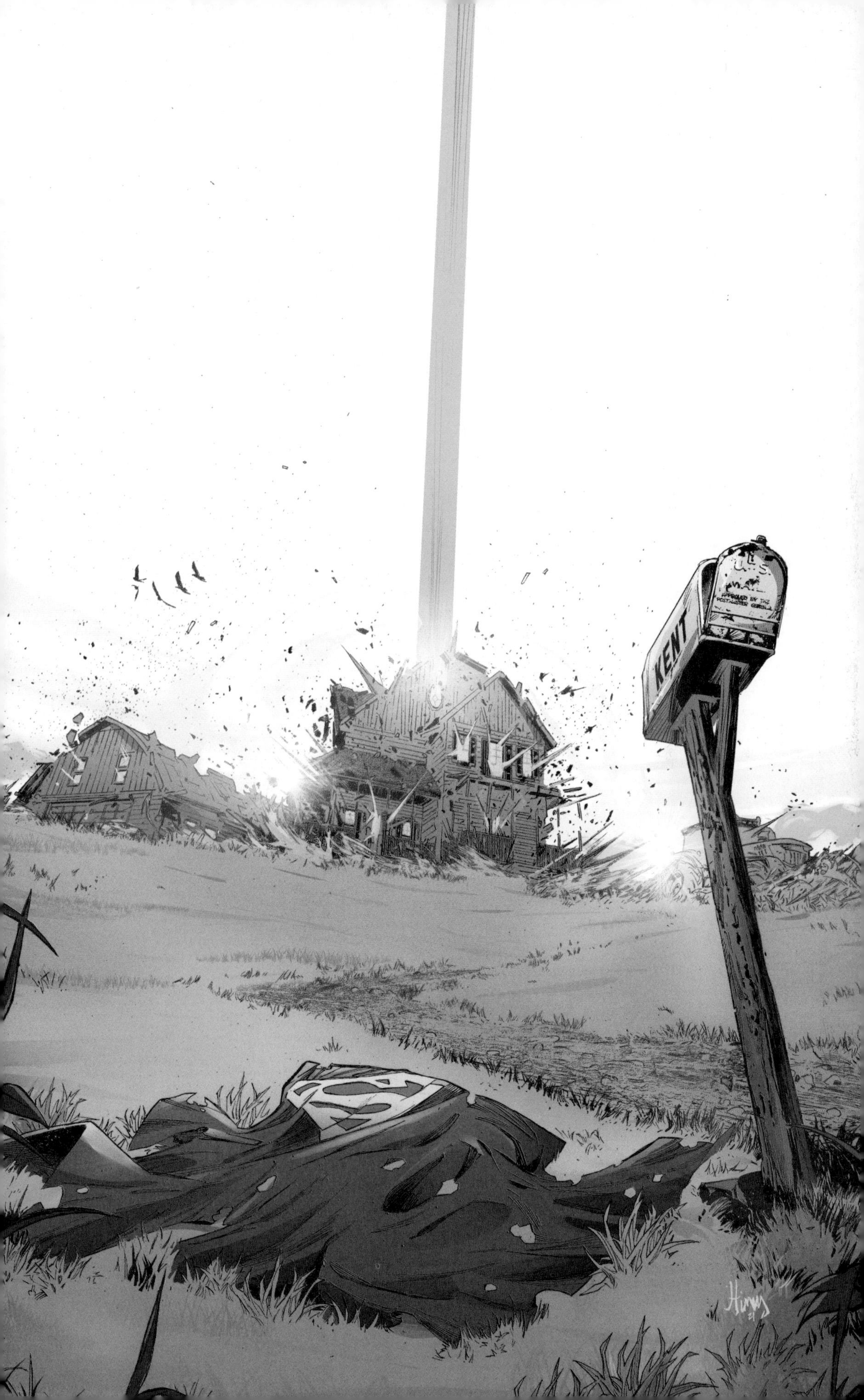
KENT
U.S.

Superman: Son of Kal-El #4 variant cover art by **INHYUK LEE**

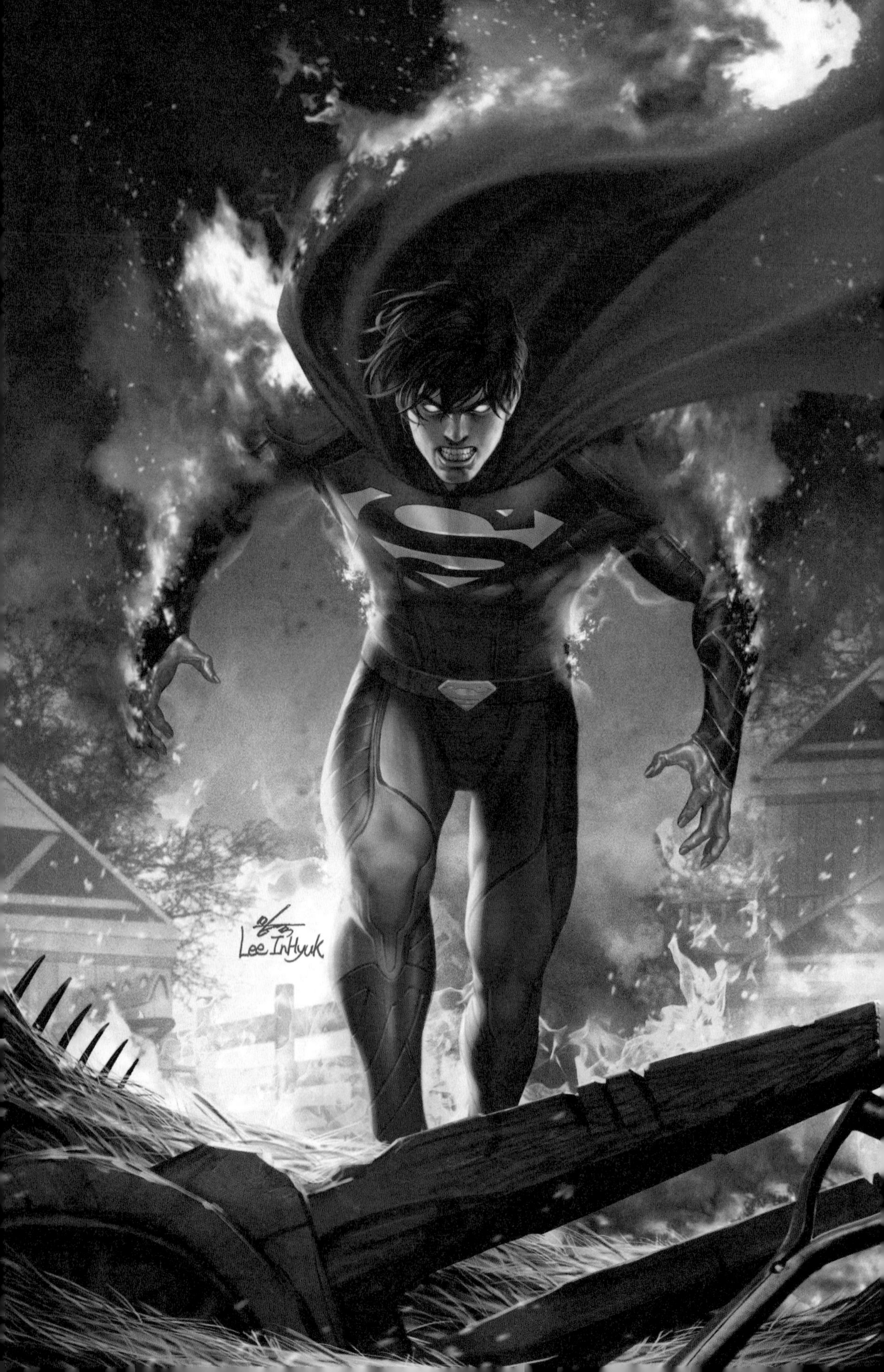
Lee InHyuk

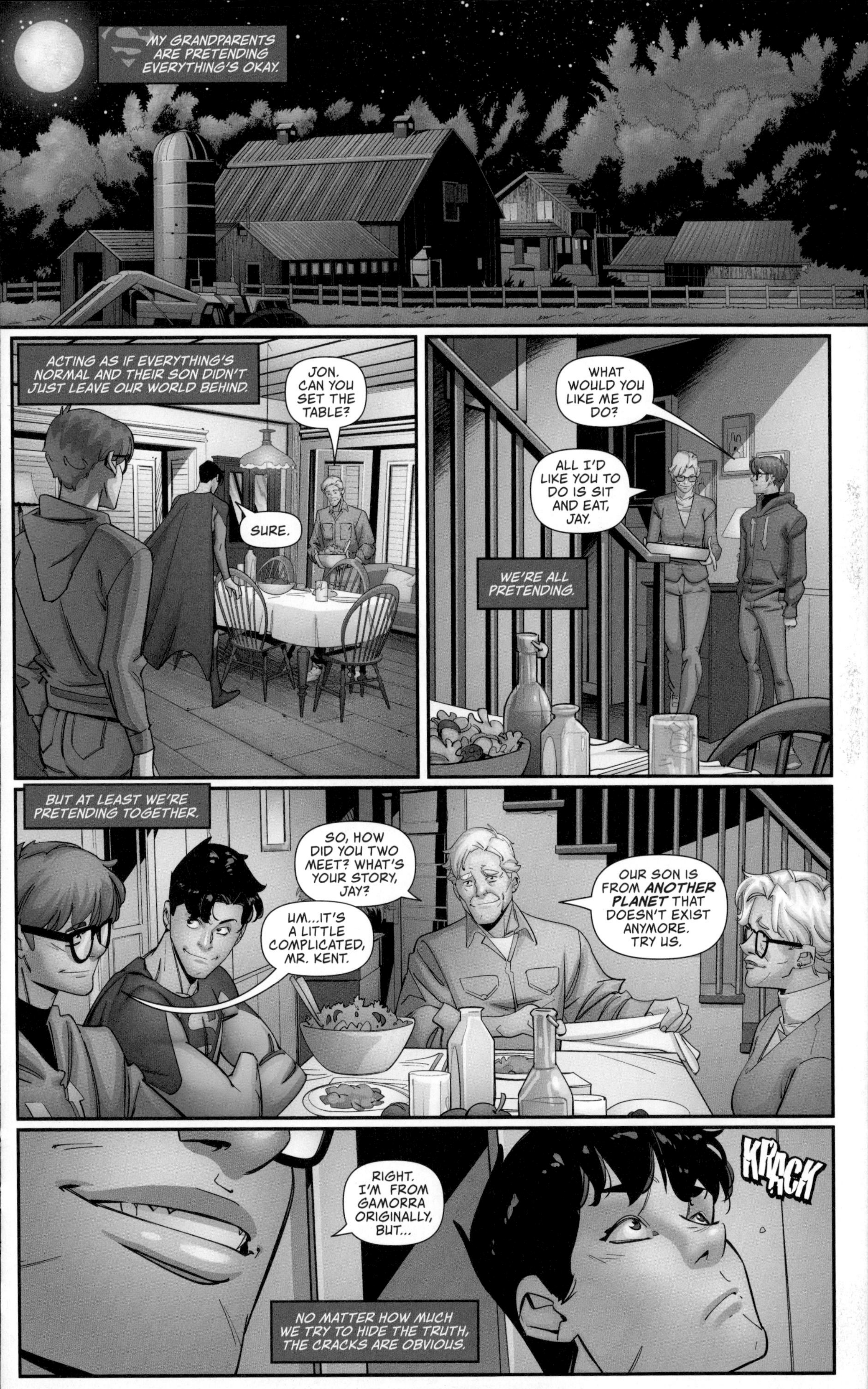
MY GRANDPARENTS ARE PRETENDING EVERYTHING'S OKAY.
ACTING AS IF EVERYTHING'S NORMAL AND THEIR SON DIDN'T JUST LEAVE OUR WORLD BEHIND.
JON. CAN YOU SET THE TABLE?
SURE.
WHAT WOULD YOU LIKE ME TO DO?
ALL I'D LIKE YOU TO DO IS SIT AND EAT, JAY.
WE'RE ALL PRETENDING.
BUT AT LEAST WE'RE PRETENDING TOGETHER.
SO, HOW DID YOU TWO MEET? WHAT'S YOUR STORY, JAY?
UM...IT'S A LITTLE COMPLICATED, MR. KENT.
OUR SON IS FROM ANOTHER PLANET THAT DOESN'T EXIST ANYMORE. TRY US.
RIGHT. I'M FROM GAMORRA ORIGINALLY, BUT...
KRACK
NO MATTER HOW MUCH WE TRY TO HIDE THE TRUTH, THE CRACKS ARE OBVIOUS.

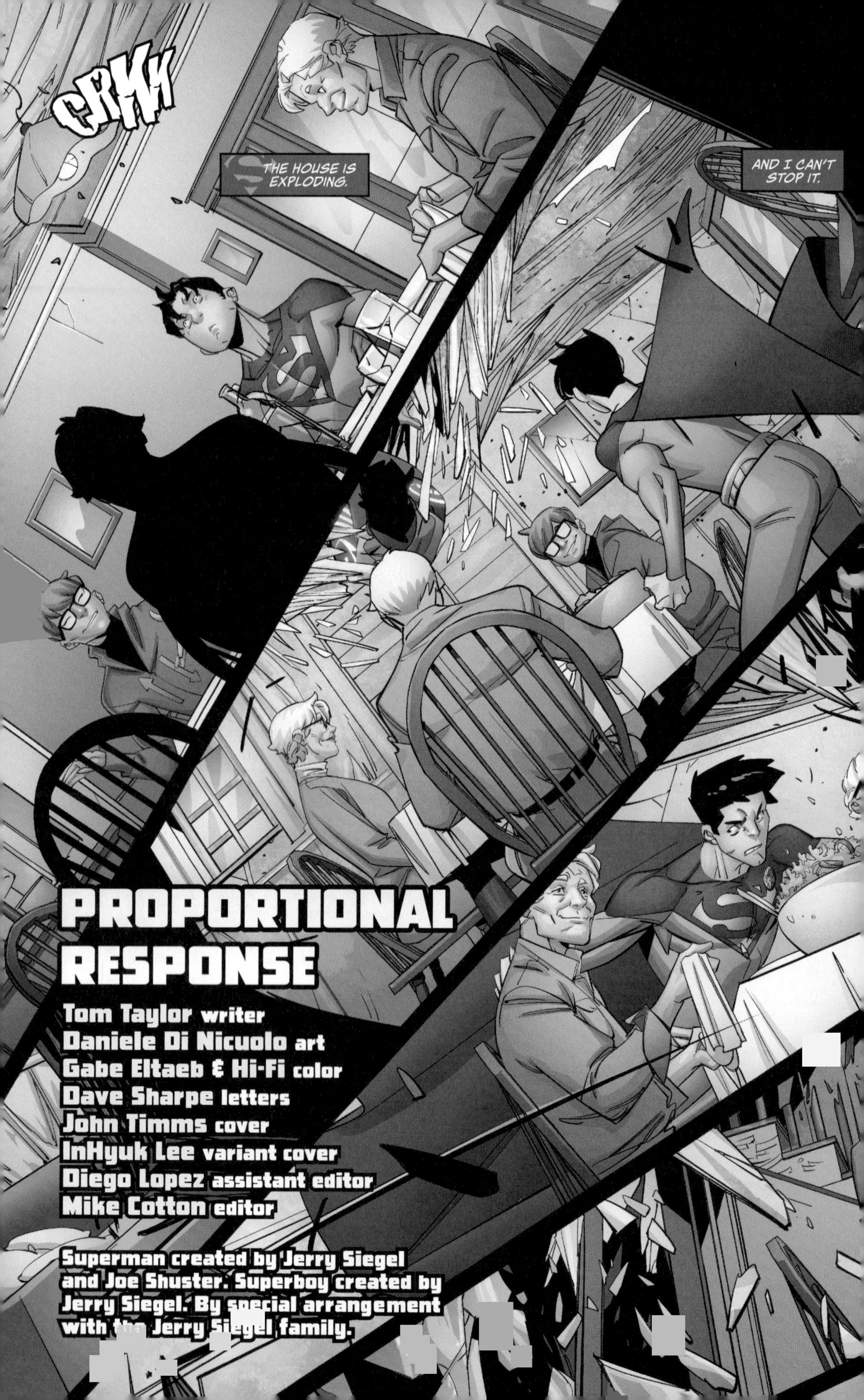
CRKK
THE HOUSE IS EXPLODING.
AND I CAN'T STOP IT.
PROPORTIONAL RESPONSE
Tom Taylor writer
Daniele Di Nicuolo art
Gabe Eltaeb & Hi-Fi color
Dave Sharpe letters
John Timms cover
InHyuk Lee variant cover
Diego Lopez assistant editor
Mike Cotton editor
Superman created by Jerry Siegel and Joe Shuster. Superboy created by Jerry Siegel. By special arrangement with the Jerry Siegel family.

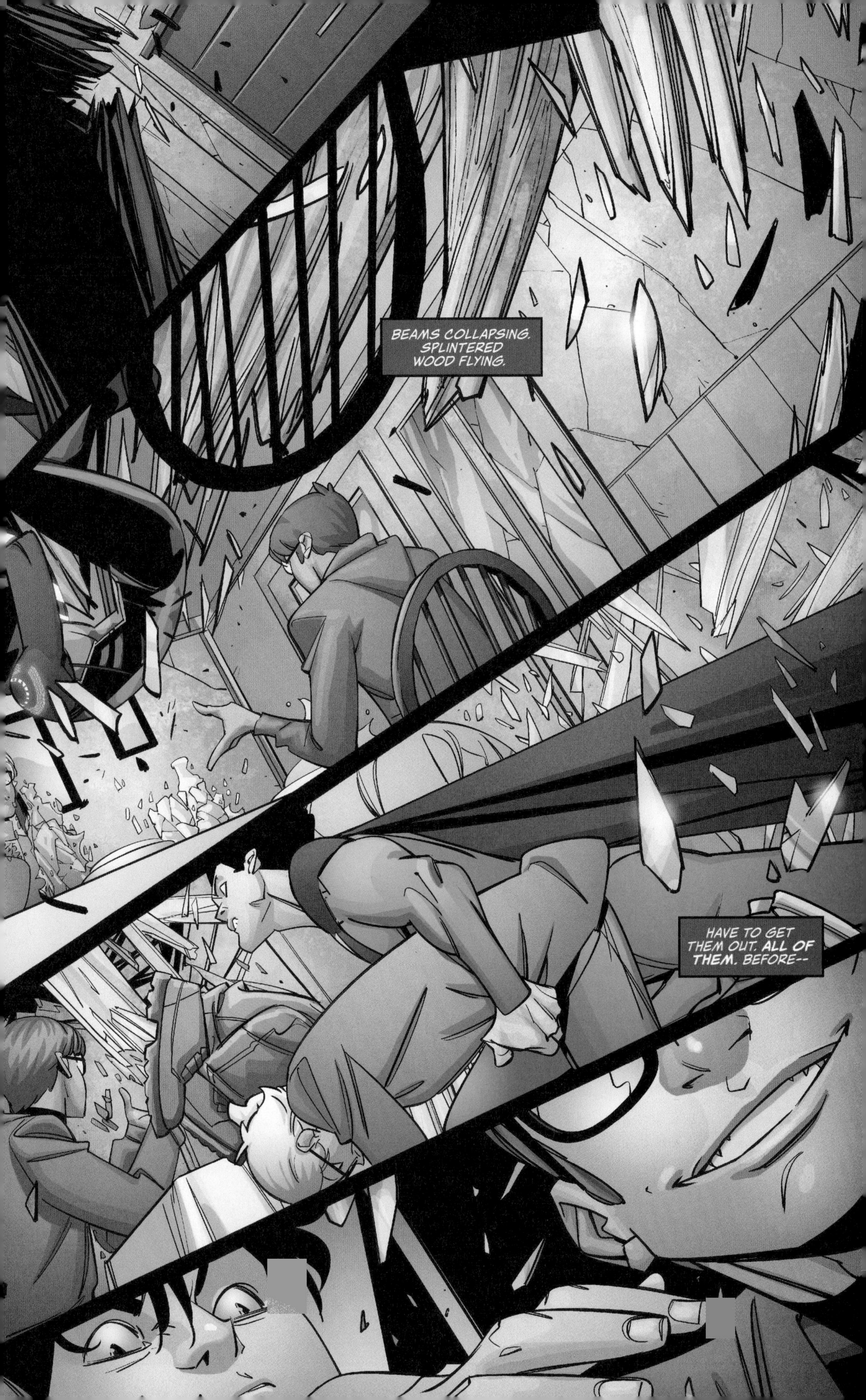
BEAMS COLLAPSING. SPLINTERED WOOD FLYING.
HAVE TO GET THEM OUT. ALL OF THEM. BEFORE--

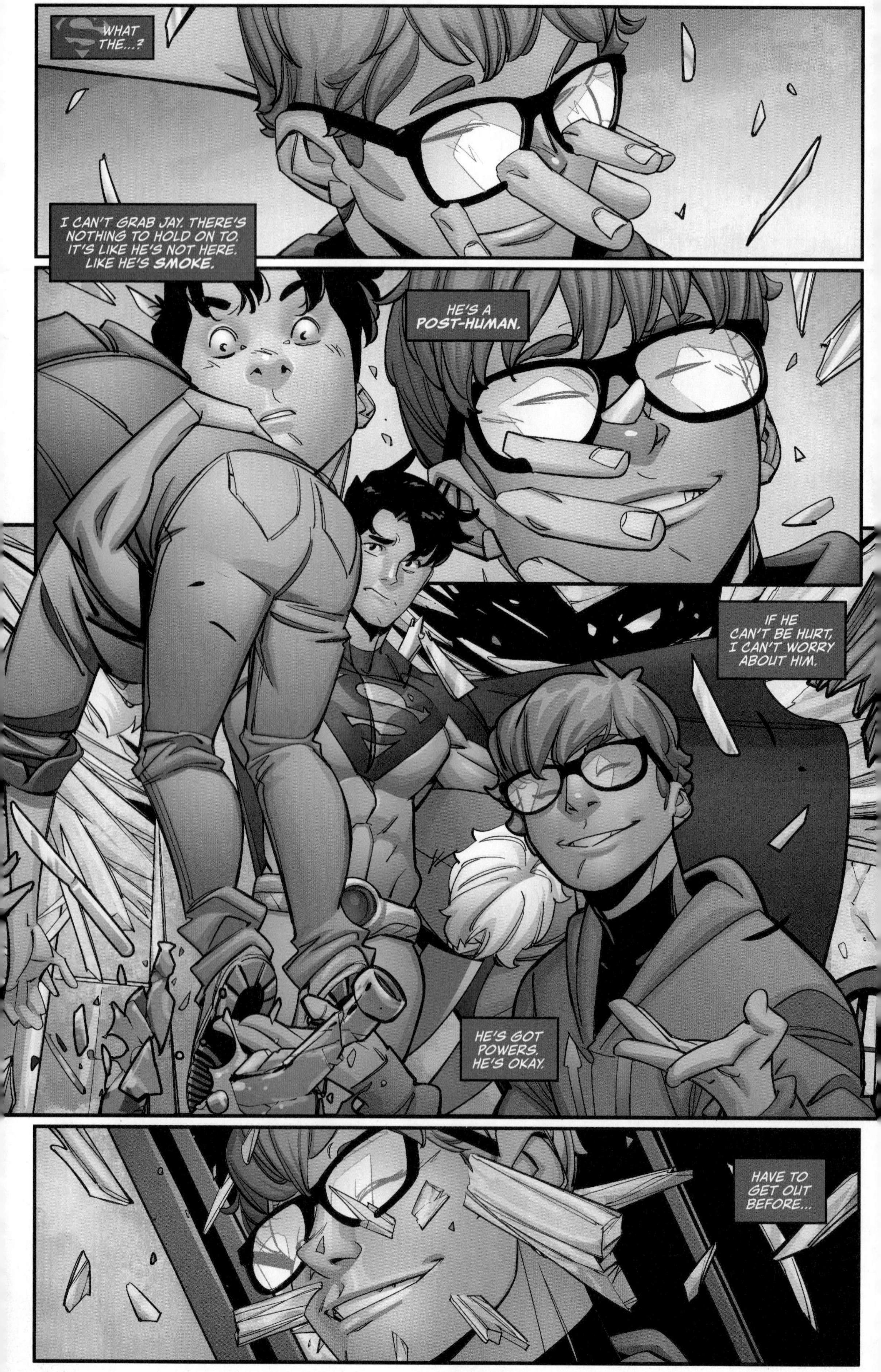
WHAT THE...?
I CAN'T GRAB JAY. THERE'S NOTHING TO HOLD ON TO. IT'S LIKE HE'S NOT HERE. LIKE HE'S SMOKE.
HE'S A POST-HUMAN.
IF HE CAN'T BE HURT, I CAN'T WORRY ABOUT HIM.
HE'S GOT POWERS. HE'S OKAY.
HAVE TO GET OUT BEFORE...

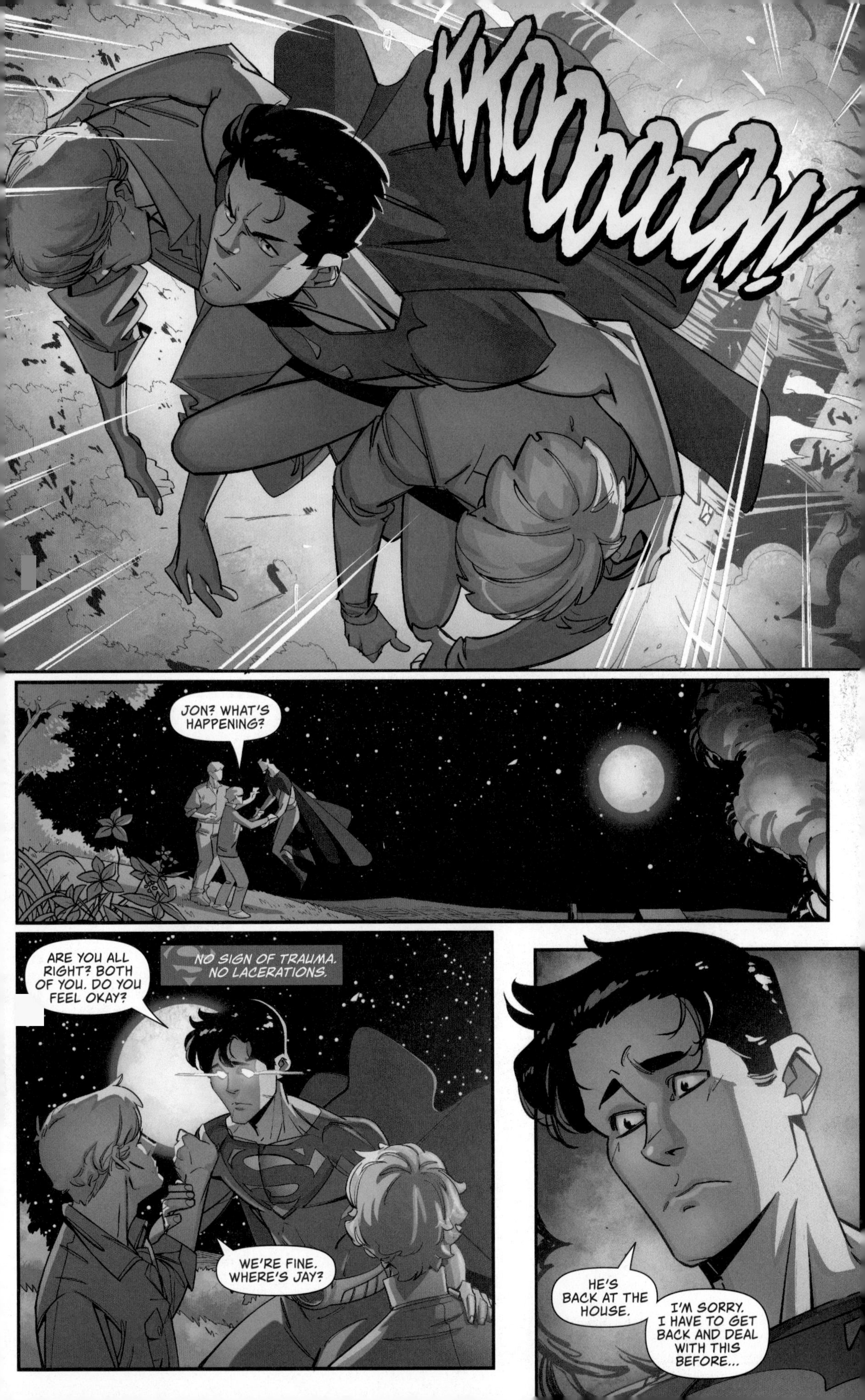
KKOOOOOOM!!
JON? WHAT'S HAPPENING?
ARE YOU ALL RIGHT? BOTH OF YOU. DO YOU FEEL OKAY?
NO SIGN OF TRAUMA. NO LACERATIONS.
WE'RE FINE. WHERE'S JAY?
HE'S BACK AT THE HOUSE.
I'M SORRY. I HAVE TO GET BACK AND DEAL WITH THIS BEFORE...

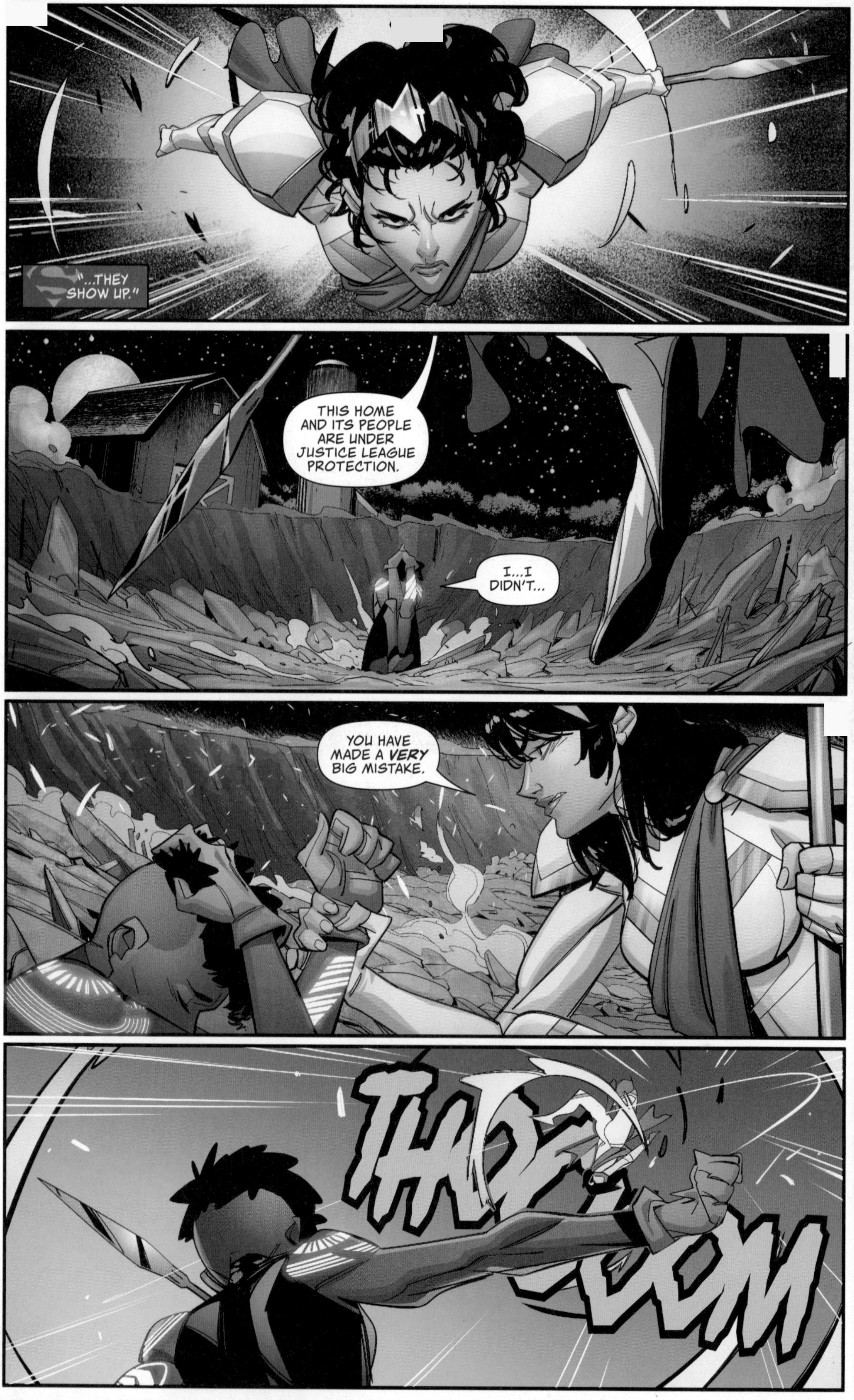
"...THEY SHOW UP."
THIS HOME AND ITS PEOPLE ARE UNDER JUSTICE LEAGUE PROTECTION.
I...I DIDN'T...
YOU HAVE MADE A *VERY* BIG MISTAKE.

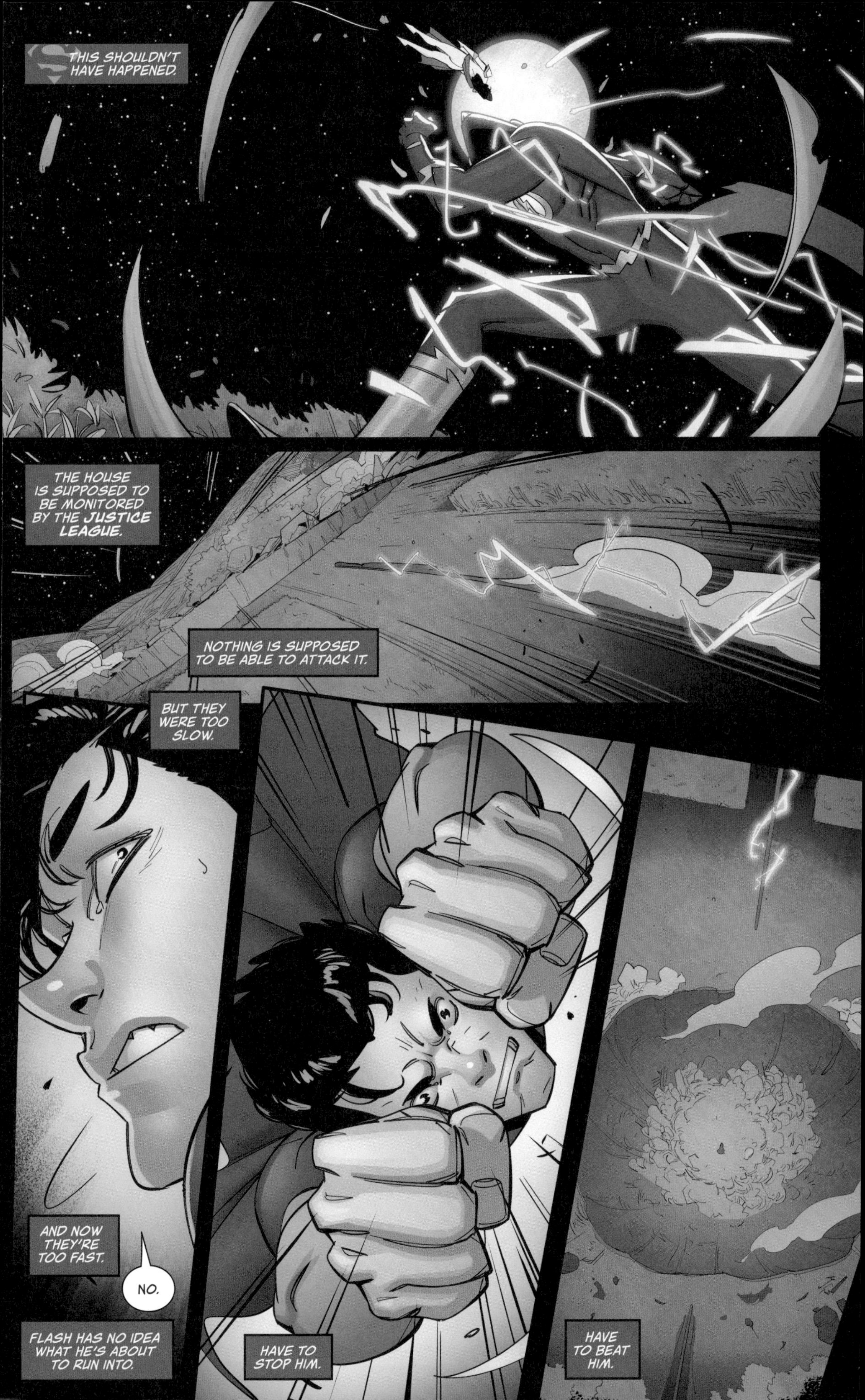
THIS SHOULDN'T HAVE HAPPENED.
THE HOUSE IS SUPPOSED TO BE MONITORED BY THE JUSTICE LEAGUE.
NOTHING IS SUPPOSED TO BE ABLE TO ATTACK IT.
BUT THEY WERE TOO SLOW.
AND NOW THEY'RE TOO FAST.
NO.
FLASH HAS NO IDEA WHAT HE'S ABOUT TO RUN INTO.
HAVE TO STOP HIM.
HAVE TO BEAT HIM.

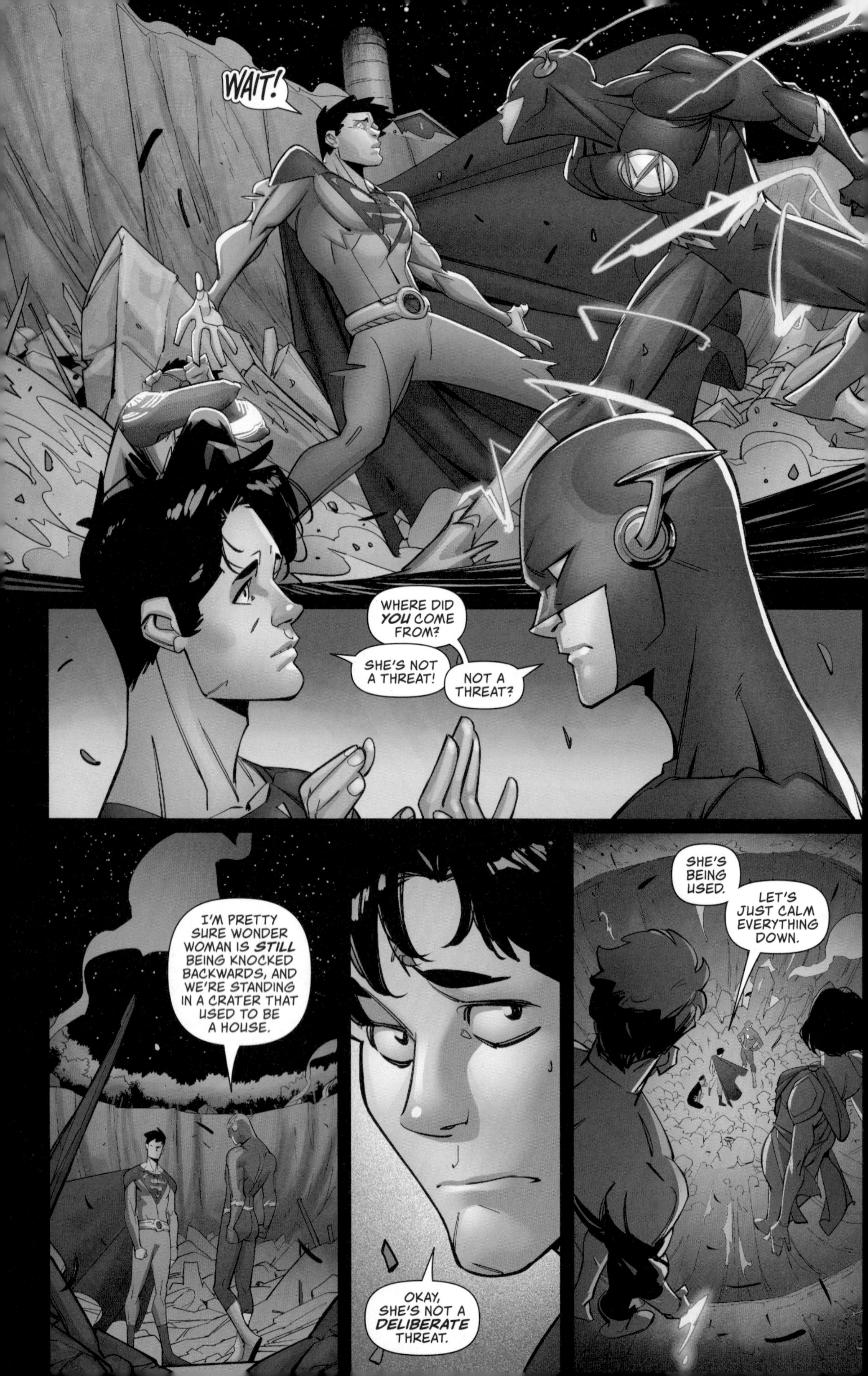
WAIT!
WHERE DID YOU COME FROM?
SHE'S NOT A THREAT!
NOT A THREAT?
I'M PRETTY SURE WONDER WOMAN IS STILL BEING KNOCKED BACKWARDS, AND WE'RE STANDING IN A CRATER THAT USED TO BE A HOUSE.
OKAY, SHE'S NOT A DELIBERATE THREAT.
SHE'S BEING USED.
LET'S JUST CALM EVERYTHING DOWN.

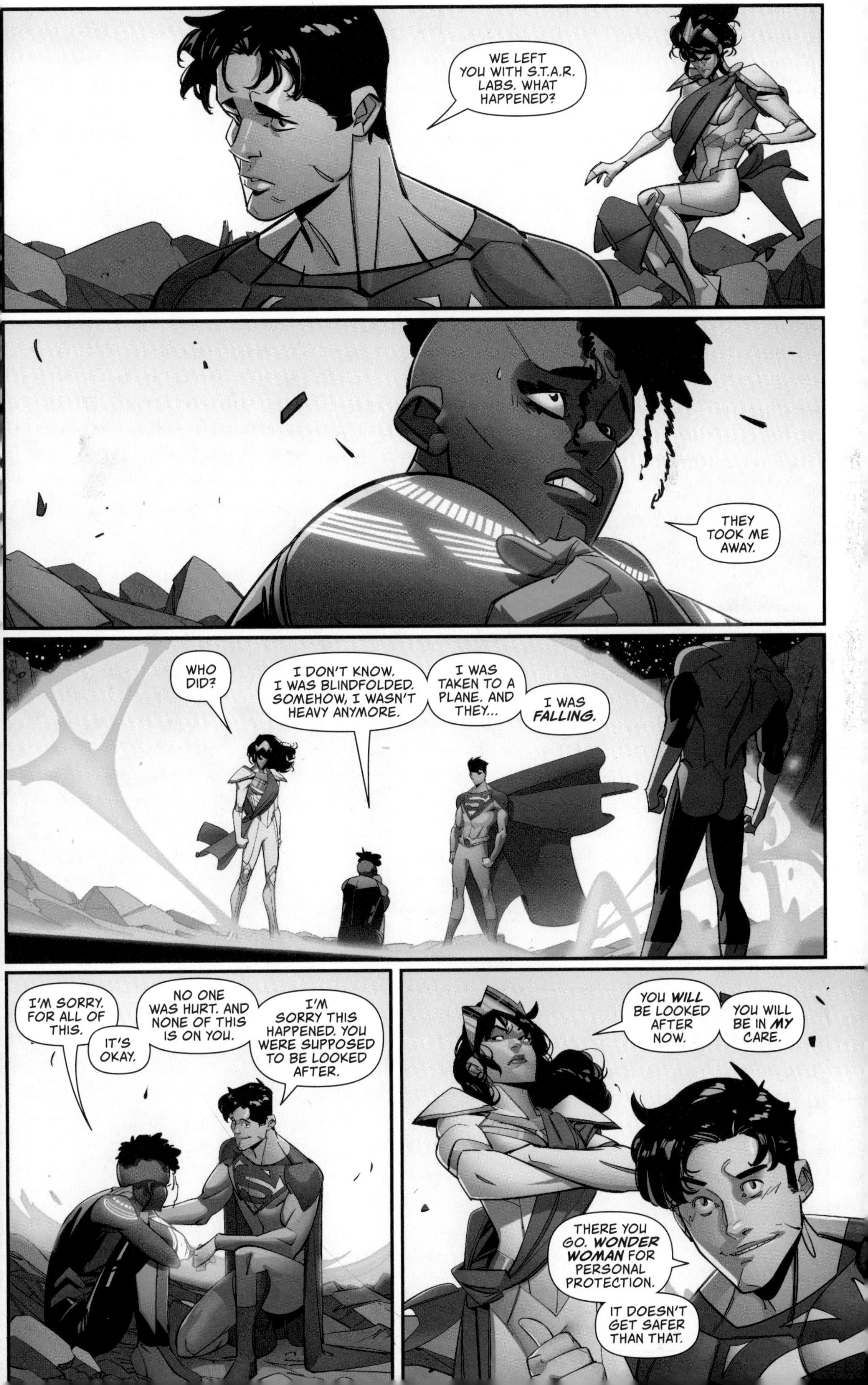
WE LEFT YOU WITH S.T.A.R. LABS. WHAT HAPPENED?
THEY TOOK ME AWAY.
WHO DID?
I DON'T KNOW. I WAS BLINDFOLDED. SOMEHOW, I WASN'T HEAVY ANYMORE.
I WAS TAKEN TO A PLANE. AND THEY...
I WAS *FALLING.*
I'M SORRY. FOR ALL OF THIS.
IT'S OKAY.
NO ONE WAS HURT. AND NONE OF THIS IS ON YOU.
I'M SORRY THIS HAPPENED. YOU WERE SUPPOSED TO BE LOOKED AFTER.
YOU *WILL* BE LOOKED AFTER NOW.
YOU WILL BE IN *MY* CARE.
THERE YOU GO. *WONDER WOMAN* FOR PERSONAL PROTECTION.
IT DOESN'T GET SAFER THAN THAT.

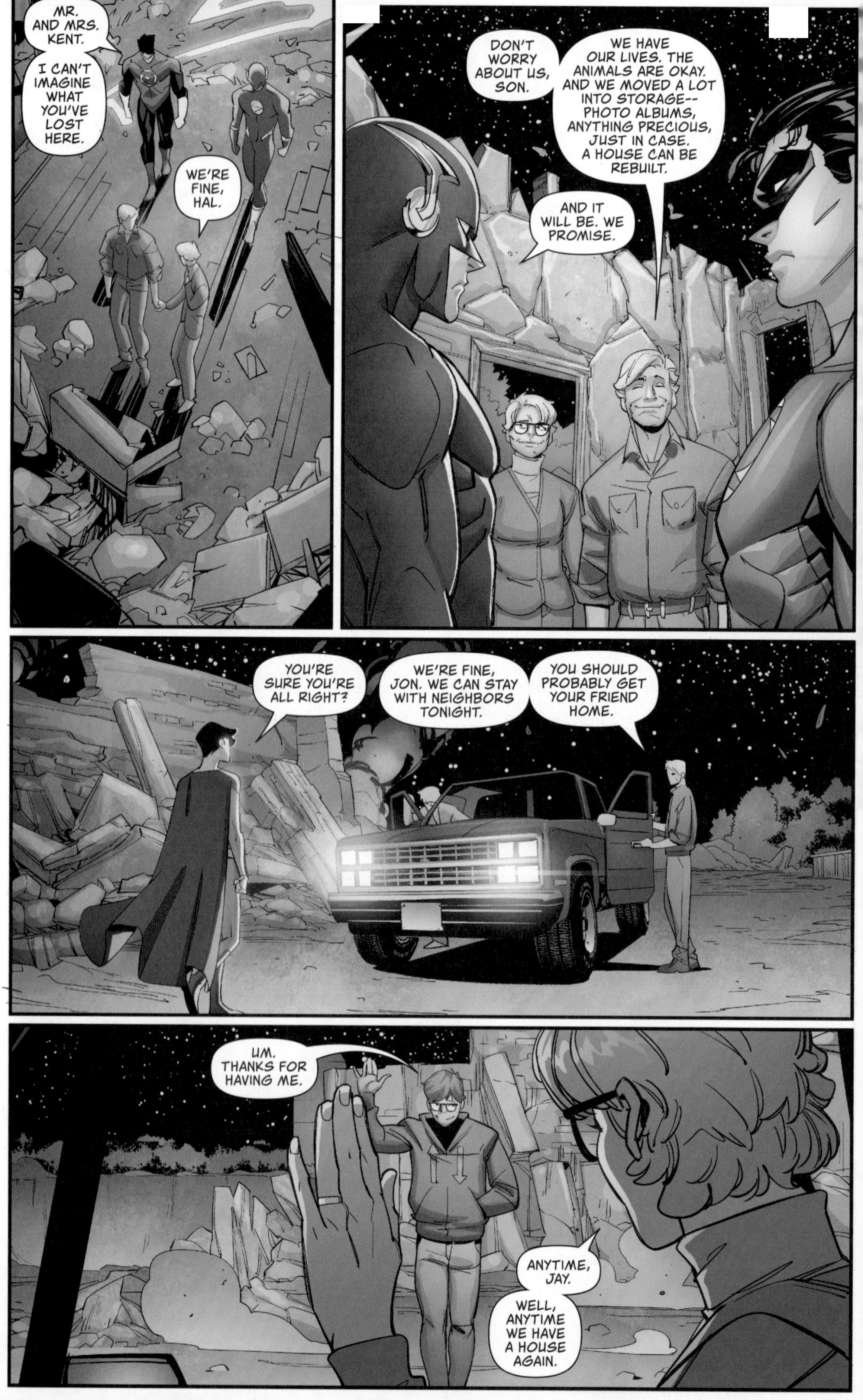
MR. AND MRS. KENT.
I CAN'T IMAGINE WHAT YOU'VE LOST HERE.
WE'RE FINE, HAL.
DON'T WORRY ABOUT US, SON.
WE HAVE OUR LIVES. THE ANIMALS ARE OKAY. AND WE MOVED A LOT INTO STORAGE-- PHOTO ALBUMS, ANYTHING PRECIOUS, JUST IN CASE. A HOUSE CAN BE REBUILT.
AND IT WILL BE. WE PROMISE.
YOU'RE SURE YOU'RE ALL RIGHT?
WE'RE FINE, JON. WE CAN STAY WITH NEIGHBORS TONIGHT.
YOU SHOULD PROBABLY GET YOUR FRIEND HOME.
UM. THANKS FOR HAVING ME.
ANYTIME, JAY.
WELL, ANYTIME WE HAVE A HOUSE AGAIN.

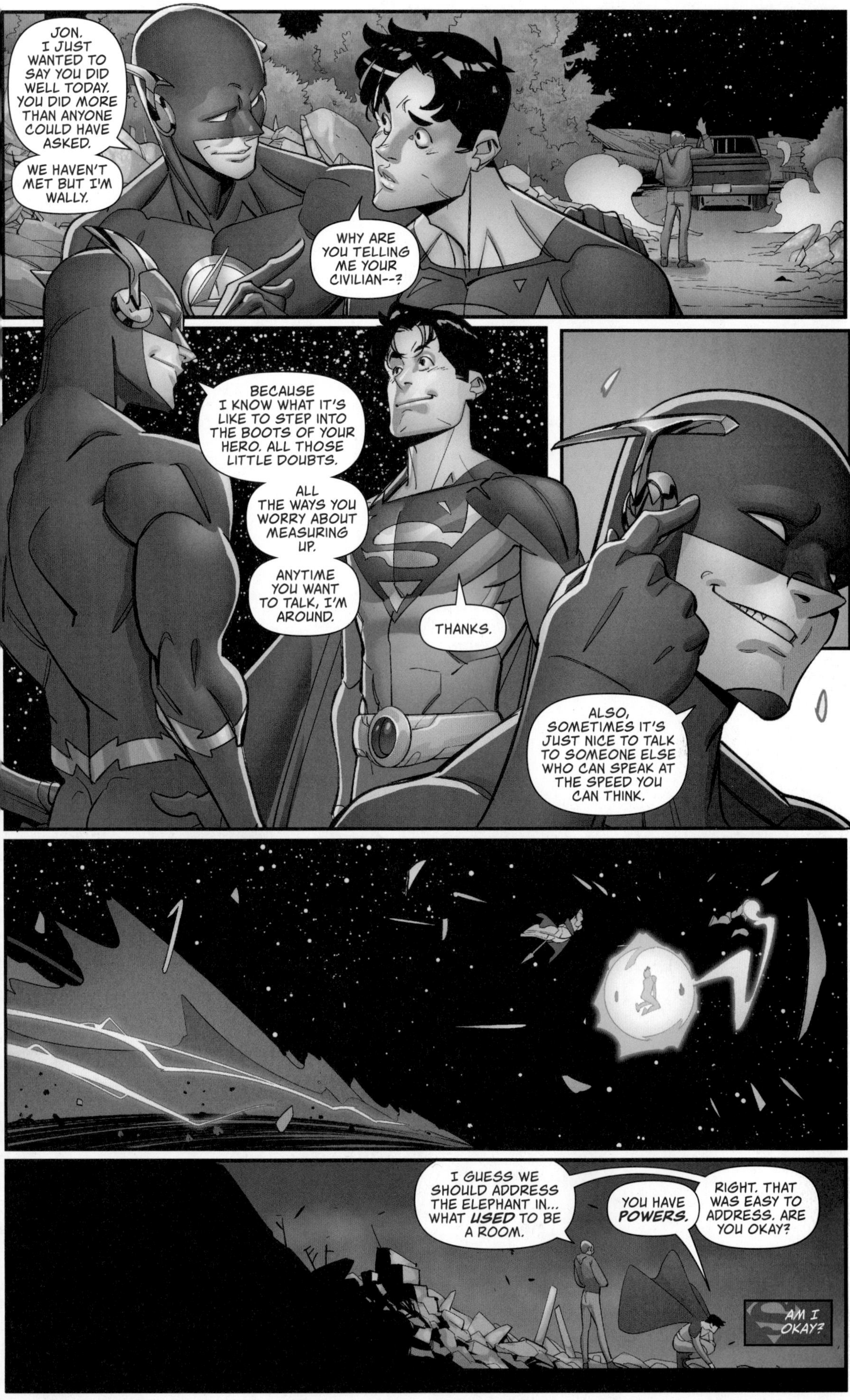

JON. I JUST WANTED TO SAY YOU DID WELL TODAY. YOU DID MORE THAN ANYONE COULD HAVE ASKED.
WE HAVEN'T MET BUT I'M WALLY.
WHY ARE YOU TELLING ME YOUR CIVILIAN--?
BECAUSE I KNOW WHAT IT'S LIKE TO STEP INTO THE BOOTS OF YOUR HERO. ALL THOSE LITTLE DOUBTS.
ALL THE WAYS YOU WORRY ABOUT MEASURING UP.
ANYTIME YOU WANT TO TALK, I'M AROUND.
THANKS.
ALSO, SOMETIMES IT'S JUST NICE TO TALK TO SOMEONE ELSE WHO CAN SPEAK AT THE SPEED YOU CAN THINK.
I GUESS WE SHOULD ADDRESS THE ELEPHANT IN... WHAT **USED** TO BE A ROOM.
YOU HAVE **POWERS.**
RIGHT. THAT WAS EASY TO ADDRESS. ARE YOU OKAY?
AM I OKAY?

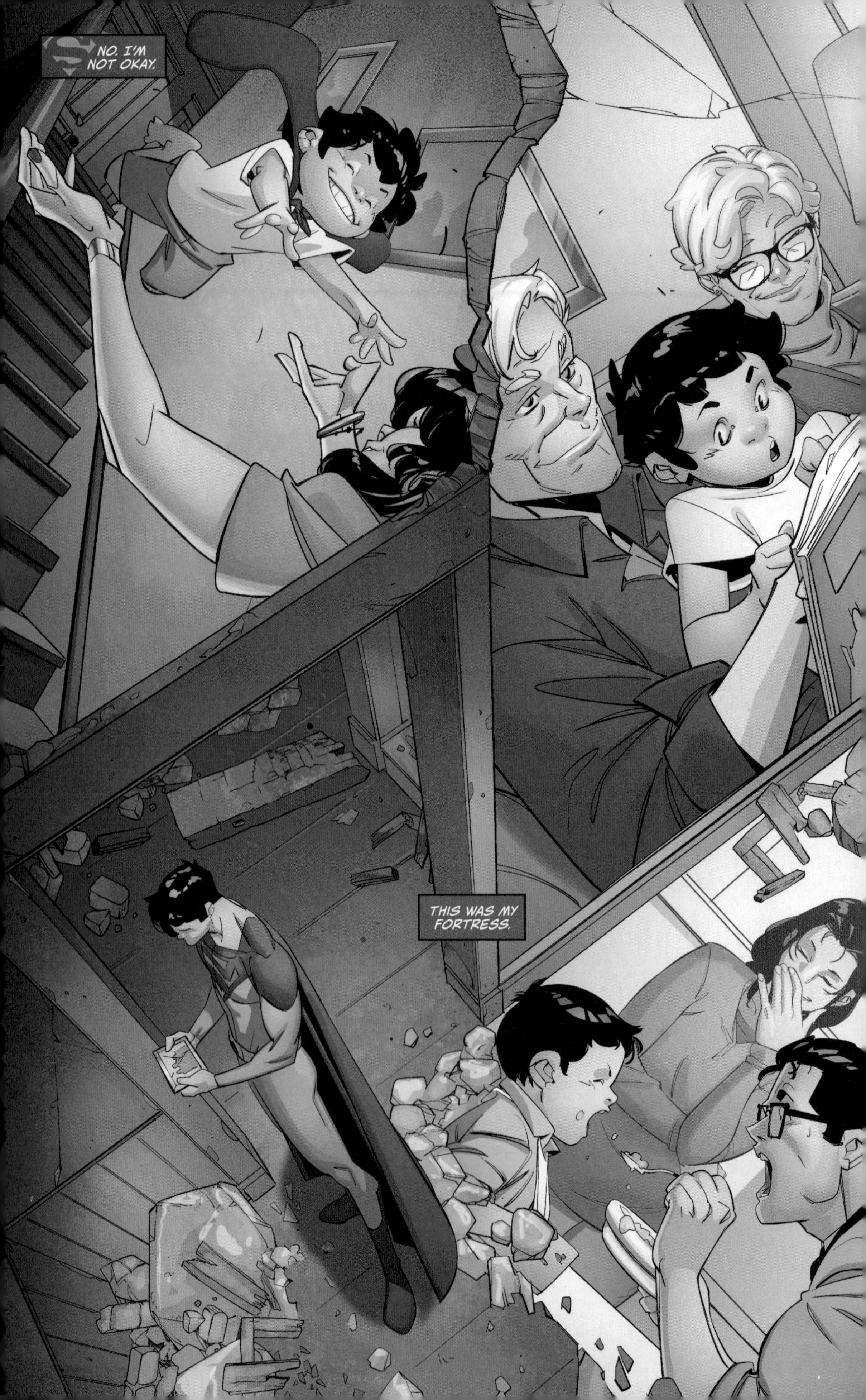
NO. I'M NOT OKAY.
THIS WAS MY FORTRESS.

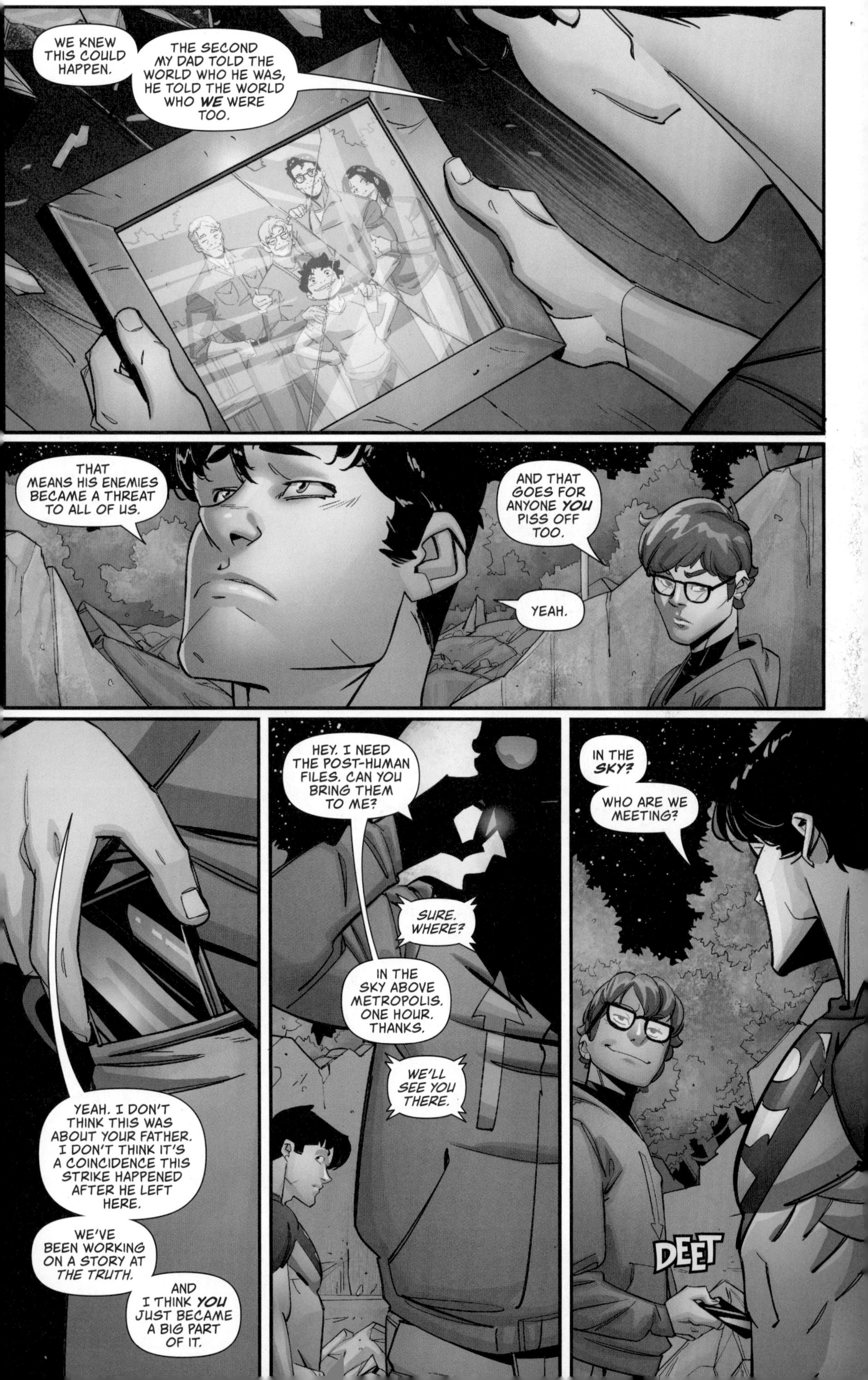
WE KNEW THIS COULD HAPPEN.
THE SECOND MY DAD TOLD THE WORLD WHO HE WAS, HE TOLD THE WORLD WHO WE WERE TOO.
THAT MEANS HIS ENEMIES BECAME A THREAT TO ALL OF US.
AND THAT GOES FOR ANYONE YOU PISS OFF TOO.
YEAH.
YEAH. I DON'T THINK THIS WAS ABOUT YOUR FATHER. I DON'T THINK IT'S A COINCIDENCE THIS STRIKE HAPPENED AFTER HE LEFT HERE.
WE'VE BEEN WORKING ON A STORY AT THE TRUTH.
AND I THINK YOU JUST BECAME A BIG PART OF IT.
HEY. I NEED THE POST-HUMAN FILES. CAN YOU BRING THEM TO ME?
SURE. WHERE?
IN THE SKY ABOVE METROPOLIS. ONE HOUR. THANKS.
WE'LL SEE YOU THERE.
IN THE SKY?
WHO ARE WE MEETING?
DEET

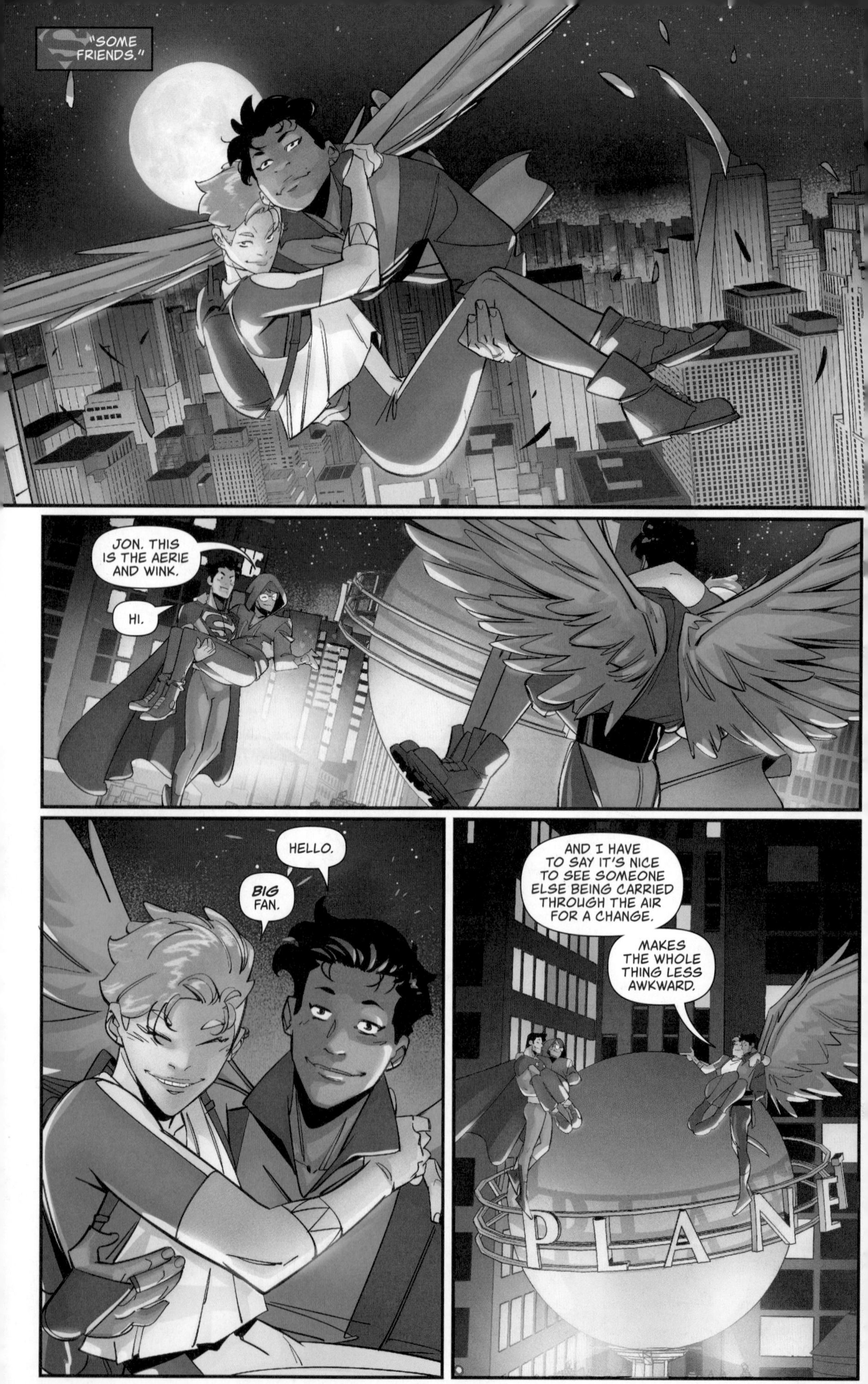
"SOME FRIENDS."
JON. THIS IS THE AERIE AND WINK.
HI.
HELLO.
BIG FAN.
AND I HAVE TO SAY IT'S NICE TO SEE SOMEONE ELSE BEING CARRIED THROUGH THE AIR FOR A CHANGE.
MAKES THE WHOLE THING LESS AWKWARD.
PLANE

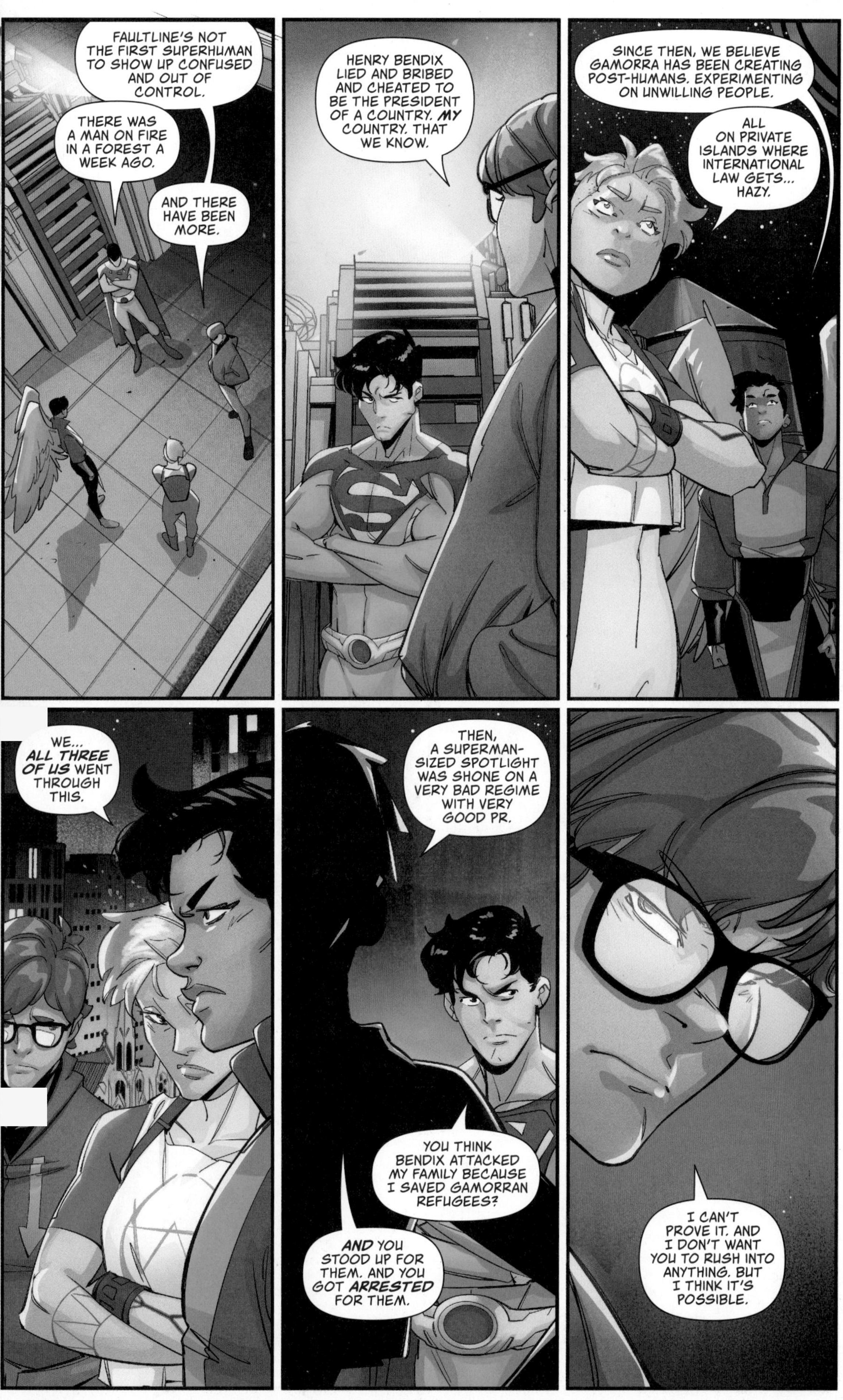
FAULTLINE'S NOT THE FIRST SUPERHUMAN TO SHOW UP CONFUSED AND OUT OF CONTROL.
THERE WAS A MAN ON FIRE IN A FOREST A WEEK AGO.
AND THERE HAVE BEEN MORE.
HENRY BENDIX LIED AND BRIBED AND CHEATED TO BE THE PRESIDENT OF A COUNTRY. *MY* COUNTRY. THAT WE KNOW.
SINCE THEN, WE BELIEVE GAMORRA HAS BEEN CREATING POST-HUMANS. EXPERIMENTING ON UNWILLING PEOPLE.
ALL ON PRIVATE ISLANDS WHERE INTERNATIONAL LAW GETS... HAZY.
WE... *ALL THREE OF US* WENT THROUGH THIS.
THEN, A SUPERMAN-SIZED SPOTLIGHT WAS SHONE ON A VERY BAD REGIME WITH VERY GOOD PR.
YOU THINK BENDIX ATTACKED MY FAMILY BECAUSE I SAVED GAMORRAN REFUGEES?
AND YOU STOOD UP FOR THEM. AND YOU GOT *ARRESTED* FOR THEM.
I CAN'T PROVE IT. AND I DON'T WANT YOU TO RUSH INTO ANYTHING. BUT I THINK IT'S POSSIBLE.

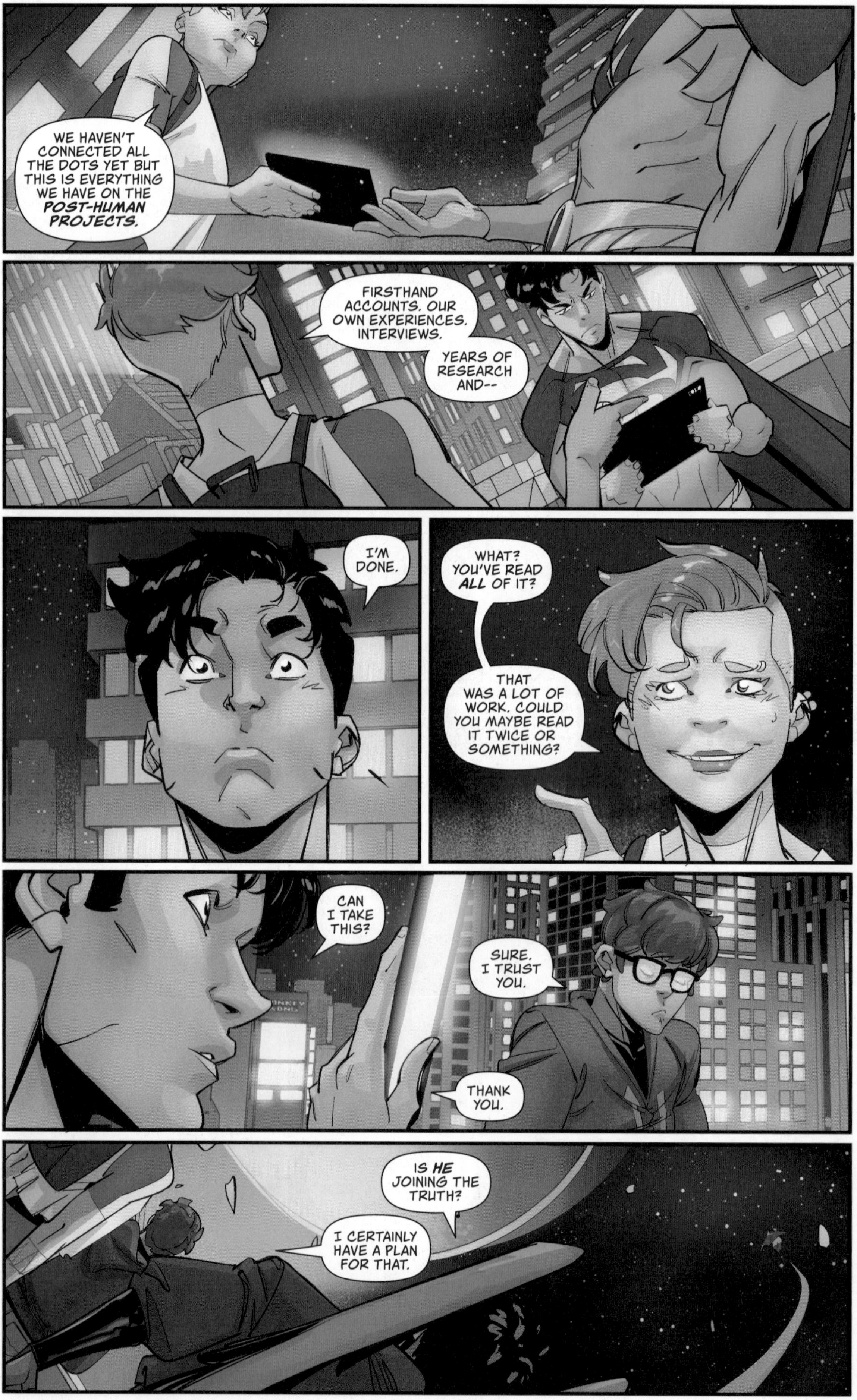
WE HAVEN'T CONNECTED ALL THE DOTS YET BUT THIS IS EVERYTHING WE HAVE ON THE POST-HUMAN PROJECTS.
FIRSTHAND ACCOUNTS. OUR OWN EXPERIENCES. INTERVIEWS.
YEARS OF RESEARCH AND--
I'M DONE.
WHAT? YOU'VE READ ALL OF IT?
THAT WAS A LOT OF WORK. COULD YOU MAYBE READ IT TWICE OR SOMETHING?
CAN I TAKE THIS?
SURE. I TRUST YOU.
THANK YOU.
IS HE JOINING THE TRUTH?
I CERTAINLY HAVE A PLAN FOR THAT.

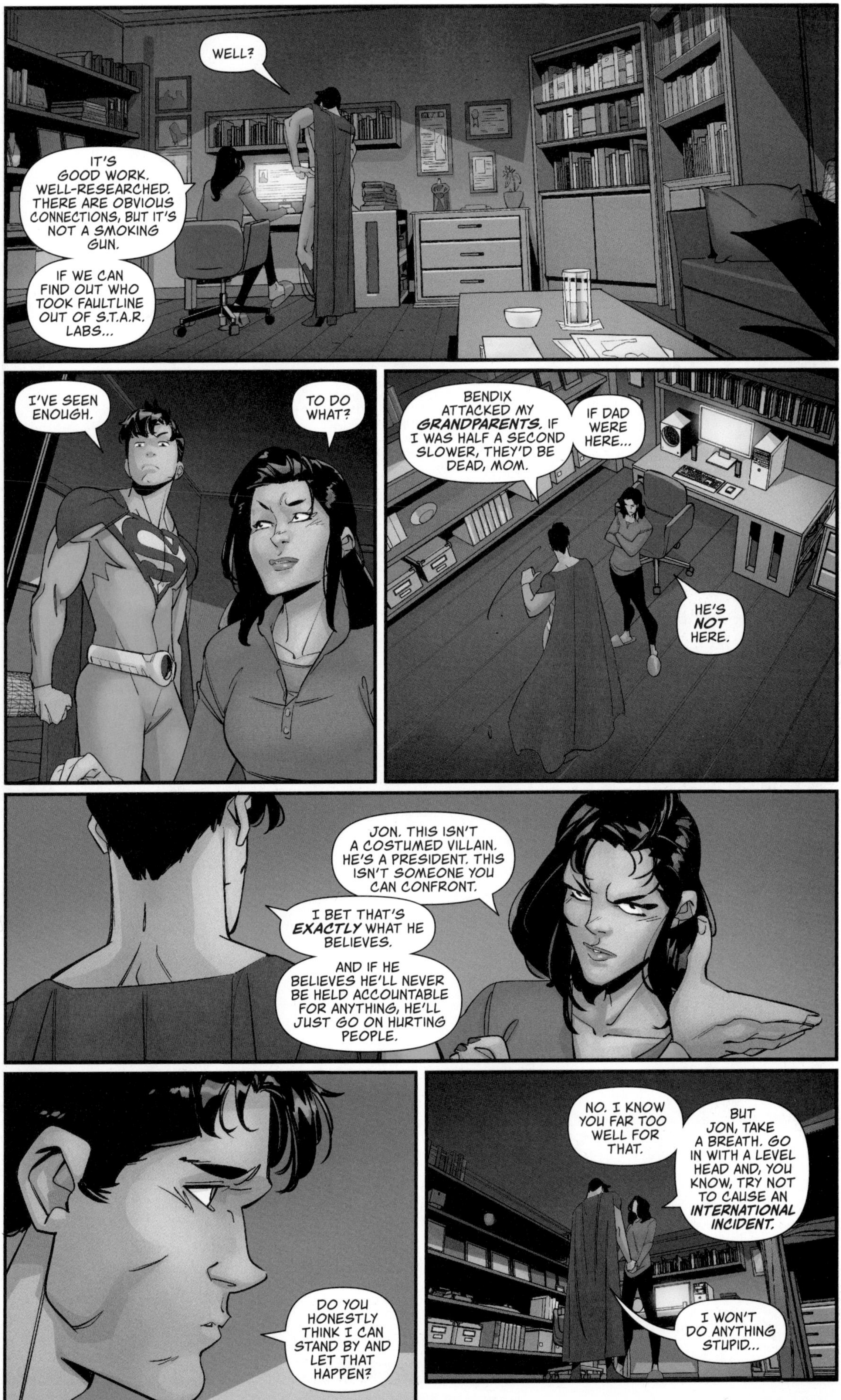
WELL?
IT'S GOOD WORK. WELL-RESEARCHED. THERE ARE OBVIOUS CONNECTIONS, BUT IT'S NOT A SMOKING GUN.
IF WE CAN FIND OUT WHO TOOK FAULTLINE OUT OF S.T.A.R. LABS...
I'VE SEEN ENOUGH.
TO DO WHAT?
BENDIX ATTACKED MY **GRANDPARENTS.** IF I WAS HALF A SECOND SLOWER, THEY'D BE DEAD, MOM.
IF DAD WERE HERE...
HE'S **NOT** HERE.
JON. THIS ISN'T A COSTUMED VILLAIN. HE'S A PRESIDENT. THIS ISN'T SOMEONE YOU CAN CONFRONT.
I BET THAT'S **EXACTLY** WHAT HE BELIEVES.
AND IF HE BELIEVES HE'LL NEVER BE HELD ACCOUNTABLE FOR ANYTHING, HE'LL JUST GO ON HURTING PEOPLE.
DO YOU HONESTLY THINK I CAN STAND BY AND LET THAT HAPPEN?
NO. I KNOW YOU FAR TOO WELL FOR THAT.
BUT JON, TAKE A BREATH. GO IN WITH A LEVEL HEAD AND, YOU KNOW, TRY NOT TO CAUSE AN **INTERNATIONAL INCIDENT.**
I WON'T DO ANYTHING STUPID...

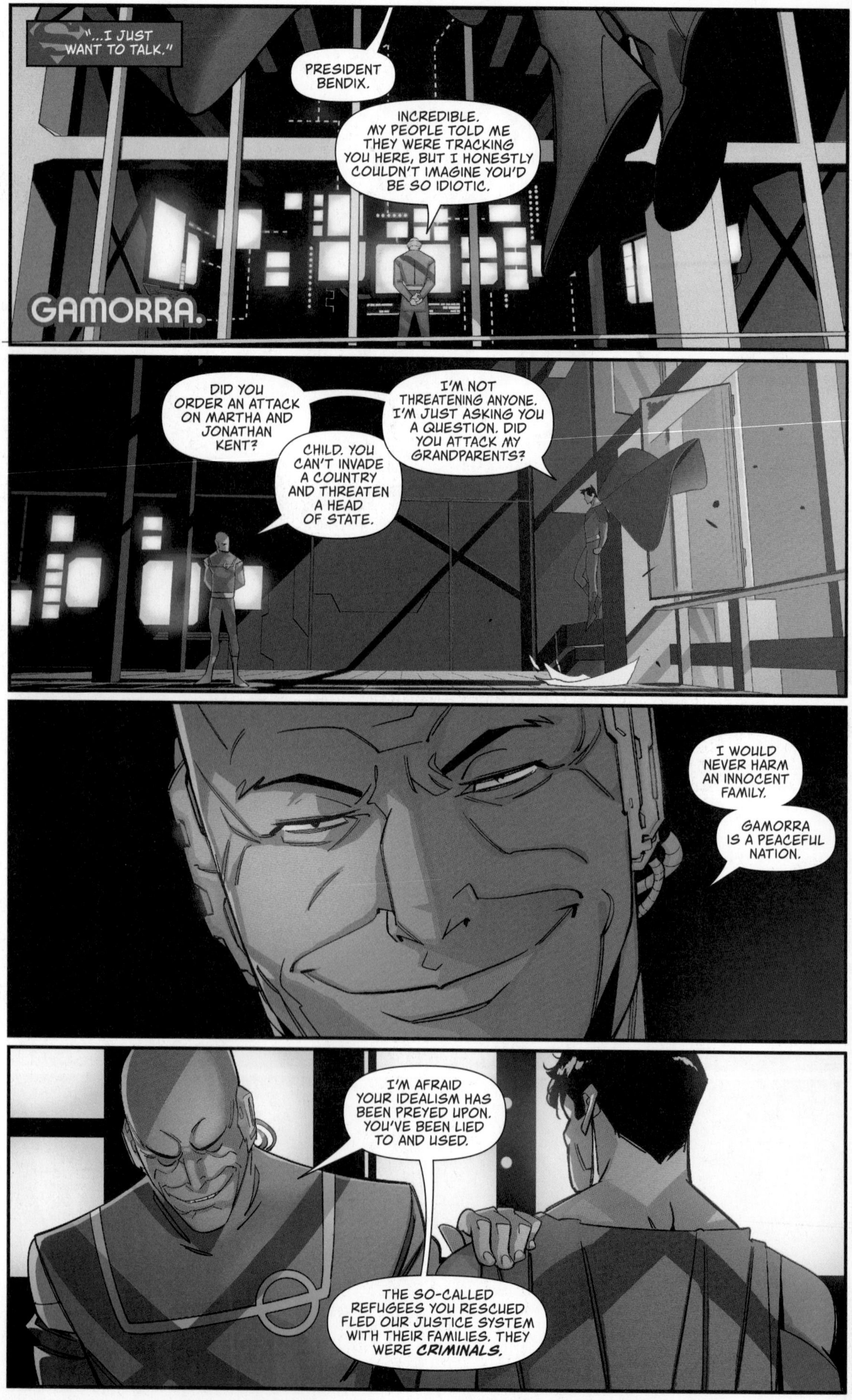
"...I JUST WANT TO TALK."
PRESIDENT BENDIX.
INCREDIBLE. MY PEOPLE TOLD ME THEY WERE TRACKING YOU HERE, BUT I HONESTLY COULDN'T IMAGINE YOU'D BE SO IDIOTIC.
GAMORRA.
DID YOU ORDER AN ATTACK ON MARTHA AND JONATHAN KENT?
CHILD. YOU CAN'T INVADE A COUNTRY AND THREATEN A HEAD OF STATE.
I'M NOT THREATENING ANYONE. I'M JUST ASKING YOU A QUESTION. DID YOU ATTACK MY GRANDPARENTS?
I WOULD NEVER HARM AN INNOCENT FAMILY.
GAMORRA IS A PEACEFUL NATION.
I'M AFRAID YOUR IDEALISM HAS BEEN PREYED UPON. YOU'VE BEEN LIED TO AND USED.
THE SO-CALLED REFUGEES YOU RESCUED FLED OUR JUSTICE SYSTEM WITH THEIR FAMILIES. THEY WERE ***CRIMINALS.***

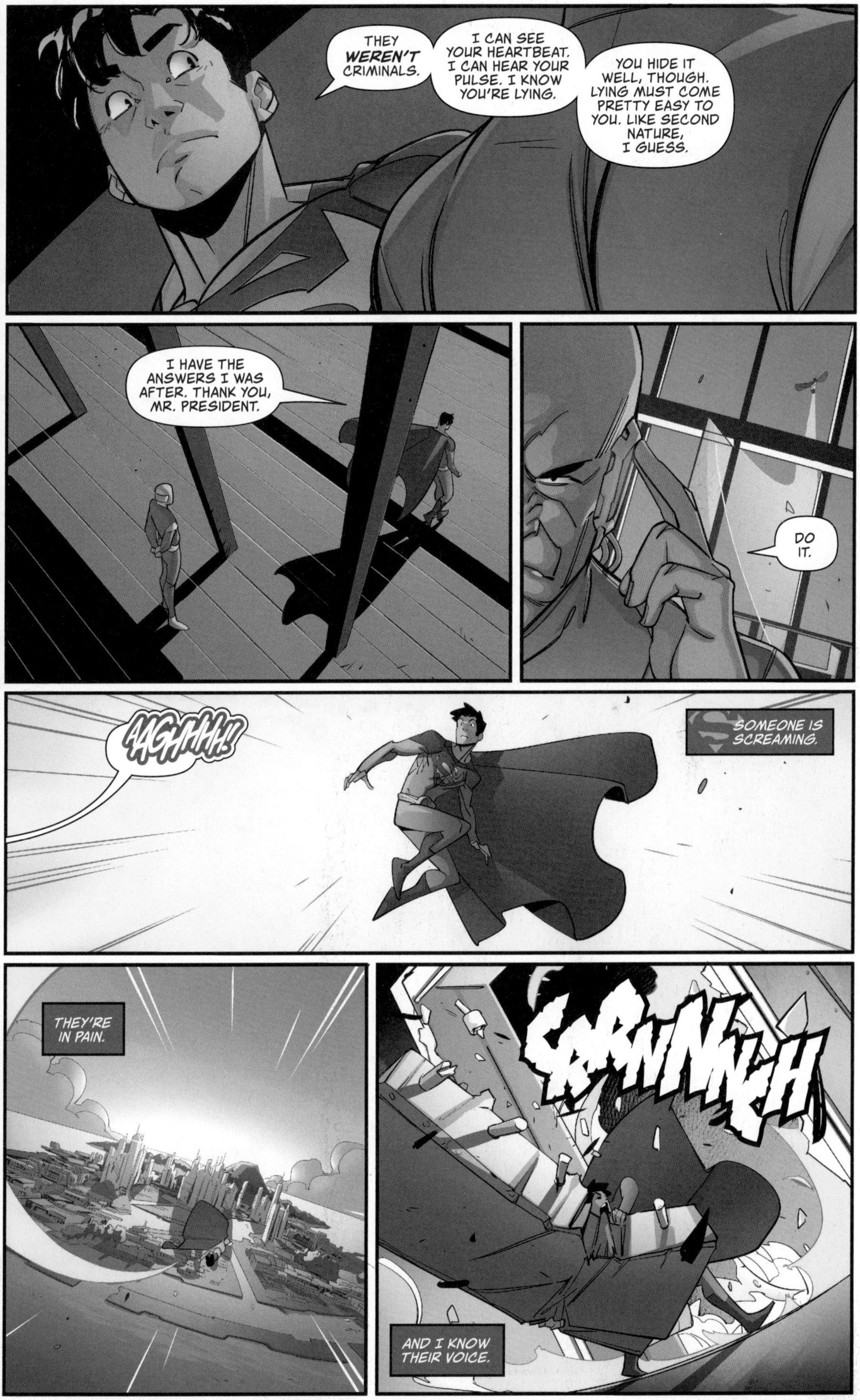
THEY WEREN'T CRIMINALS.
I CAN SEE YOUR HEARTBEAT. I CAN HEAR YOUR PULSE. I KNOW YOU'RE LYING.
YOU HIDE IT WELL, THOUGH. LYING MUST COME PRETTY EASY TO YOU. LIKE SECOND NATURE, I GUESS.
I HAVE THE ANSWERS I WAS AFTER. THANK YOU, MR. PRESIDENT.
DO IT.
AAGHHHH!!
SOMEONE IS SCREAMING.
THEY'RE IN PAIN.
SKRUNNCH
AND I KNOW THEIR VOICE.

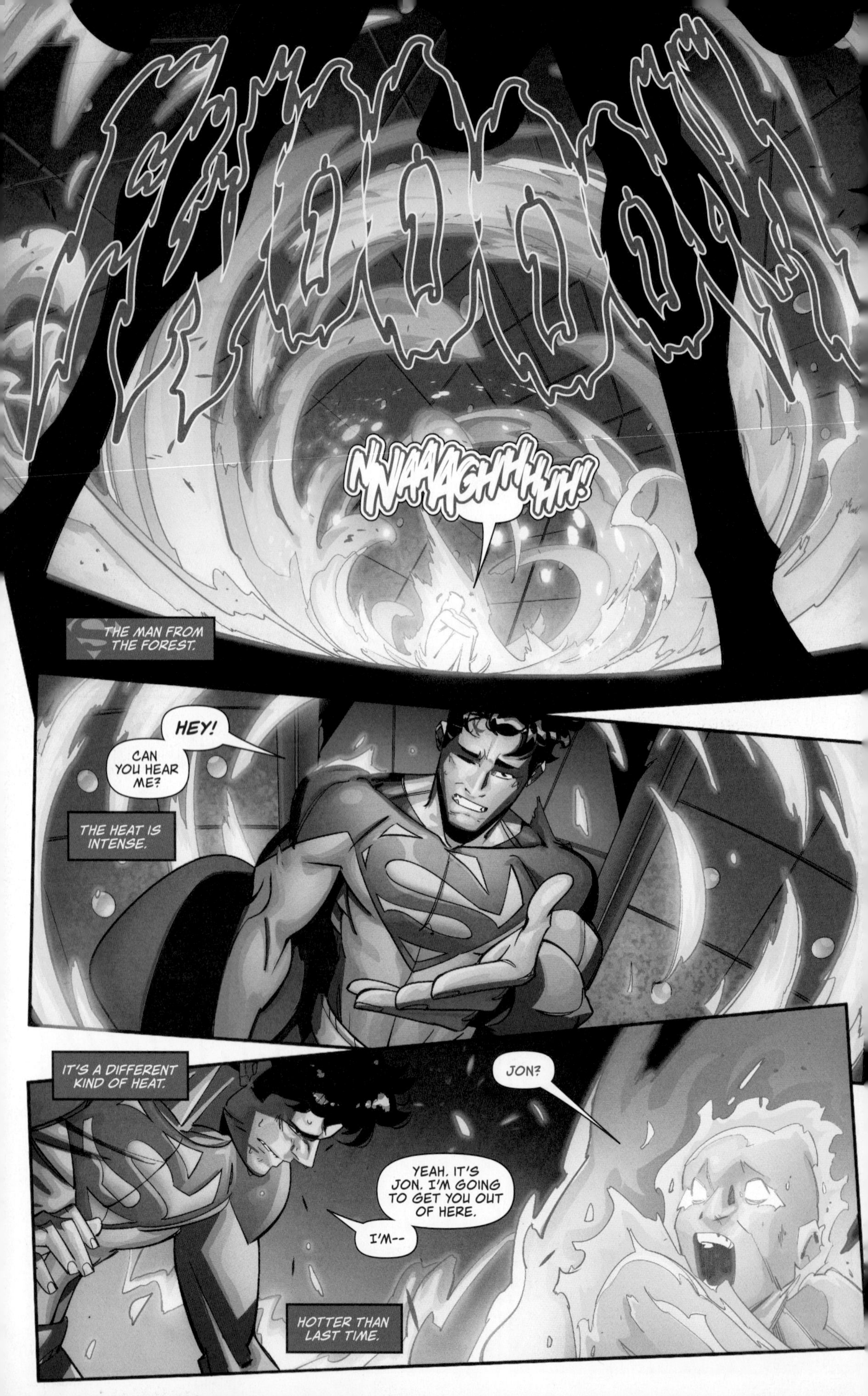

NWAAAGHHHHH!
THE MAN FROM THE FOREST.
HEY!
CAN YOU HEAR ME?
THE HEAT IS INTENSE.
IT'S A DIFFERENT KIND OF HEAT.
JON?
YEAH. IT'S JON. I'M GOING TO GET YOU OUT OF HERE.
I'M--
HOTTER THAN LAST TIME.

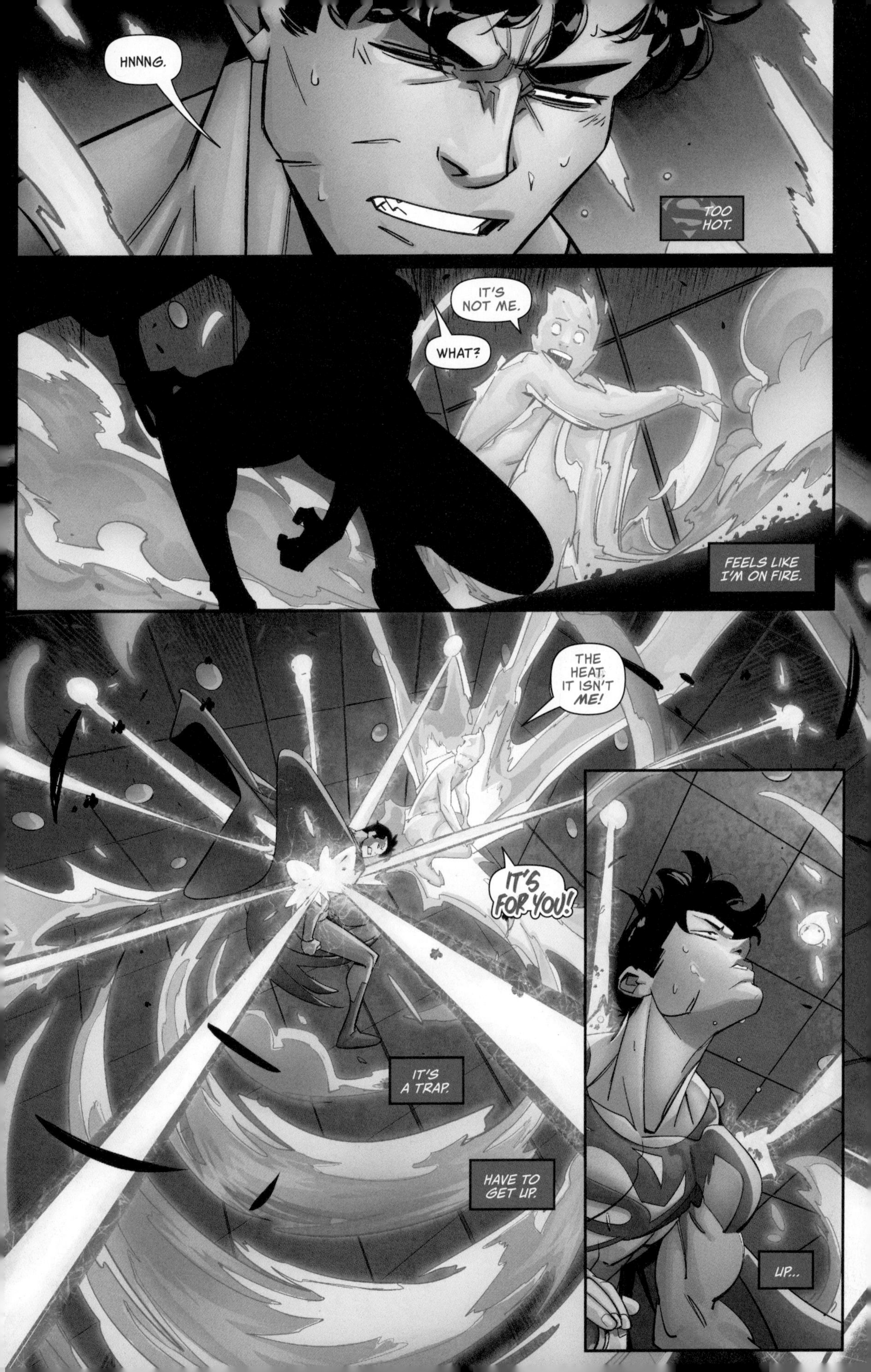
HNNNG.
TOO HOT.
IT'S NOT ME.
WHAT?
FEELS LIKE I'M ON FIRE.
THE HEAT. IT ISN'T ME!
IT'S FOR YOU!
IT'S A TRAP.
HAVE TO GET UP.
UP...

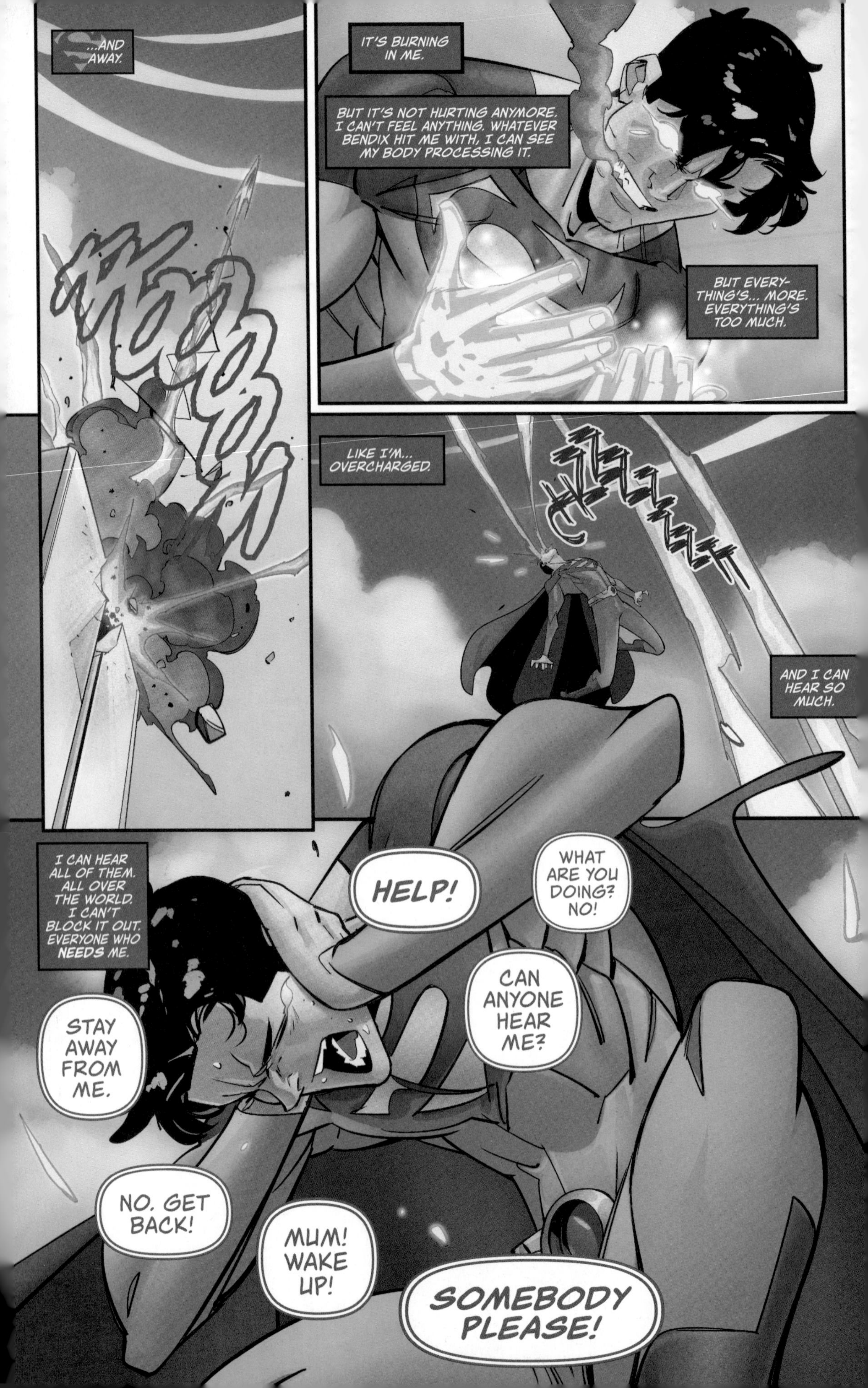
...AND AWAY.
IT'S BURNING IN ME.
BUT IT'S NOT HURTING ANYMORE. I CAN'T FEEL ANYTHING. WHATEVER BENDIX HIT ME WITH, I CAN SEE MY BODY PROCESSING IT.
BUT EVERY-THING'S... MORE. EVERYTHING'S TOO MUCH.
LIKE I'M... OVERCHARGED.
AND I CAN HEAR SO MUCH.
I CAN HEAR ALL OF THEM. ALL OVER THE WORLD. I CAN'T BLOCK IT OUT. EVERYONE WHO NEEDS ME.
HELP!
WHAT ARE YOU DOING? NO!
CAN ANYONE HEAR ME?
STAY AWAY FROM ME.
NO. GET BACK!
MUM! WAKE UP!
SOMEBODY PLEASE!

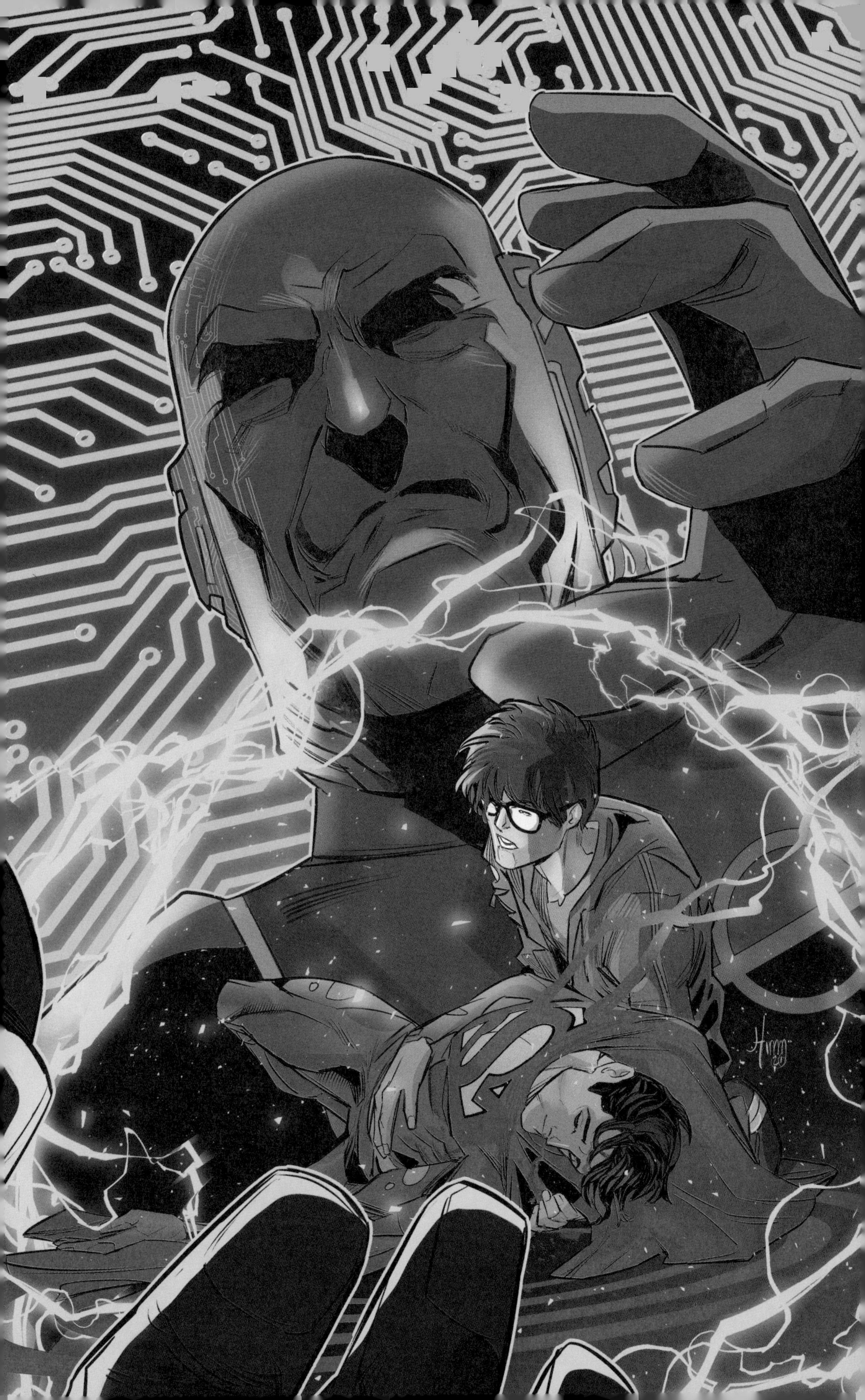

Superman: Son of Kal-El #5 variant cover art by **INHYUK LEE**

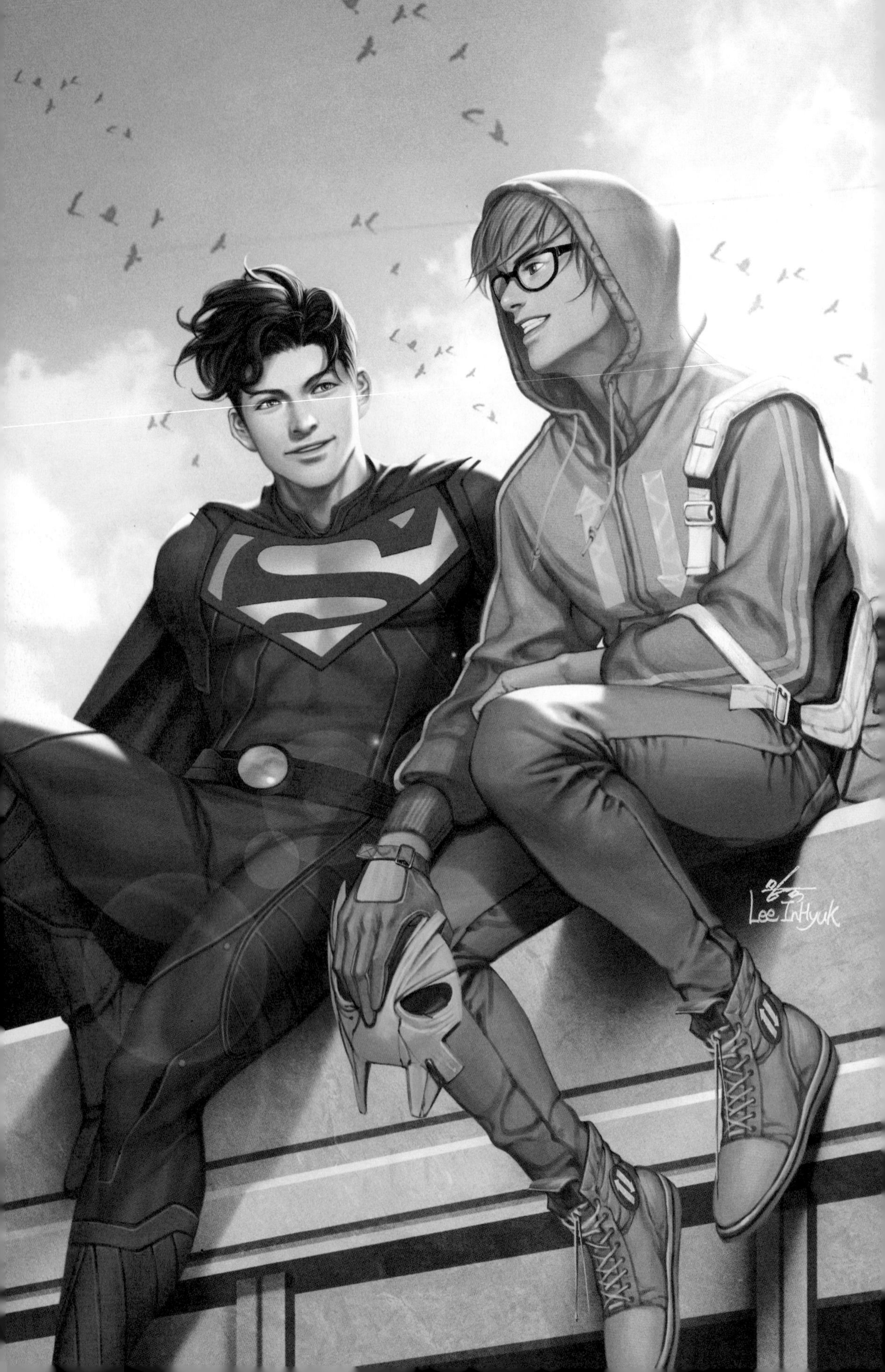
Lee InHyuk

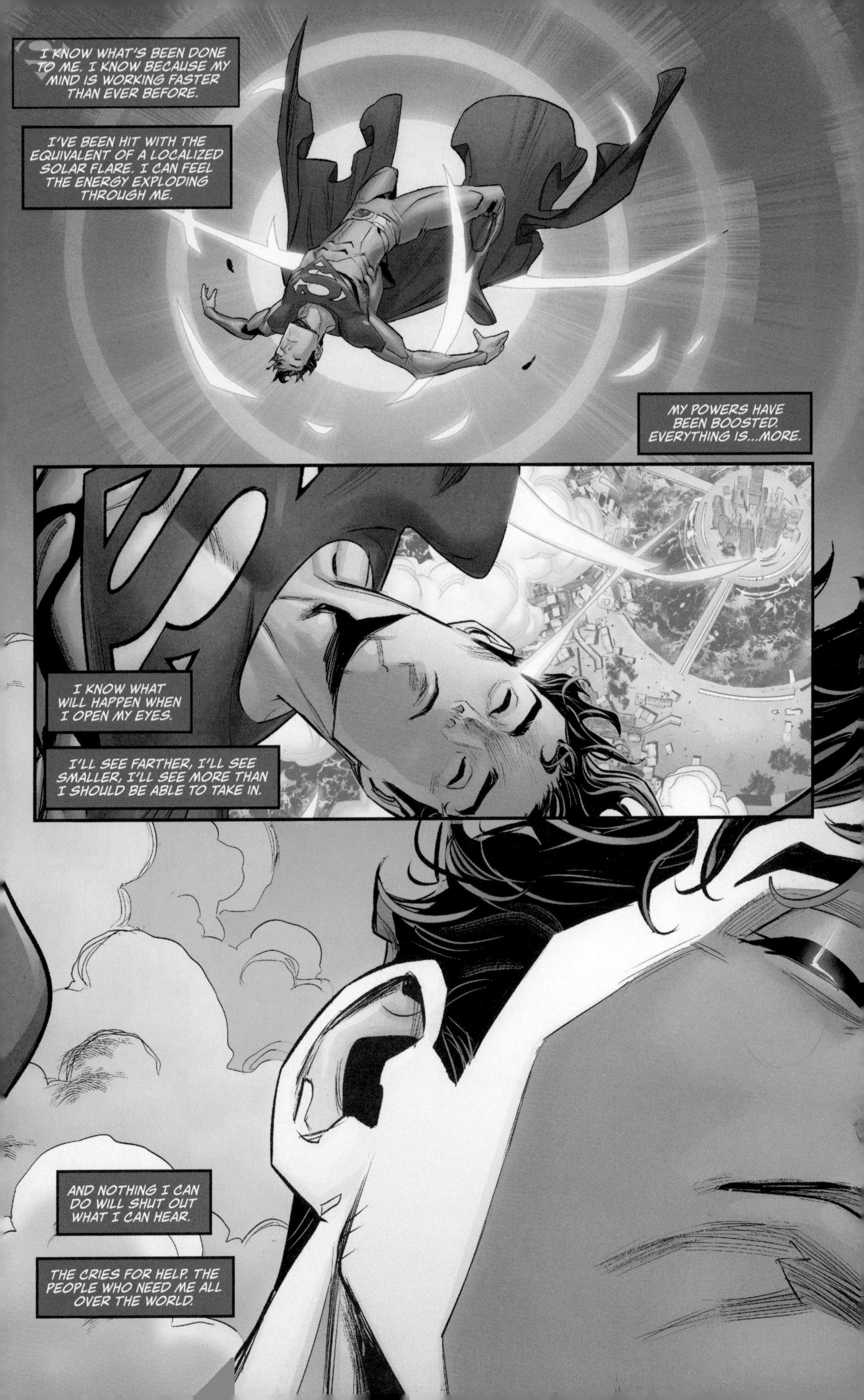
I KNOW WHAT'S BEEN DONE TO ME. I KNOW BECAUSE MY MIND IS WORKING FASTER THAN EVER BEFORE.
I'VE BEEN HIT WITH THE EQUIVALENT OF A LOCALIZED SOLAR FLARE. I CAN FEEL THE ENERGY EXPLODING THROUGH ME.
MY POWERS HAVE BEEN BOOSTED. EVERYTHING IS...MORE.
I KNOW WHAT WILL HAPPEN WHEN I OPEN MY EYES.
I'LL SEE FARTHER, I'LL SEE SMALLER, I'LL SEE MORE THAN I SHOULD BE ABLE TO TAKE IN.
AND NOTHING I CAN DO WILL SHUT OUT WHAT I CAN HEAR.
THE CRIES FOR HELP. THE PEOPLE WHO NEED ME ALL OVER THE WORLD.

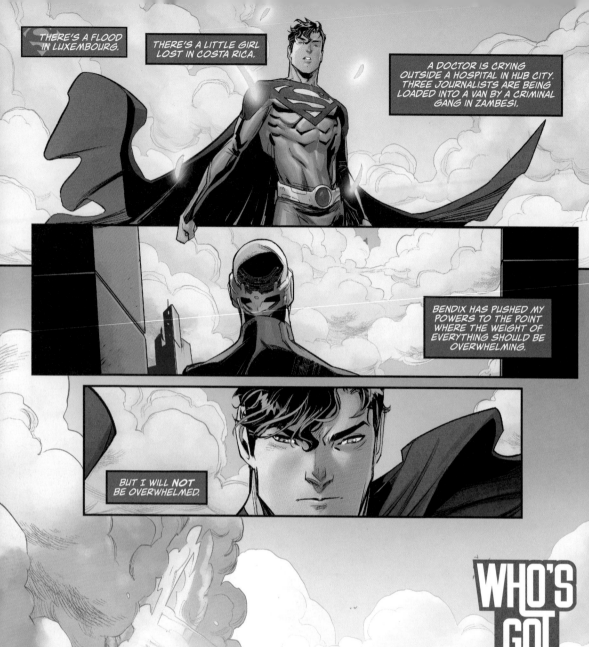

THERE'S A FLOOD IN LUXEMBOURG.

THERE'S A LITTLE GIRL LOST IN COSTA RICA.

A DOCTOR IS CRYING OUTSIDE A HOSPITAL IN HUB CITY. THREE JOURNALISTS ARE BEING LOADED INTO A VAN BY A CRIMINAL GANG IN ZAMBESI.

BENDIX HAS PUSHED MY POWERS TO THE POINT WHERE THE WEIGHT OF EVERYTHING SHOULD BE OVERWHELMED.

BUT I WILL **NOT** BE OVERWHELMED.

WHO'S GOT YOU?

TOM TAYLOR SCRIPT
JOHN TIMMS ART
HI-FI COLOR
DAVE SHARPE LETTERS
JOHN TIMMS COVER
INHYUK LEE,
TRAVIS MOORE AND
TAMRA BONVILLAIN
VARIANT COVERS
JILLIAN GRANT &
DIEGO LOPEZ
ASSISTANT EDITOR
MIKE COTTON EDITOR

SUPERMAN CREATED
BY JERRY SIEGEL
AND JOE SHUSTER.
SUPERBOY CREATED
BY JERRY SIEGEL.
BY SPECIAL
ARRANGEMENT WITH THE
JERRY SIEGEL FAMILY.

THE "PROGRESS" PRIDE
FLAG IN THE DC LOGO
DESIGNED BY
DANIEL QUASAR.

I CAN SAVE THEM ALL.

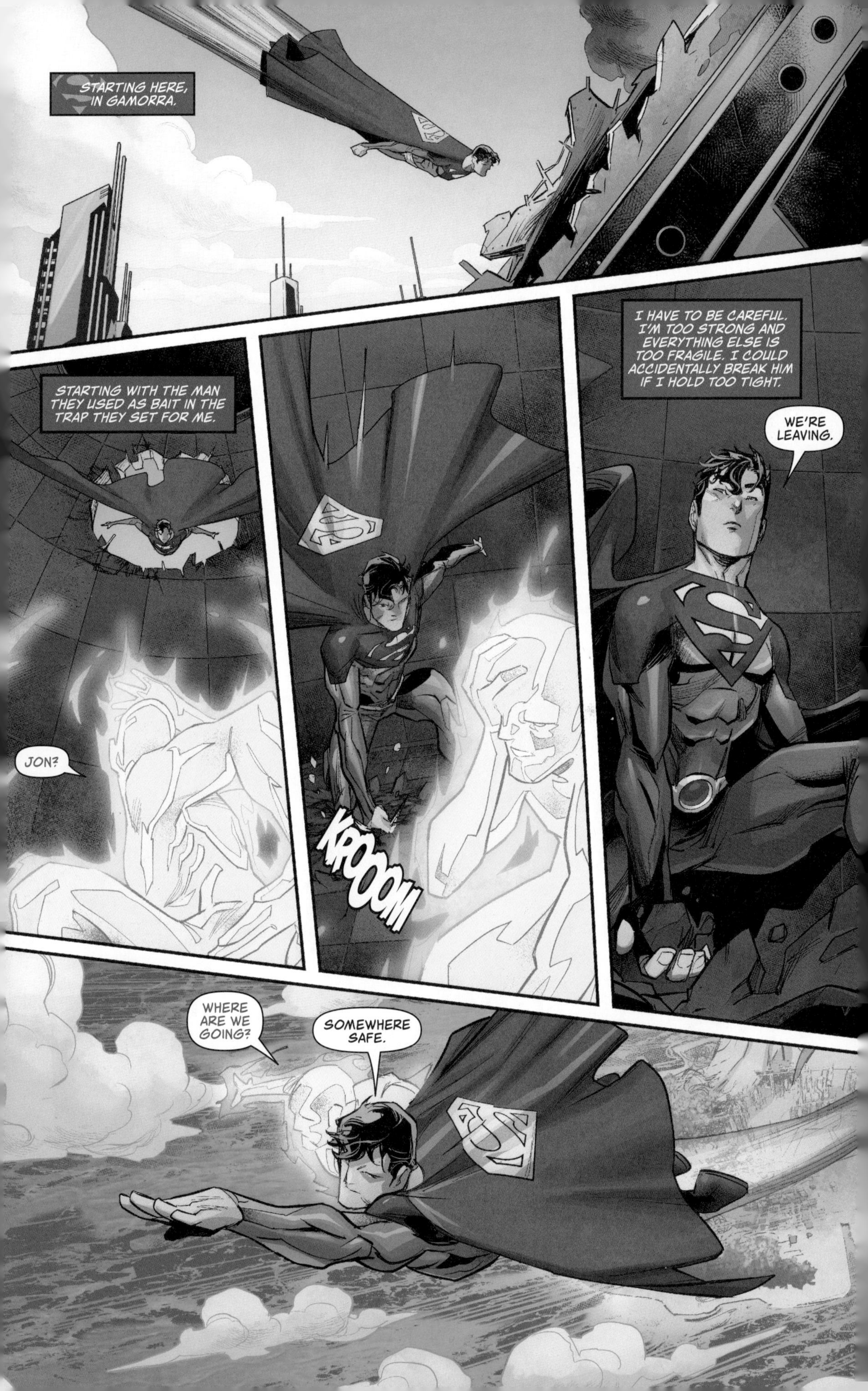
STARTING HERE, IN GAMORRA.
STARTING WITH THE MAN THEY USED AS BAIT IN THE TRAP THEY SET FOR ME.
JON?
KROOOOM
I HAVE TO BE CAREFUL. I'M TOO STRONG AND EVERYTHING ELSE IS TOO FRAGILE. I COULD ACCIDENTALLY BREAK HIM IF I HOLD TOO TIGHT.
WE'RE LEAVING.
WHERE ARE WE GOING?
SOMEWHERE SAFE.

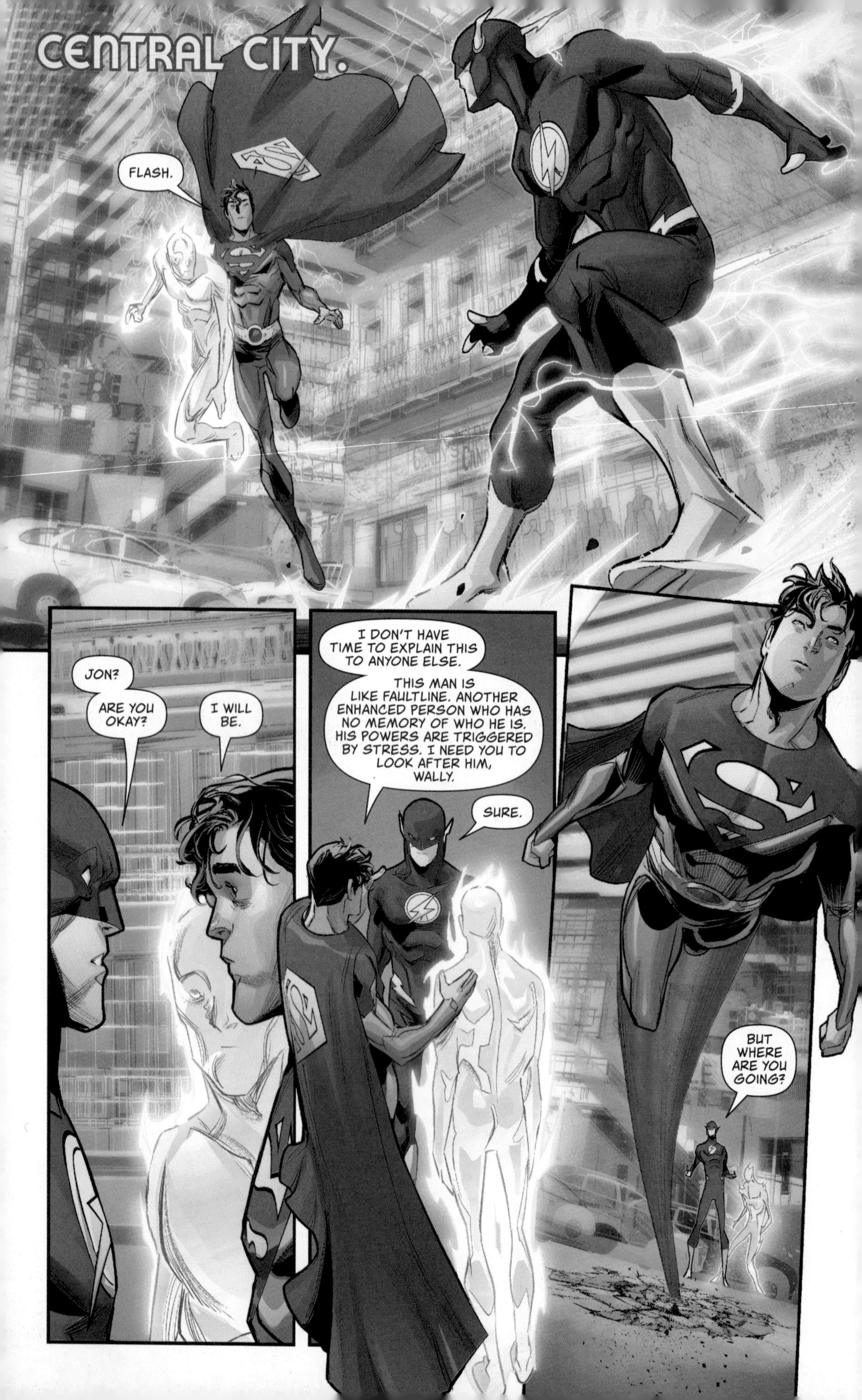
CENTRAL CITY.
FLASH.
JON?
ARE YOU OKAY?
I WILL BE.
I DON'T HAVE TIME TO EXPLAIN THIS TO ANYONE ELSE.
THIS MAN IS LIKE FAULTLINE. ANOTHER ENHANCED PERSON WHO HAS NO MEMORY OF WHO HE IS. HIS POWERS ARE TRIGGERED BY STRESS. I NEED YOU TO LOOK AFTER HIM, WALLY.
SURE.
BUT WHERE ARE YOU GOING?

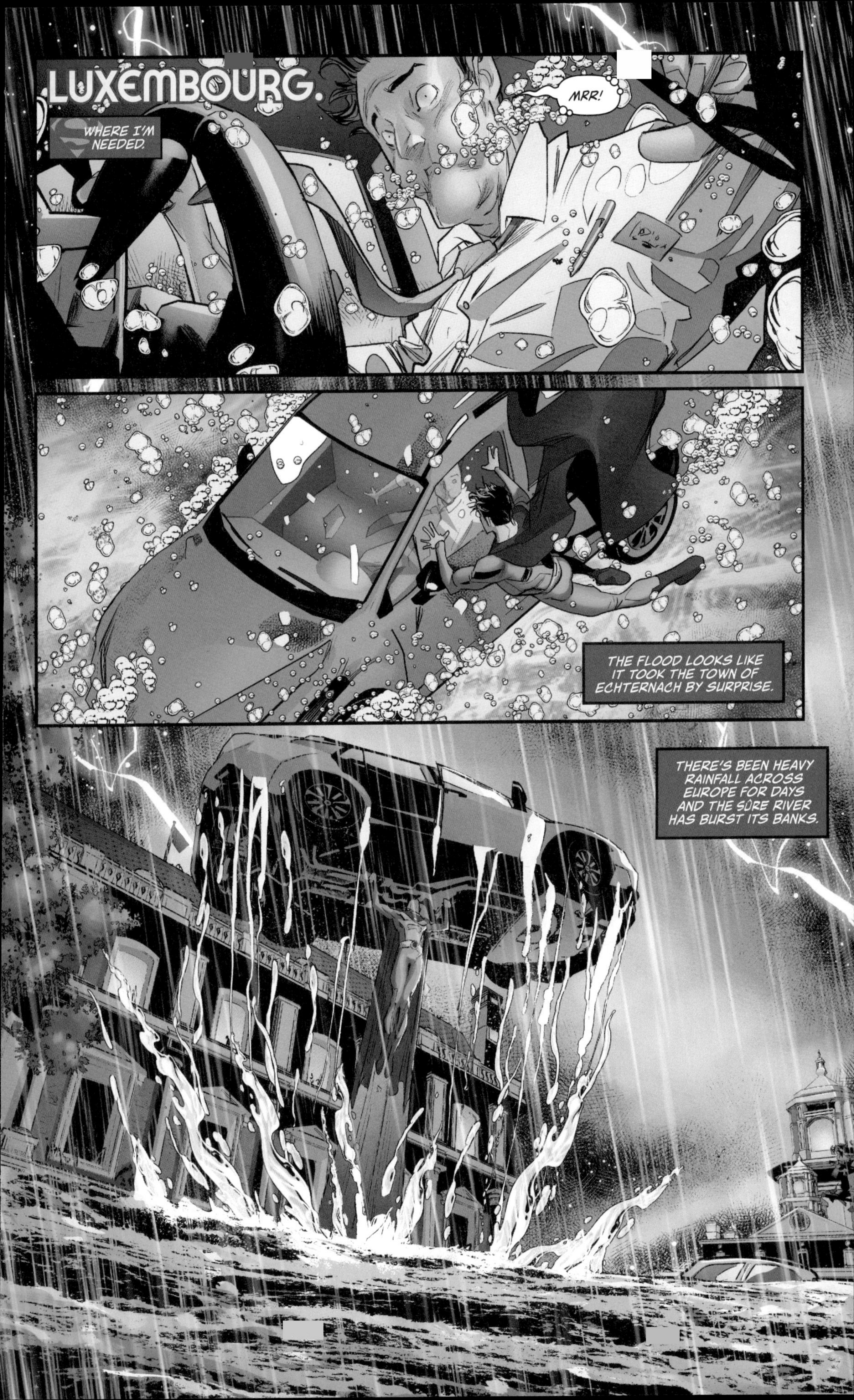
LUXEMBOURG.
WHERE I'M NEEDED.
MRR!
THE FLOOD LOOKS LIKE IT TOOK THE TOWN OF ECHTERNACH BY SURPRISE.
THERE'S BEEN HEAVY RAINFALL ACROSS EUROPE FOR DAYS AND THE SÛRE RIVER HAS BURST ITS BANKS.

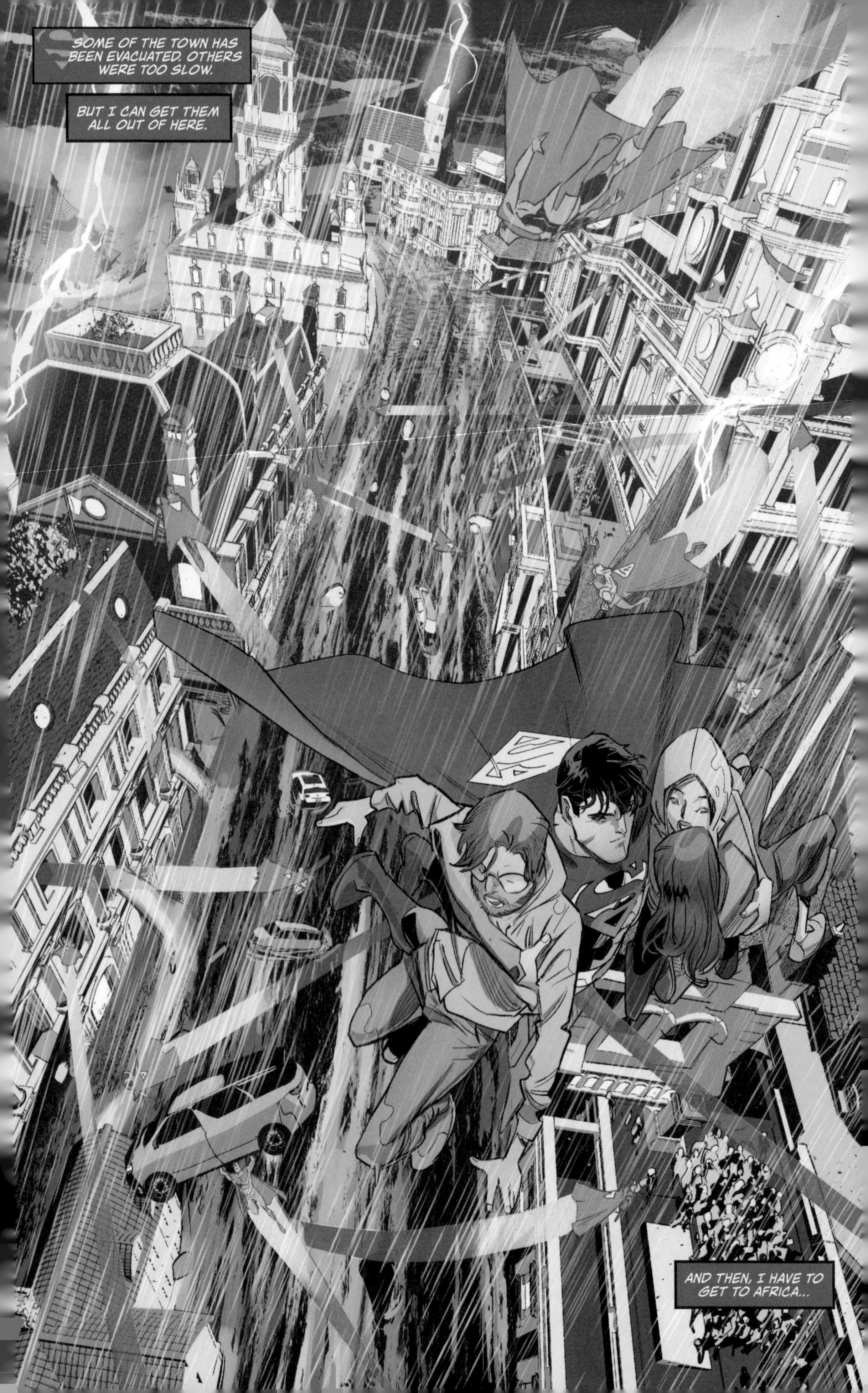
SOME OF THE TOWN HAS BEEN EVACUATED. OTHERS WERE TOO SLOW.
BUT I CAN GET THEM ALL OUT OF HERE.
AND THEN, I HAVE TO GET TO AFRICA...

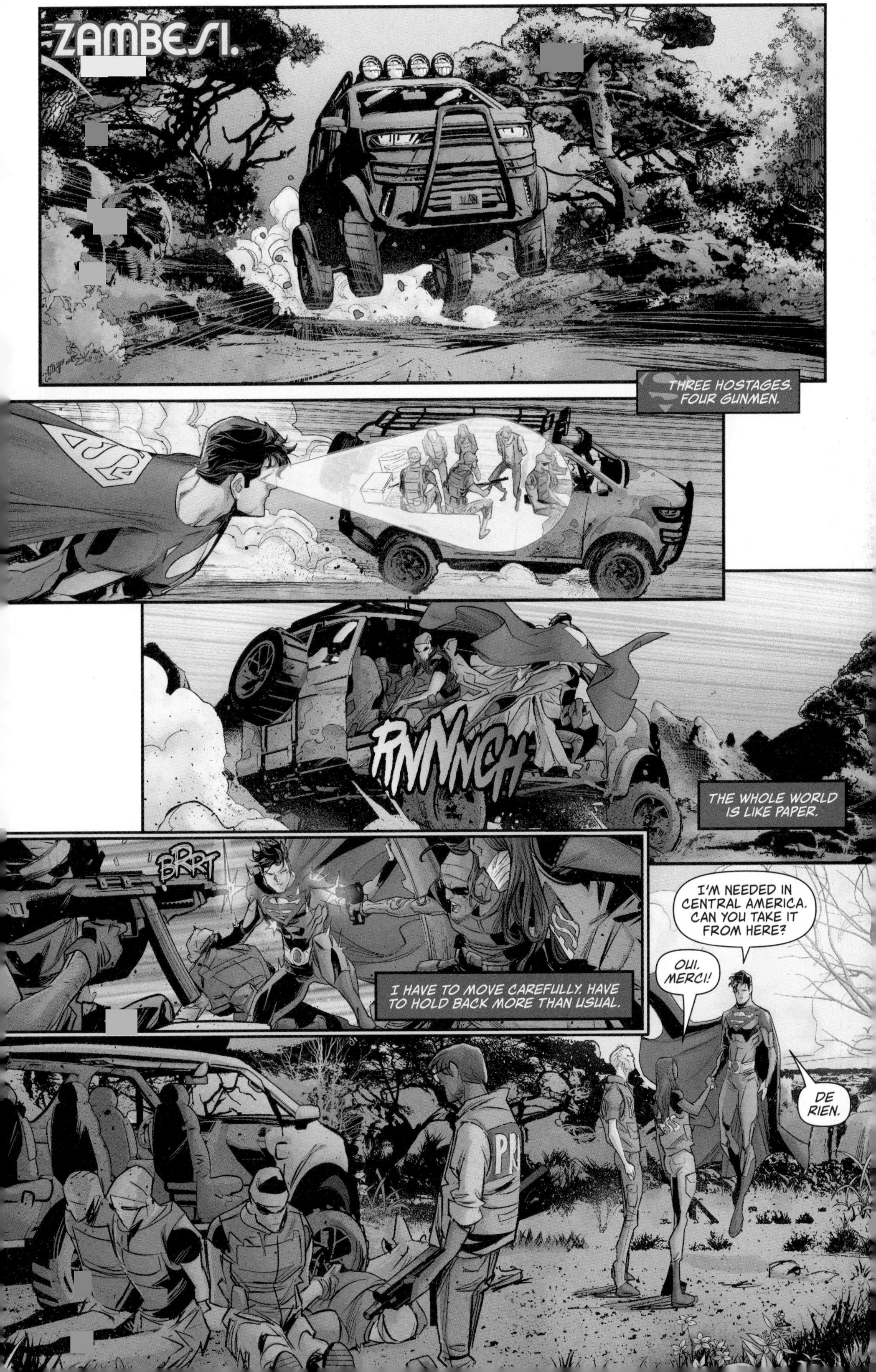
ZAMBESI.
THREE HOSTAGES. FOUR GUNMEN.
RNNNCH
THE WHOLE WORLD IS LIKE PAPER.
BRRT
I HAVE TO MOVE CAREFULLY. HAVE TO HOLD BACK MORE THAN USUAL.
I'M NEEDED IN CENTRAL AMERICA. CAN YOU TAKE IT FROM HERE?
OUI. MERCI!
DE RIEN.

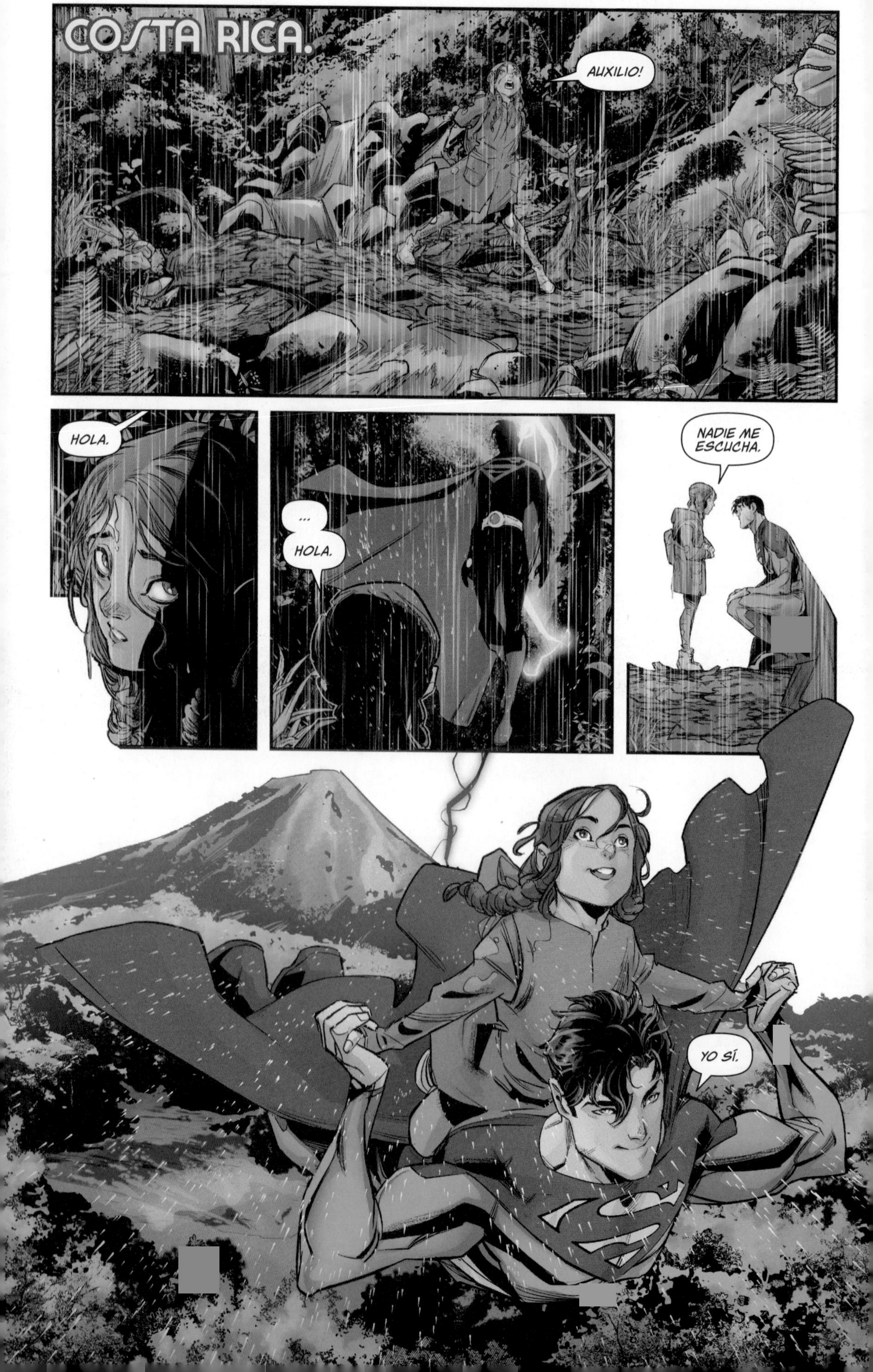
COSTA RICA.
AUXILIO!
HOLA.
...
HOLA.
NADIE ME ESCUCHA.
YO SÍ.

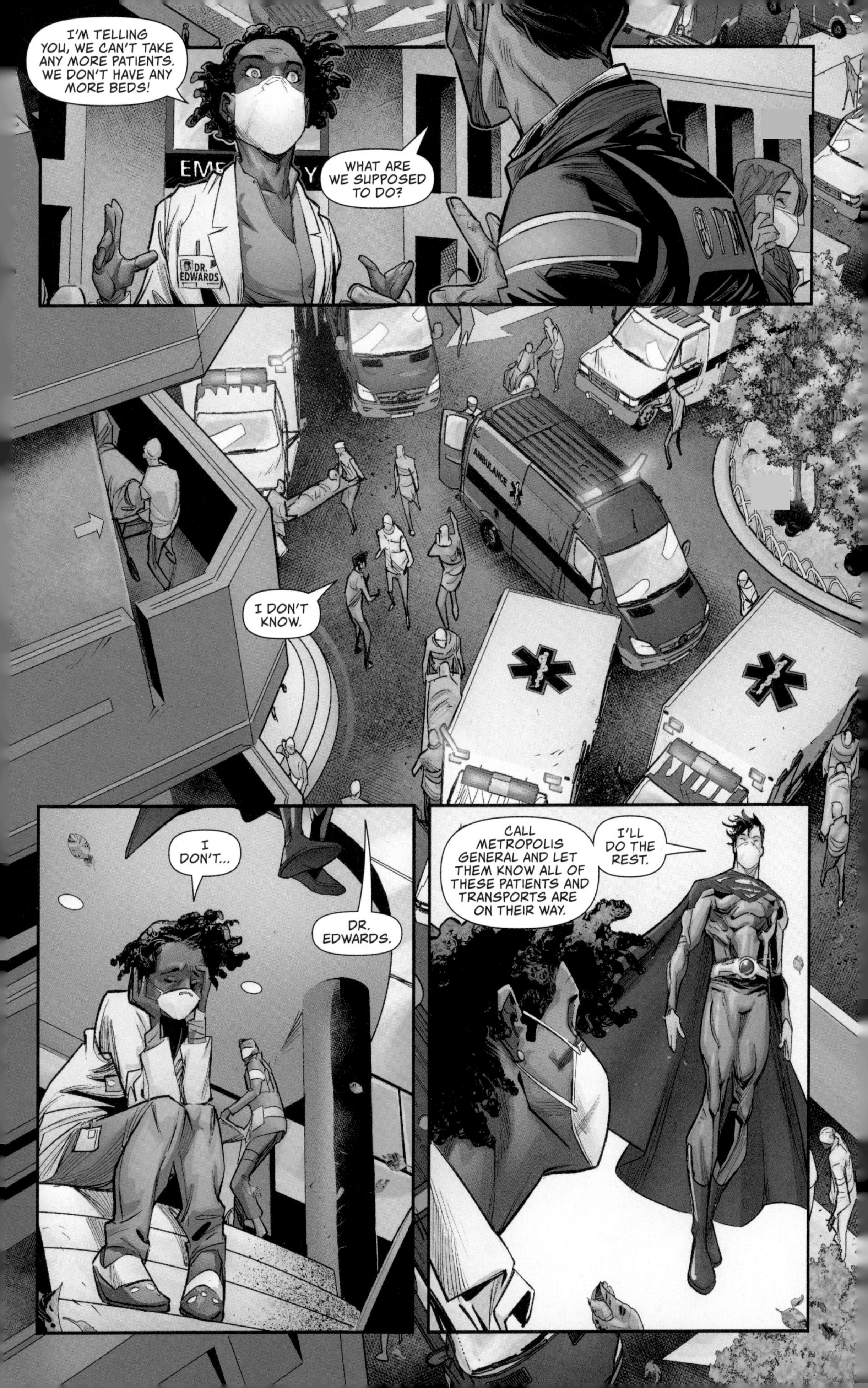
I'M TELLING YOU, WE CAN'T TAKE ANY MORE PATIENTS. WE DON'T HAVE ANY MORE BEDS!
DR. EDWARDS
WHAT ARE WE SUPPOSED TO DO?
AMBULANCE
I DON'T KNOW.
I DON'T...
DR. EDWARDS.
CALL METROPOLIS GENERAL AND LET THEM KNOW ALL OF THESE PATIENTS AND TRANSPORTS ARE ON THEIR WAY.
I'LL DO THE REST.

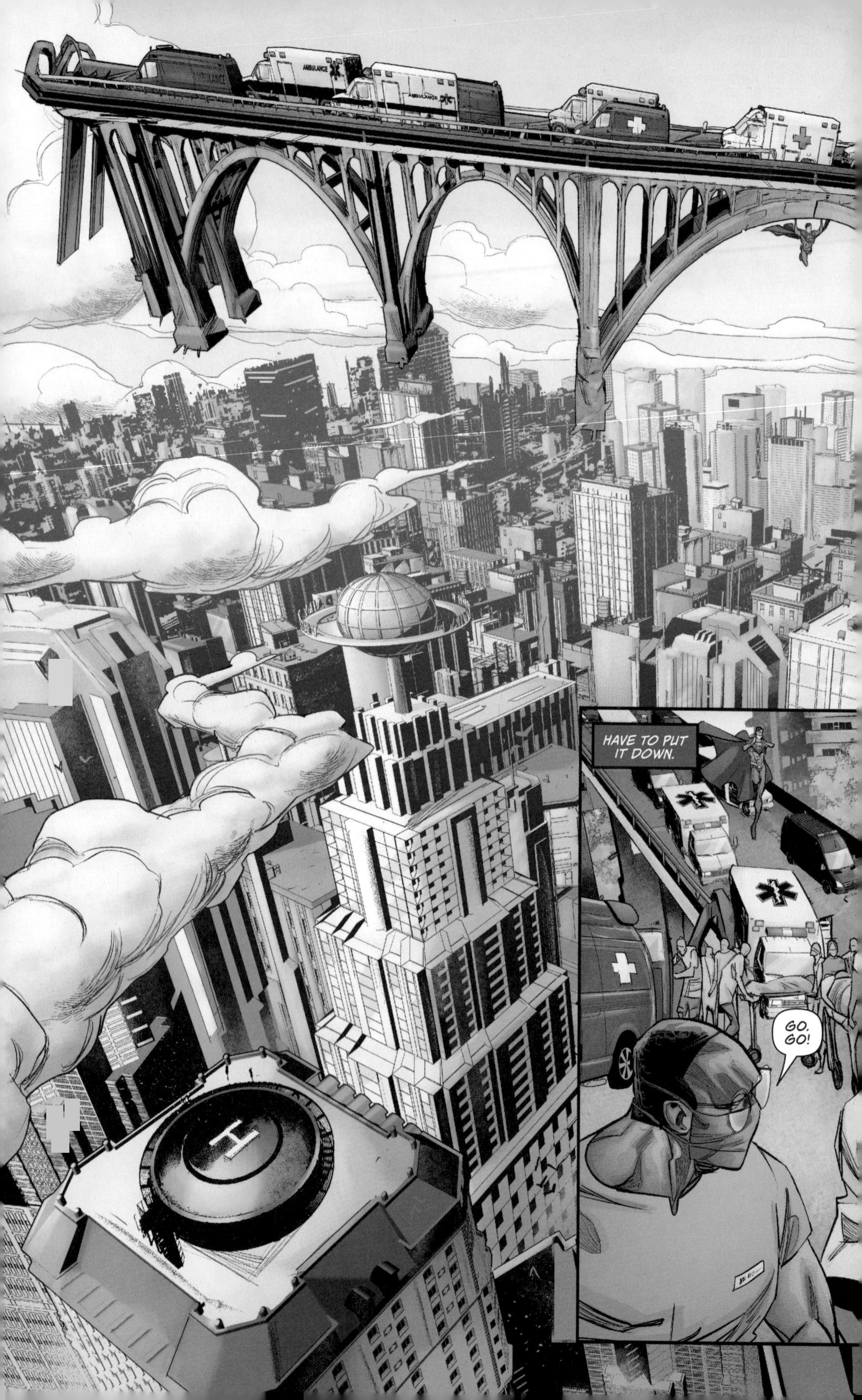
HAVE TO PUT IT DOWN.
GO. GO!

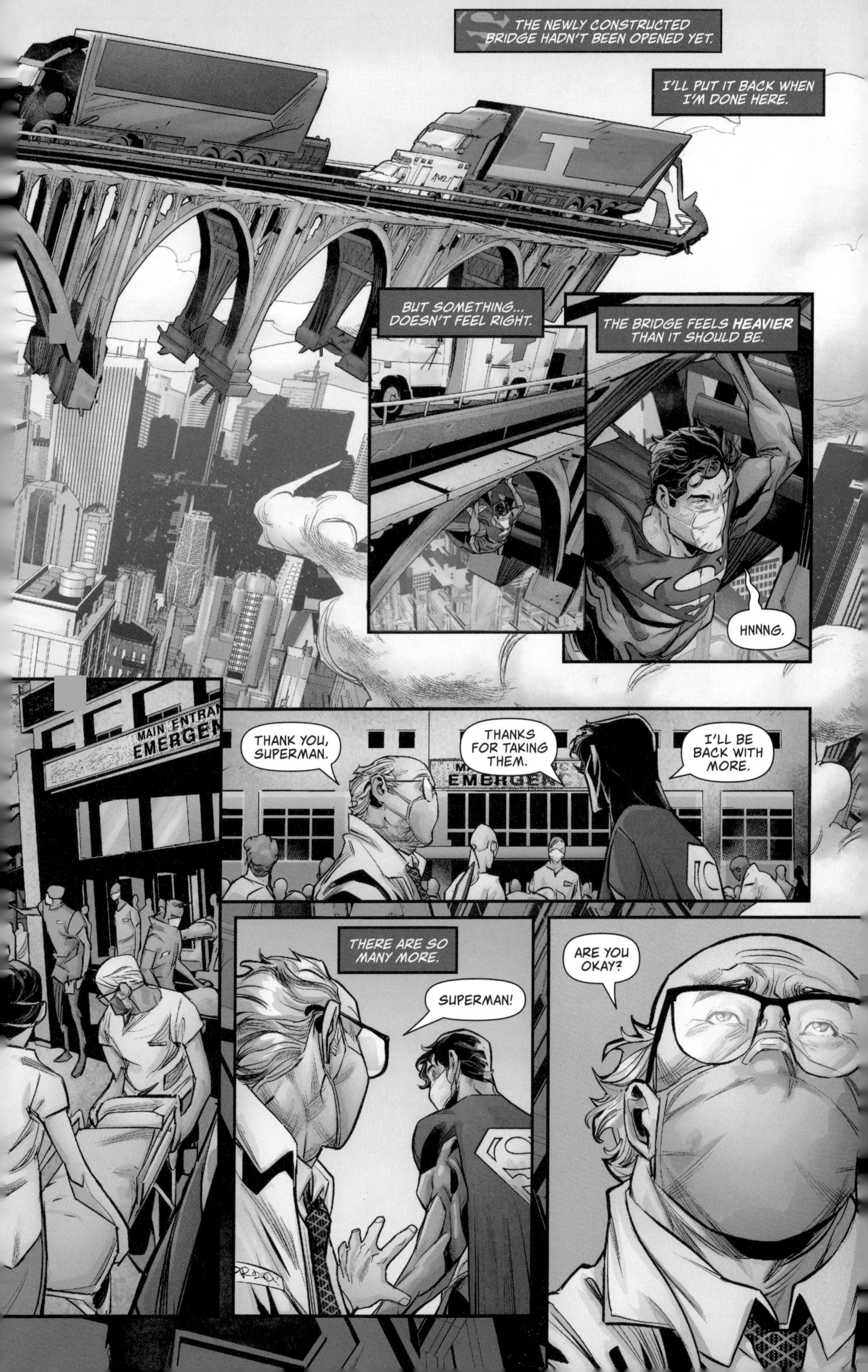
THE NEWLY CONSTRUCTED BRIDGE HADN'T BEEN OPENED YET.
I'LL PUT IT BACK WHEN I'M DONE HERE.
BUT SOMETHING... DOESN'T FEEL RIGHT.
THE BRIDGE FEELS **HEAVIER** THAN IT SHOULD BE.
HNNNG.
MAIN ENTRAN
EMERGEN
THANK YOU, SUPERMAN.
THANKS FOR TAKING THEM.
I'LL BE BACK WITH MORE.
THERE ARE SO MANY MORE.
SUPERMAN!
ARE YOU OKAY?

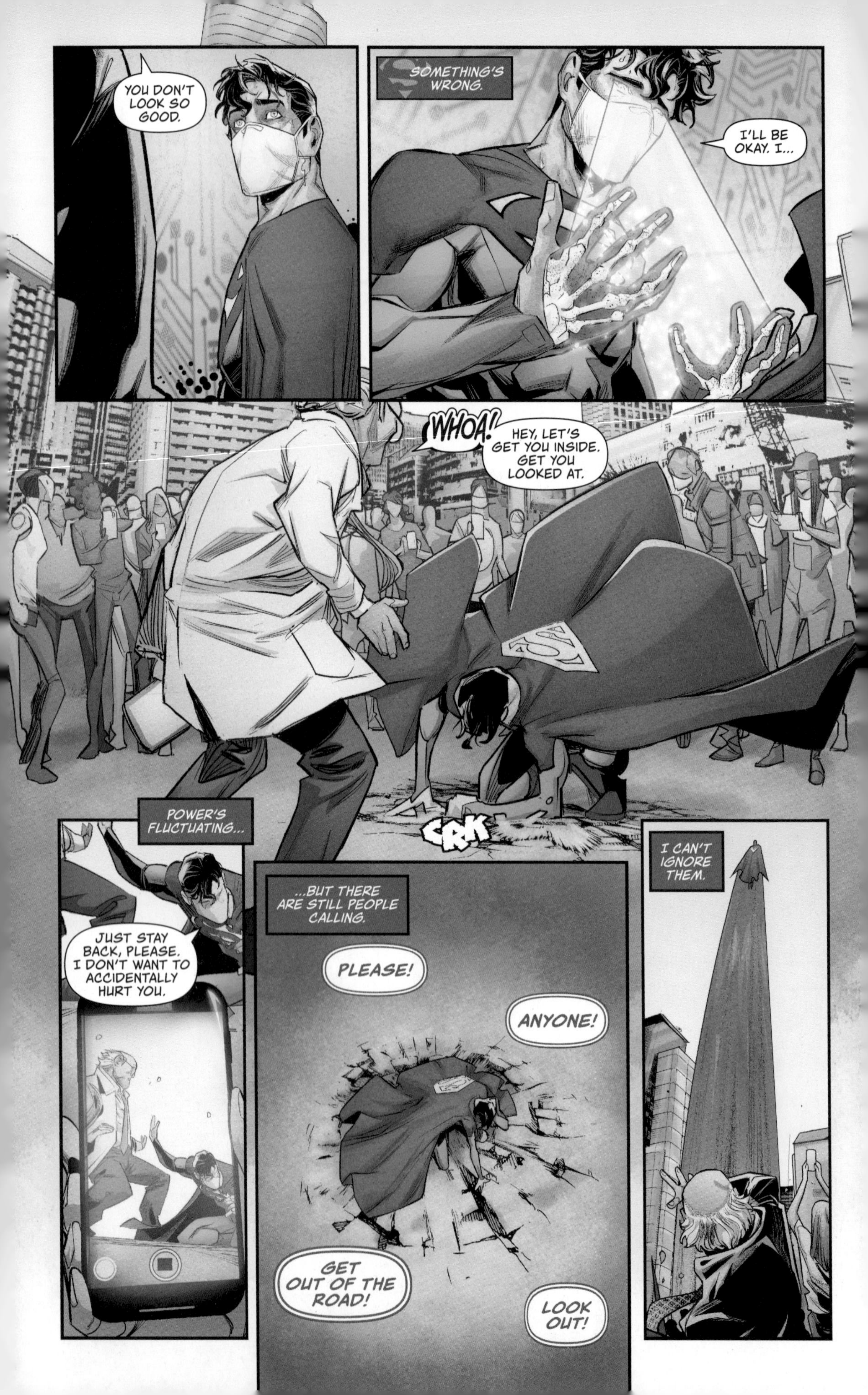
YOU DON'T LOOK SO GOOD.
SOMETHING'S WRONG.
I'LL BE OKAY. I...
WHOA!
HEY, LET'S GET YOU INSIDE. GET YOU LOOKED AT.
CRK
POWER'S FLUCTUATING...
JUST STAY BACK, PLEASE. I DON'T WANT TO ACCIDENTALLY HURT YOU.
...BUT THERE ARE STILL PEOPLE CALLING.
PLEASE!
ANYONE!
GET OUT OF THE ROAD!
LOOK OUT!
I CAN'T IGNORE THEM.

I CAN'T STOP.

MOVE!

HEY! GET OUT OF THE WAY!

SSCREEEEE

I STOP, AND PEOPLE DIE.

SSCREEEEE

AGHHHH!

AGHHHHH!

HEY, I NEED YOU TO STOP SCREAMING. PLEASE.

MY ARM!

WHAT?

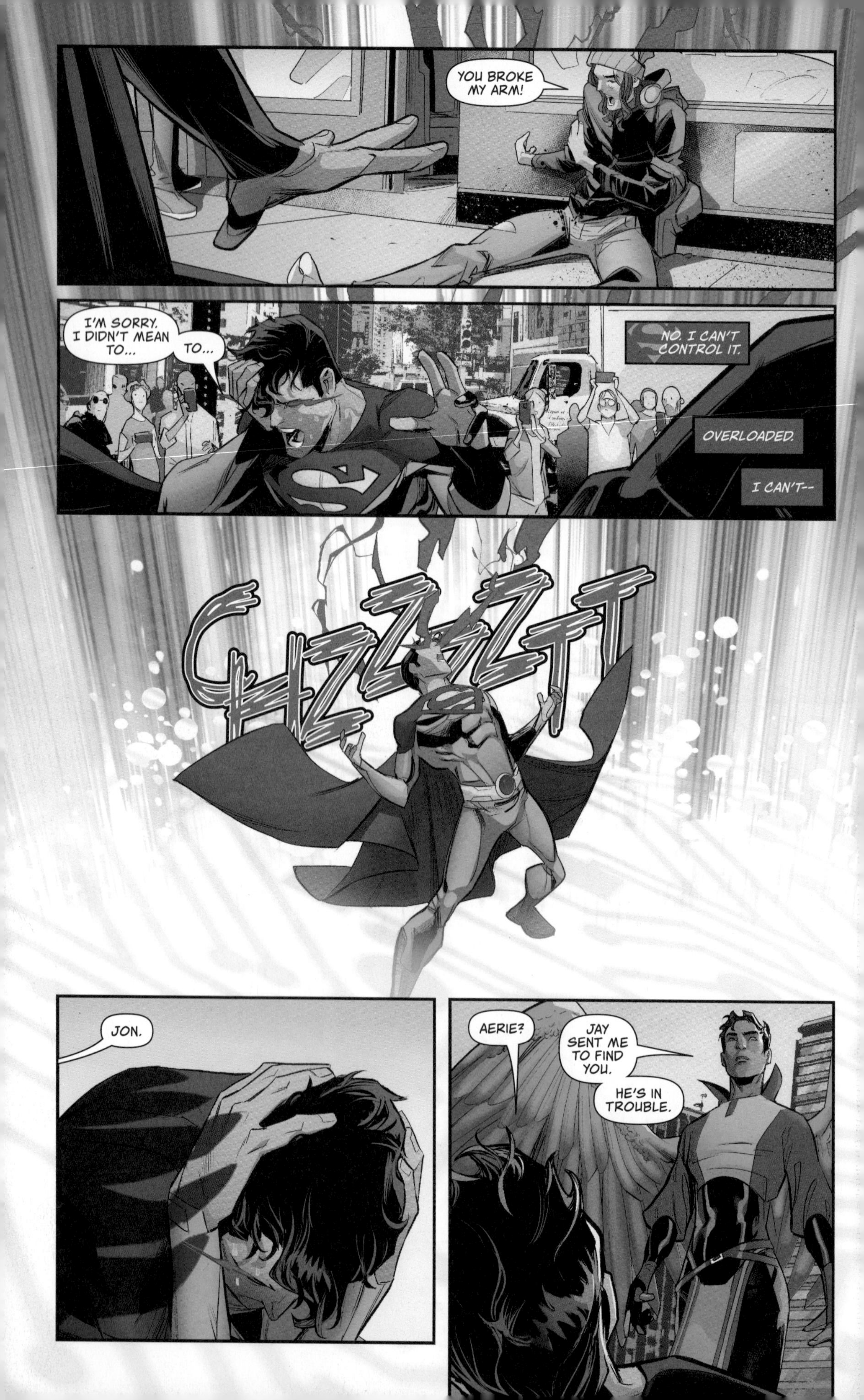
YOU BROKE MY ARM!
I'M SORRY. I DIDN'T MEAN TO...
TO...
NO. I CAN'T CONTROL IT.
OVERLOADED.
I CAN'T--
CHZZZZTT
JON.
AERIE?
JAY SENT ME TO FIND YOU.
HE'S IN TROUBLE.

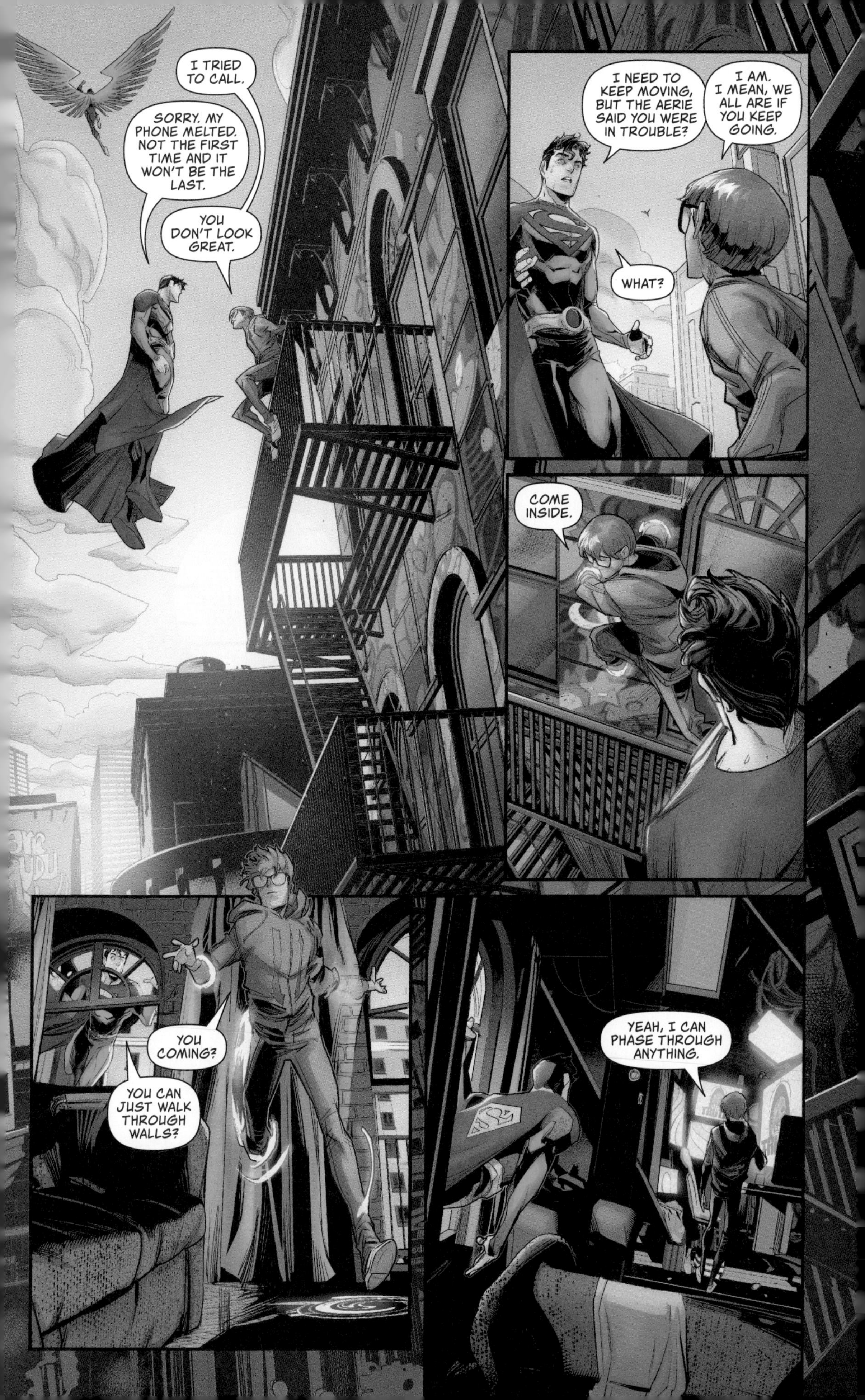
I TRIED TO CALL.
SORRY. MY PHONE MELTED. NOT THE FIRST TIME AND IT WON'T BE THE LAST.
YOU DON'T LOOK GREAT.
I NEED TO KEEP MOVING, BUT THE AERIE SAID YOU WERE IN TROUBLE?
I AM. I MEAN, WE ALL ARE IF YOU KEEP GOING.
WHAT?
COME INSIDE.
YOU COMING?
YOU CAN JUST WALK THROUGH WALLS?
YEAH, I CAN PHASE THROUGH ANYTHING.

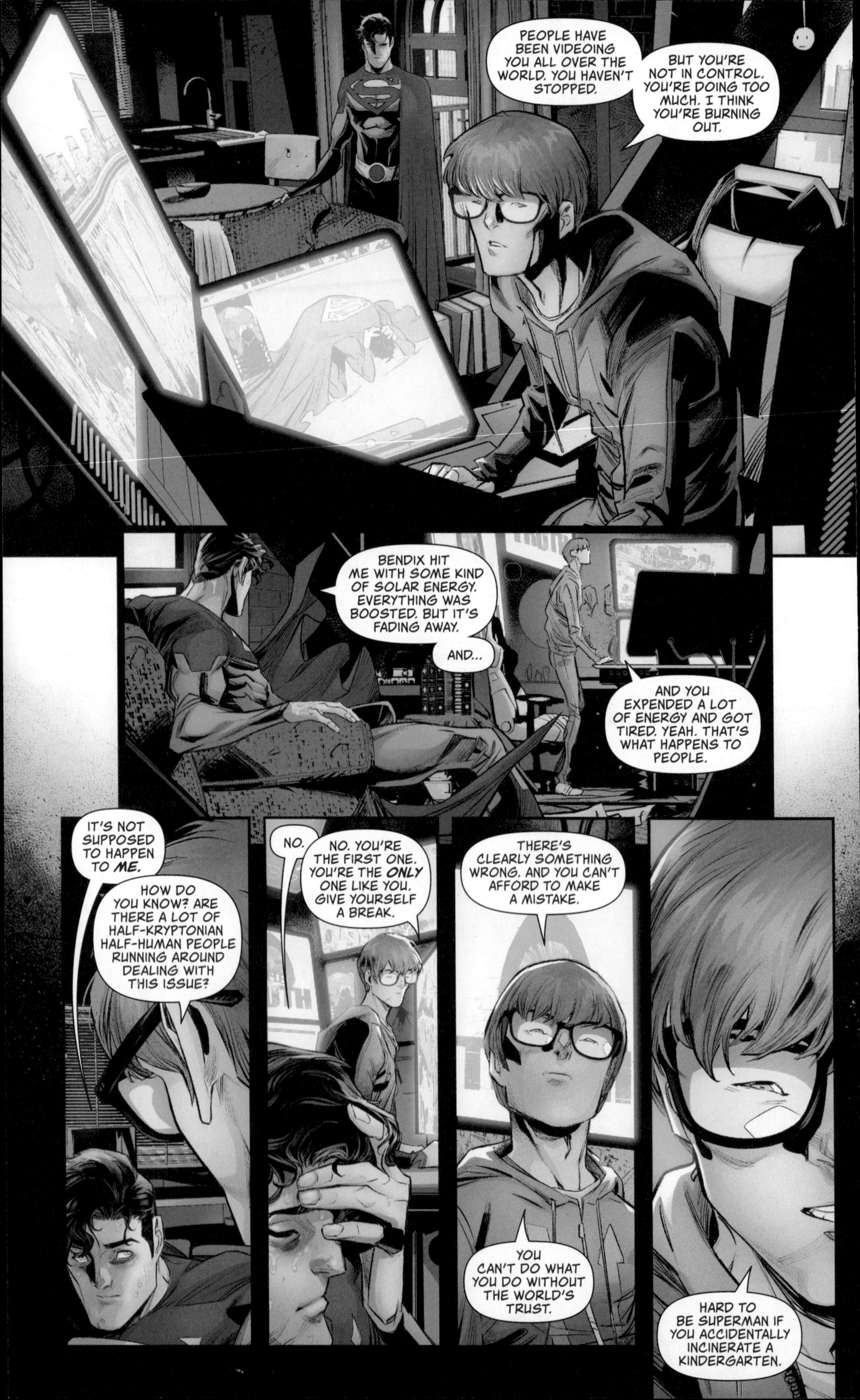
PEOPLE HAVE BEEN VIDEOING YOU ALL OVER THE WORLD. YOU HAVEN'T STOPPED.
BUT YOU'RE NOT IN CONTROL. YOU'RE DOING TOO MUCH. I THINK YOU'RE BURNING OUT.
BENDIX HIT ME WITH SOME KIND OF SOLAR ENERGY. EVERYTHING WAS BOOSTED. BUT IT'S FADING AWAY.
AND...
AND YOU EXPENDED A LOT OF ENERGY AND GOT TIRED. YEAH. THAT'S WHAT HAPPENS TO PEOPLE.
IT'S NOT SUPPOSED TO HAPPEN TO *ME.*
HOW DO YOU KNOW? ARE THERE A LOT OF HALF-KRYPTONIAN HALF-HUMAN PEOPLE RUNNING AROUND DEALING WITH THIS ISSUE?
NO.
NO. YOU'RE THE FIRST ONE. YOU'RE THE *ONLY* ONE LIKE YOU. GIVE YOURSELF A BREAK.
THERE'S CLEARLY SOMETHING WRONG. AND YOU CAN'T AFFORD TO MAKE A MISTAKE.
YOU CAN'T DO WHAT YOU DO WITHOUT THE WORLD'S TRUST.
HARD TO BE SUPERMAN IF YOU ACCIDENTALLY INCINERATE A KINDERGARTEN.

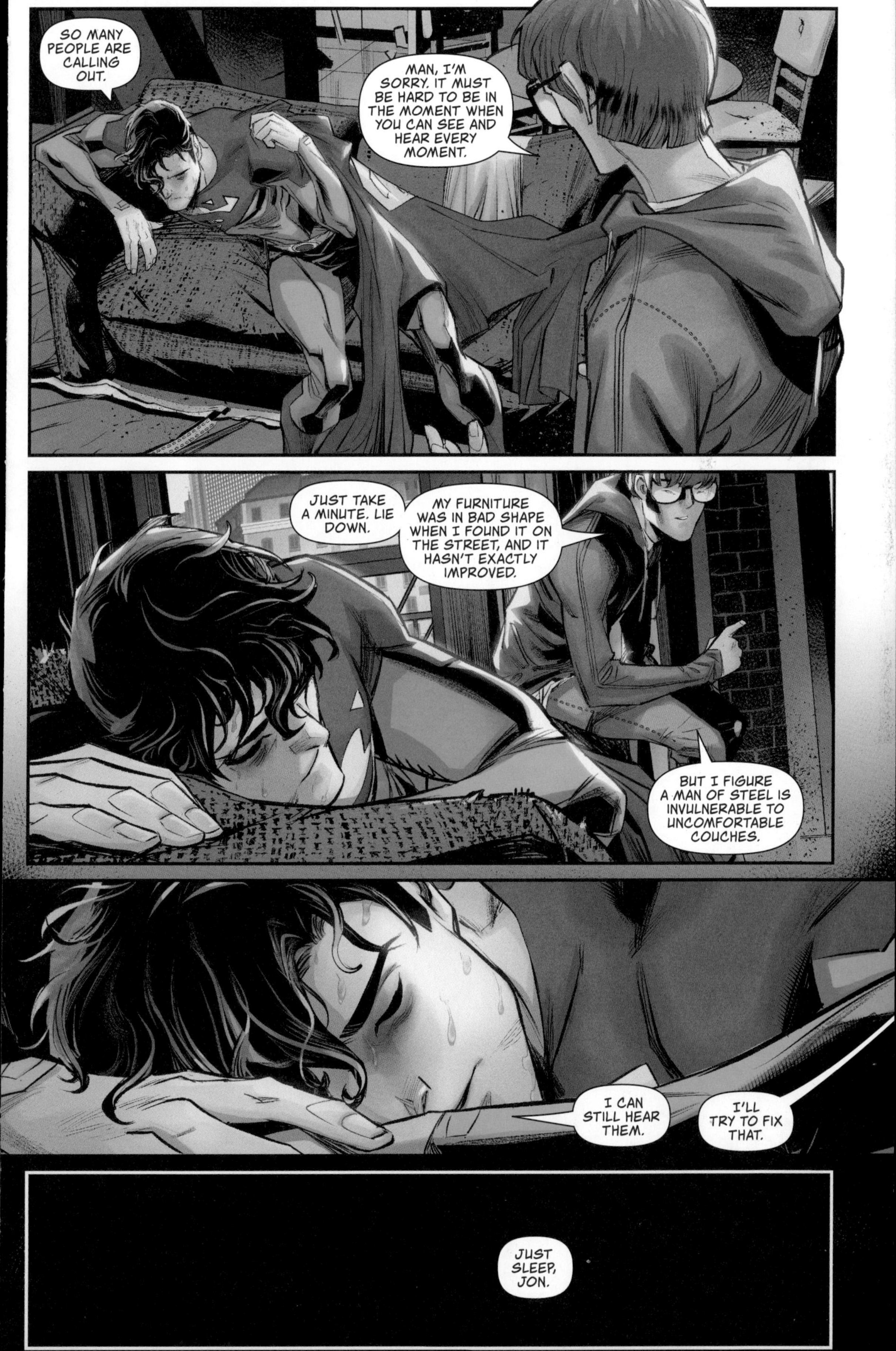
SO MANY PEOPLE ARE CALLING OUT.
MAN, I'M SORRY. IT MUST BE HARD TO BE IN THE MOMENT WHEN YOU CAN SEE AND HEAR EVERY MOMENT.
JUST TAKE A MINUTE. LIE DOWN.
MY FURNITURE WAS IN BAD SHAPE WHEN I FOUND IT ON THE STREET, AND IT HASN'T EXACTLY IMPROVED.
BUT I FIGURE A MAN OF STEEL IS INVULNERABLE TO UNCOMFORTABLE COUCHES.
I CAN STILL HEAR THEM.
I'LL TRY TO FIX THAT.
JUST SLEEP, JON.

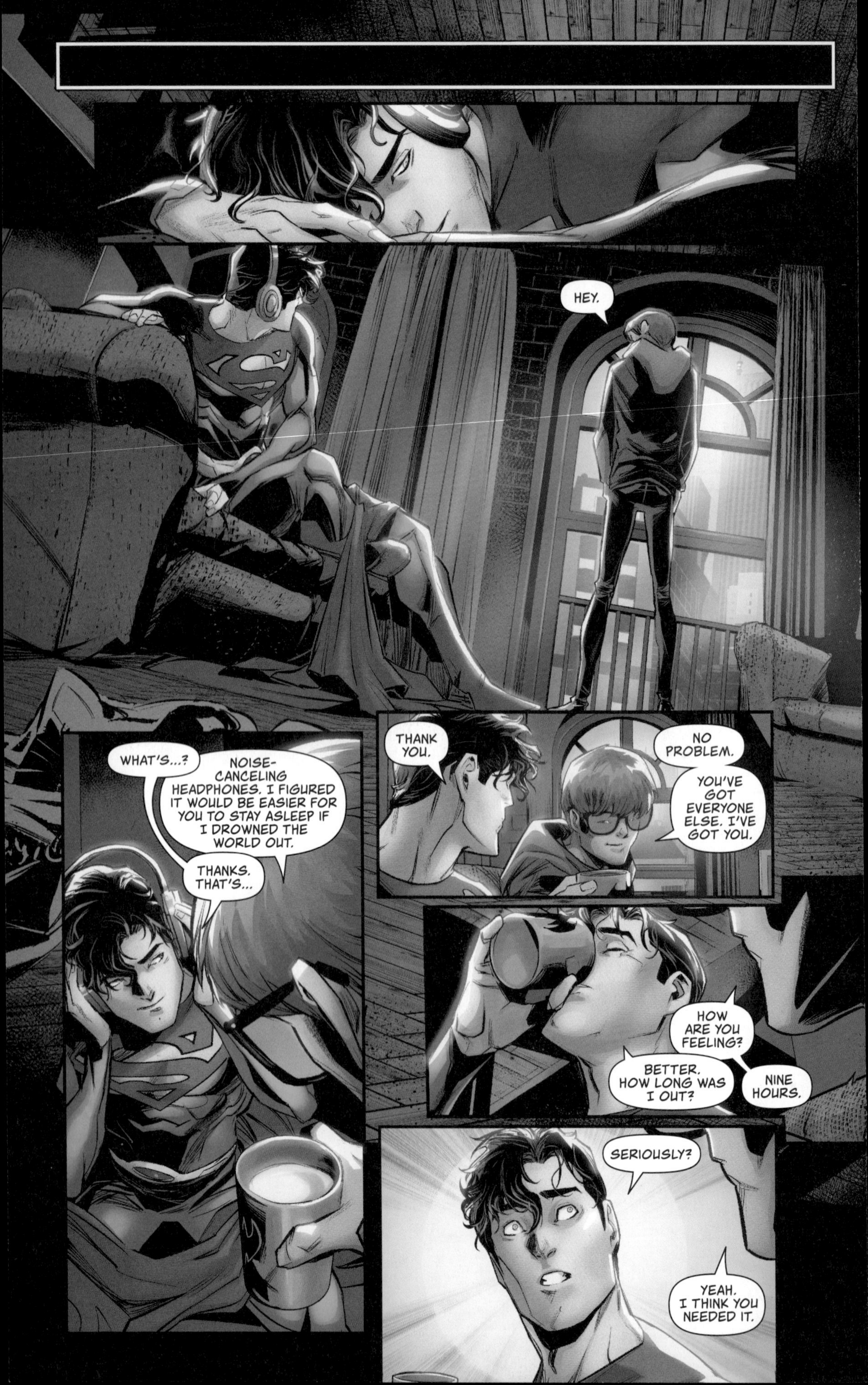
[redacted]
HEY.
WHAT'S...?
NOISE-CANCELING HEADPHONES. I FIGURED IT WOULD BE EASIER FOR YOU TO STAY ASLEEP IF I DROWNED THE WORLD OUT.
THANKS. THAT'S...
THANK YOU.
NO PROBLEM.
YOU'VE GOT EVERYONE ELSE. I'VE GOT YOU.
HOW ARE YOU FEELING?
BETTER. HOW LONG WAS I OUT?
NINE HOURS.
SERIOUSLY?
YEAH. I THINK YOU NEEDED IT.

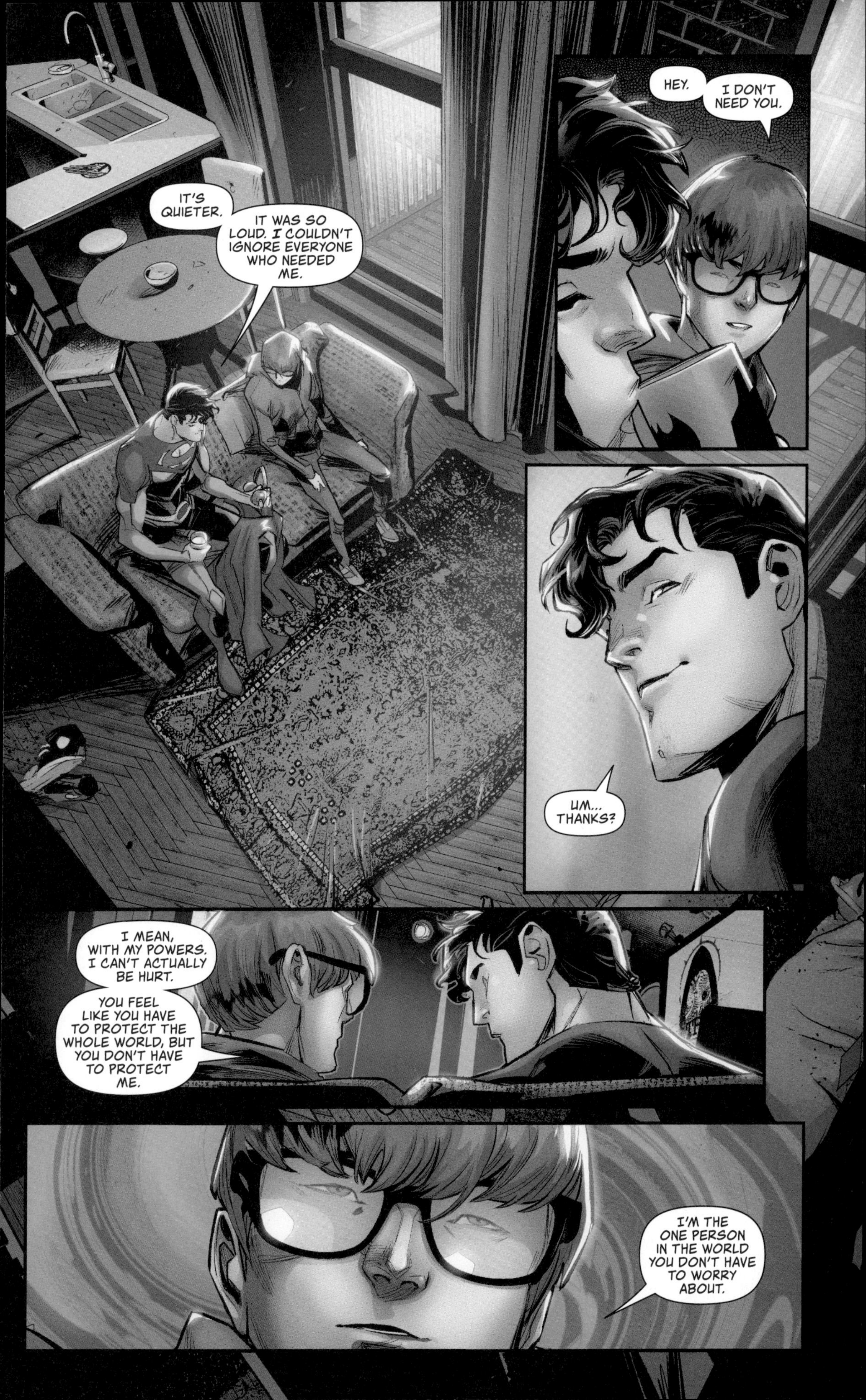
IT'S QUIETER.
IT WAS SO LOUD. I COULDN'T IGNORE EVERYONE WHO NEEDED ME.
HEY.
I DON'T NEED YOU.
UM... THANKS?
I MEAN, WITH MY POWERS. I CAN'T ACTUALLY BE HURT.
YOU FEEL LIKE YOU HAVE TO PROTECT THE WHOLE WORLD, BUT YOU DON'T HAVE TO PROTECT ME.
I'M THE ONE PERSON IN THE WORLD YOU DON'T HAVE TO WORRY ABOUT.

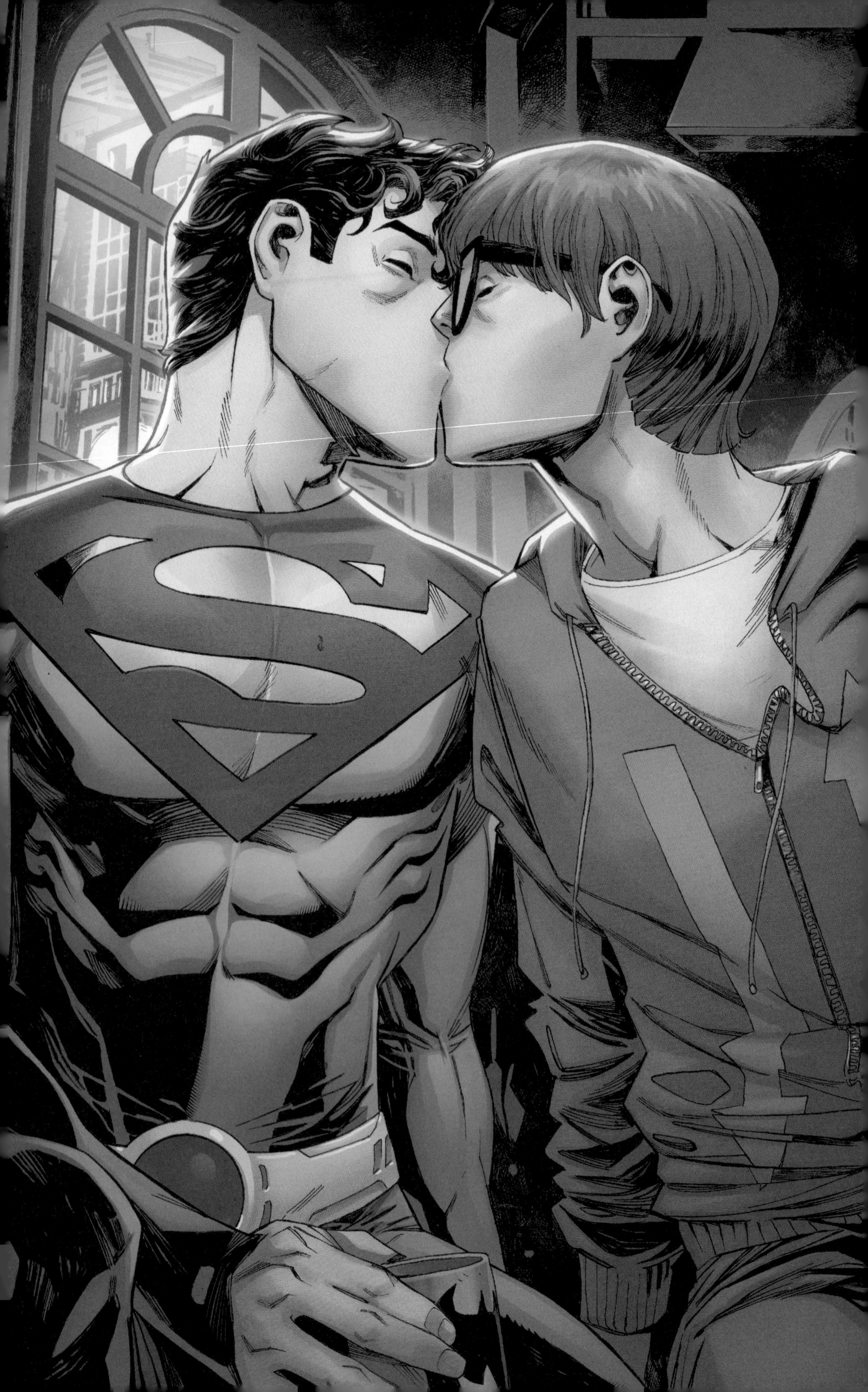

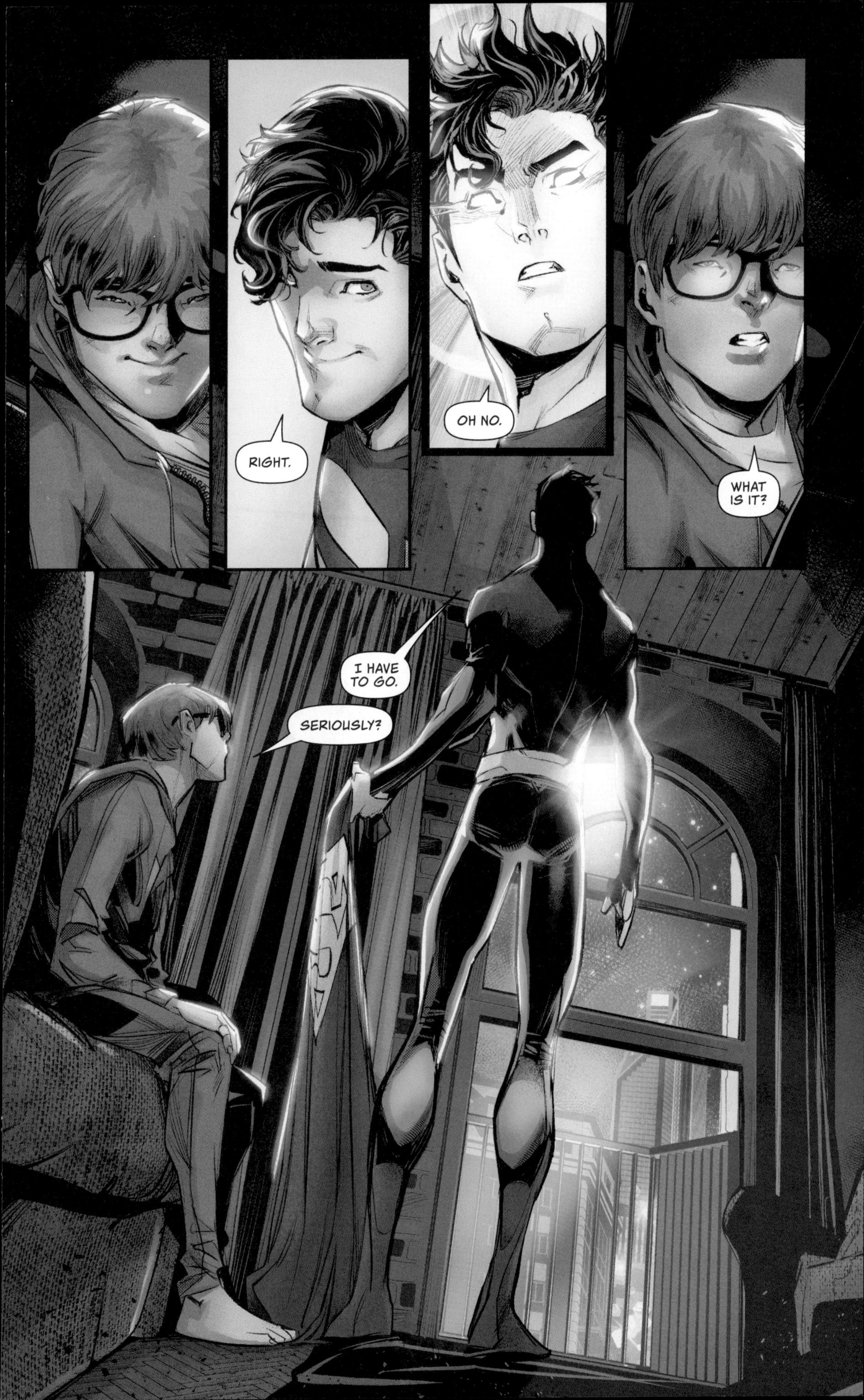
RIGHT.
OH NO.
WHAT IS IT?
I HAVE TO GO.
SERIOUSLY?

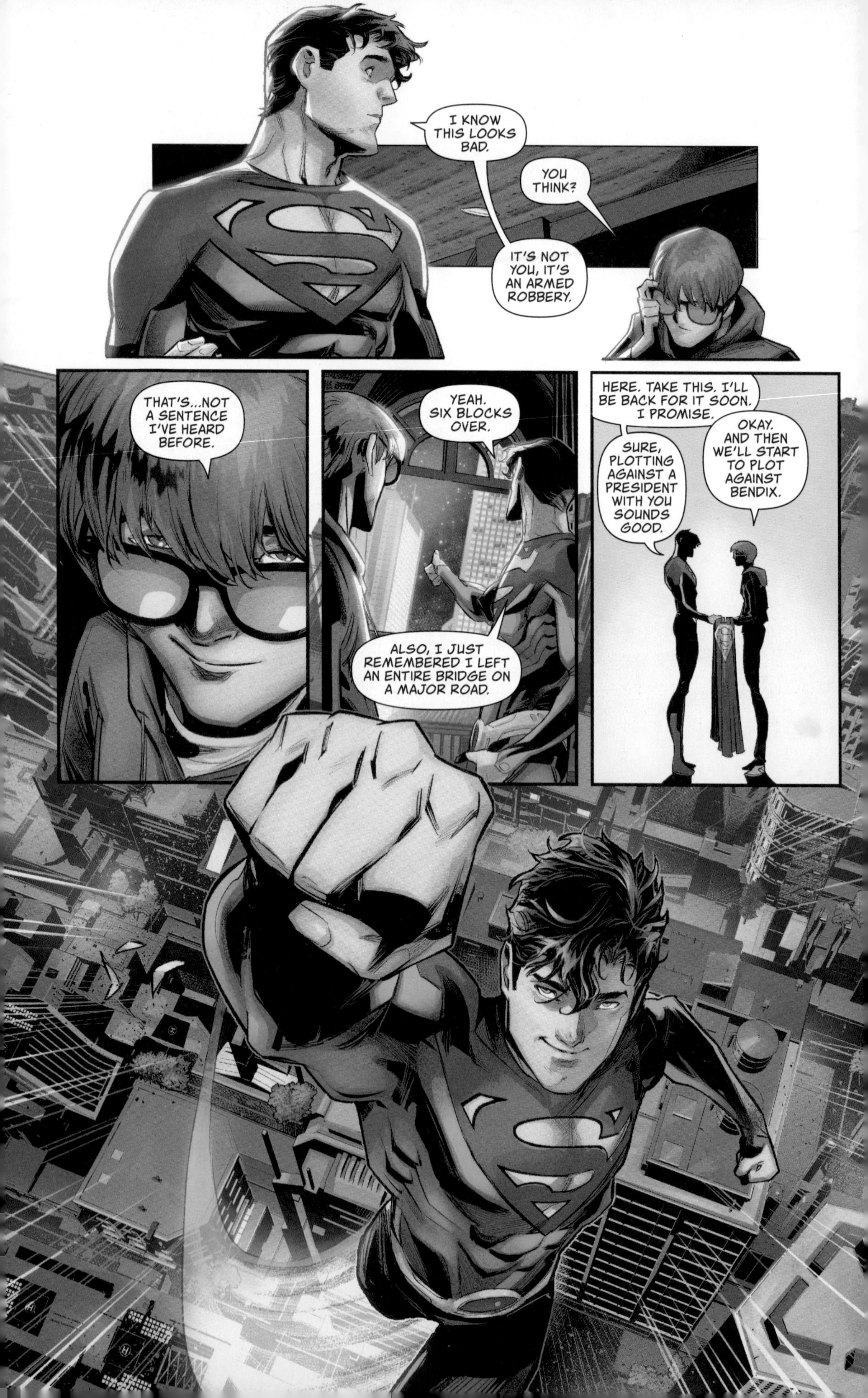
I KNOW THIS LOOKS BAD.
YOU THINK?
IT'S NOT YOU, IT'S AN ARMED ROBBERY.
THAT'S...NOT A SENTENCE I'VE HEARD BEFORE.
YEAH. SIX BLOCKS OVER.
ALSO, I JUST REMEMBERED I LEFT AN ENTIRE BRIDGE ON A MAJOR ROAD.
HERE. TAKE THIS. I'LL BE BACK FOR IT SOON. I PROMISE.
SURE, PLOTTING AGAINST A PRESIDENT WITH YOU SOUNDS GOOD.
OKAY. AND THEN WE'LL START TO PLOT AGAINST BENDIX.

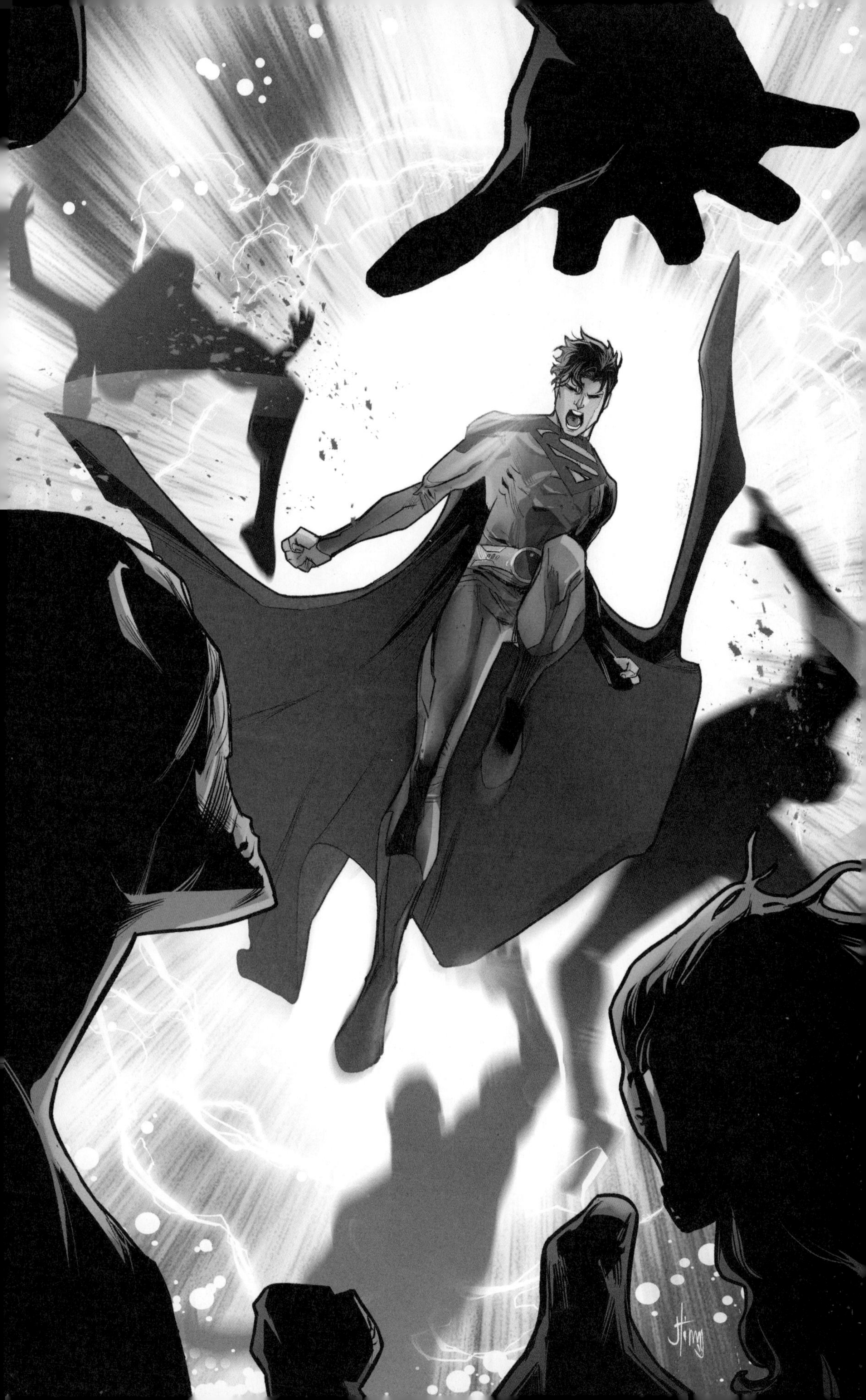

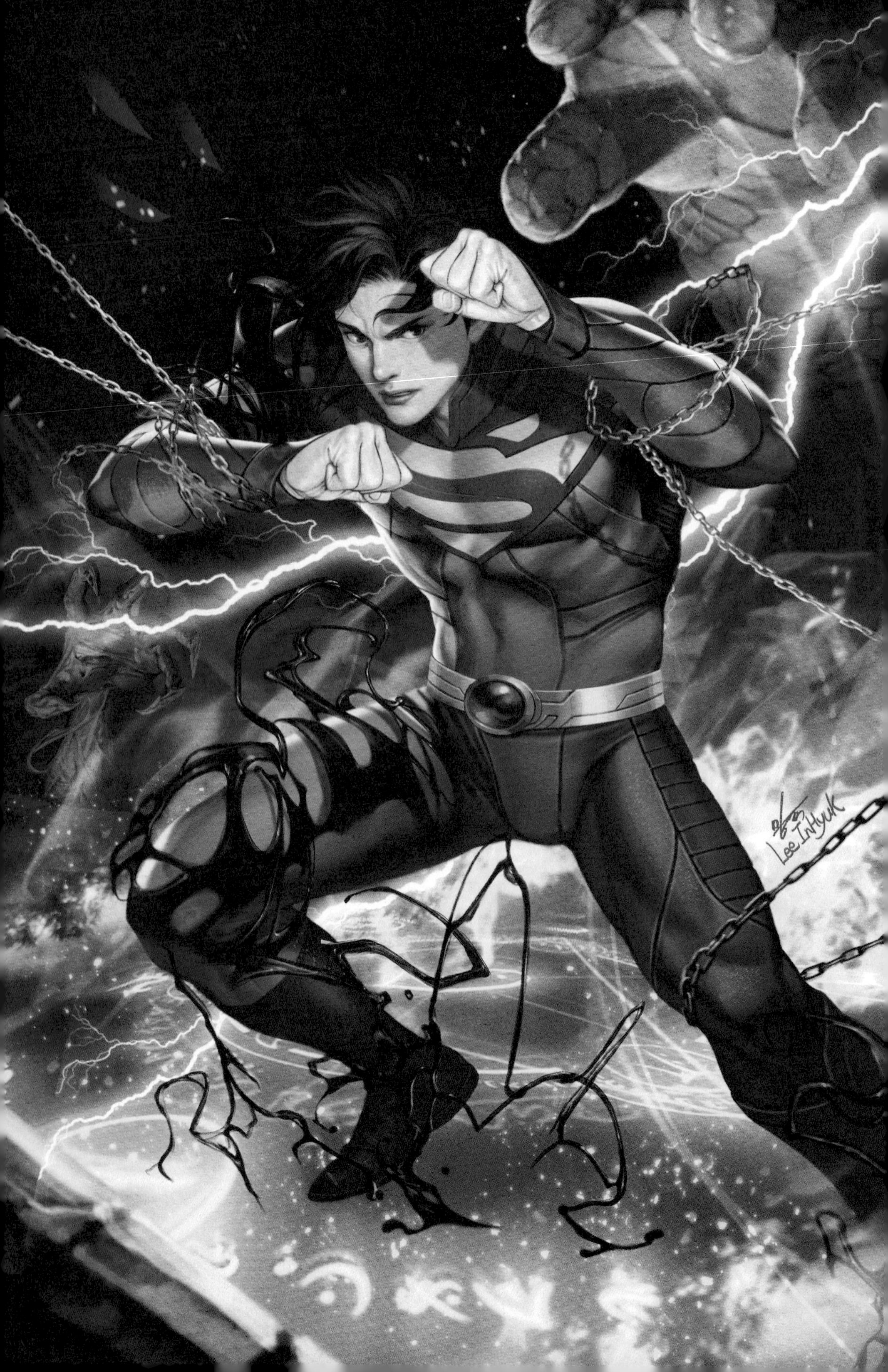
Lee InHyuk

Superman: Son of Kal-El #6 variant cover art by **INHYUK LEE**

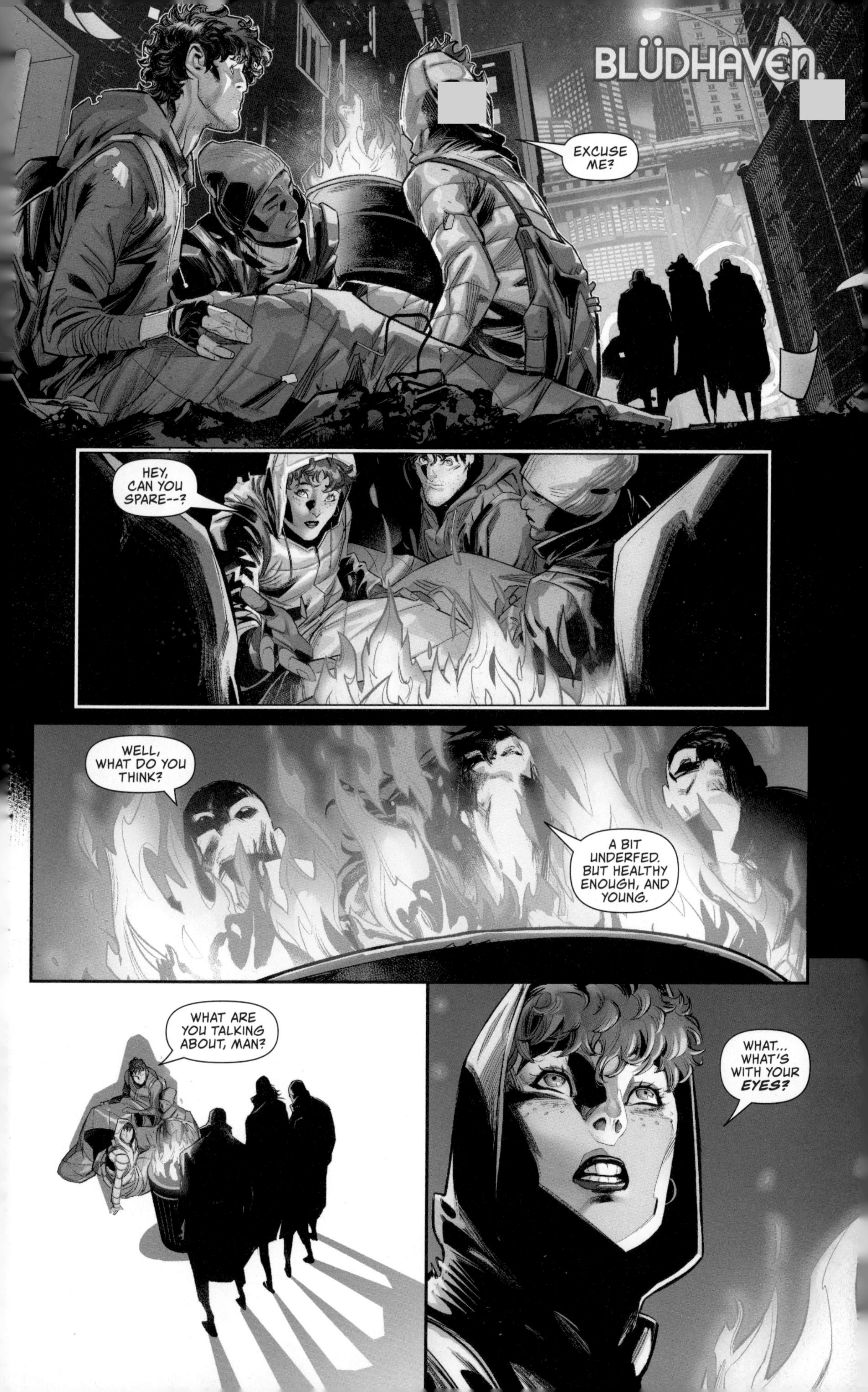
BLÜDHAVEN.
EXCUSE ME?
HEY, CAN YOU SPARE--?
WELL, WHAT DO YOU THINK?
A BIT UNDERFED. BUT HEALTHY ENOUGH, AND YOUNG.
WHAT ARE YOU TALKING ABOUT, MAN?
WHAT... WHAT'S WITH YOUR *EYES?*

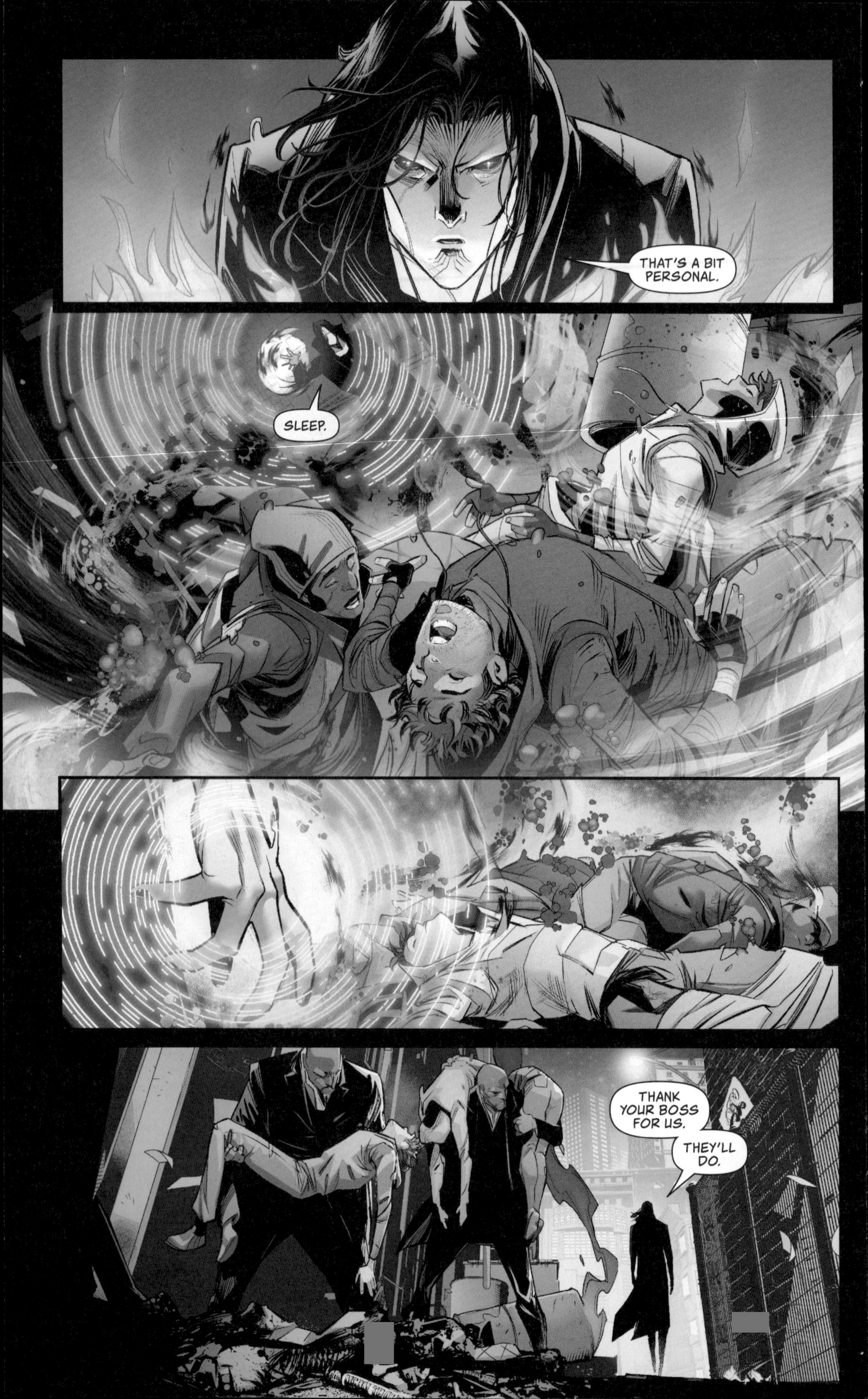
THAT'S A BIT PERSONAL.
SLEEP.
THANK YOUR BOSS FOR US.
THEY'LL DO.

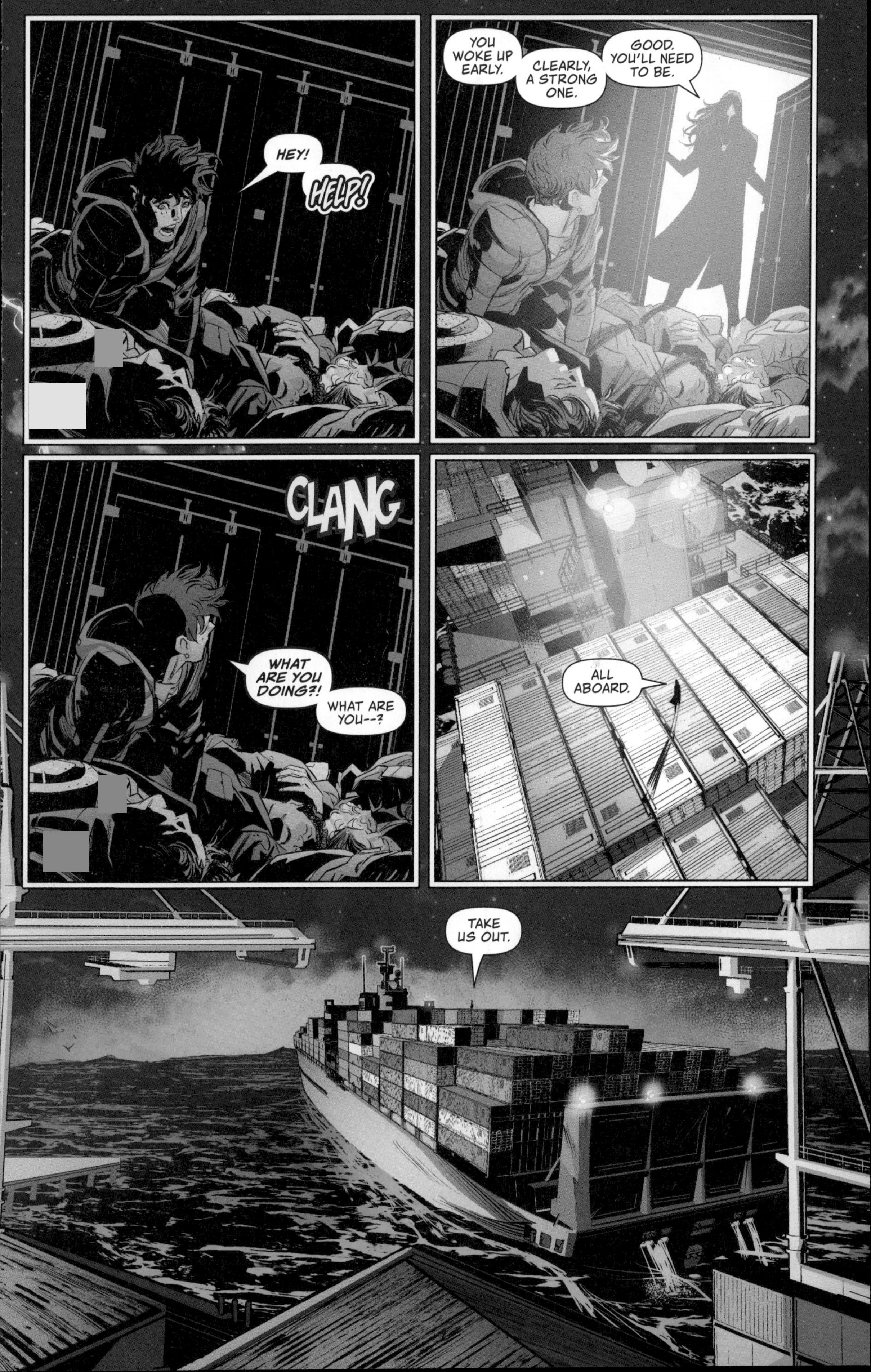
HEY!
HELP!
YOU WOKE UP EARLY.
CLEARLY, A STRONG ONE.
GOOD. YOU'LL NEED TO BE.
CLANG
WHAT ARE YOU DOING?!
WHAT ARE YOU--?
ALL ABOARD.
TAKE US OUT.

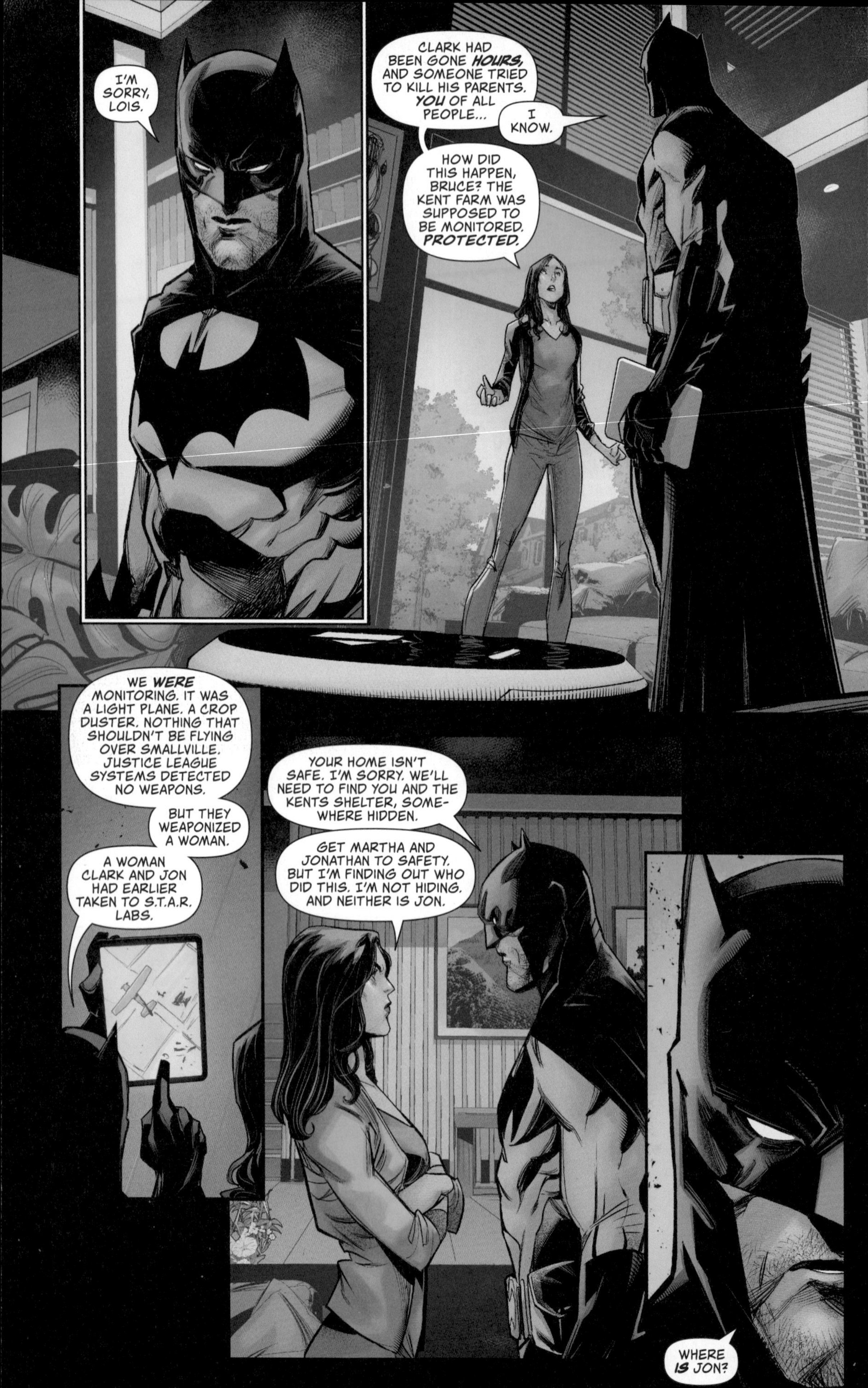
I'M SORRY, LOIS.
CLARK HAD BEEN GONE HOURS, AND SOMEONE TRIED TO KILL HIS PARENTS. YOU OF ALL PEOPLE...
I KNOW.
HOW DID THIS HAPPEN, BRUCE? THE KENT FARM WAS SUPPOSED TO BE MONITORED. PROTECTED.
WE WERE MONITORING. IT WAS A LIGHT PLANE. A CROP DUSTER. NOTHING THAT SHOULDN'T BE FLYING OVER SMALLVILLE. JUSTICE LEAGUE SYSTEMS DETECTED NO WEAPONS.
BUT THEY WEAPONIZED A WOMAN.
A WOMAN CLARK AND JON HAD EARLIER TAKEN TO S.T.A.R. LABS.
YOUR HOME ISN'T SAFE. I'M SORRY. WE'LL NEED TO FIND YOU AND THE KENTS SHELTER, SOMEWHERE HIDDEN.
GET MARTHA AND JONATHAN TO SAFETY. BUT I'M FINDING OUT WHO DID THIS. I'M NOT HIDING. AND NEITHER IS JON.
WHERE IS JON?

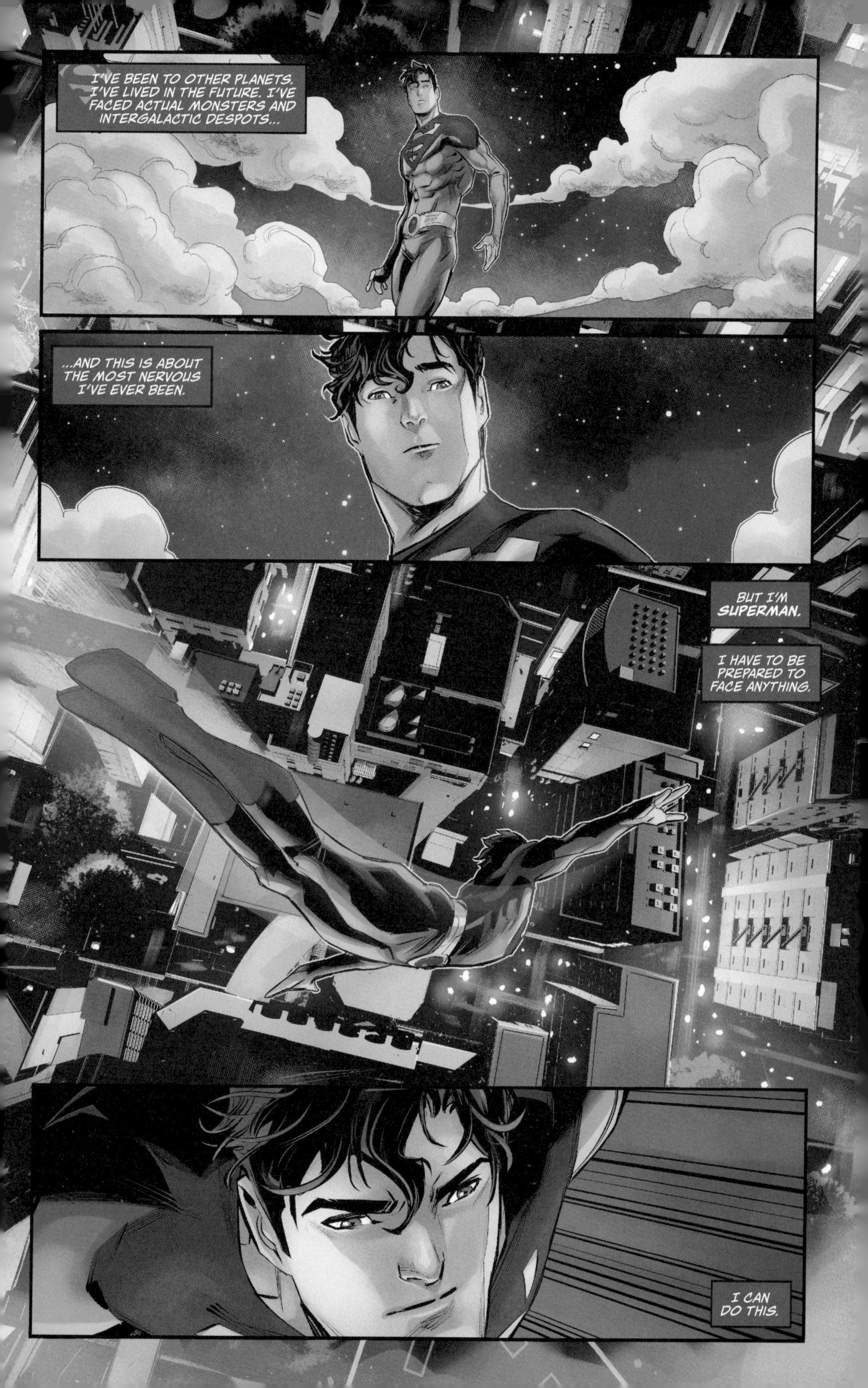
I'VE BEEN TO OTHER PLANETS. I'VE LIVED IN THE FUTURE. I'VE FACED ACTUAL MONSTERS AND INTERGALACTIC DESPOTS...
...AND THIS IS ABOUT THE MOST NERVOUS I'VE EVER BEEN.
BUT I'M **SUPERMAN.**
I HAVE TO BE PREPARED TO FACE ANYTHING.
I CAN DO THIS.

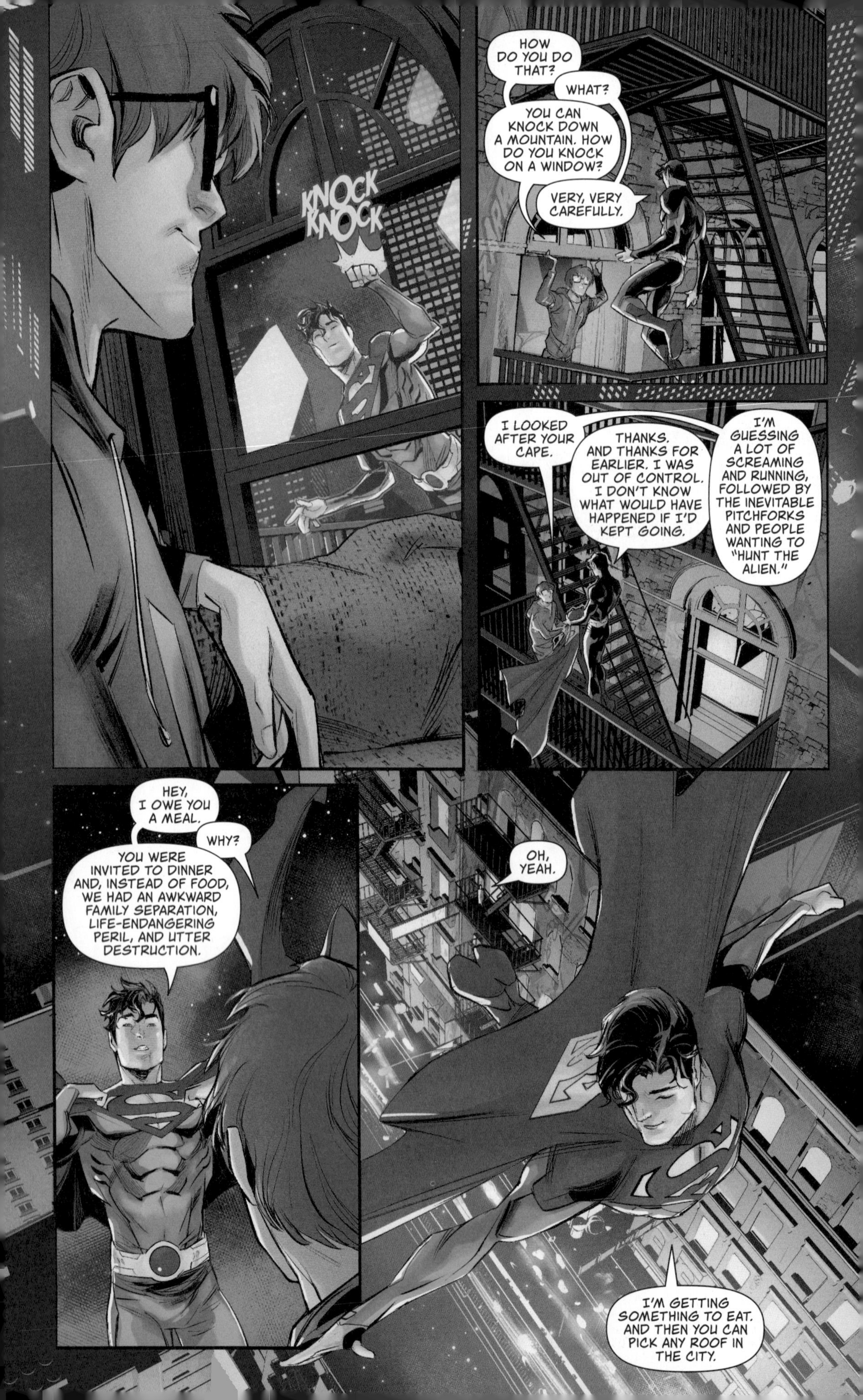
KNOCK KNOCK
HOW DO YOU DO THAT?
WHAT?
YOU CAN KNOCK DOWN A MOUNTAIN. HOW DO YOU KNOCK ON A WINDOW?
VERY, VERY CAREFULLY.
I LOOKED AFTER YOUR CAPE.
THANKS. AND THANKS FOR EARLIER. I WAS OUT OF CONTROL. I DON'T KNOW WHAT WOULD HAVE HAPPENED IF I'D KEPT GOING.
I'M GUESSING A LOT OF SCREAMING AND RUNNING, FOLLOWED BY THE INEVITABLE PITCHFORKS AND PEOPLE WANTING TO "HUNT THE ALIEN."
HEY, I OWE YOU A MEAL.
WHY?
YOU WERE INVITED TO DINNER AND, INSTEAD OF FOOD, WE HAD AN AWKWARD FAMILY SEPARATION, LIFE-ENDANGERING PERIL, AND UTTER DESTRUCTION.
OH, YEAH.
I'M GETTING SOMETHING TO EAT. AND THEN YOU CAN PICK ANY ROOF IN THE CITY.

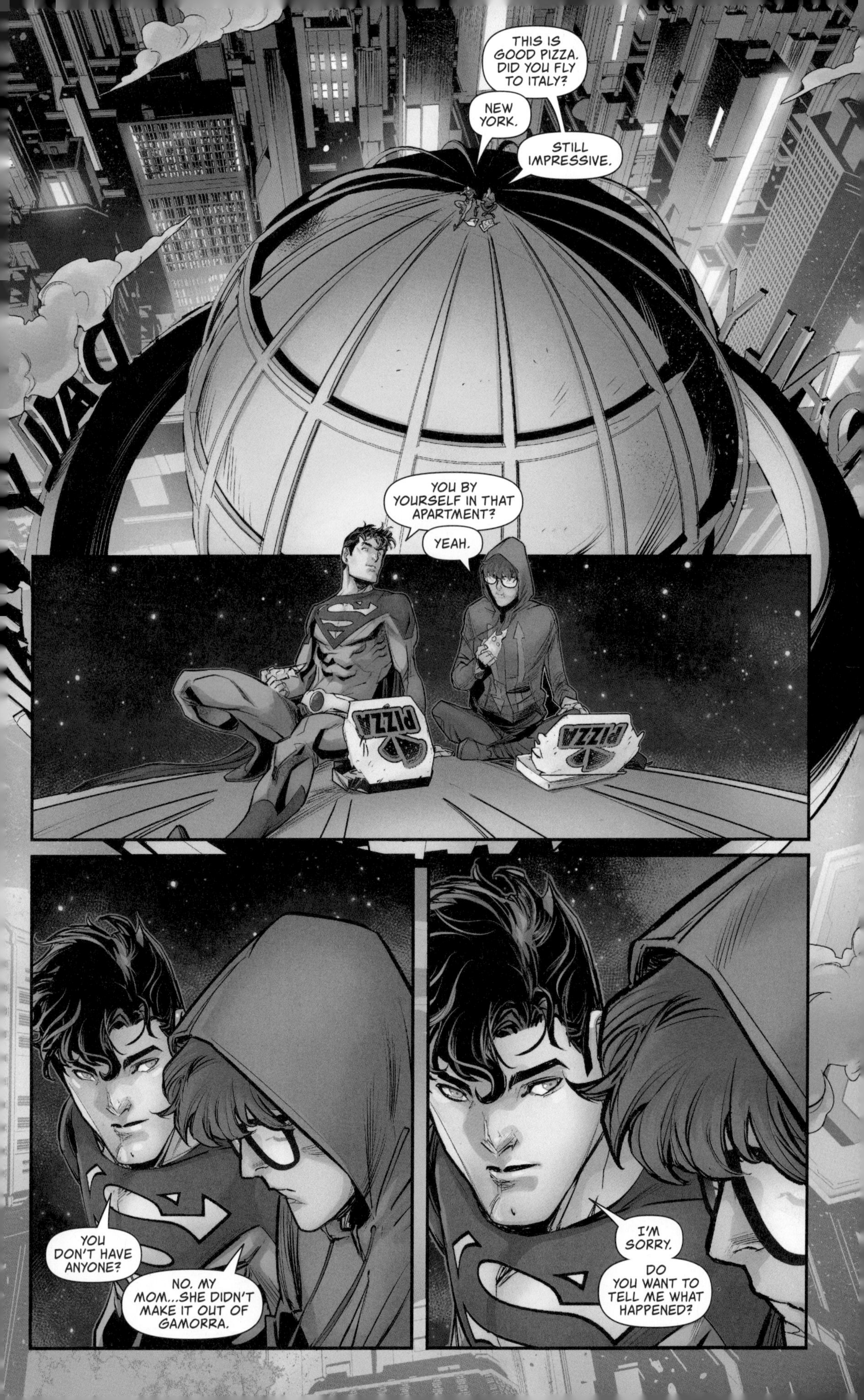
THIS IS GOOD PIZZA. DID YOU FLY TO ITALY?
NEW YORK.
STILL IMPRESSIVE.
YOU BY YOURSELF IN THAT APARTMENT?
YEAH.
PIZZA
PIZZA
YOU DON'T HAVE ANYONE?
NO. MY MOM...SHE DIDN'T MAKE IT OUT OF GAMORRA.
I'M SORRY.
DO YOU WANT TO TELL ME WHAT HAPPENED?

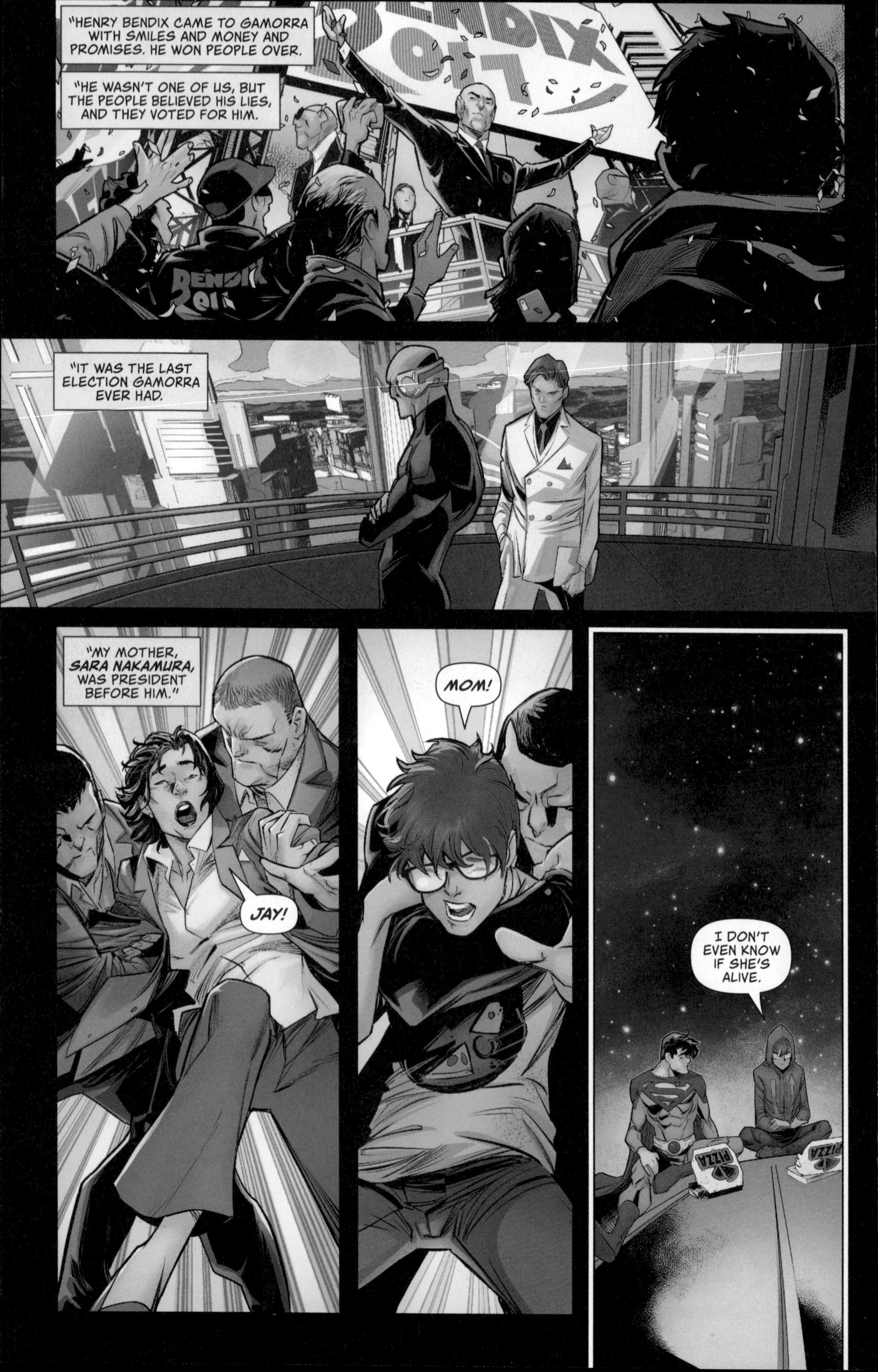
"HENRY BENDIX CAME TO GAMORRA WITH SMILES AND MONEY AND PROMISES. HE WON PEOPLE OVER.
"HE WASN'T ONE OF US, BUT THE PEOPLE BELIEVED HIS LIES, AND THEY VOTED FOR HIM.
"IT WAS THE LAST ELECTION GAMORRA EVER HAD.
"MY MOTHER, *SARA NAKAMURA*, WAS PRESIDENT BEFORE HIM."
JAY!
MOM!
I DON'T EVEN KNOW IF SHE'S ALIVE.
PIZZA
PIZZA

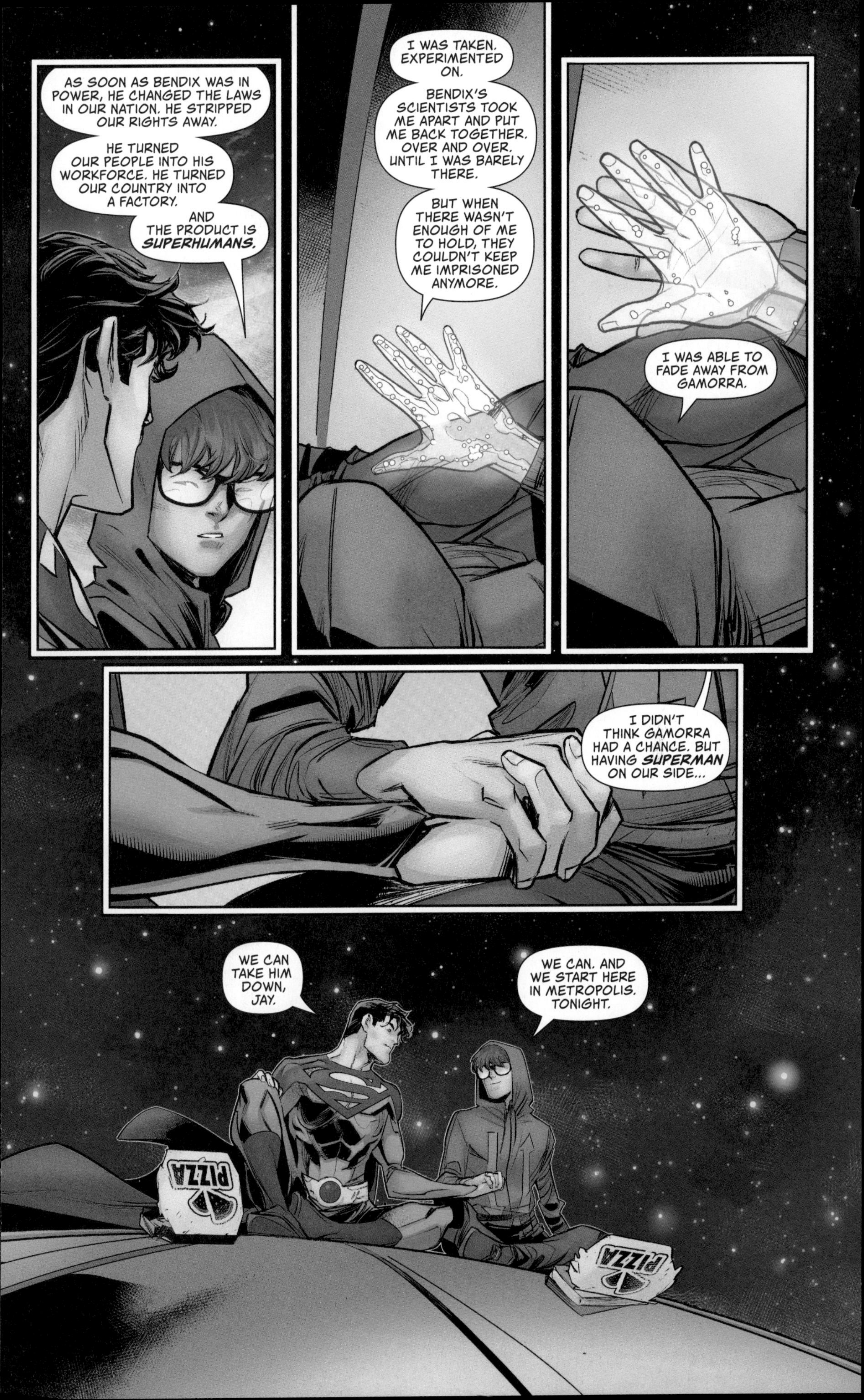
AS SOON AS BENDIX WAS IN POWER, HE CHANGED THE LAWS IN OUR NATION. HE STRIPPED OUR RIGHTS AWAY.
HE TURNED OUR PEOPLE INTO HIS WORKFORCE. HE TURNED OUR COUNTRY INTO A FACTORY.
AND THE PRODUCT IS *SUPERHUMANS.*
I WAS TAKEN. EXPERIMENTED ON.
BENDIX'S SCIENTISTS TOOK ME APART AND PUT ME BACK TOGETHER. OVER AND OVER. UNTIL I WAS BARELY THERE.
BUT WHEN THERE WASN'T ENOUGH OF ME TO HOLD, THEY COULDN'T KEEP ME IMPRISONED ANYMORE.
I WAS ABLE TO FADE AWAY FROM GAMORRA.
I DIDN'T THINK GAMORRA HAD A CHANCE. BUT HAVING *SUPERMAN* ON OUR SIDE...
WE CAN TAKE HIM DOWN, JAY.
WE CAN. AND WE START HERE IN METROPOLIS. TONIGHT.
PIZZA
PIZZA

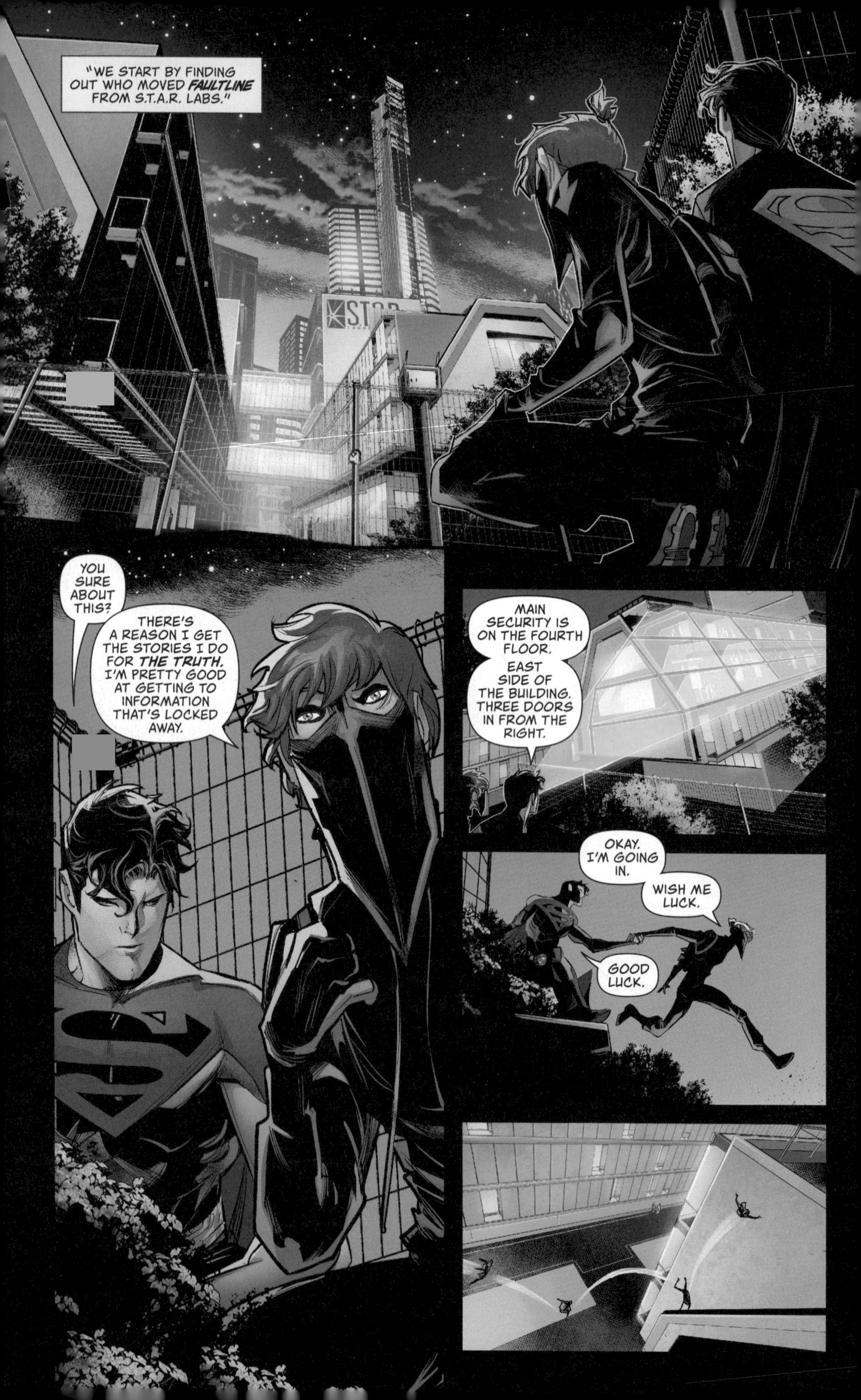
"WE START BY FINDING OUT WHO MOVED *FAULTLINE* FROM S.T.A.R. LABS."
YOU SURE ABOUT THIS?
THERE'S A REASON I GET THE STORIES I DO FOR *THE TRUTH.* I'M PRETTY GOOD AT GETTING TO INFORMATION THAT'S LOCKED AWAY.
MAIN SECURITY IS ON THE FOURTH FLOOR.
EAST SIDE OF THE BUILDING. THREE DOORS IN FROM THE RIGHT.
OKAY. I'M GOING IN.
WISH ME LUCK.
GOOD LUCK.

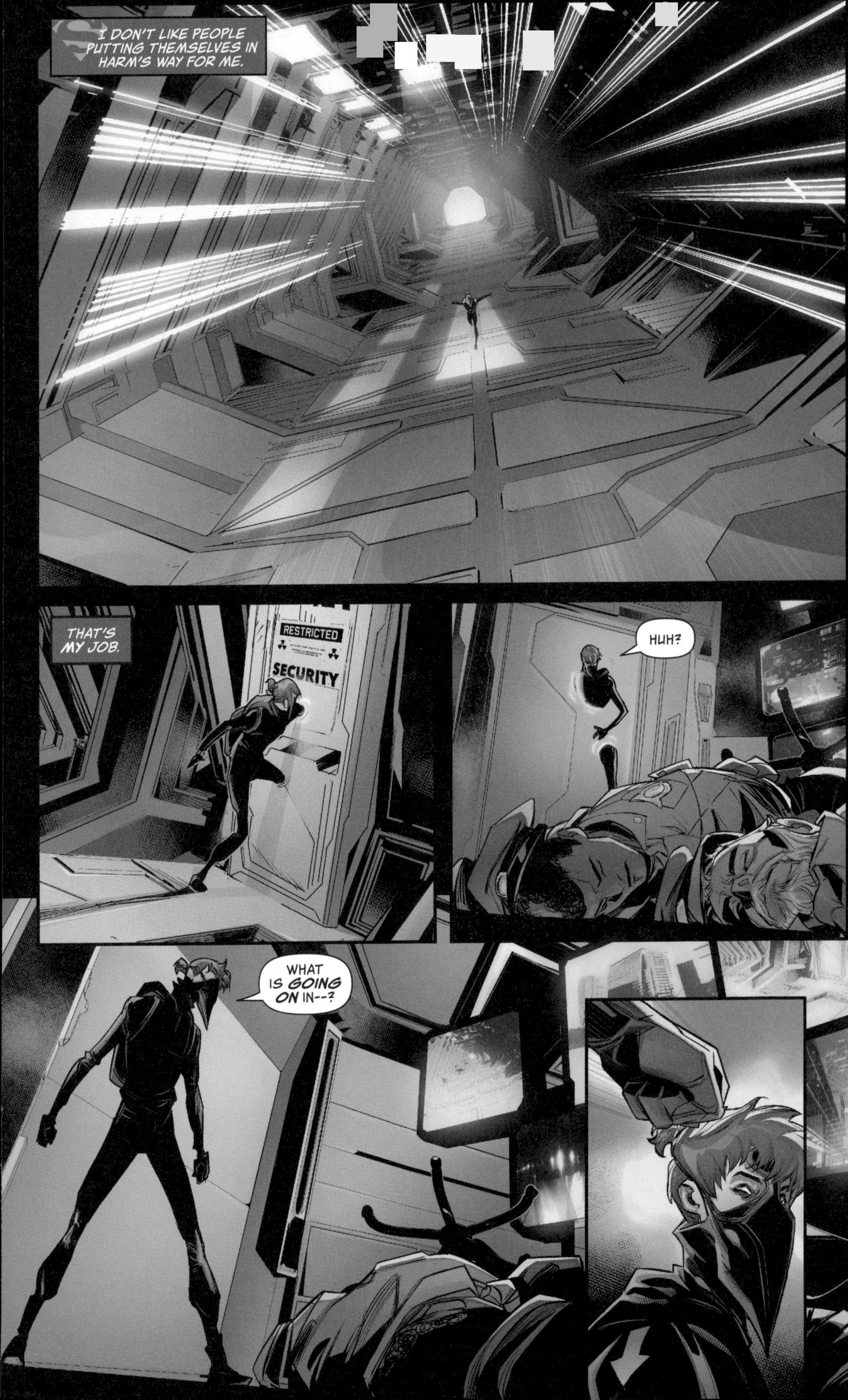
I DON'T LIKE PEOPLE PUTTING THEMSELVES IN HARM'S WAY FOR ME.
THAT'S MY JOB.
RESTRICTED
SECURITY
HUH?
WHAT IS GOING ON IN--?

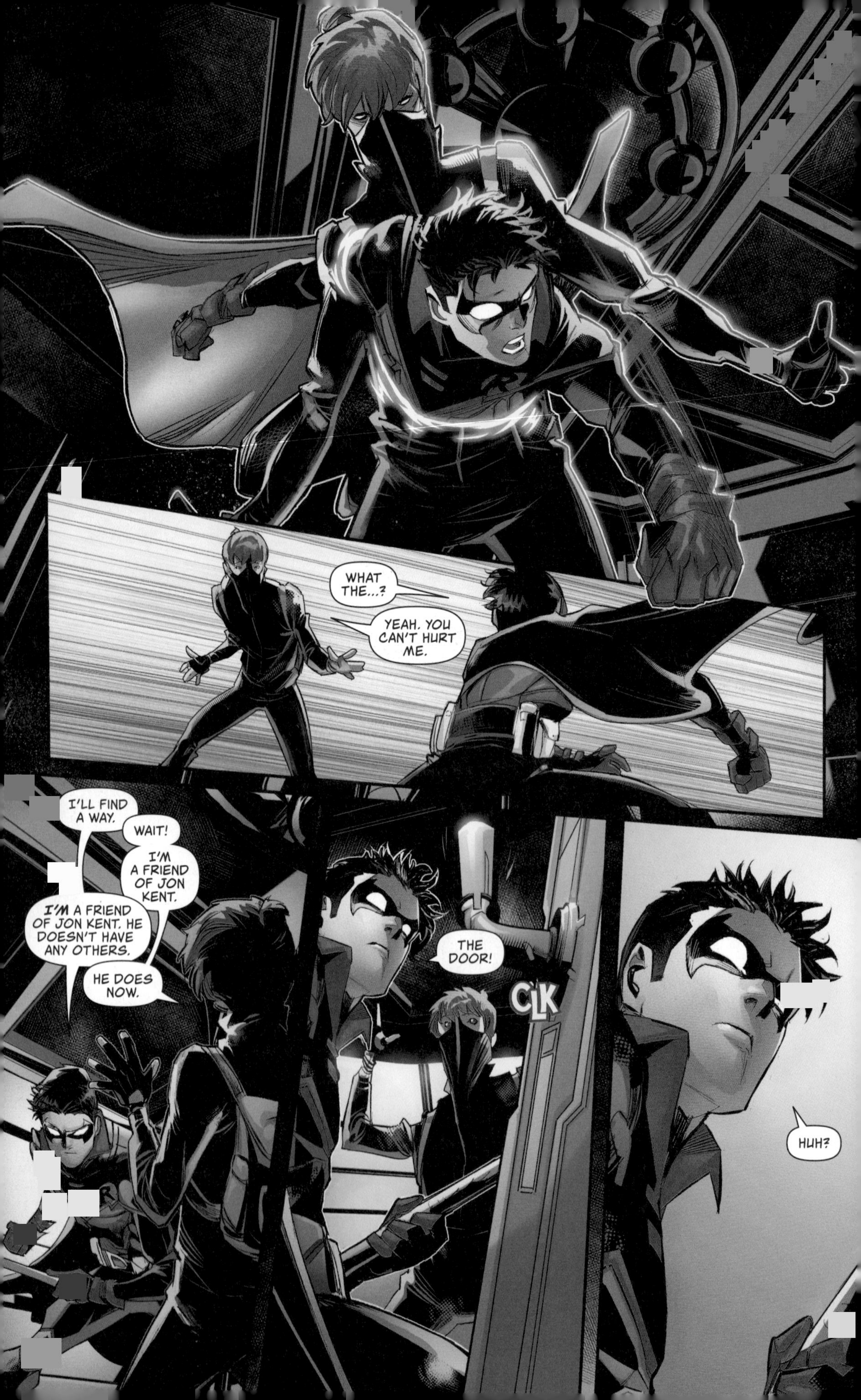
WHAT THE...?
YEAH. YOU CAN'T HURT ME.
I'LL FIND A WAY.
WAIT!
I'M A FRIEND OF JON KENT.
I'M A FRIEND OF JON KENT. HE DOESN'T HAVE ANY OTHERS.
HE DOES NOW.
THE DOOR!
CLK
HUH?

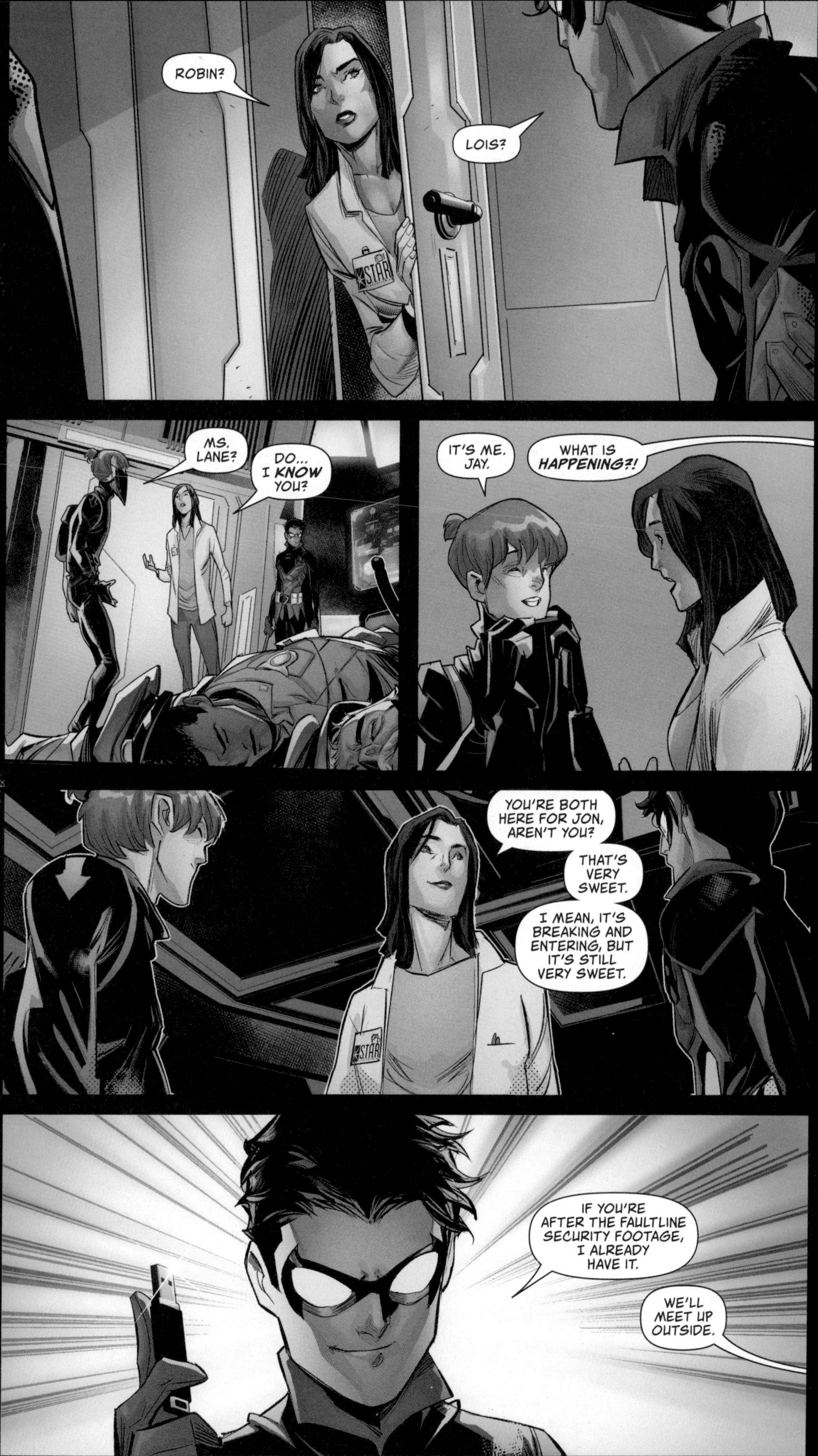
ROBIN?
LOIS?
MS. LANE?
DO... I **KNOW** YOU?
IT'S ME. JAY.
WHAT IS **HAPPENING?!**
YOU'RE BOTH HERE FOR JON, AREN'T YOU?
THAT'S VERY SWEET.
I MEAN, IT'S BREAKING AND ENTERING, BUT IT'S STILL VERY SWEET.
IF YOU'RE AFTER THE FAULTLINE SECURITY FOOTAGE, I ALREADY HAVE IT.
WE'LL MEET UP OUTSIDE.

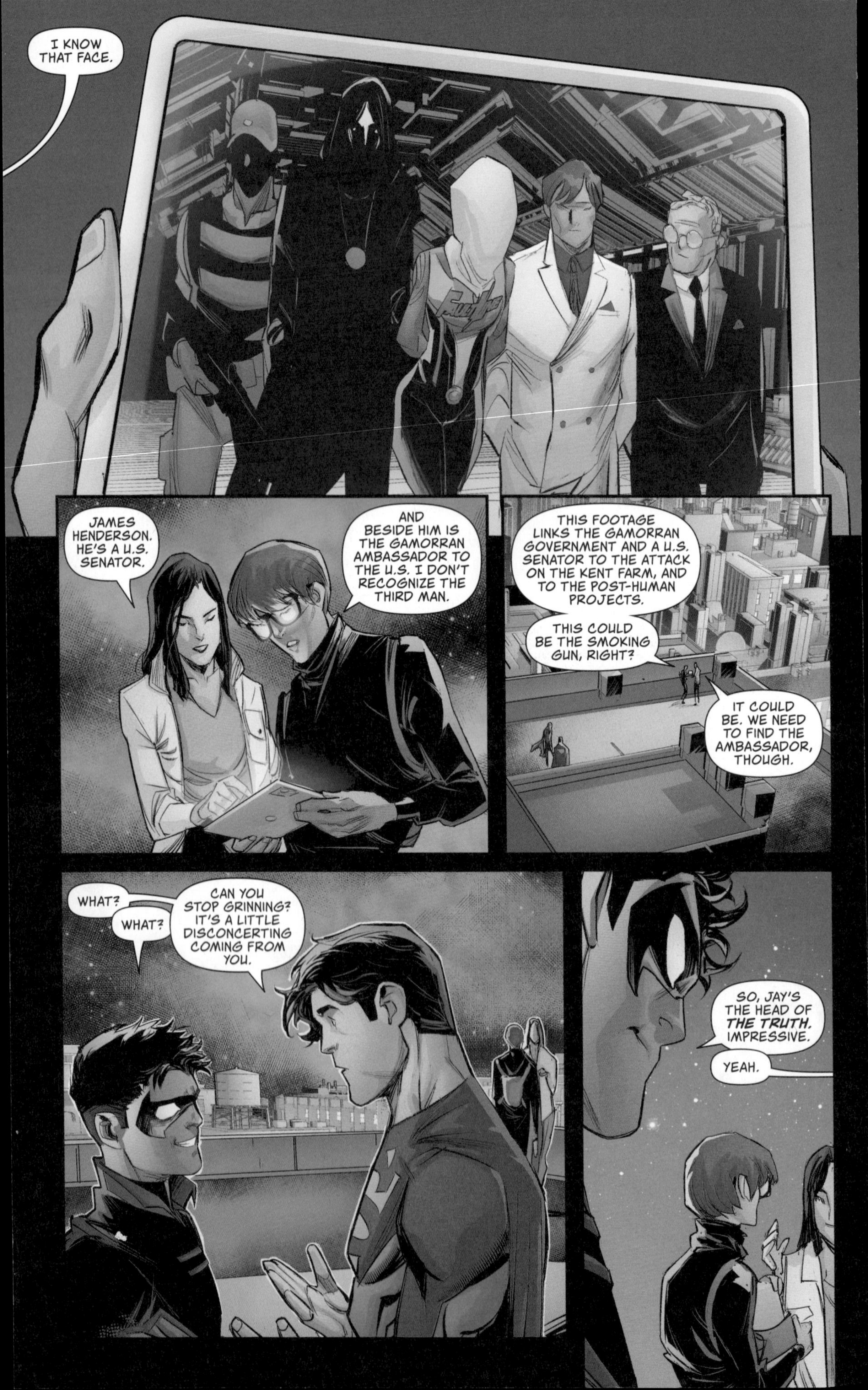
I KNOW THAT FACE.
JAMES HENDERSON. HE'S A U.S. SENATOR.
AND BESIDE HIM IS THE GAMORRAN AMBASSADOR TO THE U.S. I DON'T RECOGNIZE THE THIRD MAN.
THIS FOOTAGE LINKS THE GAMORRAN GOVERNMENT AND A U.S. SENATOR TO THE ATTACK ON THE KENT FARM, AND TO THE POST-HUMAN PROJECTS.
THIS COULD BE THE SMOKING GUN, RIGHT?
IT COULD BE. WE NEED TO FIND THE AMBASSADOR, THOUGH.
WHAT?
WHAT?
CAN YOU STOP GRINNING? IT'S A LITTLE DISCONCERTING COMING FROM YOU.
SO, JAY'S THE HEAD OF *THE TRUTH.* IMPRESSIVE.
YEAH.

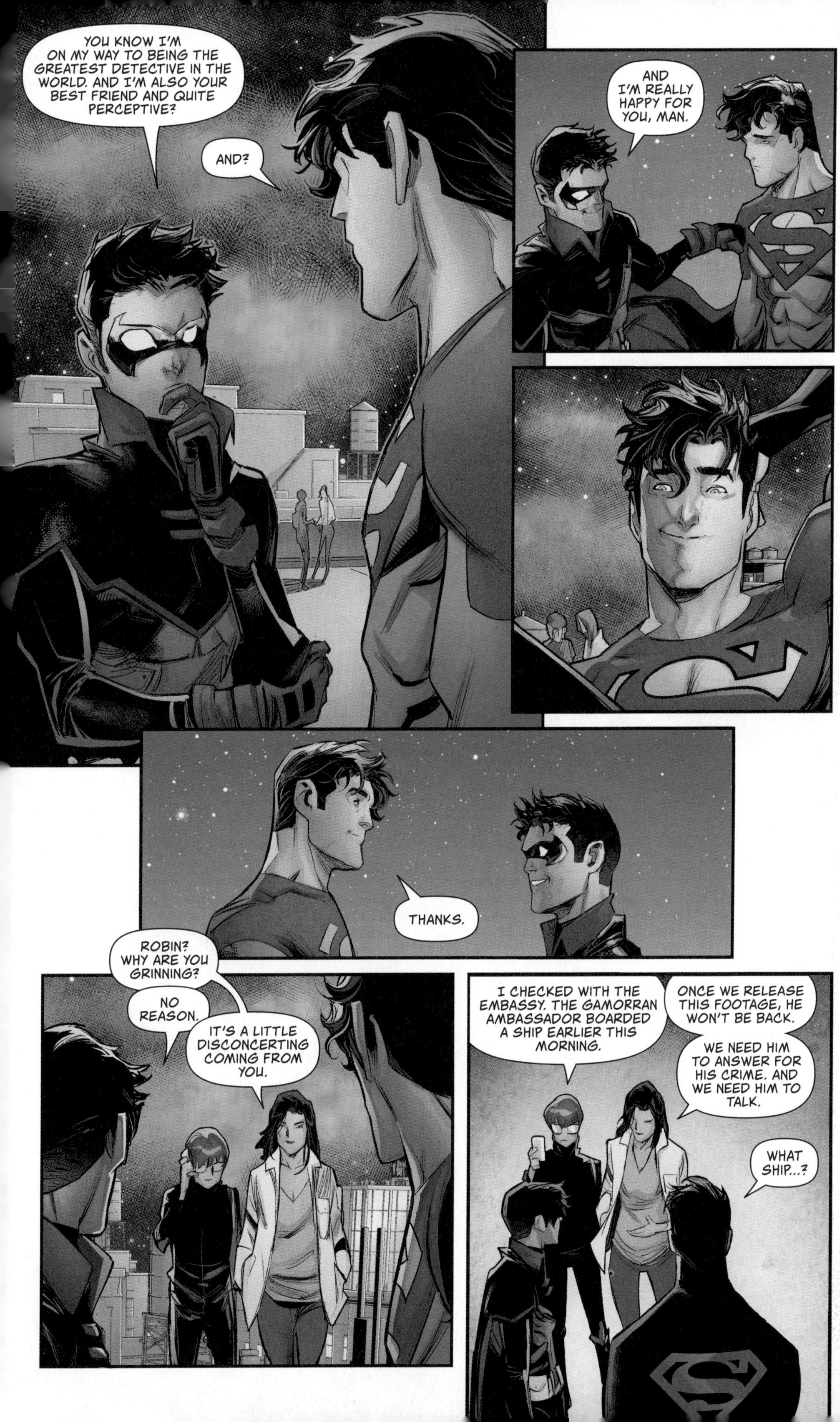
YOU KNOW I'M ON MY WAY TO BEING THE GREATEST DETECTIVE IN THE WORLD. AND I'M ALSO YOUR BEST FRIEND AND QUITE PERCEPTIVE?
AND?
AND I'M REALLY HAPPY FOR YOU, MAN.
THANKS.
ROBIN? WHY ARE YOU GRINNING?
NO REASON.
IT'S A LITTLE DISCONCERTING COMING FROM YOU.
I CHECKED WITH THE EMBASSY. THE GAMORRAN AMBASSADOR BOARDED A SHIP EARLIER THIS MORNING.
ONCE WE RELEASE THIS FOOTAGE, HE WON'T BE BACK.
WE NEED HIM TO ANSWER FOR HIS CRIME. AND WE NEED HIM TO TALK.
WHAT SHIP...?

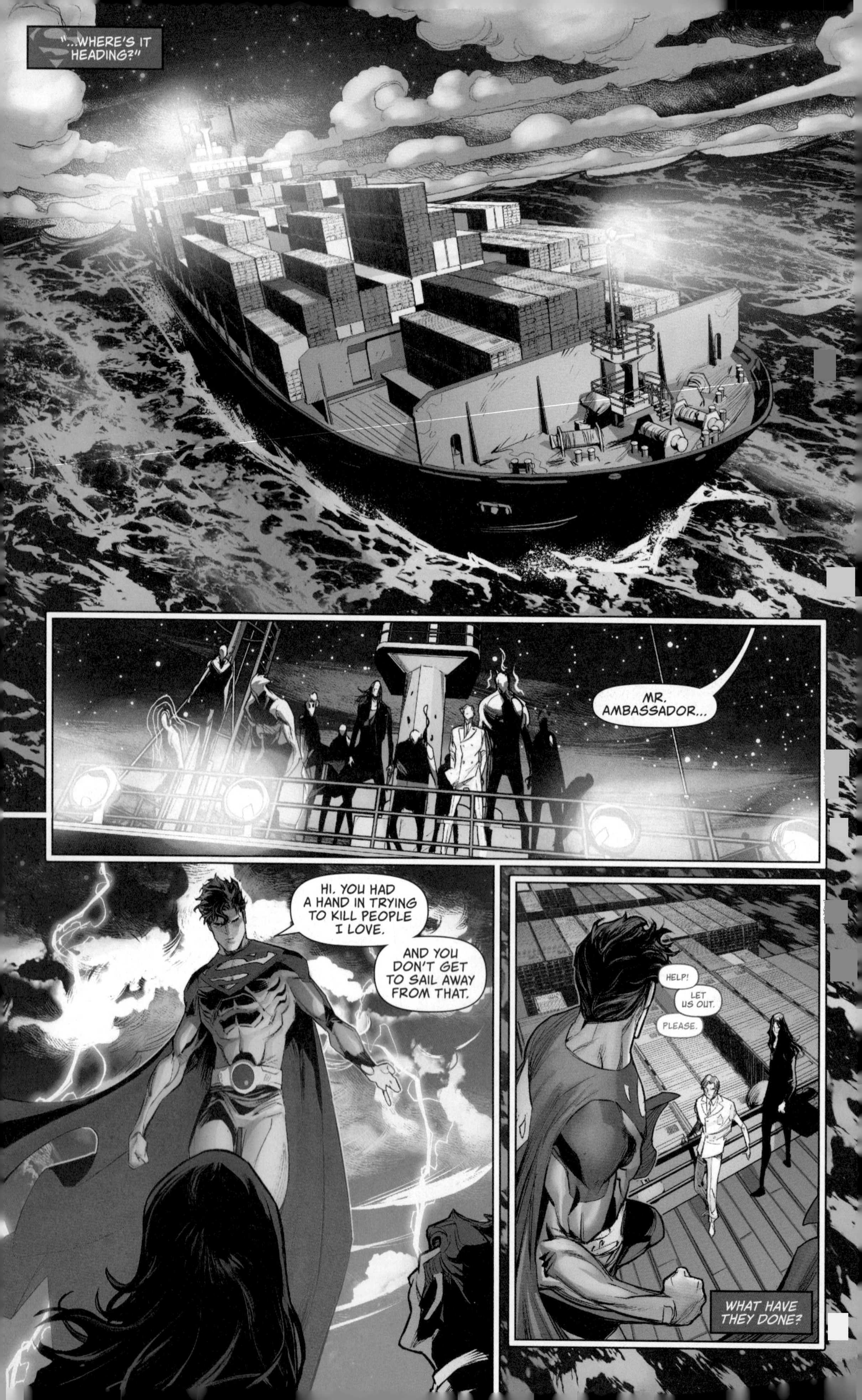
"...WHERE'S IT HEADING?"
MR. AMBASSADOR...
HI. YOU HAD A HAND IN TRYING TO KILL PEOPLE I LOVE.
AND YOU DON'T GET TO SAIL AWAY FROM THAT.
HELP!
LET US OUT.
PLEASE.
WHAT HAVE THEY DONE?

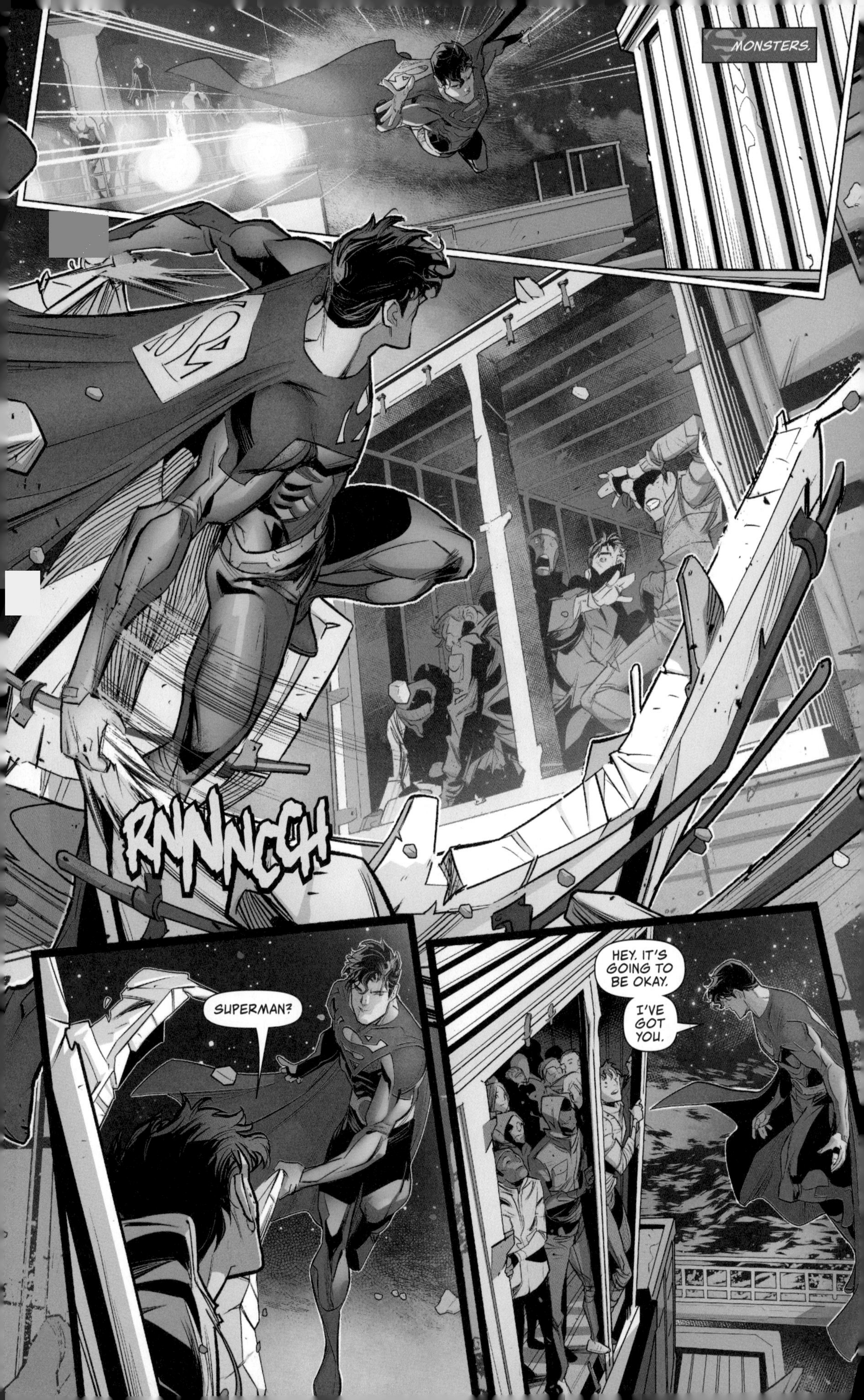
MONSTERS.
RNNNCCH
SUPERMAN?
HEY. IT'S GOING TO BE OKAY.
I'VE GOT YOU.

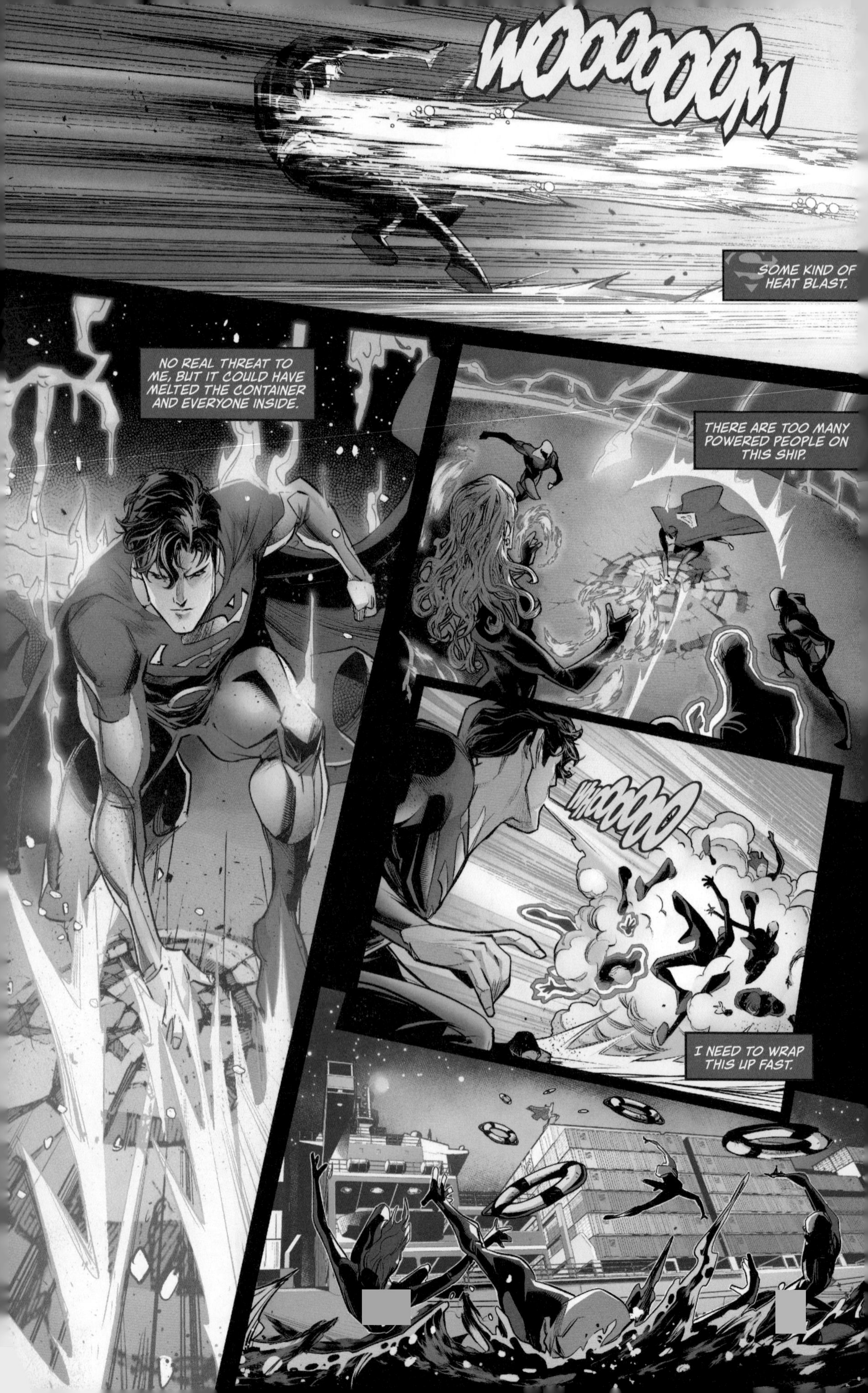
WOOOOOOM
SOME KIND OF HEAT BLAST.
NO REAL THREAT TO ME, BUT IT COULD HAVE MELTED THE CONTAINER AND EVERYONE INSIDE.
THERE ARE TOO MANY POWERED PEOPLE ON THIS SHIP.
WHOOOOO
I NEED TO WRAP THIS UP FAST.

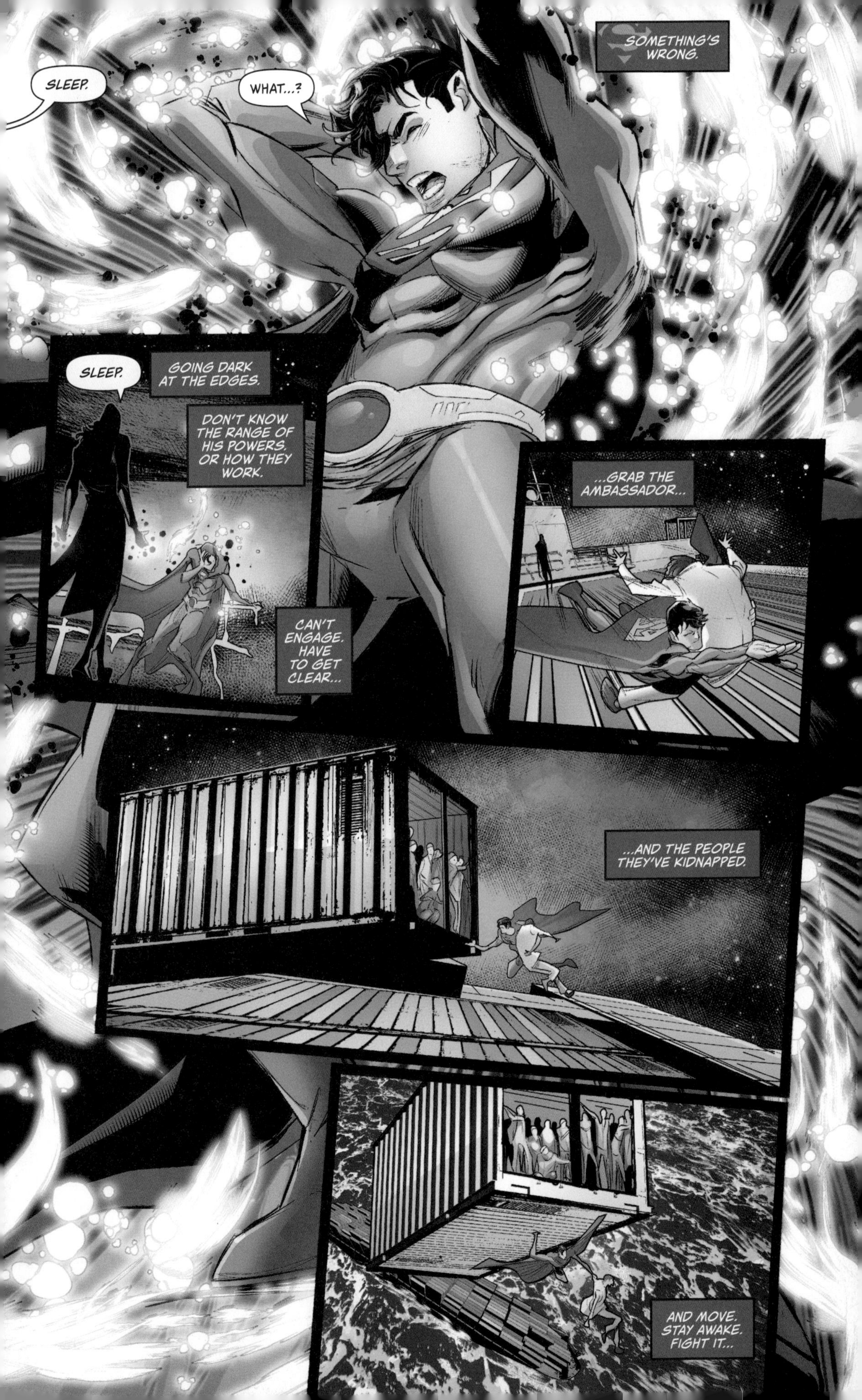
SOMETHING'S WRONG.
SLEEP.
WHAT...?
SLEEP.
GOING DARK AT THE EDGES.
DON'T KNOW THE RANGE OF HIS POWERS. OR HOW THEY WORK.
CAN'T ENGAGE. HAVE TO GET CLEAR...
...GRAB THE AMBASSADOR...
...AND THE PEOPLE THEY'VE KIDNAPPED.
AND MOVE. STAY AWAKE. FIGHT IT...

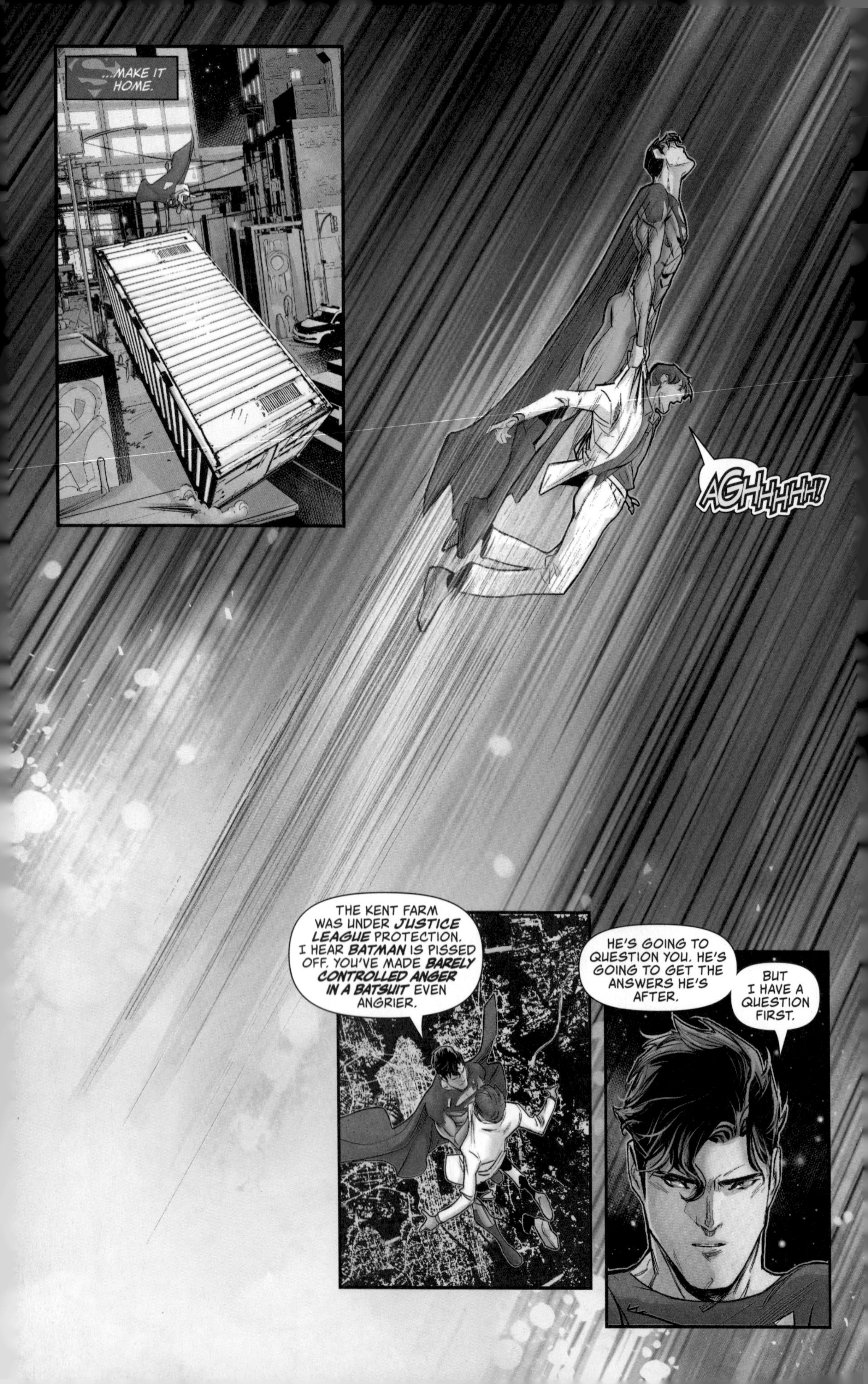
...MAKE IT HOME.
AGHHHHH!
THE KENT FARM WAS UNDER JUSTICE LEAGUE PROTECTION. I HEAR BATMAN IS PISSED OFF. YOU'VE MADE BARELY CONTROLLED ANGER IN A BATSUIT EVEN ANGRIER.
HE'S GOING TO QUESTION YOU. HE'S GOING TO GET THE ANSWERS HE'S AFTER.
BUT I HAVE A QUESTION FIRST.

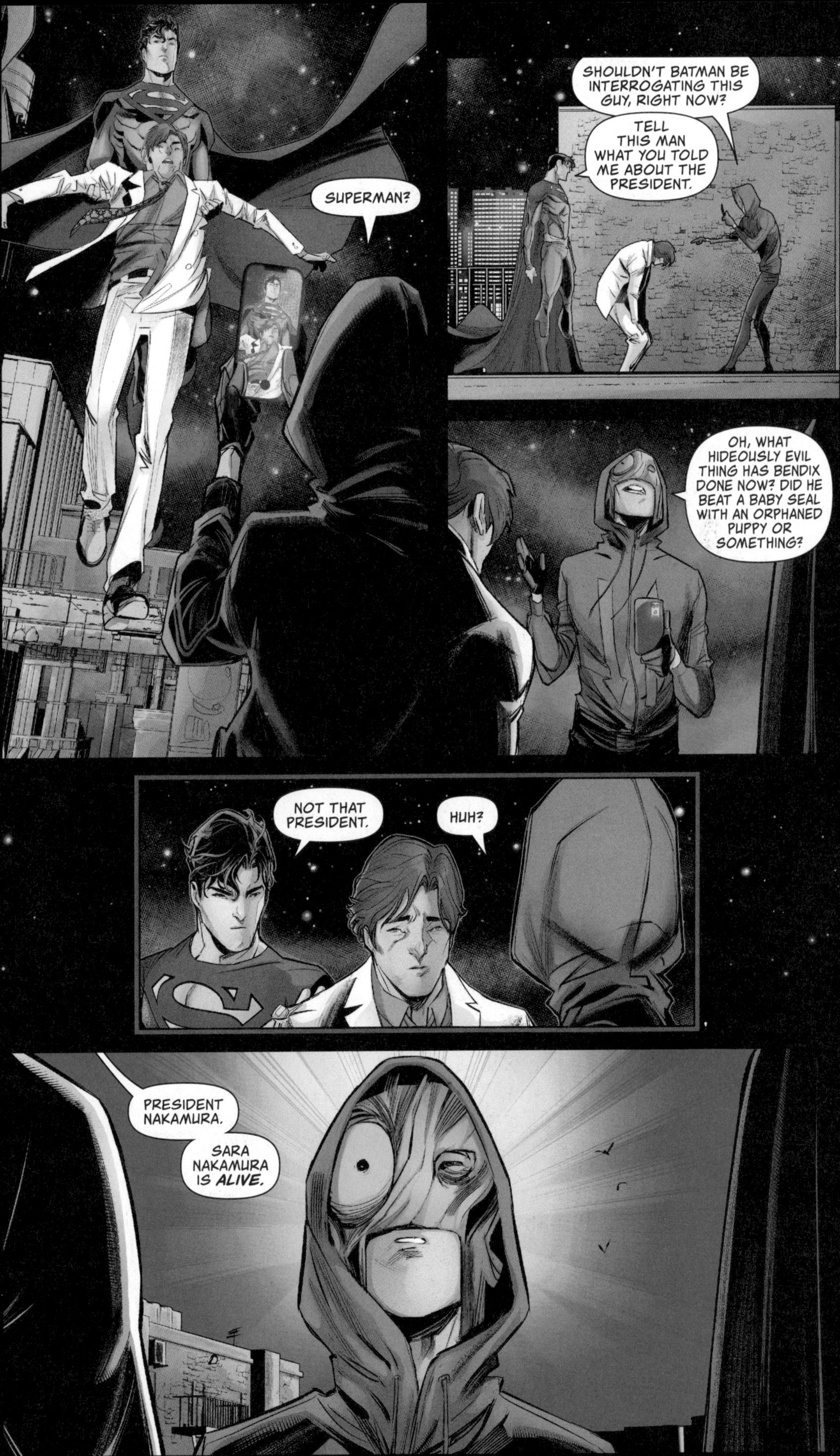
SUPERMAN?
SHOULDN'T BATMAN BE INTERROGATING THIS GUY, RIGHT NOW?
TELL THIS MAN WHAT YOU TOLD ME ABOUT THE PRESIDENT.
OH, WHAT HIDEOUSLY EVIL THING HAS BENDIX DONE NOW? DID HE BEAT A BABY SEAL WITH AN ORPHANED PUPPY OR SOMETHING?
NOT THAT PRESIDENT.
HUH?
PRESIDENT NAKAMURA.
SARA NAKAMURA IS ALIVE.

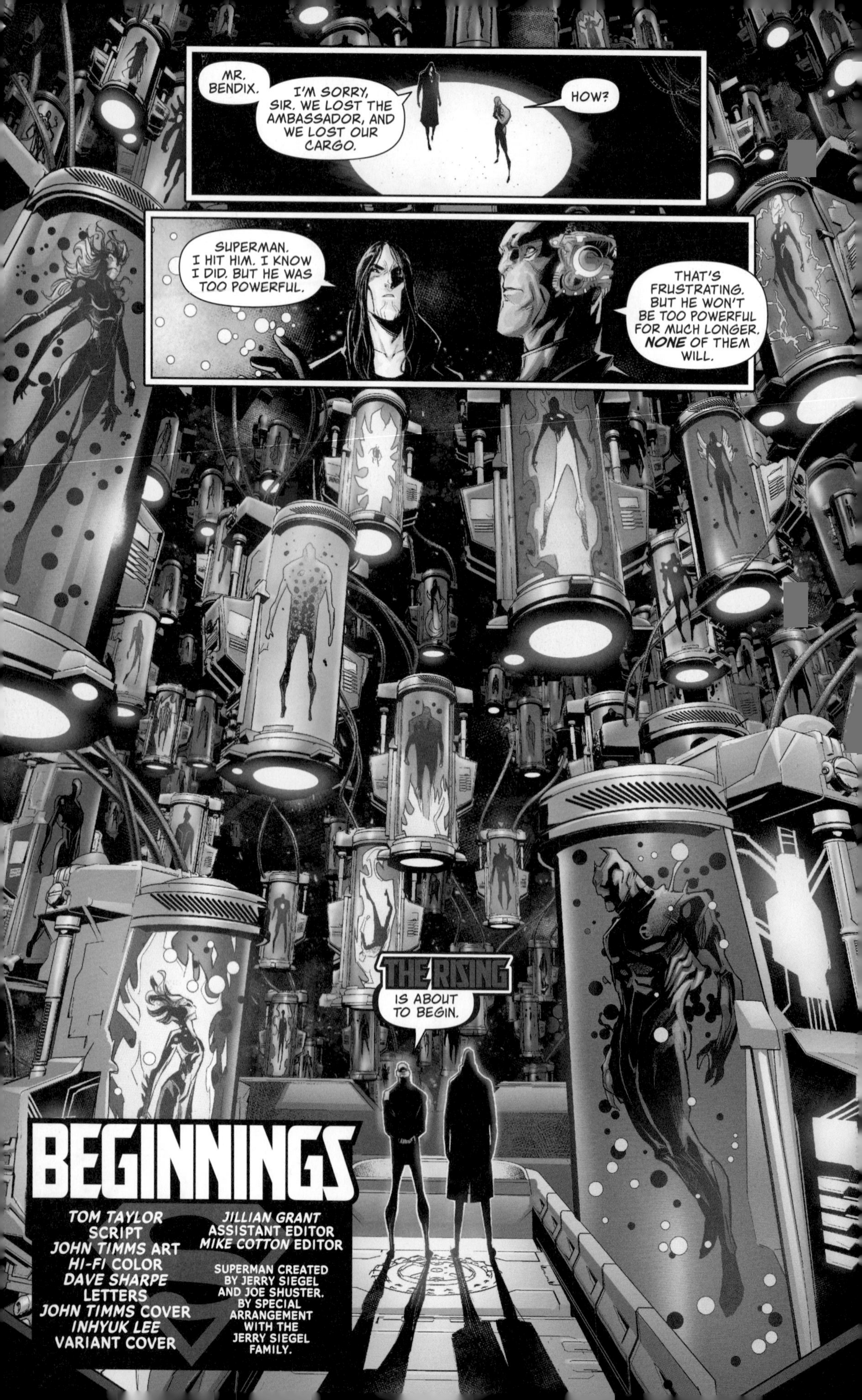
MR. BENDIX.
I'M SORRY, SIR. WE LOST THE AMBASSADOR, AND WE LOST OUR CARGO.
HOW?
SUPERMAN. I HIT HIM. I KNOW I DID. BUT HE WAS TOO POWERFUL.
THAT'S FRUSTRATING. BUT HE WON'T BE TOO POWERFUL FOR MUCH LONGER. NONE OF THEM WILL.
THE RISING IS ABOUT TO BEGIN.
BEGINNINGS
TOM TAYLOR SCRIPT
JOHN TIMMS ART
HI-FI COLOR
DAVE SHARPE LETTERS
JOHN TIMMS COVER
INHYUK LEE VARIANT COVER
JILLIAN GRANT ASSISTANT EDITOR
MIKE COTTON EDITOR
SUPERMAN CREATED BY JERRY SIEGEL AND JOE SHUSTER. BY SPECIAL ARRANGEMENT WITH THE JERRY SIEGEL FAMILY.

BONUS VARIANT COVERS

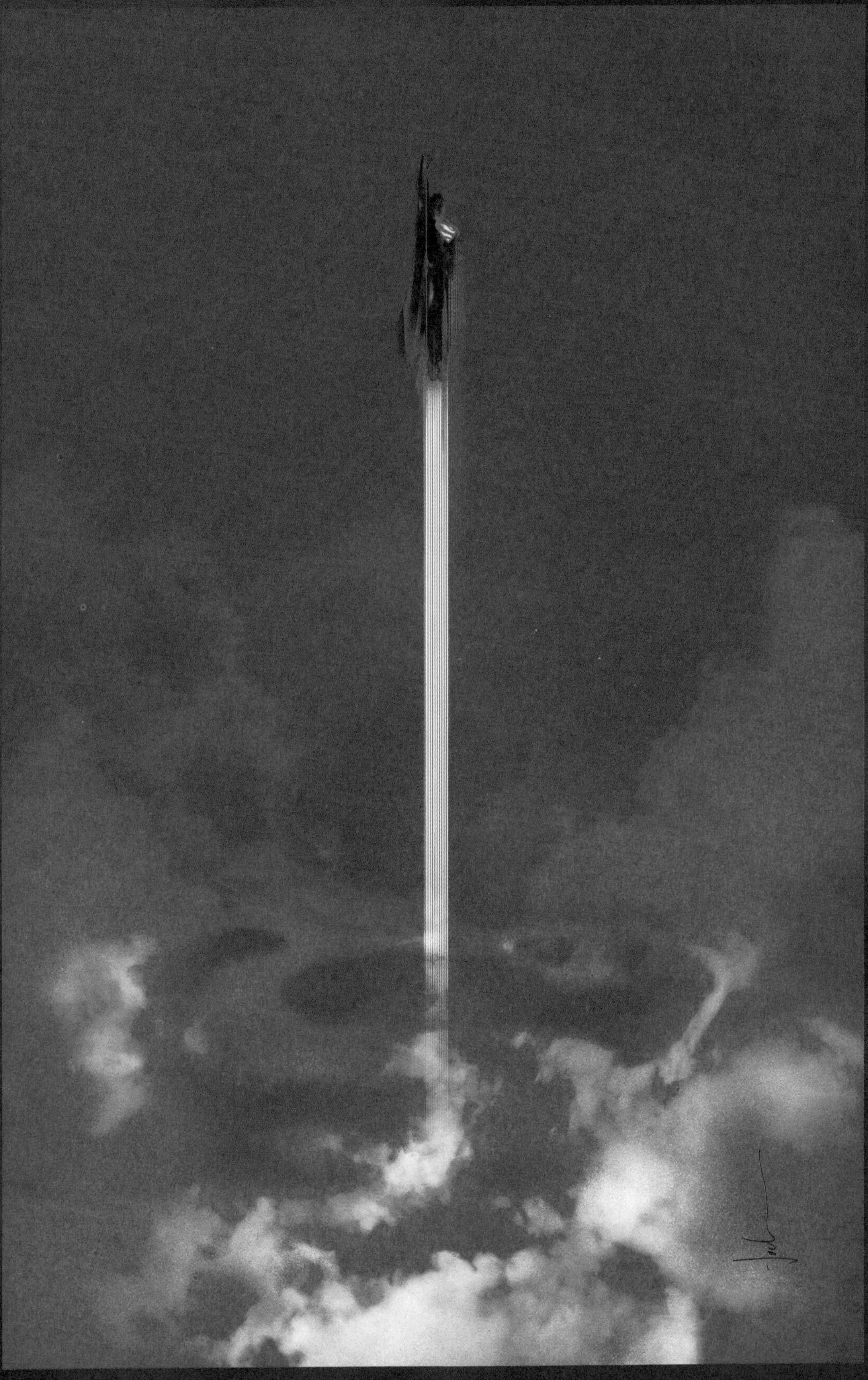

Superman: Son of Kal-El #1 variant cover art by **JOCK**

Superman: Son of Kal-El #1 variant cover art by **STEPHEN BYRNE**

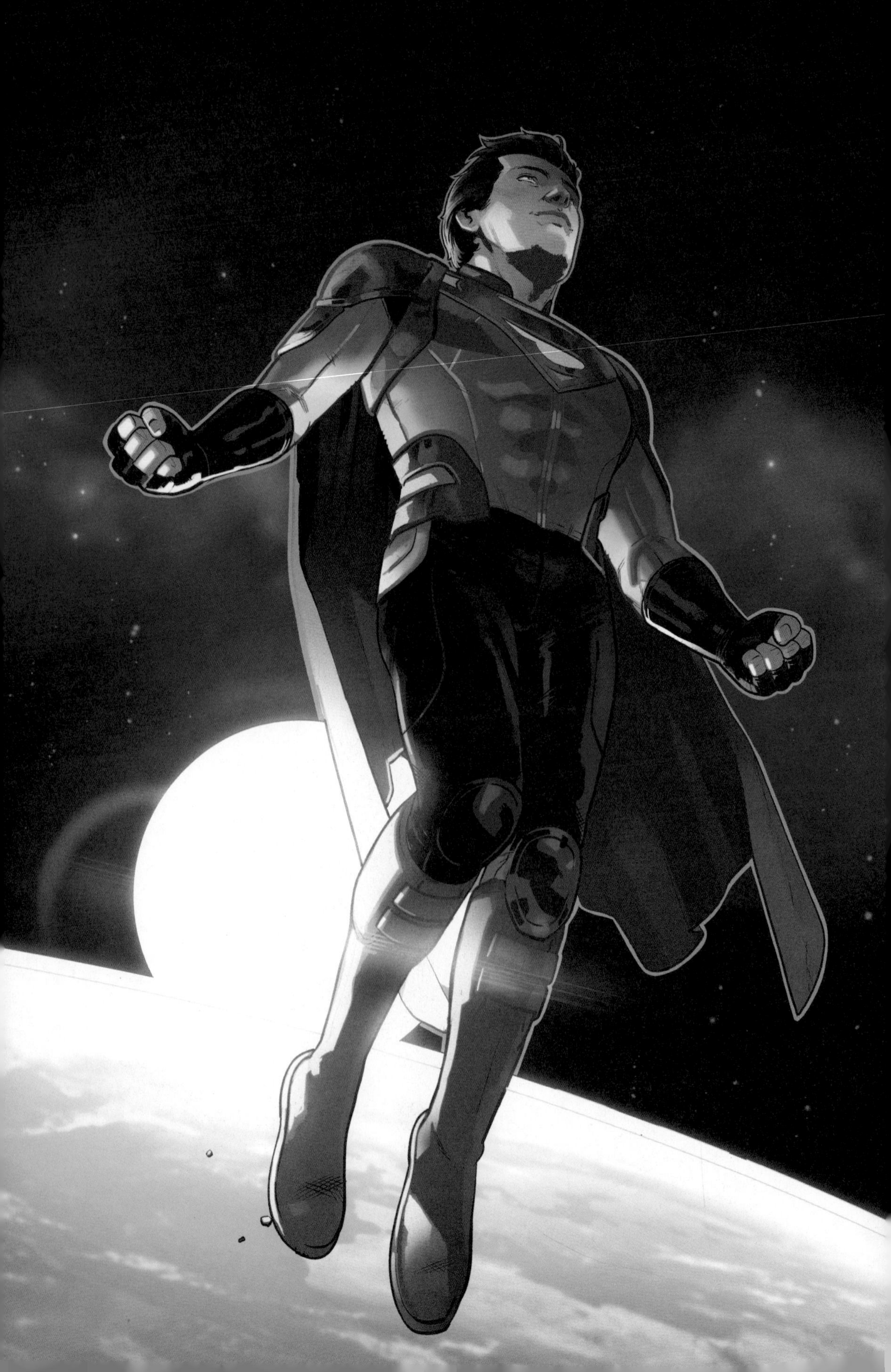

Superman: Son of Kal-El #1 variant cover art by **JEN BARTEL**

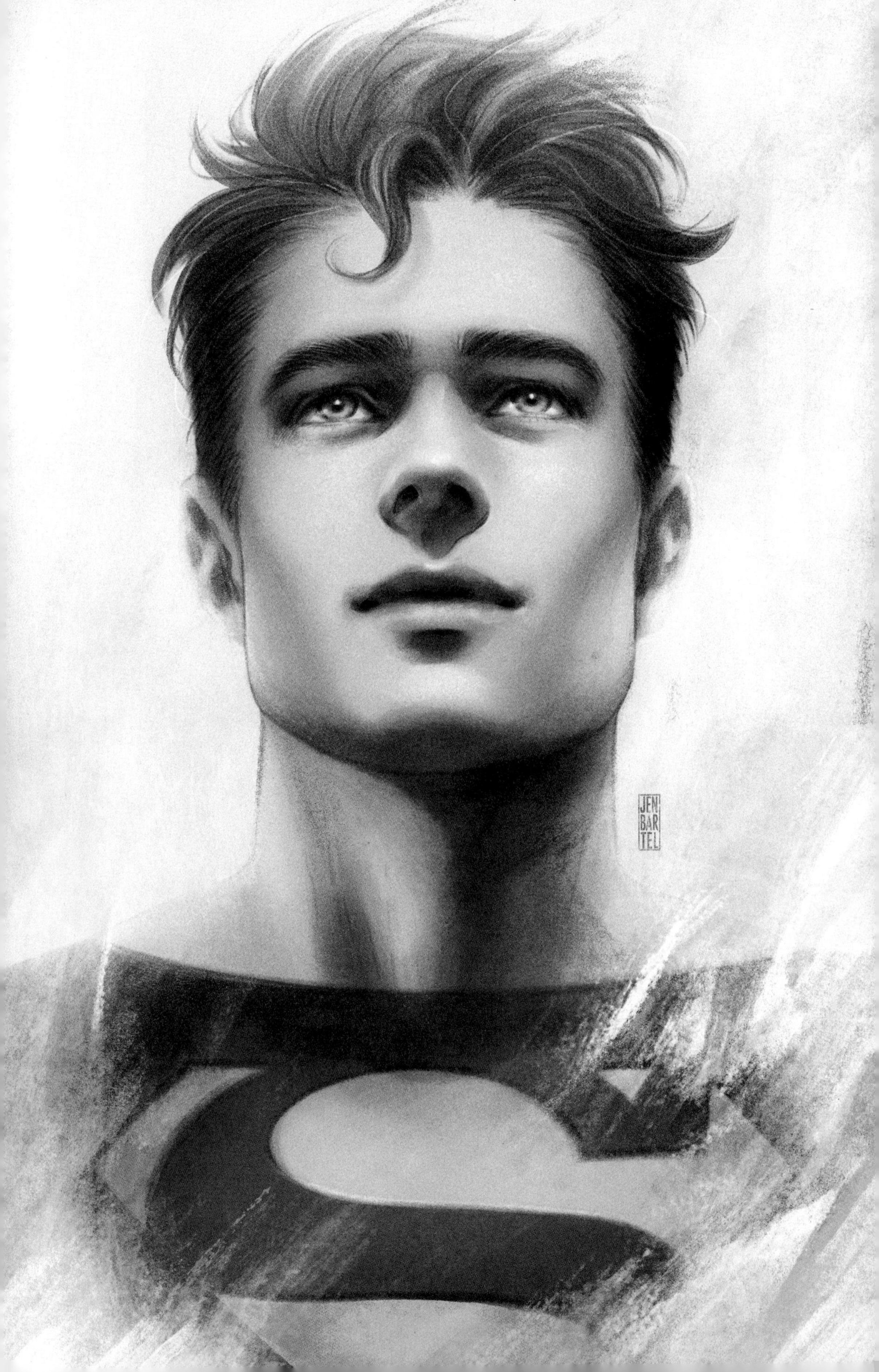
JEN BARTEL

Superman: Son of Kal-El #5 variant cover art by **TRAVIS MOORE** & **TAMRA BONVILLAIN**

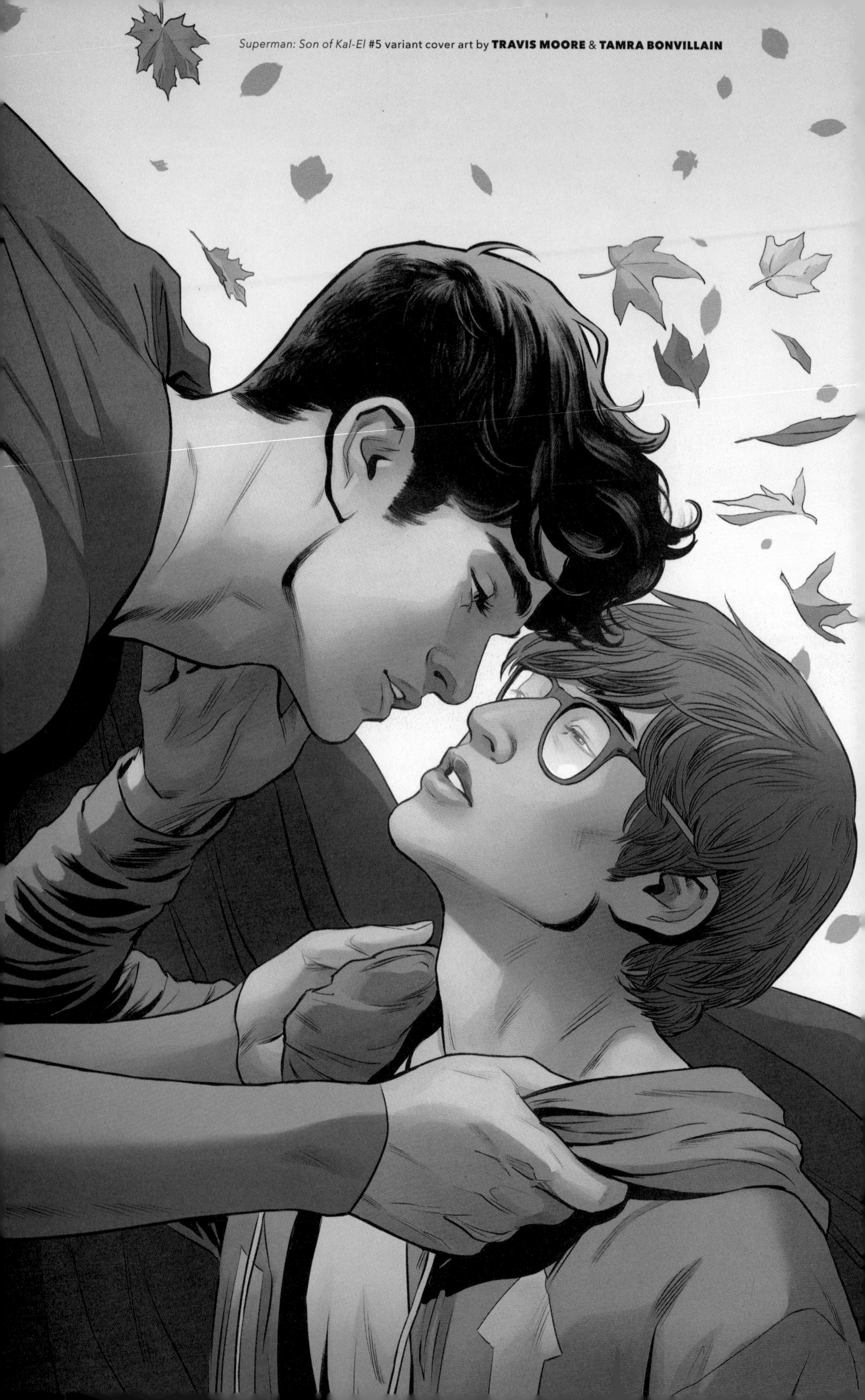

SKETCHBOOK GALLERY BY **JOHN TIMMS**

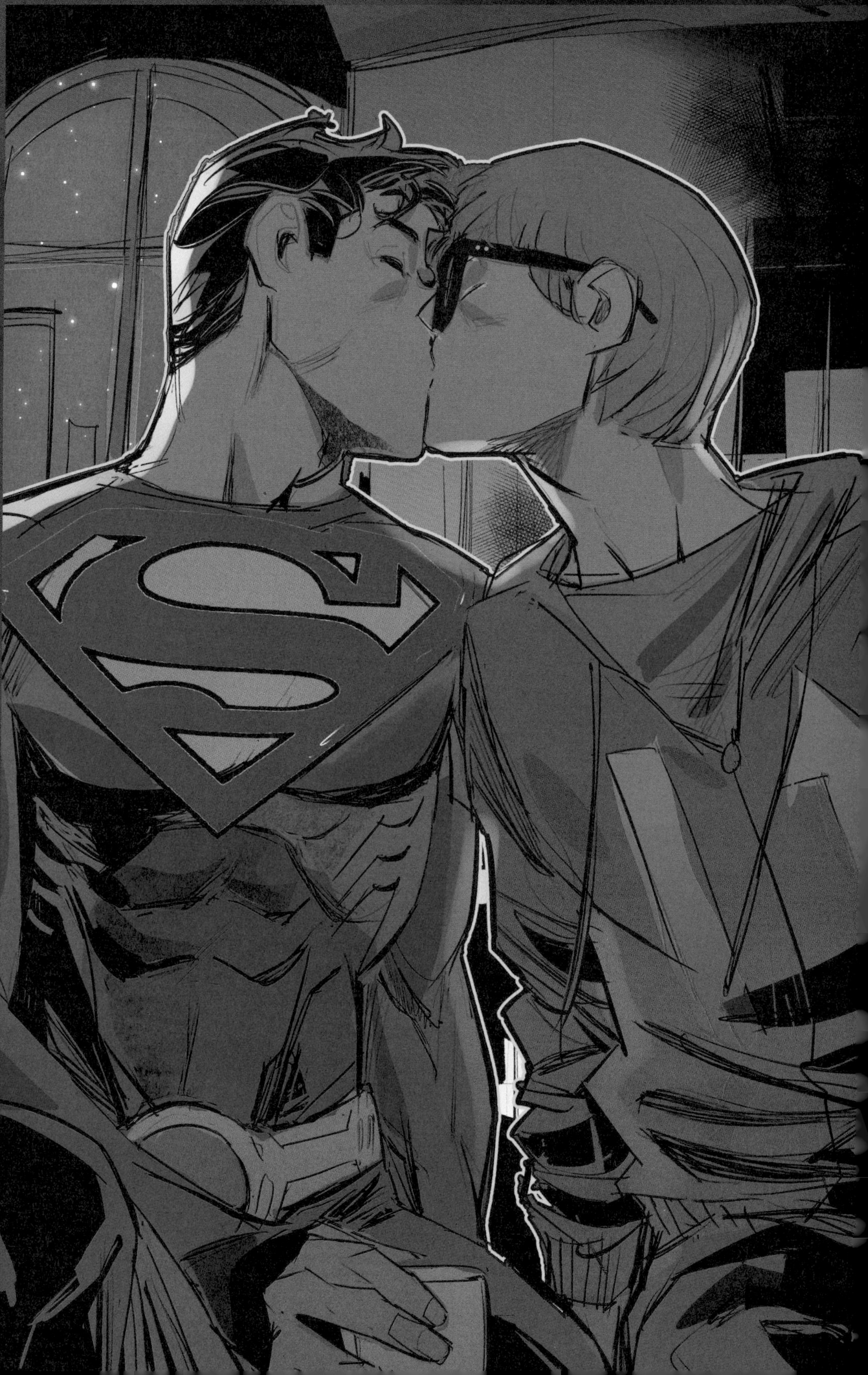

MAIN COVER CONCEPTS FOR *SUPERMAN: SON OF KAL-EL* #1-6 BY

JOHN TIMMS

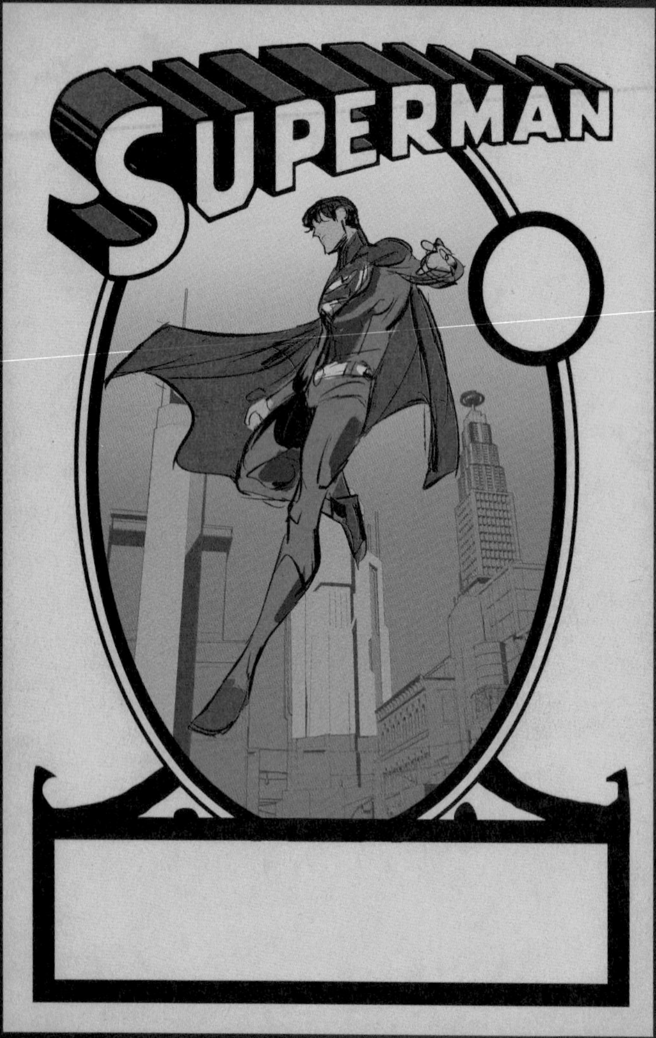
SUPERMAN

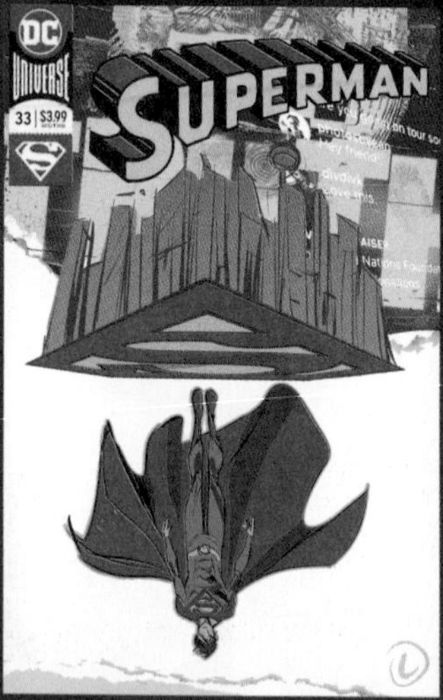
DC
UNIVERSE
33 | $3.99
SUPERMAN

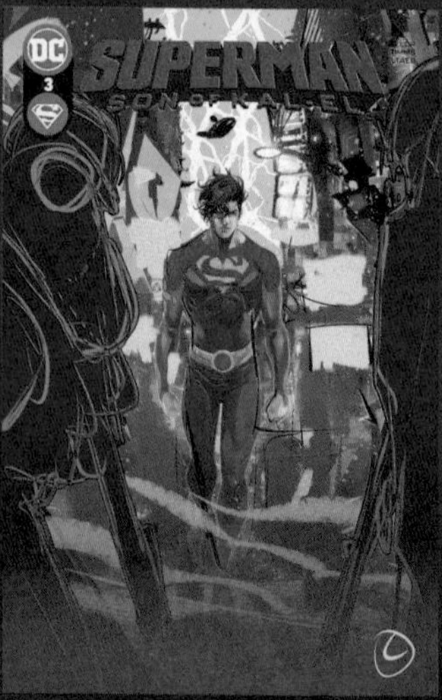
DC
3
SUPERMAN
SON OF KAL-EL

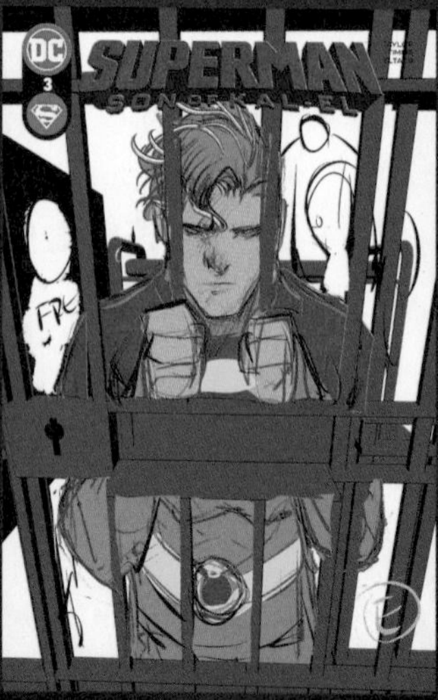
DC
3
SUPERMAN
SON OF KAL-EL

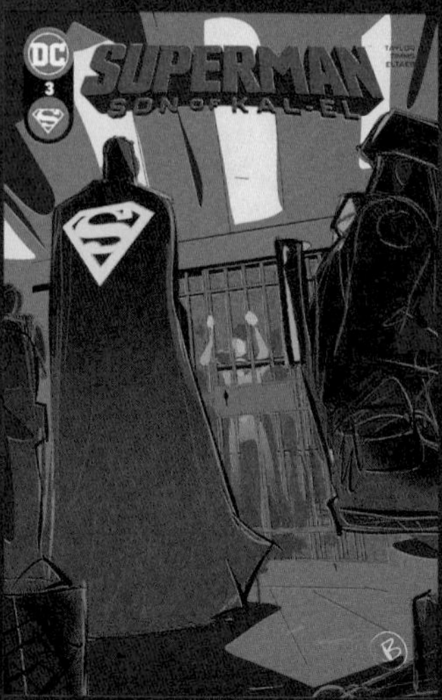
DC
3
SUPERMAN
SON OF KAL-EL

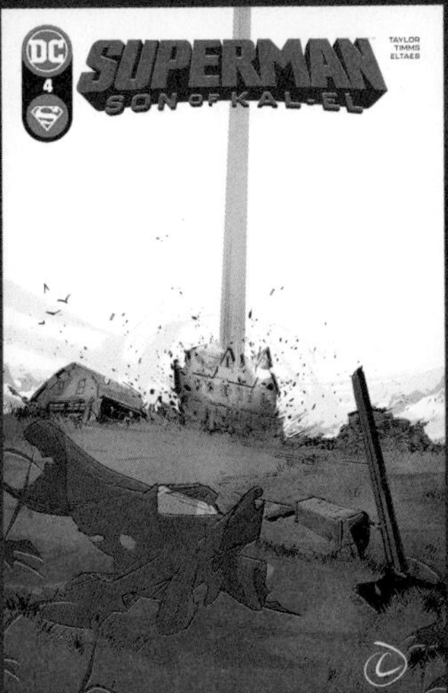
DC
4
SUPERMAN
SON OF KAL-EL
TAYLOR
TIMMS
ELTAEB

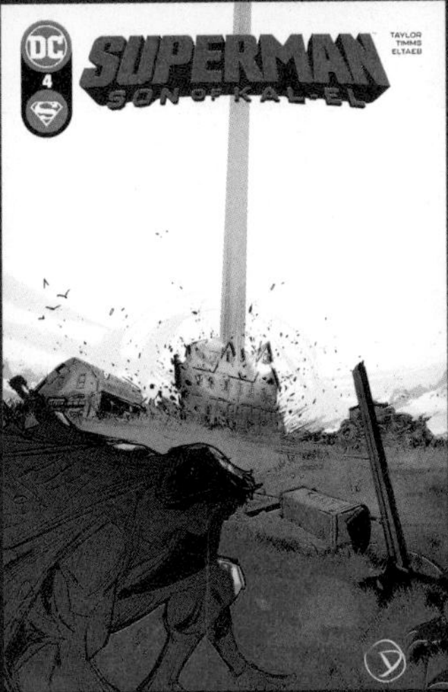
DC
4
SUPERMAN
SON OF KAL-EL
TAYLOR
TIMMS
ELTAEB

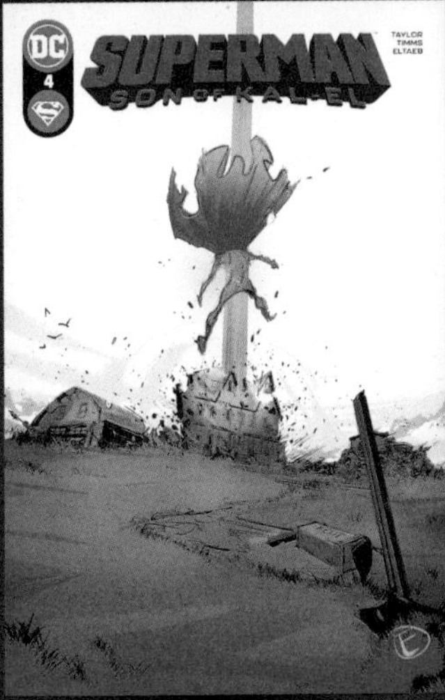
DC
4
SUPERMAN
SON OF KAL-EL
TAYLOR
TIMMS
ELTAEB

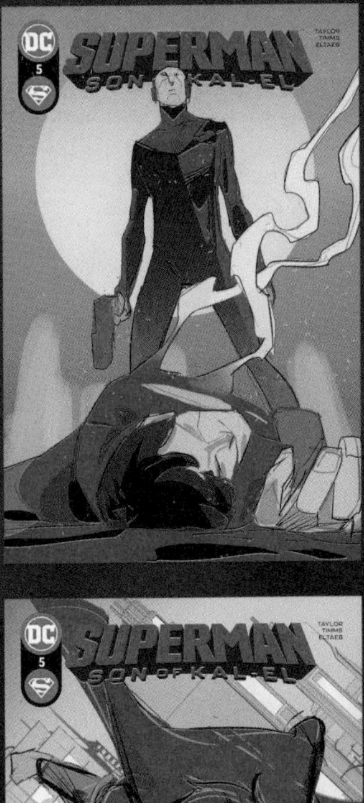
DC
5
SUPERMAN
SON OF KAL-EL
TAYLOR
TIMMS
ELTAEB

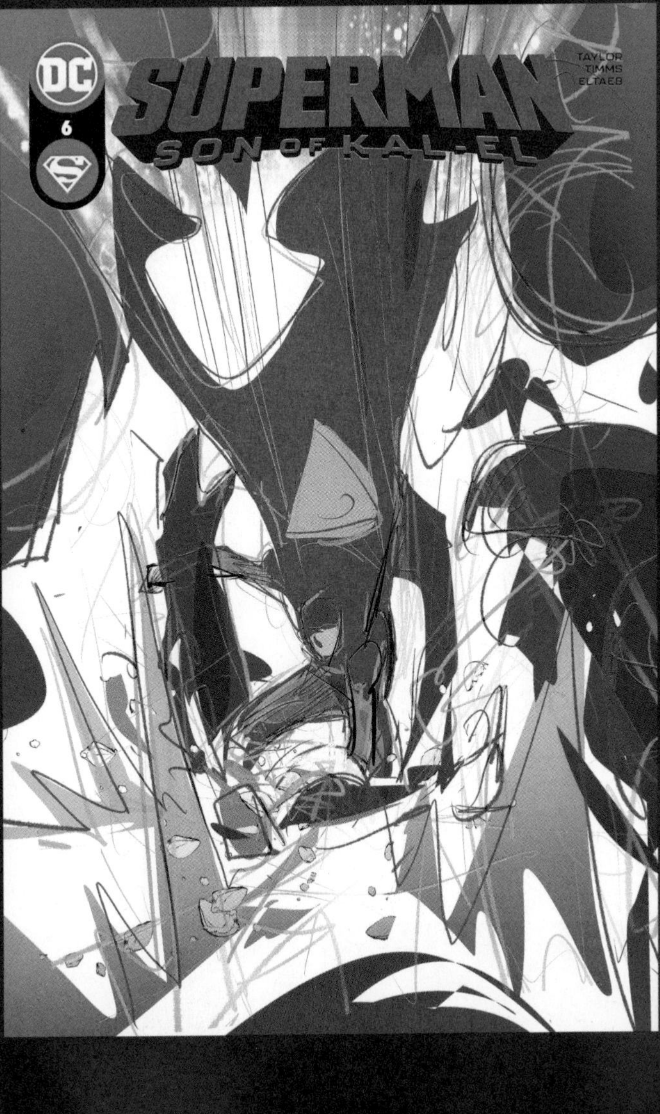
DC
6
SUPERMAN
SON OF KAL-EL
TAYLOR
TIMMS
ELTAEB

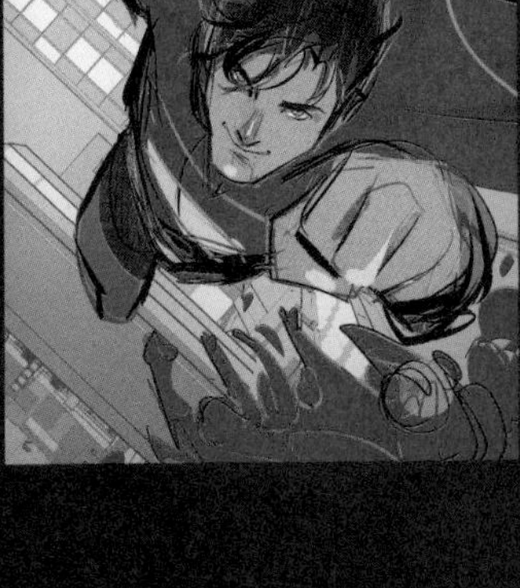
DC
5
SUPERMAN
SON OF KAL-EL
TAYLOR
TIMMS
ELTAEB

CHARACTER DESIGNS & CONCEPT ART BY

JOHN TIMMS

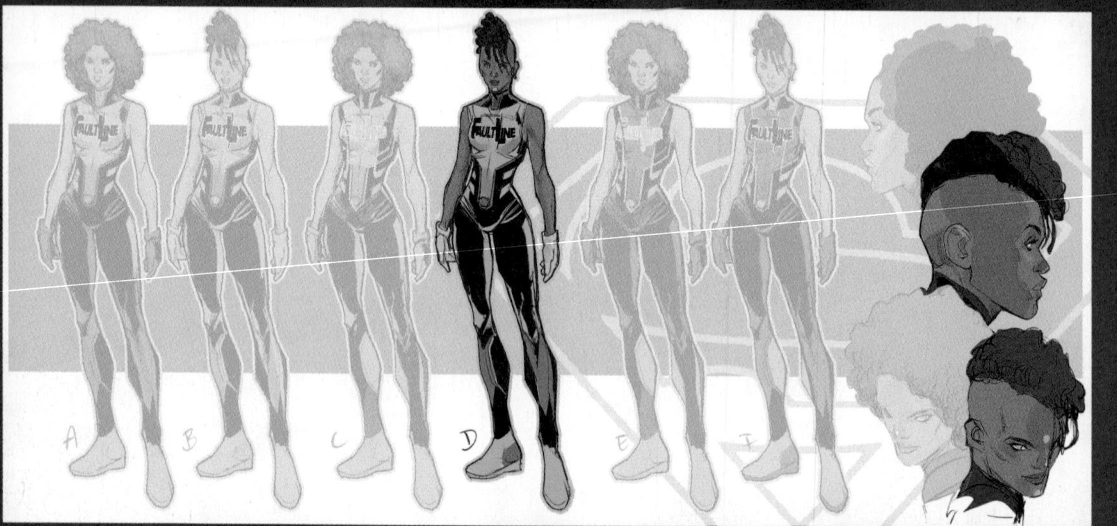
FAULTLINE
A
B
C
D
E
F

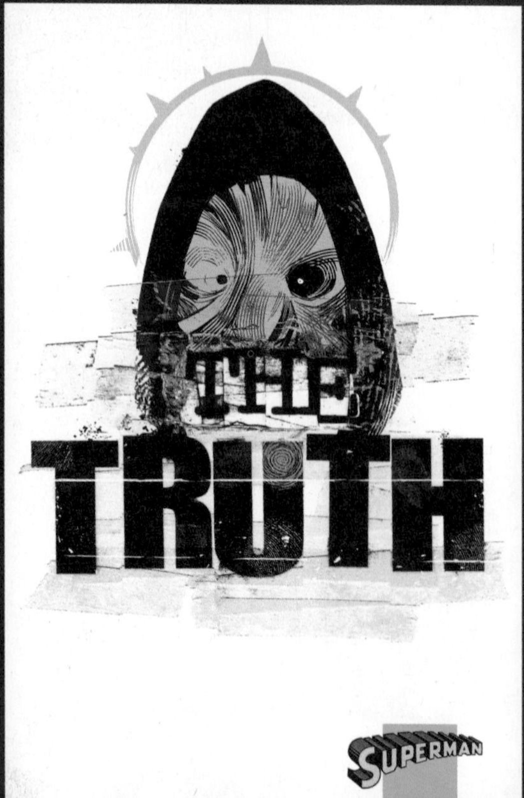
THE
TRUTH
SUPERMAN

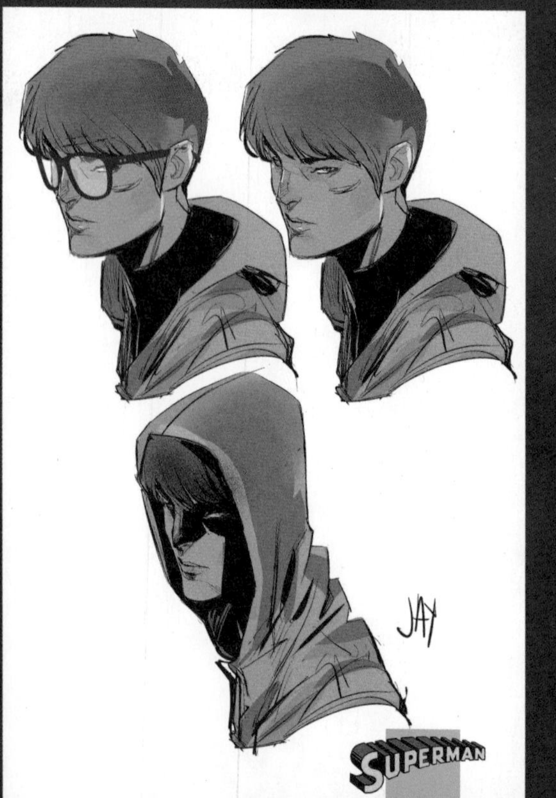
SUPERMAN

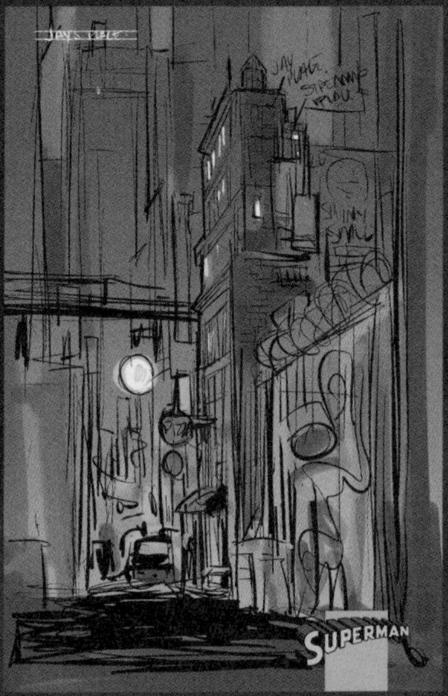
SUPERMAN

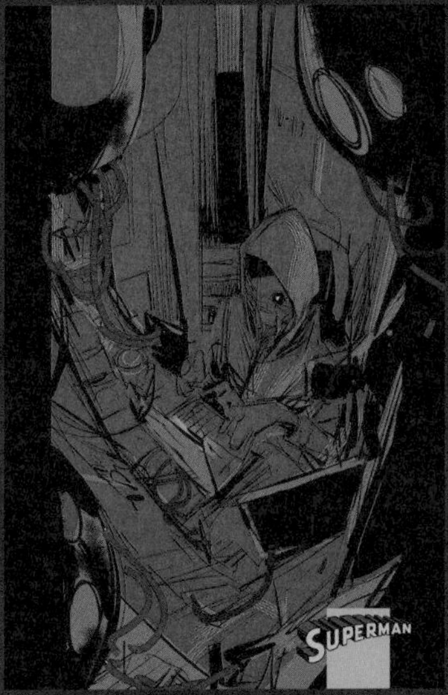
SUPERMAN

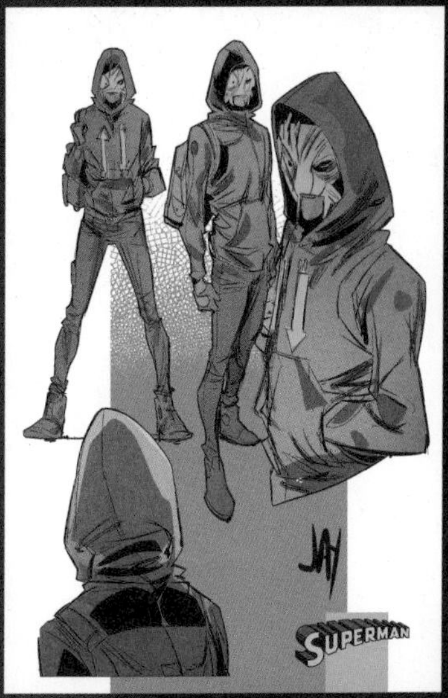
SUPERMAN

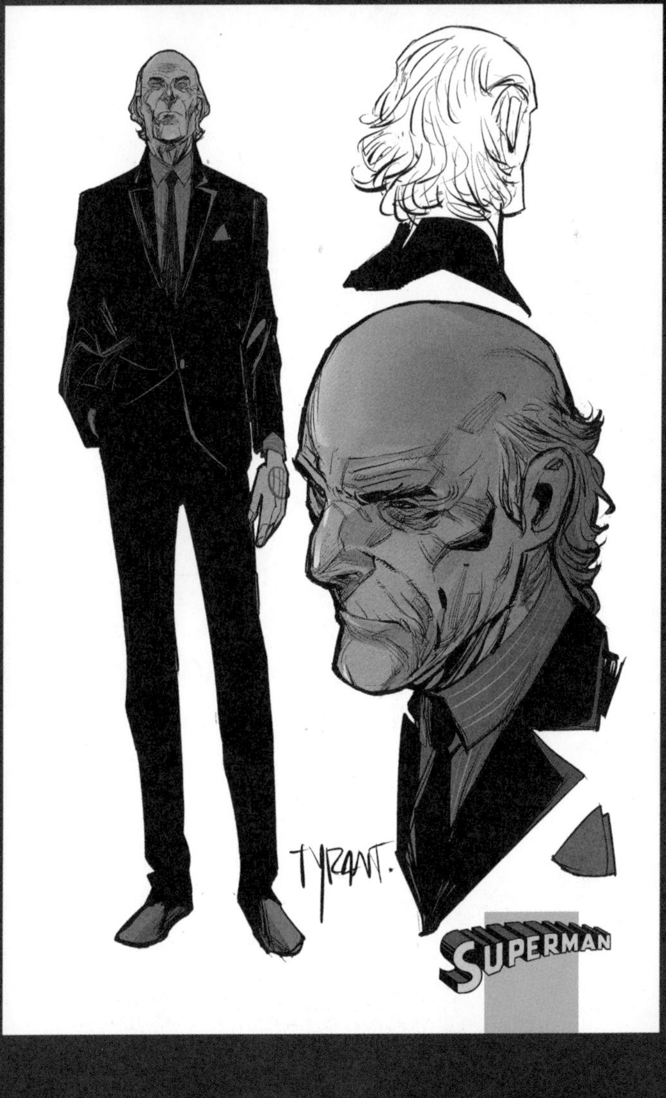
TYRANT.
SUPERMAN

PAGE LAYOUTS BY

JOHN TIMMS

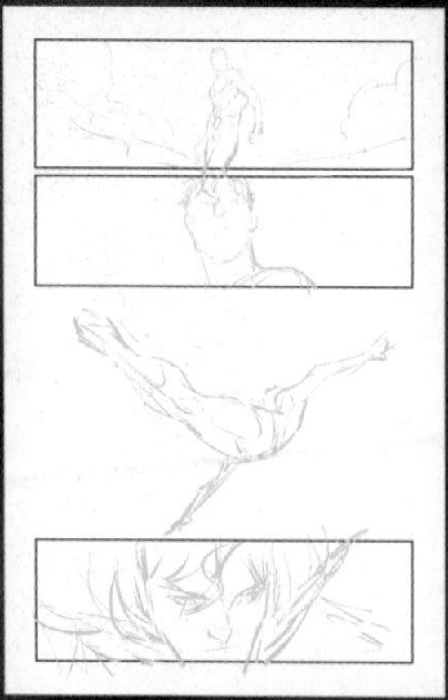

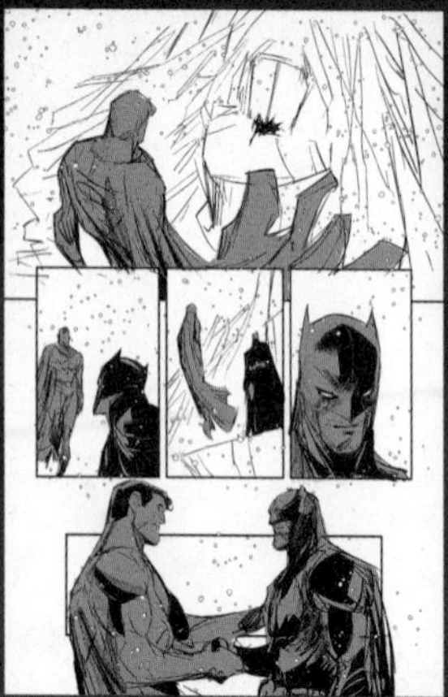

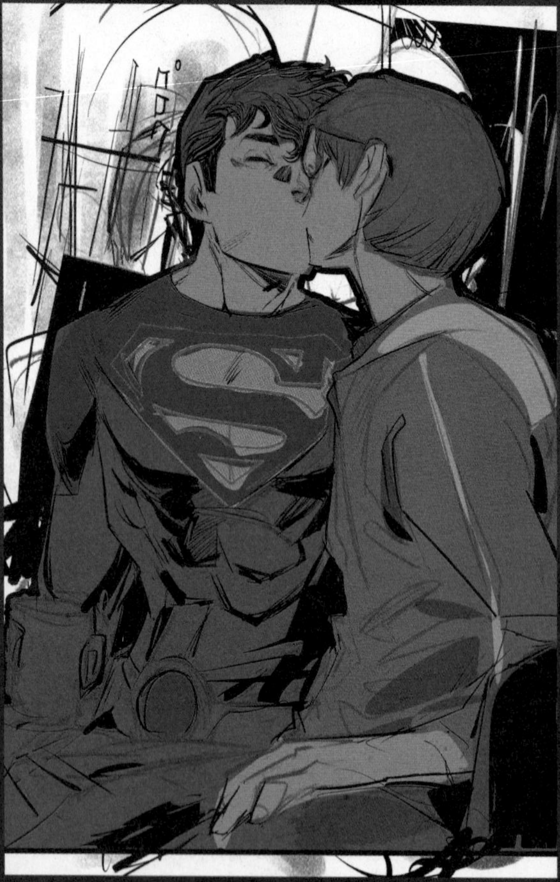

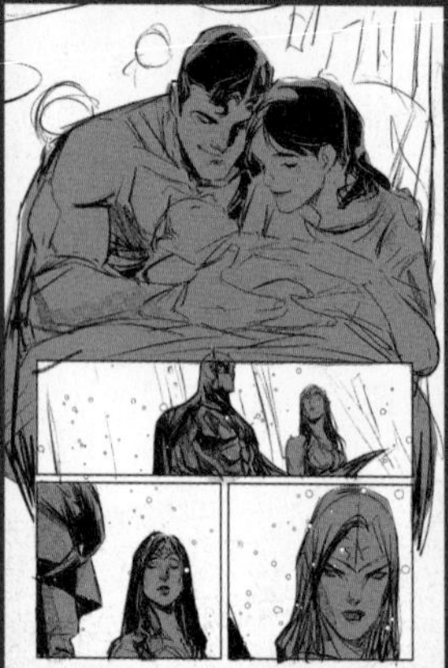

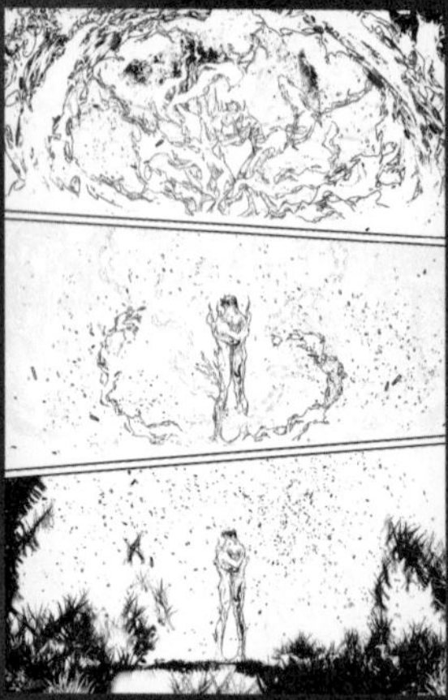

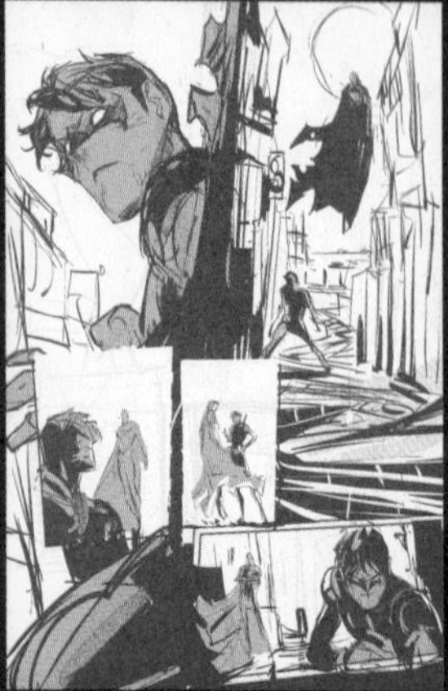

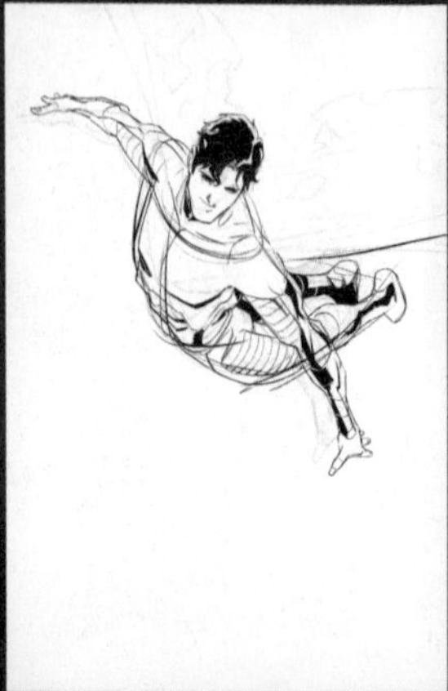

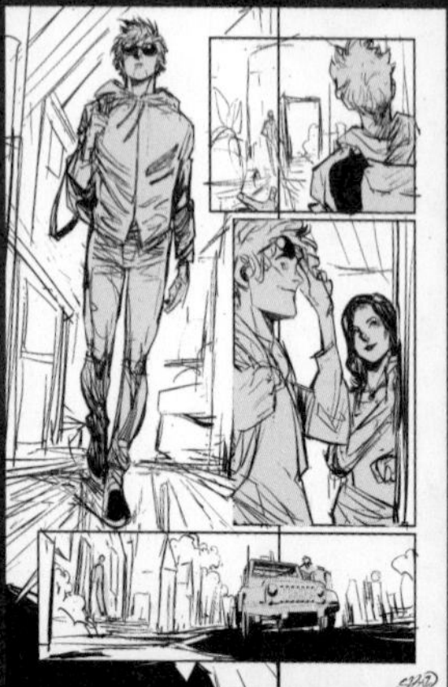

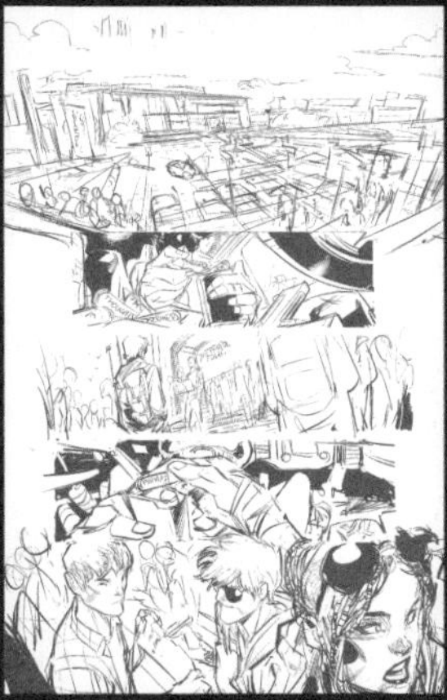
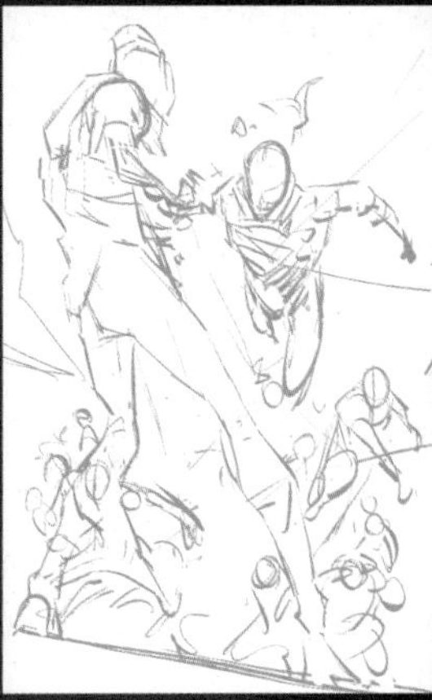
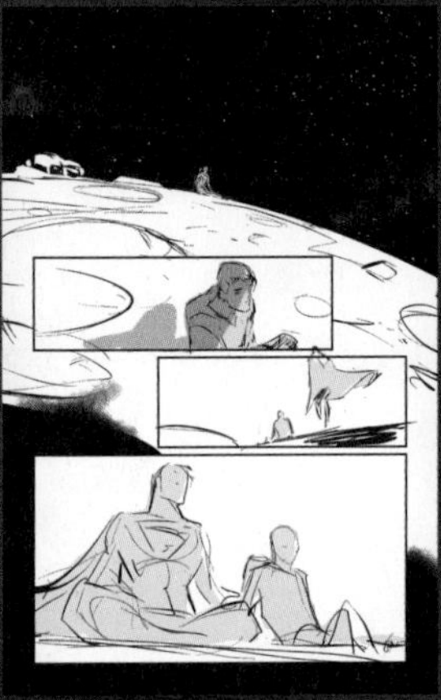
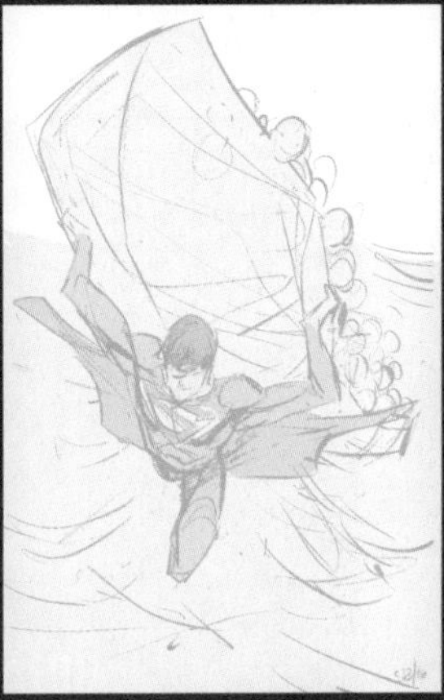
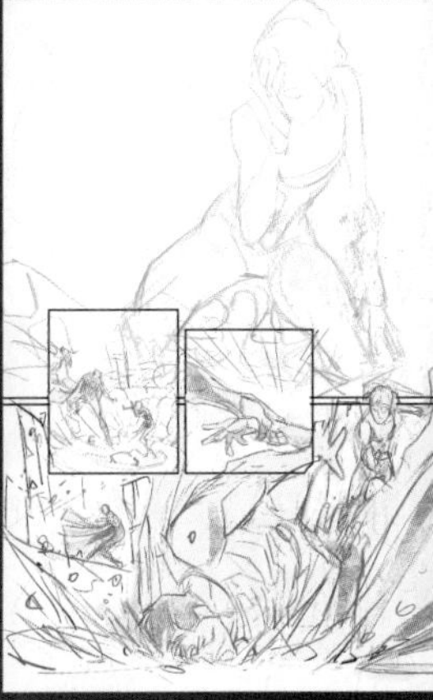
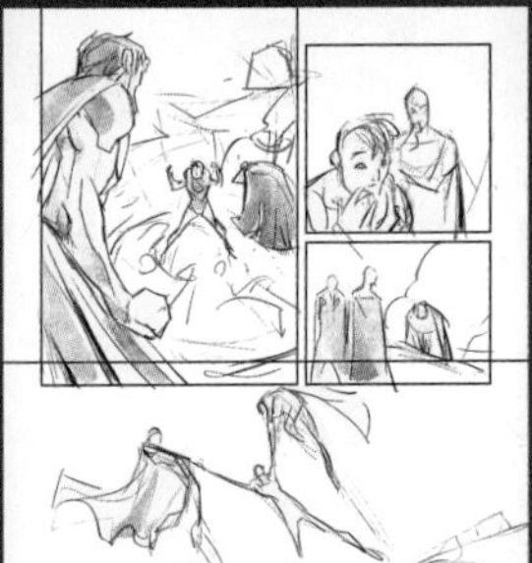
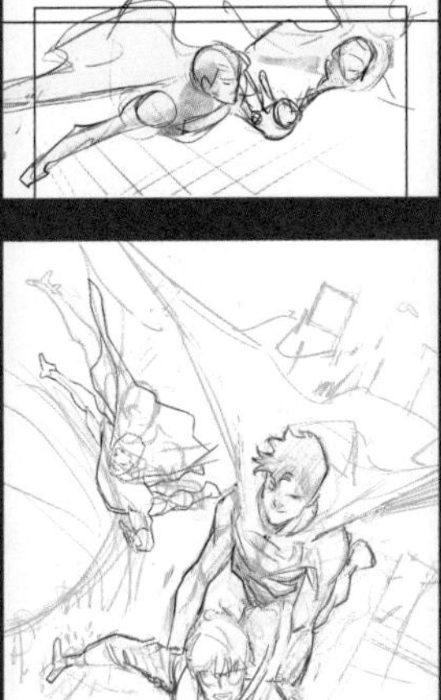
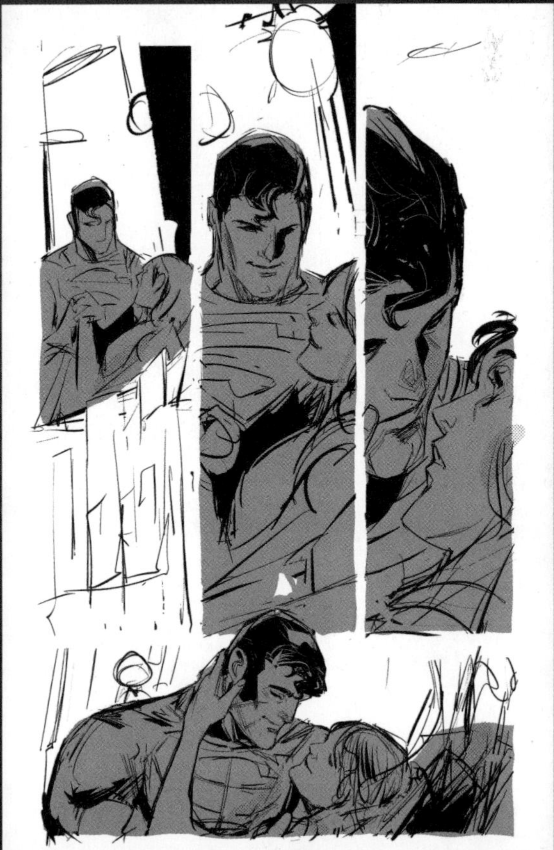

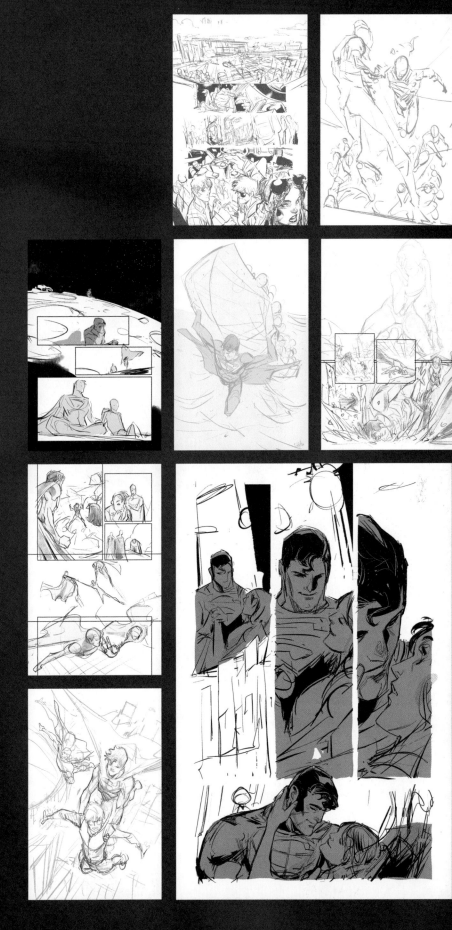

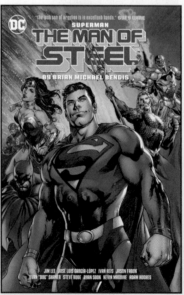

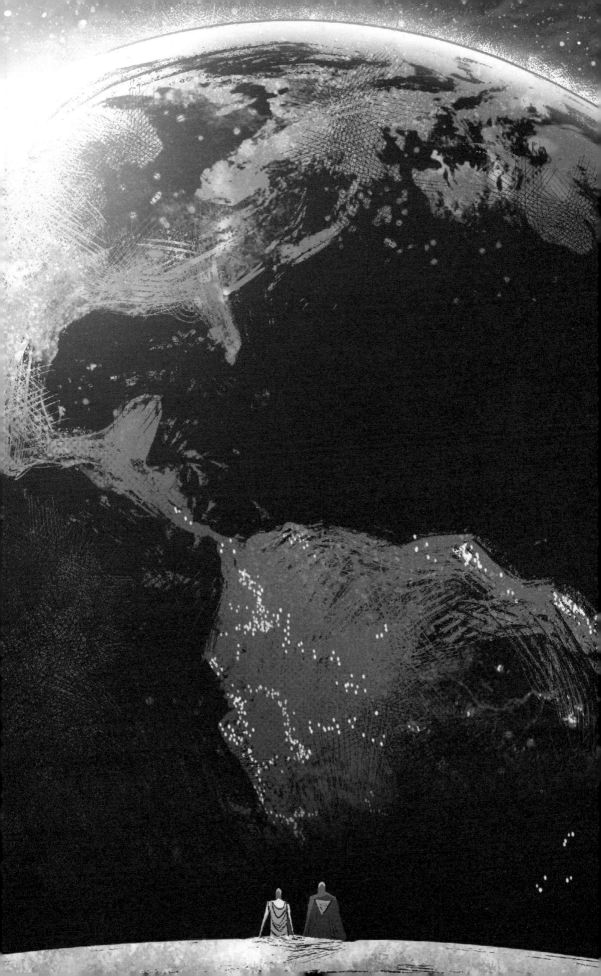

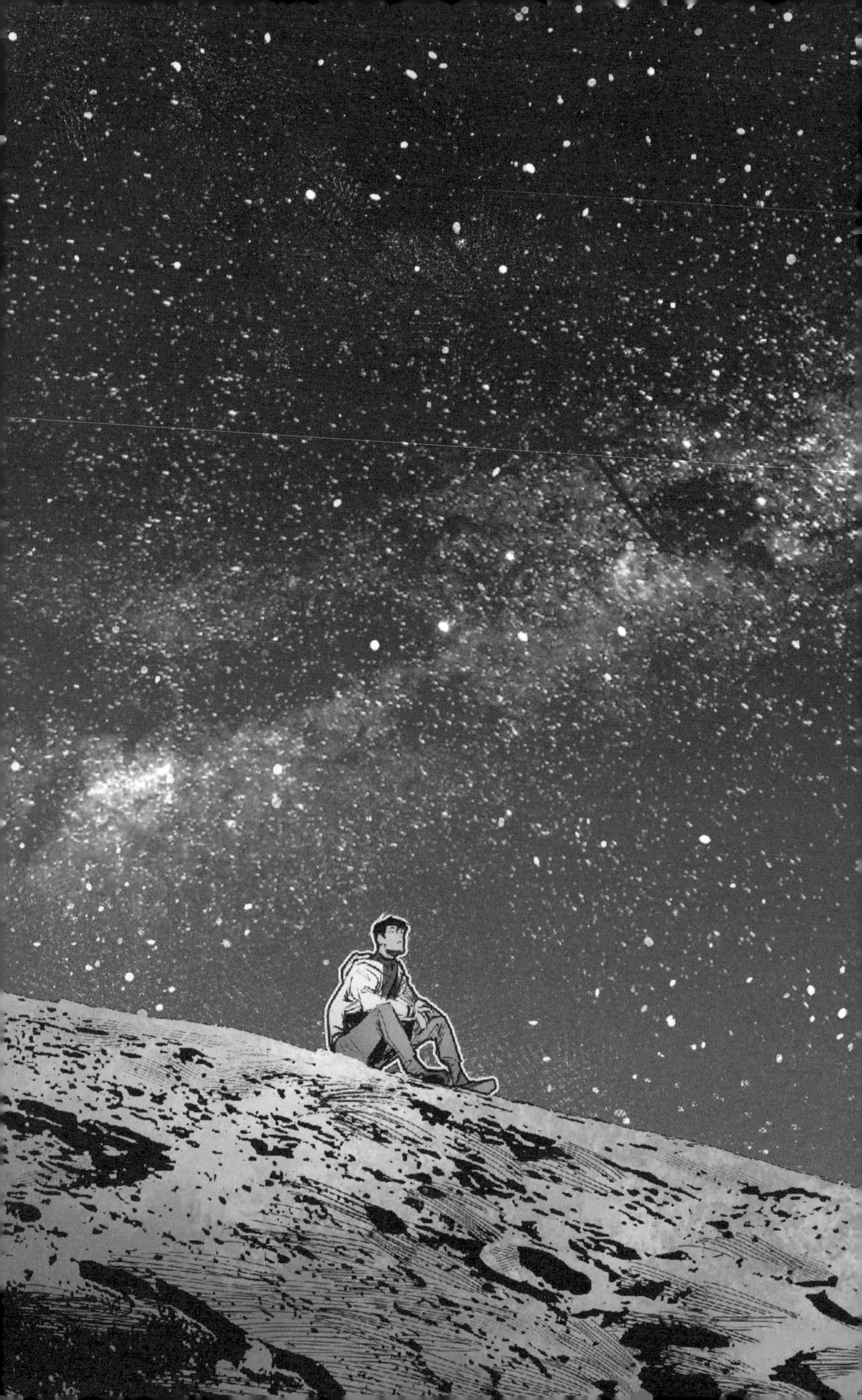